PROPRIETARY CLAIMS AND INSOLVENCY

AUSTRALIA
LBC Information Services
Sydney

CANADA and USA
Carswell
Toronto

NEW ZEALAND
Brooker's
Auckland

SINGAPORE and MALAYSIA
Thomson Information (S.E. Asia)
Singapore

PROPRIETARY CLAIMS AND INSOLVENCY

by

Gerard McCormack, B.C.L., LL.M., Barrister at Law
(Dublin)

Reader in Law at the University of Essex, Colchester

LONDON
SWEET & MAXWELL
1997

Published in 1997 by Sweet & Maxwell Limited of
100 Avenue Road, Swiss Cottage
London NW3 3PF
Phototypeset by Selwood Systems Limited
Midsomer Norton
Printed and bound in Great Britain by
Butler and Tanner Ltd
Frome and London

No Natural forests were destroyed to make this product;
only farmed timber was used and replanted

**A CIP catalogue record for this book is available from the
British Library**

ISBN 0421 564 806

PREFACE

It is a fundamental principle of the law that when a legal person becomes insolvent any available assets of that person must be distributed to their creditors within the same class on a rateable basis. Some may argue that the principle of rateable or *pari passu* distribution of available assets is somewhat shallow and superficial in that there may be different classes of creditors and some classes of creditor may be paid off ahead of other classes. Moreover, the legislature has designated a particular category of creditors that are deemed particularly worthy of payment – namely preferential creditors. Preferential creditors enjoy priority over general creditors who are left very much at the end of the queue for payment and may receive only a small proportion of what is owed to them.

At a very general level one may say that the function of equity is to mitigate the rigours of the law. The question therefore arises whether a person who would otherwise be within the category of general creditors, may invoke the assistance of equity to leapfrog the queue of creditors. In particular, may such a person assert a proprietary right in some asset held by the insolvent that would allow him to take priority over other creditors of the insolvent. As a general proposition the courts are loath to entertain such claims. Judicial reticence is reflected in the remarks of Judge Paul Baker in *Re Stapylton Fletcher Ltd* [1995] 1 All E.R. 192 at 213–214. He said: "The court must be very cautious in devising equitable interests and remedies which erode the statutory scheme for distribution on insolvency. It cannot do it because of some perceived injustice arising as a consequence of the insolvency."

Not all judges sing from the same hymn sheet however, so to speak. In this connection one might cite the observations of Lord Browne-Wilkinson in *Westdeutsche Bank v. Islington L.B.C.* [1996] 2 W.L.R. 802 at 839. He said that the introduction into English law of the remedial constructive trust may provide a more satisfactory road forward and added:

> "The court by way of remedy might impose a constructive trust on a defendant who knowingly retains property of which the plaintiff has been unjustly deprived. Since the remedy can be tailored to the circumstances of the particular case, innocent third parties would not be prejudiced and restitutionary defences, such as change of position, are capable of being given effect. However, whether English law should follow the United States and Canada by adopting the remedial constuctive trust will have to be decided in some future case when the point is directly in issue."

In this book the approach of English law towards the recognition of equitable proprietary claims is considered and analysed in detail. Commonwealth comparisons are drawn where appropriate. The book stands very much at the intersection between three branches of law that are traditionally thought of as discrete – Trusts, Restitution and Insolvency. There is no other text directly in point. In the writing of this book however, many intellectual debts have been incurred. This is apparent from an appraisal of the text. The writings of a troika of distinguished Professors have been plundered – those of Professor Birks on the Law of Restitution, Professor Goode on the Law of Insolvency and Professor Hayton on the Law of Trusts. Of course I am not always in agreement with their views nor with the varying views expressed by Her Majesty's Judges. I would also like to thank my colleagues Alan Ward and Janet Dine for reading portions of the manuscript and making many helpful comments. Finally, I hope that the book is useful to both practitioners and academics.

Gerard McCormack
Wivenhoe Park, Essex
October 30, 1996

Contents

Chapter Six

Chapter Seven

Chapter Eight

Contents

Chapter Nine

The Identification Principles of Equitable Tracing   192

Chapter Ten

Knowing Receipt of Trust Property: Liability of   212
Recipient to make Restitution

Chapter Eleven

Assisting in a Breach of Trust: Principles of Accessory   226
Liability

TABLE OF CASES

Table of Cases

Table of Cases

Table of Cases

Table of Cases

Table of Cases

Table of Cases

Table of Cases

Table of Cases

Table of Cases

TABLE OF STATUTES

TABLE OF STATUTORY INSTRUMENTS

CHAPTER ONE

Introduction—Insolvency and the Handling of Trust Assets

The focus of this book is on the treatment of trust assets in insolvency. In the context of insolvency the difference between merely personal rights and proprietary rights is of huge significance. If one has a breach of contract or tort claim against a company that has become insolvent then one has little hope of recovering anything from the corporate carcass, as it were. One is said to be an unsecured creditor and the entitlement of an unsecured creditor to be paid ranks after the entitlements of those of numerous other creditors of the company.[1] When a company becomes insolvent the order of distribution of the assets of the company is roughly as follows:

(1) expenses of realisations;
(2) fixed charge holders;
(3) preferential debts;
(4) floating charges holders;
(5) unsecured debts.

Persons who have merely unsecured claims against the assets of the company are at the end of the queue of creditors and in the preponderance of cases there will be little, if anything, left for them. The hallowed concept of *pari passu* distribution is in fact extremely hollow because all it means is that creditors within the same class should be treated equally provided that there is no other factor to displace the principle of equality. The bulk of business is of course transacted through the corporate form so that the above-mentioned state of affairs is the order of the day. Even if the insolvent is an individual or a partnership the general regime applicable in the event of insolvency is largely the same. The main difference lies in the fact that it is not possible for individuals or partnerships to create floating charges over their assets.[2]

There are various mechanisms that a person who might superficially be regarded as extending credit on an unsecured basis to a company could potentially employ so as to elevate his claim for payment into something approaching "secured" status. One such device that is available to a supplier of goods is the reservation of title clause.[3] There are many variants to the simple

---

[1] Debts due to members in their capacity as members are paid after all other debts of the company.
[2] A floating charge enable a company to dispose of assets within the category covered by the charge in the ordinary course of its business without reference to, or the consent of the person entitled to the benefit of the charge. This state of affairs continues until the charge is said to crystallise, *i.e.* becomes converted into a fixed charge on the assets then in the possession of the company and within the scope of the charge. See generally, *Re Yorkshire Woolcombers Association Ltd* [1903] 2 Ch. 284; *Illingworth v. Houldsworth* [1904] A.C. 355; *Re Brightlife Ltd* [1987] Ch. 200; Eilis Ferran "Floating Charges—the nature of the security" [1988] C.L.J. 213.
[3] For a comprehensive study of the operation of reservation of title clauses in sale of goods contracts see McCormack *Reservation of Title* (Sweet & Maxwell, 2nd ed. 1995). See also Iwan Davies *Effective Retention of Title* (1991) and for a detailed empirical study of the operation of reservation of title clauses in commercial practice see also Sally Wheeler *Reservation of Title Clauses* (1991).

clause but basically the supplier is retaining title to goods supplied under a particular contract of sale until the goods have been paid for notwithstanding the fact that the goods have been delivered to the buyer. Of course the reservation of title clause is not a technique of general availability. The state of insolvency law and practice was reviewed by an important and influential Department of Trade review committee under the chairmanship of Sir Kenneth Cork which reported in June 1982.[4] The committee pointed out that while the supplier of goods was able to achieve protection by adopting reservation of title clauses, no similar protection was open to the supplier of consumables or of services. The report commented[5]:

> "Fuel supplied to heat furnaces, or fodder supplied for livestock, disappears on consumption and paint applied to the fabric of a factory becomes attached to the realty; the supplier on credit is necessarily left with an unsecured claim in the insolvency of the customer. The canteen operator, the contractor who cleans the factory, the pensions consultant all extend credit with no means of protection similar to that of the supplier of goods."

THE TRUST DEVICE

A device that is potentially of more benefit to such persons is that of the trust. If what might be termed assets in the broadest sense have been delivered, in a physical or non-physical sense, to a company under the umbrella of a trust with the company holding them as trustee, then the person delivering the assets is not relegated to the status of an unsecured creditor. Rather he is the beneficiary under a trust of the assets and as such has a proprietary claim to these assets. Such assets as a general proposition fall outside the grasp of the company's fixed and floating charge holders and are not available for distribution to them.[6] This general principle will be examined in this chapter but first it is useful and appropriate to say something about the different forms of insolvency procedure in English law, both individual and corporate. Four different forms of procedure will be looked at: liquidation, administrative receivership, administration and bankruptcy. The latter procedure relates to individuals whereas the others are applicable with respect to companies.

INSOLVENCY PROCEDURES

When talking about liquidations it is appropriate at the outset to distinguish between the two different types of liquidations, namely compulsory and voluntary liquidations. A compulsory liquidation stems from a winding-up order made by the court following the presentation of a petition.[7] Winding up orders are normally made by the court on the ground that the company is unable to pay

---

[4] Cmnd. 8558.
[5] *Op. cit.* at para. 1619.
[6] s. 283(3)(a) of the Insolvency Act 1986 lays down that any property held by the bankrupt on trust for any other person does not constitute part of a bankrupt's estates for the purposes of the legislation. There is no equivalent procedure in the case of corporate insolvencies but there is no doubt that a similar principle applies. A liquidator has no power to expropriate assets belonging to third parties.
[7] s. 124 of the Insolvency Act.

its debts.[8] A voluntary winding up, on the other hand, is initiated by the company itself passing a winding up resolution and it may be either a solvent winding-up (in which case it is a member's voluntary winding up) or insolvent (in which case it is a creditors voluntary winding up).

For the winding up to be a members voluntary winding up, (and therefore one over which the members retain control) the directors must have made a statutory declaration as required by section 89 of the Insolvency Act 1986 to the effect that they have formed the opinion that the company will be able to pay its debts in full, within such period, not exceeding 12 months from the commencement of the winding up, as may be specified in the declaration.[9] A creditors voluntary winding up may arise in one of two ways. First, the directors may never have made a declaration of solvency so from the outset it was a creditors voluntary winding up. The second situation arises where the directors have made a declaration of solvency but the liquidator is of the opinion that the company will be unable to pay its debts in full (together with interest) within the period stated in the declaration of solvency. In such circumstances the liquidator must take steps which have the effect of transforming the members voluntary winding into a creditors voluntary winding up.[10]

The basic task of the liquidator in all the different types of liquidation is to collect in and realise the assets of the company. Then it is his duty to distribute the assets or the proceeds of realisation amongst the company creditors, and if there is a surplus after paying off the company's debts and liabilities in full, between the company shareholders and other persons entitled thereto. To fulfill these basic duties liquidators are invested with a wide array of powers. These powers are set out in Schedule 4 to the Insolvency Act 1986. Some of these powers may be exercised by a liquidator on his own volition. Others require appropriate consent. The consent necessary is that of the court or liquidation committee in a compulsory winding up or creditors voluntary winding up. The liquidation committee is comprised of member and creditor representatives and carries out various functions in the liquidation. The consent is that of the members, appropriately enough, in a members voluntary winding up given in the form of an extraordinary resolution. One of the powers exercisable by a liquidator only with prior authorisation is that of paying any class of creditors in full. This power however, does not give a liquidator any leeway to change the order of priority. Before utilising this facility a liquidator must therefore ensure that the remaining assets of the company are adequate to enable him to pay also all debts and liabilities of the company which rank prior to, or *pari passu* with, the class of creditors who have been paid off first chronologically.[11]

Liquidation may fairly be described as a terminal process. At the end of the day once the liquidator has completed the task of collecting in, realising and distributing the assets of the company the company is struck off the register of

[8] s. 122(1)(f) of the Insolvency Act. s. 123 contains a definition of inability to pay debts. Another possible ground of winding up is that it is just and equitable that the company should be wound up.

[9] It should be noted that a director making a declaration without having reasonable grounds for the opinion that the company will be able to pay its debts in full within the period specified is liable to a fine and/or imprisonment. If its debts are not paid in full within the period specified it is to be presumed (unless the contrary is shown) that the director did not have reasonable grounds for his opinion: see s. 89(4) and (5) of the Insolvency Act.

[10] See s. 95.

[11] See Rajak *Company Liquidations* (1988) p. 225.

companies and dissolved. This is legal death so to speak with the concomitant loss of legal personality though the company may be brought back to life for certain purposes however.[12]

The legal regime of bankruptcy which is confined to individuals is very much the equivalent of liquidation though there are significant differences in the two forms of procedure largely explicable on the basis that individuals cannot for practical reasons receive a legal sentence of death in the same way as companies.[13] In place of the liquidator we have the trustee in bankruptcy whose function it is to administer the estate of the bankrupt. The property of the bankrupt vests automatically in the trustee in bankruptcy. According to section 306(2) of the Insolvency Act 1986 this effect occurs without any conveyance, assignment or transfer. This is one significant difference from liquidation where an application to the court is necessary to vest company property in the liquidator.[14] In practice, because a liquidator has such wide powers, such orders are rarely made and rarely necessary. One case where an order might be sought springs from the possible requirement of a foreign jurisdiction that the liquidator have title to the company's foreign assets. It is the function of the trustee in bankruptcy to collect the assets of the bankrupt, to realise the same and to distribute the proceeds of realisation amongst the creditors of the bankrupt.

According to section 283 of the Insolvency Act the estate available for distribution encompasses "all property belonging to or vested in the bankrupt at the commencement of the bankruptcy" but there are certain exclusions. Section 283(2) for instance excludes such tools, books, vehicles and other items of equipment as are necessary to the bankrupt for use personally by him in his employment, business or vocation as well as such clothing, bedding, furniture, household equipment and provisions as are necessary for satisfying the basic domestic needs of the bankrupt and his family. Most importantly for our purposes, section 283(3) excludes any property held by the bankrupt on trust for any other person. The state of bankruptcy of an individual commences on the day on which a bankruptcy order is made and continues until the individual is discharged from bankruptcy. The concept of a discharge marks out bankruptcy from liquidation where there is no such concept. Indeed, in the preponderance of cases, time alone has a curative effect. Section 279(2) lays down that generally discharge occurs automatically three years after the making of the bankruptcy order.

ADMINISTRATION ORDERS

In 1982 the Cork Committee on Insolvency Law and Practice recommended the introduction of a wholly new corporate insolvency mechanism that was primarily designed to facilitate the rescue and rehabilitation of the viable parts

[12] See *Gower's Principles of Modern Company Law* (5th ed. 1992) p. 775: "A contrast between the death of an individual and that of a company is that, without divine intervention but merely by an order of the court, a dissolved company can be resurrected." This miracle can be performed under the aegis of ss. 651 and 653 of the Companies Act 1985 as amended to by the Companies Act 1989 so as to reverse the decision of the House of Lords in *Bradley v. Eagle Star Insurance Co.* [1989] A.C. 957. On the new legislative dispensation see *Re Workvale Ltd* [1991] 1 W.L.R. 294.
[13] Where partnerships become insolvent the winding up is conducted in accordance with the provisions of the Insolvent Partnerships Order 1986.
[14] s. 145 of the Insolvency Act 1986.

of a company's business that was in financial difficulties. The substance of these recommendations were implemented in Part 11 of the Insolvency Act 1986. A new procedure known as administration was introduced. If an administration order is made an official called an administrator, who must be a qualified insolvency practitioner, takes charge of the company's affairs.[15] According to section 9 of the Insolvency Act a petition for the appointment of an administrator may be presented either by the company, by the directors or by a creditor. A floating chargeholder has an effective veto on the appointment of an administrator.[16] There is a statutorily-imposed moratorium on the enforcement of claims against the company following the presentation of a petition for the appointment of an administrator and after the making of an order.[17] The purpose of the moratorium is to give the company a breathing space in which the administrator may formulate his proposals.

According to section 8 of the Insolvency Act the court has power to make an administration order if it is satisfied that the company is or is likely to become unable to pay its debts and secondly, if it considers that the making of an order would be likely to achieve one or more of certain stated objectives. The prime of these objectives is the survival of the company, and the whole or any part of it's undertaking, as a going concern. Another possible objective is the more advantageous realisation of the company's assets than would be effected on a winding up. The fact that floating charge holders have a veto on the appointment of an administrator has led to the drafting of so-called lightweight floating charges. These floating charges have been brought into being expressly for the purpose of conferring such a veto and have no other purpose in that there are no free assets on which the floating charge might bite.[18] The lender is already secured up to the hilt by fixed charges on all the company's assets. The grant of the veto may be viewed as part of a delicate balancing act by the legislature and gives to the floating chargeholder what section 19(5) in a sense takes away. The latter subsection stipulates that debts and expenses incurred by the administrator while in office, are payable out of the property of the company in his custody or control in priority to the claims of a floating chargeholder. So post-administration expenses have a form of super-priority but a beneficiary under a trust is unaffected by this legislative imposition. Such a beneficiary is however caught by the embargo contained in section 11(3)(d) of the Insolvency Act which lays down that after the making of an administration order no proceedings may be commenced or continued against the company or its property except with the consent of the administrator or the leave of the court and subject (where the court gives leave) to such terms as the court may impose.[19]

---

[15] s. 8 of the Act sets out the circumstances in which the court may make an administration order.
[16] s. 9(3) of the Insolvency Act.
[17] ss. 10 and 11 of the Insolvency Act.
[18] See *Re Croftbell Ltd* [1990] B.C.L.C. 844 on which see Oditah [1991] J.B.L. 49.
[19] For the circumstances in which leave may be granted see the Court of Appeal judgments in *Bristol Airports plc v. Powdrill* [1990] Ch. 744 and and *Re Atlantic Computer Systems (No. 1)* [1991] B.C.L.C. 606. The basic message is that an administration should not be conducted at the expense of those who have proprietary rights which they are seeking to exercise save to the degree that this may be inevitable if the purpose of the administration is to succeed and then only to a limited extent. After the presentation of a petition for the appointment of an administrator but before the making of an administration order a similar embargo against the commencement or continuance of proceedings exists, and in this case it is only the court that may grant leave: s. 10(1)(c).

RECEIVERSHIP

Liquidation, bankruptcy and administration are all collective insolvency procedures premised on the assumption that collective effort in the collection, realisation and distribution of assets or in the attainment of the goal of corporate rehabilitation is better than the unseemly free-for-all of action by individual creditors.[20] Receivership is different in that essentially it means the realisation of assets for the benefit of the secured creditor by whom the receiver was appointed.[21] Having said that, once the receiver is appointed, certain duties are owed over and above those to the appointor. For instance, prior ranking charge holders and preferential creditors must be paid off first out of assets covered by the floating charge.[22] A debenture containing a floating charge will normally specify a number of events that entitle the debenture holder to appoint a receiver. In addition, a debenture holder is entitled to apply to the court for the appointment of a receiver if his security is in jeopardy.[23]

The Insolvency Act 1986 has introduced the concept of an administrative receiver as defined in section 29(2) of the Act. Basically this is a receiver of the whole or substantially the whole of the company's property appointed by a floating charge holder. Sections 28–49 of the Insolvency Act put a lot of the law relating to receivers on a statutory footing but it is still necessary to refer to common law principles. The receiver displaces the board of directors from management functions insofar as the charged assets are concerned.[24] They continue in office, however, and are still required and able to do certain things.[25] The fundamental task of a receiver is to realise the assets of the company covered by the charge for the benefit of the debenture holder who made the appointment. To facilitate the accomplishment of this goal of optimum realisation the receiver is normally invested with extensive powers to manage the affairs of the company by the debenture. In the case of an administrative receiver, Schedule 1 to the Insolvency Act 1986 confers various far-reaching powers which are possessed by the administrative receiver unless a contrary provision appears in the debenture. Section 43 gives an administrative receiver the power, with leave of the court, to dispose of property that is subject to a prior or equal security interest. It is a condition of any order made by the court that the net proceeds of the disposal, and, where those proceeds are less than such amount as may be determined by the court to be the net amount which would be realised on the sale of the property in the open market by a willing vendor, such sums as may be required to make good the deficiency, shall be applied towards discharging the sums secured by the security. Does this section encompass

---

[20] See generally R. M. Goode *Principles of Corporate Insolvency Law* (1990) Chaps. 1 and 2.

[21] See generally *Downsview Nominees Ltd v. First City Corp. Ltd* [1993] 3 All E.R. 626. See also *China & South Sea Bank v. Tan* [1989] 3 All E.R. 839.

[22] s. 40 of the Insolvency Act 1986 lays down that the preferential debts of a company shall be paid out of the assets coming to the hands of the receiver in priority to any claims for principal or interest in respect of the debentures.

[23] See *McMahon v. North Kent Co.* [1891] 2 Ch. 148; *Edwards v. Standard Rolling Stock* [1893] 1 Ch. 574; *Re Victoria Steamboats Co.* [1897] 1 Ch. 158; *Re Tilt Cove Copper Co.* [1913] 2 Ch. 588 and *Re New York Taxicab Co.* [1913] 1 Ch. 1.

[24] *Re Emmadart Ltd* [1979] Ch. 540; *Gomba Holdings U.K. Ltd v. Homan* [1986] 1 W.L.R. 1301.

[25] It was held in *Newhart Developments Ltd v. Co-operative Bank Ltd* [1978] Q.B. 814 that the directors could bring an action on behalf of the company against a debentureholder for the improper exercise of his powers but *cf. Tudor Grange Holdings Ltd v. Citibank N.A.* [1992] Ch. 53.

property that is held by the company on trust? The section talks about the disposal of property which is subject to a security. The word "security" is defined in section 248(b) of the Insolvency Act as meaning "any mortgage, charge, lien or other security." This definition appears to exclude trust property. This does not mean however that an administrative receiver will automatically incur liability by disposing of property that is held by the company on trust. Section 234 of the Insolvency Act 1986 lays down that where an administrative receiver disposes of property which is not property of the company, he is not liable to the true owner if, at the time of seizure or disposal, he believes and has reasonable grounds to believe that he is entitled to seize or dispose of the property. Liability arises only insofar as any loss or damage was caused by his own negligence. Furthermore, the administrator has a lien on the propety or the proceeds of its sale for such expenses as were incurred in connection with the seizure or disposal. The beneficiary under the trust has the right to trace the proceeds of sale. Section 234 and the exemption from liability therein contained applies not only to an administrator but also to an administrative receiver, a liquidator and a provisional liquidator. Section 304 of the Insolvency Act embodies a similar exemption from liability insofar as the trustee in bankruptcy is concerned. However, when the provision is read in conjunction with section 283 it is clear that property which was held by the bankrupt on trust does not form part of the bankrupt's estate and the only barrier between the trustee and liability is that erected by section 304.

EXCLUSION OF TRUST ASSETS FROM THE DISTRIBUTABLE PROPERTY OF AN INSOLVENT

As we have seen the assets of an insolvent available for distribution among its creditors do not include assets held by the insolvent on trust for others. There is an express statutory statement of this proposition with respect to individual insolvency. Section 283(a) of the Insolvency Act states that any property which is held by the bankrupt on trust for any other person does not constitute part of of the bankrupt's estate for the purpose of the legislation. Somewhat suprisingly, there is no equivalent provision as regards corporate insolvency though it is clear that a similar principle obtains. The liquidator, etc., can have no better claim to the assets than the company as trustee had. While not directly in point the decision of the House of Lords in the Scottish appeal *Heritable Reversionary Company Ltd v. Millar*[26] does have some bearing on the matter. In that case Lord Watson said[27]:

> "An apparent title to land or personal estate, carrying no real right of property with it, does not, in the ordinary or in any true legal sense, make such land or personal estate the property of the person who holds the title. That which, in legal as well as conventional language, is described as a man's property is estate, whether heritable or moveable, in which he has a beneficial interest which the law allows him to dispose of. It does not include estate in which he has no beneficial interest, and which he cannot dispose of without committing a fraud."

[26] [1892] A.C. 598. See generally Hamish Anderson "The Treatment of Trust Assets in English Insolvency Law" in Ewan McKendrick ed. *Commercial Aspects of Trusts and Fiduciary Obligations* (1992), 167, pp. 171–172.
[27] *ibid.* at 614.

7

TRUST MUST BE PROPERLY CONSTITUTED

While it is well established that trust assets do not constitute part of the estate of an insolvent, it is important to state that the trust must be properly established before the exclusion can operate.[28] It is not enough that there is a contractual right to have a trust established when the would-be trustee becomes insolvent. In such a situation all that the beneficiary has is an unsecured claim. The point is well illustrated by reference to *MacJordan Construction Ltd v. Brookmount Erostin Ltd.*[29]

Brookmount was a property developer which had become insolvent. It had entered into a building contract with the plaintiff builder which provided for interim payments to be made to the builder and also for Brookmount to retain as retention moneys 3 per cent of the amount due as interim payments. It was laid down in the contract that Brookmount's interests in the retention moneys was fiduciary as a trustee for the builder. It so happened that no sum was ever set aside in respect of the retention moneys. Brookmount had granted a floating charge over all its assets to a bank and the latter proceeded to appoint administrative receivers. The plaintiff claimed that the amount of the retention moneys were held on trust for it and that it had priority over the bank's floating charge. The Court of Appeal rejected this proposition. Although Brookmount was contractually obliged under its agreement with the plaintiff to establish a retention fund, this process had not been gone through and thus there was no fund impressed with a trust of the retention moneys. Accordingly the builder had no equitable interest that could take priority over the floating charge of the bank.

Counsel for the plaintiff builder relied on *Rayack Construction Ltd v. Lampeter Meat Co. Ltd*[30] and *Re Arthur Sanders Ltd.*[31] In the *Rayack*[32] case Vinelott J. held that a provision in a building contract similar to the one in the present case imposed upon the employer a contractual obligation "to appropriate and set aside as a separate trust fund a sum equal to that part of the sum certified in any interim certificate as due in repsect of work completed which the employer is entitled to retain ..." In *Re Arthur Sanders Ltd*[33] Nourse J. held that as between a solvent employer on the one hand and an insolvent builder on the other hand, the retention sum that the employer ought to have appropriated and set aside under a building contract should be treated as notionally set aside.

Scott L.J. who delivered the judgment of the Court of Appeal in the *MacJordan Construction* case was unimpressed by the references to these authorities. He agreed with the decision in *Re Arthur Sanders Ltd* which he said prevented the employer from obtaining, by reason of its own breach of contract in failing to set aside a rentention fund, a more extensive right of set-off that would have been available to it if it had done so. Scott L.J. commented that where however

---

[28] See generally R.M. Goode *Principles of Corporate Insolvency Law* (1990) pp. 56–57.
[29] 56 Build.L.R. 1; [1992] B.C.L.C. 350.
[30] (1979) 12 Build.L.R. 30.
[31] (1981) 17 Build.L.R. 125. See also *Re Jartay Developments Ltd* (1983) 22 Build.L.R. 134 and *Concorde Construction Co. Ltd v. Colgan Ltd* (1984) 29 Build.L.R. 120.
[32] (1979) 12 Build.L.R. 30 at 37.
[33] See (1981) 17 Build.L.R. 125 at 136. Nourse J. said in the case of a solvent employer, equity, looking on that as done which ought to be done, will not allow any advantage to be gained from his failure to set aside a fund.

the employer was insolvent, whether or not in liquidation, and where the position was being considered as between the builder and other creditors of the insolvent employer, there was no reason at all for treating the employer as having set aside the retention fund when it had not in fact done so and no reason for treating the contractor as other than an unsecured creditor.[34]

Wates Construction (London) Ltd v. Franthom Property Ltd[35] was similarly distinguishable. In that case the plaintiff builder applied for an order requiring the defendant employer to establish the requisite retention fund. There was no insolvency and no issue of priorities to be resolved involving any other creditor of the employer. The employer unsuccessfully defended the action on the basis that it ought to be allowed to continue to use all its available assets as working capital and should not be compelled by the establishment of the retention funds to deprive itself of part of its working capital.[36]

STATUTORY TRUST UPON LIQUIDATION

Trusts in favour of third parties over property held by the company as legal owner that have been created pre-liquidation must be distinguished from the statutory trust that is said to arise upon liquidation.[37] The company in liquidation remains the legal owner of its assets unless the court makes an order pursuant to section 145 of the Insolvency Act 1986 vesting them in the liquidator. It ceases however to be the beneficial owner from the commencement of the winding up. This is because the Insolvency legislation directs that the assets must be applied only for certain specified purposes, namely satisfaction of the claims of creditors with any surplus paid to contributories. The general issue was considered by the House of Lords in *Ayerst (Inspector of Taxes) v. C. & K. (Construction) Ltd.*[38] Lord Diplock pointed out that the statutory scheme for dealing with the assets of a company in the course of winding up its affairs differs in several respects from a trust of specific property created by the voluntary act of the settlor. Some of these differences were similar to those which distinguished the administration of estates of deceased persons and of bankrupts from an ordinary trust. Another difference which was peculiar to the winding-up of a company was that the actual custody, control, realisation and distribution of the proceeds of the property which was subject to the statutory scheme was taken out of the hands of the legal owner of the property, the company, and vested in a third party, the liquidator, over whom the company had no control. Notwithstanding these considerations the effect of the statute was to give to the property of a company in liquidation that essential characteristic which distinguished trust property from other property, namely, that it could not be used or disposed of by the legal owner for his own benefit, but must be used or disposed of for the benefit of other persons.[39] Retention of the legal

---

[34] [1992] B.C.L.C. 350 at 359.

[35] (1991) 53 Build.L.R. 23.

[36] See the comments of Scott L.J. in the case of *MacJordan Construction v. Brockmount Erostin* 56 Build.L.R. 1; [1992] B.C.L.C. 350 at 355–356.

[37] See generally Hamish Anderson in Ewan McKendrick ed. *Commercial Aspects of Trusts and Fiduciary Obligations* (1992) 167 p. 171.

[38] [1976] A.C. 167. See also *Re Ashpurton Estates Ltd* [1983] Ch. 110; *R. v. Registrar of Companies, ex parte Central Bank of India* [1986] 1 Q.B. 1114; *Re Lines Bros Ltd* [1983] 1 Ch. 1.

[39] *ibid.* at 180.

ownership of property did not prevent the full owner from being divested of the beneficial ownership of it. This was in fact the consequence of the Insolvency statute.[40]

STRUCTURE OF THE BOOK

Problems of structure are endemic with books that deal with an interlocking subject matter. This work is no exception. Sometimes it is difficult if not impossible to compartmentalise issues but certain branches of doctrine are more susceptible of easy segregation than others. It is a basic principle of the law of insolvency that all creditors of the same class are treated equally when it comes to the distribution of corporate assets on an insolvency. This is referred to as the *pari passu* principle. This principle and its application to trust claims is considered in Chapter 2. Particular attention is paid in this chapter to the controversial decision of the House of Lords in *British Eagle v. Air France*[41] and its ramifications in the trust sphere. Chapter 3 looks in a general sense at what might be described as the diminution of trust claims. Sometimes a trust claimant will suffer some loss of priority because of a competing security interest. Alternatively the amount of the trust claim may be reduced because of expenses properly chargeable to the trust that are incurred by an insolvency practitioner in administering the trust assets. Moreover, the trust arrangement may be adversely affected by some invalidating provision of the Insolvency Act. All these issues are considered in Chapter 3. Chapter 4 deals with conditional payments and the *Quistclose* trust. Chapter 5 looks at proprietary claims in the context of abuse of fiduciary position and bribes and secret commissions. Chapter 6 examines instances of the use of the remedial constructive trust; the granting of a proprietary remedy at the discretion of the court. Chapter 7 tackles the issue of payments made under a mistake. Chapter 8 attempts to unravel the controversial concept of tracing value, both at common law and in equity. The chapter concentrates on common law tracing and the prerequisites of an equitable tracing claim. Chapter 9 is concerned with the identification principles of equitable tracing. Chapter 10 looks at liability for receipt of trust property—what is traditionally discussed in trust textbooks under the heading of constructive trust liability for knowing receipt. Finally, Chapter 11 examines the issue of liability for rendering assistance in the disposition of trust property in breach of trust.

One might ask why I look at mistaken payments and not, say, look at payments made under coercion or duress? Apart from the factors of economy of exposition and space one might respond by stating that this does not purport to be a general treatise on the law of restitution. Mistaken payments are singled out for special consideration not only because of their proprietary effects but by reason of the perceived frequency with which they occur. The proper role of proprietary claims to assets within the overall law of insolvency is considered throughout the text but more particularly in Chapters 5, 6 and 7. At this juncture, however, it seems appropriate to discuss more generally the role of equity in commercial transactions and also to contrast equitable proprietary claims of the kind considered in this book with the floating charge which has been the mainstay of bank finance for over a century.

---

[40] *ibid.*
[41] [1975] 2 All E.R. 390.

10

EQUITY IN COMMERCIAL TRANSACTIONS

Lord Nicholls suggested in 1995 in *Royal Brunei Airlines v. Tan*[42] that the role of equity in commercial transactions is a topical one. He pointed out that recourse is had to equity in situations of insolvency. While his comments were specifically to the situation of liability for knowing assistance in a breach of trust they carry a more general resonance. The role of equity in commercial transactions has however been a topical one down through the ages. The nineteenth century saw the judicial recognition of the floating charge which might be described as a testament to the ingenuity of nineteenth century equity practitioners.[43] The characteristics of a floating charge were spelled out by Lord Macnaghten in *Governments Stock and Other Securities Investment Co. Ltd v. Manila Railway Co. Ltd*[44] who said[45]:

> "A floating security is an equitable charge on the assets for the time being of a going concern. It attaches to the subject charged in the varying condition in which it happens to be from time to time. It is the essence of such a charge that it remains dormant until the undertaking charged ceases to be a going concern or until the person in whose favour the charge is created intervenes. His right to intervene may of course be suspended by agreement. But if there is no agreement for suspension, he may exercise his right whenever he pleases after default."

The same judge distinguished between a fixed and a floating charge in *Illingworth v. Houldsworth*.[46] He stated[47]:

> "I should have thought there was not much difficulty in defining what a floating charge is in contrast to what is called a specific charge. A specific charge, I think, is one that without more fastens on ascertained and definite property or property capable of being ascertained and defined; a floating charge, on the other hand, is ambulatory and shifting in its nature, hovering and so to speak floating with the property which it is intended to affect until some event occurs or some act is done which causes it to settle and fasten on the subject of the charge within its reach and grasp."

It may be argued that there is a certain degree of vagueness associated with this definition. In particular use of the words "ambulatory" and "shifting" may serve to mystify rather than to enlighten. Be that as it may, a specific or fixed charge (the two terms are synonyms) prevents a company from disposing of an unencumbered title to the assets which form the subject-matter of the charge.

---

[42] [1995] 3 All E.R. 97. See also the comments of Lord Browne-Wilkinson in *Westdeutsche Bank v. Islington L.B.C.* [1996] 2 W.L.R. 802 at 828.
[43] For an extremely useful account of the historical evolution of the floating charge see Pennington (1960) 23 M.L.R. 630. See also Ferran [1988] C.L.J. 213.
[44] [1897] A.C. 81.
[45] *ibid.* at 86.
[46] [1904] A.C. 355.
[47] *ibid.* at 358. See also the comments of Romer L.J. in *Illingworth v. Houldsworth* on appeal where the case is reported under the name of *Re Yorkshire Woolcombers Association Ltd* [1903] 2 Ch. 284 at 295: "[I]f a charge has the three characteristics that I am about to mention it is a floating charge. (1) if it is a charge on a class of assets of a company, present and future; (2) if that class is one which, in the ordinary course of the business of the company, would be changing from time to time; and (3) if you find that by the charge it is contemplated that, until some future step is taken by or on behalf of those interested in the charge, the company may carry on its business in the ordinary way as far as concerns the particular class of assets I am dealing with."

With a floating charge, on the other hand, the chargor is entitled to dispose of assets within the category covered by the charge in the ordinary course of its business without the consent of, or reference to, the person who has the benefit of the charge.

GENESIS OF THE FLOATING CHARGE

In 1982 the high-powered Cork committee[48] which looked at the state of British Insolvency Law and Practice took the view that the flaoting charge had become so fundamental a part of the financial structure of the United Kingdom that its abolition could not be contemplated.[49] The judicial development of the floating charge was a specific response to the persistent needs of companies for more capital.[50] The Industrial Revolution meant that only a small proportion of a company's wealth might be tied up in buildings and fixed equipment with the bulk of its assets being in the form of raw materials, manufactured goods or goods in the process of manufacture, stock-in-trade and debts owed to the company by trade customers. The existing fixed charge form of security meant that the main part of a company's assets were not available to secure loans made to it. Initially it appeared that creditors were prepared to lend on an unsecured basis but the pace of industrial and commercial expansion carried in its wake a number of corporate collapses. Creditors became reticient about lending on a totally unsecured basis and the advent of the limited liability company made matters worse from a creditor perspective. There were two principal judicial responses to this phenomenon. First, in *Holroyd v. Marshall*[51] the House of Lords held that it was legally possible for a company to create fixed charges over its after-acquired assets. Secondly, the concept of a floating charge was given the seal of judicial approval. The landmark decision is generally taken to be that of the Court of Appeal in Chancery in *Re Panama, New Zealand and Australian Royal Mail Co.*[52]

The floating charge is a creature of equity in that it was judicially recognised by courts of equity. Neverthless it arises from the agreement of the parties manifested in the instrument of charges. The contractual basis of the floating charge has been emphasised in a series of judicial decisions which hold that it is possible for the parties to agree on the events on which crystallisation will occur, *i.e.* the floating charge being converted into a fixed charge[53]. Moreover, the Court of Appeal has recently affirmed, as a matter of contractual agreement, that it is possible to combine in the same instrument of charge a fixed charge over book debts while unrealised with a floating charge over book debt proceeds.[54]

The floating charge has also been the subject of statutory consideration over the years. The genesis of the floating charge as well as the history of legislative

---

[48] The committee was chaired by Sir Kenneth Cork of Cork Gully.
[49] Cmnd. 8558 para. 1531. The committee however recommended that a fund equal to 10% of the net realisations of assets subject to a floating charge should be made available for distribution among the ordinary unsecured creditors. This recommendation has never been implemented.
[50] See generally Pennington (1960) 23 M.L.R. at 630–634.
[51] (1862) 10 H.L. Cas. 191.
[52] (1870) 5 Ch. App. 318.
[53] See e.g. *Re Brightlife Ltd* [1987] Ch. 200.
[54] *Re New Bullas Trading* [1994] B.C.C. 36; [1994] 1 B.C.L.C. 485.

intervention over the years was traced by Hoffmann J. in *Re Brightlife Ltd.*[55] He explained that the floating charge was invented by Victorian lawyers to enable manufacturing and trading companies to raise loan capital on debentures in that security could be given over the whole of a company's undertaking without inhibiting its ability to trade. The converse side of these advantages was potential prejudice to the general body of creditors, who might know nothing of the floating charge but find that all the company's assets, including the very goods which they had just delivered on credit, had been swept up by the debenture holder. The judge outlined the form of the legislative reply saying[56]:

"Parliament has responded, first, by restricting the rights of the holder of a floating charge and second, by requiring public notice of the existence and enforcement of the charge. For example, priority was given to preferential debts in 1897 and the Companies Act 1907 invalidated floating charges created within three months before the commencement of the winding up. This period has since been extended and is now one year. The registration of floating and other charges was introduced by the Companies Act 1900. The Companies Act 1907 required registration of the appointment of a receiver and the Companies Act 1929 required notice of such appointment to be given on the company's letters and invoices."

The judge went on to say that these limited and pragmatic interventions by the legislature made it wholly inappropriate for the courts to impose additional restrictive rules on grounds of public policy. While this judicial abnegation of an innovative law-making role may have some merit, the floating charge has been attacked in many quarters for being an excessive security in that it extends to future assets which have not been paid for by the company.[57] These criticisms have found a judicial echo on occasion. One might instance the observations of Buckley J. as long ago as 1905 in *Re London Pressed Hinge Co. Ltd.*[58] These comments found a more recent judicial echo in the remarks of Robert Goff L.J. in *Glough Mill Ltd v. Martin*[59] who said that the mechanism of the floating charge on which banks relied was as much open to criticism as that of the reservation of title clause which they were prone to criticise. As Hoffmann J. pointed out in *Re Brightlife Ltd* criticism of the excesses of the floating charge has led on occasion to legislative curtailment of the advantages associated with the charge. In actual fact the decision in *Re Brightlife Ltd* led to another legislative curtailment. Hoffmann J. held it was possible for chargor and chargee to agree that a floating charge should crystallise even though the chargee had not yet appointed a

---

[55] [1987] Ch. 200.

[56] *ibid.* at 215.

[57] See Cork Committee Report (Cmnd. 8558) para. 1553.

[58] [1905] 1 Ch. 576 at 581. He said: "[Where a floating charge has been granted] money is lent or goods consigned to the company in respect of which a debt accrues to a creditor, and so long as the security floats, as it is termed, and no receiver is appointed, the creditor has a possibility or expectation of being paid by the company, for, as between the company and the debenture holders, the former may pay in the ordinary course of business. He may have lent his money, or consigned his goods, to the company last week; but if he has the audacity to ask for payment and to enforce his legal remedies to obtain it, the debenture holder obtains a receiver in a proceeding to which the execution creditor is not a party and thus closes the door against him, taking his money or goods as part of the security, and leaving the creditor who supplied the money or the goods to go unpaid. I regret to be driven to the conclusion that, as the law stands, these are the rights of the debenture holder entitled to a floating charge."

[59] [1985] 1 W.L.R. 111.

receiver nor had the company gone into liquidation nor ceased to carry on business in the ordinary way. In a liquidation or receivership preferential creditors are paid ahead of floating charge holders but after fixed charge holders. If a floating charge became fixed prior to liquidation or receivership then the debenture holder would become entitled to be paid before the preferential creditors. In the wake of the *Brightlife* decision the position was changed by the Insolvency Act 1986 which, for the purpose of the Act, defines a floating charge as a charge which as created was a floating charge.[60] In a liquidation or receivership therefore, the floating charge holder will now have to be paid after preferential creditors even if the floating charge has crystallised prior to the commencement of liquidation or receivership.

THE FLOATING CHARGE VERSUS EQUITABLE PROPRIETARY CLAIMS

Preferential creditor claims consist mainly of claims by the Inland Revenue to payment of certain taxes and certain employee claims.[61] Enhancing the legal effectiveness of floating charge will work to the advantage of banks and other lending institutions holding such charges and may work to the disadvantage of the Revenue and the Trade Union lobby representing employees. One may take the equivalent of judicial notice by saying that the latter groups may carry significant weight in legislative circles. Less influential possibly is the ordinary unsecured creditor though the significance of the small business sector that essentially makes up the category of the unsecured creditor should not be underestimated. The usual counterweight to arguments that focus on the disadvantaged position of the unsecured creditor are considerations of commercial convenience and the importance for the economy of maintaining a supply of credit.[62] One leading commentator has argued strongly for a strengthening of the position of the floating charge holder.[63] He says[64]:

"[The] highest policy objective should be to confer on the typical bank floating charge a clear-cut first-ranking priority status. Fundamental commercial objectives of the solvent corporate borrowing sector are best achieved in the generality of cases through enhancing access to mainstream bank finance sources, facilitated by improving the priority effectivess of the floating charge as the most convenient form of business security."

Recognising and enforcing to the full provisions in a debenture embodying a floating charge clearly favours banks. The impact on the position of banks of judicial validation of equitable proprietary claims is not so clearcut. With some

---

[60] s. 251.

[61] The categories of preferential debt are set out in Schedule 6 to the Insolvency Act 1986.

[62] This point was mentioned in a consultative letter from the Department of Trade and Industry (July 7, 1988) that was concerned with possible limitations on so-called automatic crystallisation clauses in floating charges. The letter said: "Such clauses may often be inserted precisely because neither the chargee nor the company will know at the time that the crystallising event has occurred. A requirement to notify lenders could undermine the reason for such clauses, and, in doing so, prevent potential lenders from offering loans where they might do so now given the protection conferred by automatic crystallisation. Lenders could be deprived of the opportunity for profitable business and companies could be deprived of a means of raising finance."

[63] See W.J. Gough *Company Charges* (2nd ed. 1996).

[64] *ibid*, Preface, p. vii.

types of proprietary claim banks and other conventional lenders are the beneficiaries. With other types of proprietary claim the contrary is the case. For example, banks may benefit from a *Quistclose* trust in many instances. If money is lent by a bank for a particular purpose and that purpose is not fulfilled the money is said to be held on a resulting trust for the lender.[65] Recognition of a trust claim in this example clearly improves the relative ranking of the bank if the original loan had been made on an unsecured basis. The *Quistclose* case is an example of a particular kind of conditional payment that gave rise to a trust. Other conditional payment situations may be contemplated such as where a consumer has prepaid for goods or services on the basis that if the goods or services are not supplied the money should be returned. In these cases recognition and enforcement of a trust is to the detriment of banks. So too with equitable proprietary claims in the generality of other scenarios. There may be cases however where affording a person proprietary rights may not impact adversely on the position of banks. It is a mistake to suppose that in all cases the prime reason for invoking proprietary remedies is to gain priority over other creditors. We will see in Chapter 5 that proprietary relief is sometimes sought so as to circumvent difficulties in the assessment of damages or in the enforcement of judgments across international frontiers. In that chapter the case is made for a more discretionary approach towards the award of proprietary remedies in cases of breach of fiduciary duty. Such relief may be tailored so as to take account of the position of third party creditors who have acquired rights against the property of the company. Where however equitable proprietary rights are relied upon so as to gain a priority advantage over secured lenders it is suggested that judicial caution should be the order of the day.[66] While both the equitable proprietary claim and the floating charge are, in a broad sense, the creatures or would-be creatures of equity, there is a sharp differentiation. The floating charge security has arisen as a result of express contractual stipulation whereas there is no such stipulation in the case of the equitable proprietary claim. The floating charge holder has bargained for rights of a proprietary nature whereas the other claimant has not. In this connection one might cite the observations of Lord Browne-Wilkinson in the recent case *Westdeutsche Bank v Islington L.B.C.*[67] Along with many other judges he warned against the wholesale importation into commercial law of equitable principles inconsistent with the speed and certainty which were essential requirements for the orderly conduct of business affairs. Lord Browne-Wilkinson said that otherwise[68]:

"[A] businessman who has entered into transactions relating to or dependent upon property rights could find that assets which apparently belong to one person in fact belong to another: that these are 'off balance sheet' liabilities of which he cannot be aware; that the property rights and liabilities arise from circumstances unknown not only to himself but also to anybody else who has been involved in the transactions. A new area of unmanagable risk will be introduced into commercial dealings."

---

[65] *Barclays Bank Ltd v. Quistclose Investments Ltd* [1970] A.C. 567.
[66] See the comments of Judge Paul Baker Q.C. in *Re Stapylton Fletcher Ltd* [1995] 1 All E.R. 192 at 213–214: "The court must be very cautious in devising equitable interests and remedies which evade the statutory scheme for distribution on insolvency. It cannot do it because of some perceived injustice arising as a consequence only of the insolvency."
[67] [1996] 2 W.L.R. 802; [1996] All E.R. 961. The *Westdeutsche* case seems bound to generate an enormous academic literature. For an early taste see Birks [1996] *Restitution Law Review* 3.
[68] *ibid.* at 828.

CHAPTER TWO

Equality of Treatment for Creditors in an Insolvency—Trust Claims and *Pari Passu* Distribution of Available Assets

Section 107 of the Insolvency Act 1986 provides that subject to the provisions of the Act as to preferential payments, the company's property in a voluntary winding up shall be applied in satisfaction of the company's liabilities *pari passu*. The same dispensation holds good for both compulsory winding up and bankruptcy proceedings.[1] How does this principle impact upon the use of the trust mechanism to achieve payment in the event of insolvency. The basic requirement is that the trust must be properly constituted at the onset of liquidation/bankruptcy. If the trust has not been duly established before the onset of insolvency then there is a risk of conflict with the principle of *pari passu* distribution of an insolvent's estate among creditors. In this chapter the interaction of the principle of *pari passu* distribution with the mounting of trust claims to available assets will be discussed.

The *locus classicus* on the application of the *pari passu* principle in the insolvency context is the decision of the House of Lords in *British Eagle v. Air France*.[2] That case demonstrates a strict approach towards the practical working out of the *pari passu* doctrine and has provoked considerable controversy and debate. The decision will be examined in detail in this chapter. The chapter then goes on to consider the practical implications of the *British Eagle* case with particular reference to direct payment clauses and forfeiture clauses in construction contracts. In the direct payment situation a long standing construction industry practice has been put in doubt by the decision. A change in contracting practice was felt by practitioners in the field to be necessary to overcome the perceived problem thrown up by the interpretation placed by the House of Lords on the *pari passu* principle in *British Eagle*. This chapter will consider whether or not the change was in fact necessary.

British Eagle has also shone the spotlight of legal uncertainty on forfeiture clauses in construction contracts. A liquidator is said to take the property of the company as he finds it. In other words the liquidator of a company takes the company's property subject to pre-existing "equities" or trusts. A person who benefits under the equity or trust is not in any way infringing the rule of *pari passu* or equal distribution of available assets by advancing his claim to enforcement of the equity or trust. There is a fine line however between this state of affairs and a clause which invalidly purports to divest an insolvent of his property on an insolvency. The dividing line will be explored in the chapter.

Exploration of this demarcation necessitates a more general, albeit brief,

---

[1] With regard to compulsory winding up r. 4.181(1) of the Insolvency Rules 1986 provide: "Debts other than preferential debts rank equally between themselves in the winding up." A similar provision is found in s. 328 of Insolvency Act 1986 in respect of bankruptcy proceedings.
[2] [1975] 2 All E.R. 390.

consideration of the distinction between conditional and determinable interests in property. The chapter then proceeds to examine the interaction between the *pari passu* principle of distribution and debt subordination agreements. Because the concept of debt subordination is somewhat difficult to grasp there is a short discussion of the reasons behind the use of debt subordination agreements and the techniques of debt subordination, namely contractual debt subordination and debt subordination by trust. The legal objections to the use of debt subordination agreements are then considered. It has been argued that debt subordination agreements fly in the face of the *pari passu* principle as expounded by the House of Lords in *British Eagle* but the argument is difficult to sustain in the light of recent case law. The recent cases are examined and so too is the argument that a debt subordination trust constitutes a registrable security interest.

BRITISH EAGLE AND PARI PASSU DISTRIBUTION

In *British Eagle* the appellants and the respondents were both members of the International Air Transport Association (IATA), which is an organisation originally incorporated in 1945 by an Act of the Canadian Parliament. IATA operated a clearing-house system for ticket sales by member airlines with all payments being channelled through IATA, so that if one company sold a ticket for a journey but another actually carried the passenger, the former would reimburse the latter through the clearing house. In fact, at the end of an accounting period, all the debits and credits due to transactions during that period were totalled, to arrive at a net figure for the debit or credit of the individual airline as against IATA, in order to avoid multiplicity of payments. British Eagle went into liquidation being net debtors towards IATA, in respect of services provided by the other airlines to them, but in credit as against Air France. The liquidator was of the opinion that the clearing house arrangements were not binding on him. In due course the plaintiff instituted proceedings against the defendant claiming payment of the credit balance on its IATA account with the defendant. The defendant, Air France, claimed that the clearing house arrangements were binding on the British Eagle liquidator. Accordingly Air France contended that any net balances owed by airlines in respect of services provided for them by the plaintiff should be applied in reduction of the net amount owed by the plaintiff in respect of services provided by other airlines for it and that it was for the clearing house to submit a proof in the liquidation for the net deficiency. It followed, in their view, that by virtue of the clearing house arrangements nothing was owed by the defendant to the plaintiff.

A majority of the House of Lords held that Air France was bound to pay the money it owed to British Eagle for services provided through the IATA scheme to the liquidator of British Eagle, on the ground that for Air France to have paid the money to IATA, for distribution to airlines which were creditors of British Eagle under the IATA scheme, was repugnant to the principle of *pari passu* distribution of an insolvent's property. The rationale of the decision was that if Air France had paid the money to IATA it would have resulted in making the airlines owed money by British Eagle into secured creditors; to the extent that the money paid by Air France could satisfy their debts they would be paid in full, instead of being obliged to prove in British Eagle's liquidation and receive the same dividend as other unsecured creditors.

This being the case, the provisions of the IATA scheme were contrary to public policy. It was irrelevant that the parties to the clearing house arrangements had sound business reasons for entering into them and did not direct their minds to the question how the arrangements might be affected by the insolvency of one or more of the parties.[3] Accordingly, on liquidation, the plaintiff became entitled to recover payment of the sums payable to it by other airlines for services rendered by it during the relevant period and that airlines which had rendered services to it during that period became entitled to prove in the liquidation for the sums payable to them.

The majority in *British Eagle* consisted of Lords Cross, Diplock and Edmund-Davies. The only substantive judgment was delivered by Lord Cross who cited the well known observations of James L.J. in *Ex parte Mackay*[4] to the effect that a man is not allowed, by stipulation with a creditor, to provide for a different distribution of his effects in the event of bankuptcy from that which the law provides. According to Lord Cross the "clearing house" creditors were clearly not secured creditors. They were claiming nevertheless that they ought not to be treated in the liquidation as ordinary unsecured creditors but that they had achieved by the medium of the "clearing house" agreement a position analagous to that of secured creditors without the need for the creation and registration of charges on the book debts in question.[5]

The result in *British Eagle v. Air France* has not been the subject of universal approbation.[6] It should be noted that it was a bare majority decision and Lord Edmund-Davies who was an essential constitutent of the majority expressed some diffidence in arriving at the particular result reached confessing that he did not find the case an easy one. There were strong dissents from Lords Morris and Simon. In the view of Lord Morris because of the terms of the contracts which were made British Eagle had no claims against and no rights to sue other individual members of the clearing house. It was a general rule that a liquidator takes no better title to property than that which was possessed by the insolvent company. The liquidator in the present case could not be allowed to remould contracts that had been validly made. Lord Simon suggested that British Eagle had long since deprived itself of the right to claim from Air France payment for the interline services which British Eagle had performed for Air France. No party to the interline agreement had any right to claim direct payment for interline service. It merely had the right to have the value of such service respectively credited and debited in the monthly IATA clearing house settlement account.

Of course, as Professor R.M. Goode has pointed out, the crucial question in *British Eagle* was whether its debtor was Air France or IATA.[7] If IATA was creditor of the debtor airlines, and the debtor of the creditor then it would have

---

[3] [1975] 2 All E.R. 390 at 411 *per* Lord Cross.
[4] (1873) 8 Ch. App. 643 at 647.
[5] [1975] 2 All E.R. 390 at 410–411. Lord Cross rejected the proposition that the power of the court to go behind agreements, the results of which were repugnant to the insolvency legislation, was confined to cases in which the parties' dominant purpose was to evade its operation.
[6] See generally for commentary *English and International Set-Off* (1989) paras. 5–198 *et seq.*
[7] See Goode *Principles of Corporate Insolvency Law* (1990) at 62. (2) See also Goode *Legal Problems of Credit and Security* (2nd ed., 1988) at 175–176.

been entitled to combine British Eagle's credit balance on the Air France with its debits on the account with the creditor airlines. However if IATA acted merely as an agent of the airlines in operating a clearing mechanism, then at the commencement of winding up British Eagle had a claim against Air France which could not legitimately be the subject of a set-off with regard to claims by other airlines.

PARI PASSU DISTRIBUTION AND CONSTRUCTION CONTRACTS[8]

The *British Eagle* decision has provoked a lively debate that remains unresolved about the efficacy of so-called direct payment clauses in construction contracts. Almost invariably, construction contracts contain provision enabling an employer to pay sub-contractors direct if the main contractor fails to make regular payments to them. The purpose of such provision is to prevent progress on a development being halted on account of failure by a main contractor to keep a sub-contractor in funds.[9]

The argument against direct payment clauses is based on the premise that the sub-contractor is a creditor of the main contractor and that any mechanism which would result in one creditor of the main contractor receiving payment ahead of other creditors runs counter to the principle of equal treatment of creditors within the same class. Therefore, the argument continues, any authority of the employer to make direct payments to sub-contractors should cease upon the main contractor's insolvency. This in fact is what a standard form construction contract namely the 1980 version of the JCT stipulates. The 1980 redrafting of the JCT on this particular point was in response to the decision of the House of Lords in *British Eagle*. It is by no means inevitable however that the *British Eagle*[10] decision should have the effect of rendering improper any direct payment by an employer to nominated sub-contractors upon the main contractor's insolvency. To advance the argument it is appropriate to look more closely at the nature of direct payment provisions in construction contracts.

A seminal case on direct payment clauses is *Re Wilkinson, ex parte Fowler*.[11] This

---

[8] See generally McCormack [1993] *Insolvency Law and Practice* 169. For a general examination of the new peculiar legal pitfalls pertaining to insolvency in the construction industry see Richard Davis, *Construction Insolvency* (Chancery 1991). Chap. 6 of the book contains a meticulous examination of the law relating to direct payment clauses. See also Davis [1992] *Solicitors Journal* 596.

[9] Direct payments require express permission in the main contract. In the absence of such authorisation an employer who pays subcontractors direct may be liable to pay the same sum to the main contractor. This is in fact what happened in *Re Holt, ex parte Gray* (1888) 58 L.J.Q.B. 5. Cave J. said at p. 8: "Here it is clear that the work has been done which the bankrupt engaged himself to do, and the money for it is payable; but the architects have taken upon themselves to make a deduction. I am of the opinion that they have no power to do anything of the kind, and that their doing so was a pure piece of impertinence."

[10] [1975] 2 All E. R. 390. Frequently, in construction contracts, the power vested in an employer to make direct payments to sub-contractors is restricted to nominated sub-contractors. A distinction should also be drawn between discretionary and mandatory direct payment clauses. Most of the case law and discussion has centred on the situation where the employer has a discretion to make direct payments to sub-contractors but is under no obligation to do so. If, however, an employer is under an obligation to pay sub-contractors rather than the main contractor then there is no debt owing to the main contractor on which the *pari passu* principle of distribution of an insolvent main contractor's assets may bite. The arguments challenging the validity of discretionary direct payment clauses in the wake of *British Eagle* do not apply.

[11] [1905] 2 K.B. 713.

is a case where A signed a contract with a local authority to construct sewage works. The contract stipulated that certain machinery for the works was to be supplied to A by specified firms and by clause 54 that "If the engineer shall have reasonable cause to believe that the contractor is unduly delaying proper payment to the firms supplying the machinery, he shall have power if he thinks fit to order direct payment to them." A was adjudicated bankrupt and it was held that the power conferred on the engineer by clause 54 was not annulled or revoked by the bankruptcy.

According to Bingham J. the clause amounted to an authority given by the contractor—the bankrupt in this case—to the engineer representing the council to dispose of money, which would otherwise come to the bankrupt, in a certain way under certain circumstances. It was an authority which it was not competent for the bankrupt to withdraw. Therefore it was an authority which the bankruptcy of the contractor did not annul. The learned judge said *a propos* the clause[12]:

> "That clause, in my opinion, is inserted in the contract for the benefit, not only of the people who supply the machinery, but also of the council itself. It is very much to the interest of the council to see that contracts of this kind for public works into which they enter are carried out in a manner satisfactory to all persons who are concerned in the performance of them, The council certainly may make contracts of this kind, and they make them much more advantageously when the people who supply the machinery or other goods which are to be used by the contractor in the performance of the contract know that there is a reasonable probability that they will be paid. The council are enabled, by inserting a clause of this kind in their contract, to give a certain amount of confidence to people who supply goods to the contractor, and in that way they are placed in a better position when they come to make contracts again than they otherwise would be; and, therefore, I say that the clause is inserted, not only in the interests of the persons who supply goods to the contractor, but also in the interests of the council themselves."

The authority of *Re Wilkinson, ex parte Fowler* was confirmed in *Re Tout & Finch Ltd.*[13] Here two issues were raised by sub-contractors on the liquidation of the main contractor. First, they contended that in accordance with clause 21(c) of the contract the employer was entitled to pay to them amounts remaining unpaid, which had been included for transmission to them in previous certificates issued to the main contractor, on the bankruptcy of the latter. The second issue was whether the main contractor was trustee of retention money under the relevant sub-contract provisions. Wynn-Parry J., found in favour of the sub-contractors on both points. The learned judge referred approvingly to the words of Bingham J. in *Re Wilkinson* which he thought demonstrated "the importance of the policy which underlies such a clause as this."

BRITISH EAGLE AND DIRECT PAYMENT CLAUSES

Re Tout & Finch Ltd was not referred to in *British Eagle* though some construction law cases were cited in the dissenting judgment of Lord Morris. One can only speculate therefore about what their Lordships' opinion of that case might have been. A hostile view as to the post-liquidation effectiveness of direct payment

---

[12] *ibid.* at 719–720.
[13] [1954] 1 All E.R. 127; [1954] 1 W.L.R. 178.

clauses has however been taken by the New Zealand Court of Appeal in *Attorney General v. McMillan & Lockwood Ltd.*[14] The case arose out of construction contracts entered into by the local Ministry of Works and Development. Clause 19.11 of the relevant contract gave the Minister power to pay subcontractors, suppliers, employees and other persons, moneys due to them by the contractor "as if such persons were a lawful assignee of the contractor in respect of such moneys". According to Richardson and Bisson J. who constituted a majority of the court such wording presupposed that the contractor had property in those moneys. The clause went on to state from what source any such payment may be made. It was "out of moneys then due or accruing due to the contractor". The majority judges stated that on the true construction of these contracts, as at the liquidation the company had an existing proprietary right, a chose in action, measured by the value of the work done under each contract and as yet unpaid. The principle of equal sharing among creditors was fundamental to the scheme of the winding up and insolvency legislation, and it was not open to a company to contract for unequal division of its property on liquidation. Since, as the court concluded, the main contractor had an interest in property in respect of the balances due under the contracts when it went into liquidation, the continued application of Clause 19.11 was thereafter barred by the *pari passu* rule.

The court recognised that in the *Re Tout and Finch Ltd* line of authorities the relevant contractual provisions, which allowed for payment by the building owner direct to subcontractors, were held to survive liquidation. These cases, were however explained on the basis that, in terms of the contract, such a payment to the subcontractor was not made out of moneys which were due or would become due to the main contractor, nor was it payment on behalf of the main contractor. By contrast *Attorney General v. McMillan & Lockwood Ltd* was a case where it could be said that to apply the *pari passu* rule would be to accord the liquidator an interest in property not possessed by the company immediately before the liquidation.[15]

The majority decision of the New Zealand Court of Appeal in *Attorney General v. Lockwood & McMillan Ltd* was squarely grounded on the wording of the particular clause before the court. The clause referred to payments being made to the subcontractor as if he were an assignee of the main contractor. Such

---

[14] [1991] 1 N.Z.L.R. 53. See also *Administrator, Natal v. Magil, Grant and Nell (Pty.) Ltd (in liquidation)* [1967] 1 S.A.L.R. 660. Here Ogilvie Thompson J.A. said at 670: "Now, while it may, in a sense, be correct to say that, in regard to progress payments under contracts such as the one under consideration, the contractor is, in relation to moneys due by him to nominated sub-contractors, merely a conduit pipe, the legal positon of course is that the creditor–debtor relationship obtains only between the contractor and the building owner on the one hand and the contractor and the nominated sub-contractors on the other."

[15] Williamson J. dissented from the conclusions of his brethren. He preferred to tackle the issues arising in the case on the basis of broader considerations of public policy rather than on the narrow concept of available property. In *British Eagle* the relevant contractual arrangements were struck down as being contrary to public policty. In the opinion of Williamson J. a decision about the application of public policy to particular clauses in a contract required a balancing of various public policy considerations. He pointed out that insolvency legislation did not necessarily involve the equal distribution of all an insolvent company's property among its creditors. Some creditors obtained more than others because of a previous relationship with the insolvent. More directly relevant to the present case was the factor that the inclusion of such clauses in building contracts for public buildings assisted in ensuring that both the Crown and the contractor obtained the confidence of subcontrractors and suppliers in small communities. This was the point stressed in *Re Wilkinson, ex parte Fowler* [1905] 2 K.B. 713 at 719.

21

wording seems to assume that the main contractor has property that is being diverted away. Less felicitous wording from the point of view of those seeking to uphold direct payment clauses is not easy to imagine. d[20]:

A somewhat different view as to the effect of *British Eagle* on the *Re Tout & Finch Ltd* line of authorities was taken by Costello J. in the Irish case *Glow Heating Ltd v. Eastern Health Board*.[16] In his view the principle contained in *Re Tout & Finch Ltd* remained unaffected by *British Eagle*. Costello J. said that the clauses in the main contract and in the sub-contract which provided for direct payment by the employer to the nominated sub-contractor did not reduce the property of the insolvent main contractor in contravention of the principle of *pari passu* distribution of a company's property in a liquidation. The liquidator took the main contractor's property subject to such liabilities as affected it while it was in the main contractor's hands. There was nothing in *British Eagle* to conflict with this well established principle of insolvency law. The judge stated that the error in the liquidator's argument here arose from his use of the somewhat imprecise phrase "contracting out of the Companies Act". If a contract was one for the disposal of an asset belonging to the company (as the House of Lords in *British Eagle* found the IATA arrangement was) then, if the disposal was contrary to the *pari passu* principle, the contract could be avoided as being contrary to public policy. The phrase was not to be interpreted however, as meaning that every contract was void by which a party to it obtained rights over a company's assets superior to those given to ordinary creditors. Such an interpretation would mean that reservation of title clauses in contracts for the sale of goods would be void.[17] In this particular case neither the main contract nor the sub-contract could properly be regarded as a contract for the disposal of an asset of the company and so the contracts were not subject to the criticisms applied in the *British Eagle* case.

It should be noted that according to the terms of the contract in the *Glow Heating* case direct payments by the employer to subcontractors were mandatory in certain circumstances. The judge said that moneys payable to the main contractor were liable to suffer a reduction in the event of a specified default on the part of the contractor. The liquidator assumed the contractor's rights and obligations subject to this liability.[18]

Insofar as United Kingdom bearing on the post-liquidation effectiveness of direct payment clauses is concerned the climate of judicial opinion appears hostile. Certainly this was the view taken by Kerr J. in the recent Northern Ireland case *B. Mullan & Sons (Contractors) Ltd v. Ross*.[19] This case will now be examined.

---

[20] *ibid.*

[16] (1992) 8 *Construction Law Journal* 56.

[17] It may be argued that this analysis is somewhat question-begging in that it assumes the validity of reservation of title clauses in sale of goods contracts. Not all reservation of title clauses are valid. For a comprehensive analysis of the reservation of title phenomenon see McCormack, *Reservation of Title* (2nd ed., 1995).

[18] To compound the inconsistency in the common law world a categorical view as to the irreconcilability of *British Eagle* and *Re Tout & Finch Ltd* was taken in Singapore by Thean J. in *Joo Yee Construction Proprietary Ltd v. Diethelm Industries Proprietary Ltd* (1991) 7 *Construction Law Journal* 53. The decision of Thean J. has been affirmed by the Singapore Court of Appeal but only on procedural grounds – [1992] 2 S.C.R. 407. See generally Powell-Smith [1993] *International Construction Law Review* 240.

[19] H.C. of N.I., Ch.D, December 7, 1995.

THE NORTHERN IRELAND/UNITED KINGDOM VIEW OF DIRECT PAYMENT
CLAUSES

In the *Mullan* case the plaintiff was a sub-contractor to McLoughlin & Harvey
plc, who in turn were executing works for the Londonderry Port and Harbour
Commissioners when it went into administrative receivership. Three months
later McLoughlin & Harvey were wound up and the defendants were appointed
liquidators. Clause 27.4.3.2 of the main contract laid down that "the employer
may pay any supplier or sub-contractor for any materials or goods delivered or
works executed for the purposes of this contract (whether before or after the
date of determination) insofar as the price thereof has not already been paid by
the contractor". The liquidators essentially contended that this clause contravened Article 93 of the Insolvency (Northern Ireland) Order 1989 which
states that a company's property in a voluntary winding up shall be applied in
satisfaction of the company's liabilities *pari passu*. Kerr J. acceded to this
submission. He said that if the implementation of the clause conflicts with the
pari passu rule it is void irrespective of the right (or lack of it) on the part of the
contractor to revoke it or his contractual obligation to fulfil it. The judge took
the view that the *British Eagle* decision fatally impaired the efficacy of the direct
payment provision in this case. He said[20]:

> "[M]y conclusion that the payments due for the work executed by the sub-contractor
> constituted property of McLaughlin & Harvey at the time of the winding up renders
> those payments equally subject to the *pari passu* principle. The decision in *British Eagle*
> recognised the fundamental and predominant nature of the principle of *pari passu* in
> insolvency law. It appears to me that, to exclude from its ambit payments due for
> work carried out by a sub-contrctor which, before winding up, would be payable to
> the main contractor, would represent a considerable encroachment on, and compromise
> of, the efficacy of the principle. I must also reject the submission that *Ex p. Mackay*
> and *Ex p. Jay* can be distinguished on the basis that in those cases a deliberate attempt
> was made by one party to secure for itself an advantage over unsecured creditors. The
> fact that the payment to the sub-contractor is at the instance of the employer rather
> than the sub-contractor does not create a distinction of any significance in my opinion."

In reaching the conclusion that he did Kerr J. was reinforced in his opinions
by a consideration of the New Zealand case *Attorney-General v. McMillan &
Lockwood Ltd.*[21] He might also have referred to as, persuasive authority, the report
by Sir Michael Latham on procurement and contractual arrangements in the
United Kingdom construction industry.[22] The report criticised the impact of the
British Eagle decision on direct payment provisions but nevertheless accepted that
British Eagle had impinged adversely on such arrangements. The report pointed
to the practical reality now, that if the main contractor becomes insolvent, the
primary or secured creditors of the main contractor will receive some monies
which are intended for and owing to the subcontractor for work carried out.
Legislation was recommended to reverse this state of affairs by reason of the
fact that it was absolutely fundamental to trust within the construction industry

---

[20] *ibid.*
[21] [1991] 1 N.Z.L.R. 53.
[22] *Constructing the Team*, Final Report, July 1994. The report was commissioned jointly by the
Government and the construction industry.

that participants should be paid for the work which they had undertaken. The practical realities of construction were invoked and stated as follows[23]:

> "However diligently clients, contractors or subcontractors check on each other, the causes of the failure of any participant may be unrelated to the particular contract, or even to work in this country. In a difficult trading climate for construction, firms will undertake work for low (or no) margins, and will not endanger their chances of being selected by demanding prepayment or indemnities, even if they are aware that there might be a payment problem. Bad debt insurance is possible, but it is another cost overhead at a time when most firms are cutting their overheads in order to reduce their quotations for 'preliminaries' and remain competitive."

The report reviewed overseas experience in this area and suggested that the best line of protection for subcontractors was the establishment of mandatory trust funds. If a main contractor failed, it would be the duty of the fund trustee to ensure direct payment out of the trust fund to subcontractors. It was proposed that the statutory provisions should ensure that trustees were legally empowered to make full payments direct to contractors or subcontractors for work done, or materials supplied and/or already incorporated within the work, without the receiver of the failed participant being allowed to take such monies on behalf of other creditors. If sub-contractors "win" then other creditors of the main contractor will lose in any new statutory dispensation. Such creditors are likely to be banks who form a vociferous pressure group with respect to any readjustment of insolvency legislation.[24] The Latham Report recommendations pertaining to the establishment of mandatory trust funds have not been translated into any legislative initiative.[25]

In concluding the discussion on direct payment clauses one may fairly say that the controversy over the existing status of *Re Tout & Finch Ltd* is a long-running one. No easy resolution of the issue is in sight and the subject had provoked differing decisions overseas. The issue has not arisen for decision in England will partly one suspects be because the 1980 JCT standard form brings the direct payment facility to an end on the bankruptcy or insolvent liquidation of the main contractor. The necessity for a judicial decision on the post-liquidation effectiveness of a direct payment facility only becomes manifest if the parties use terms in their contractual relationships that are different from those found in the 1980 JCT.[26] One can empathise with their reluctance to buy

---

[23] *ibid.* at para. 10.4.

[24] One might refer in this connection to the legislative history surrounding the enactment of the Insolvency Act 1994 which was passed speedily by Parliament in response to the decision of the Court of Appeal in *Powdrill v. Watson* [1994] 2 All E.R. 513. The Court of Appeal decision in *Powdrill v. Watson* was later confirmed by the House of Lords at [1995] 2 All E.R. 65.

[25] The consultation paper "Fair Construction Contracts" issued by the Department of the Environment in May 1995 in response to Latham said the following: "The Government does not think it necessary to amend the Insolvency Act 1986 to reverse the British Eagle judgment (as recommended in "Constructing the Team") since it is considered that a properly constituted trust containing appropriate terms would deal adequately with the problems that have been identified in this field. It is understood, however, that some sectors of the construction industry are still concerned about problems that may arise for subcontractors or in cases where a trust fund has not in practice been established. Further thought is being given to this issue."

[26] See the comment in Lightman and Moss, *The Law of Receivers of Companies* (2nd ed., 1994), p. 279: "Since Amendment 11 to JCT 1980 has now removed the power to make direct payments after termination whatever the insolvency event there is less likelihood of this problem having to be resolved by the English courts."

a law suit that is likely to end up in the House of Lords. On balance, it is submitted that post *British Eagle* their Lordships are unlikely to uphold discretionary direct payment clauses that continue in force after insolvency of the main contractor has supervened. To borrow an analysis adopted by Professor Roy Goode in relation to the *British Eagle* decision a lot seems reducible to a simple question – namely, whether there was a debt owing to the main contractor by the employer?[27] If there is, and in the generality of cases there ought to be, any mechanism which has the effect of diverting payment away from the main contractor to a creditor of the main contractor would seem to infringe the *pari passu* principle.

A consideration which moves in the opposite direction is provided though by Part VII of the Companies Act 1989 which modifies the general law of insolvency with respect to "market contracts", *i.e.* contracts connected with a recognised investment exchange or recognised clearing house. Among the provisions modified is the principle of *pari passu* distribution of assets on an insolvency embodied in the Insolvency Act 1986, section 107. Notwithstanding *British Eagle* Part VII may offer an inducement to the courts to interpret the *pari passu* principle flexibly in the interests of good commercial practice.[28] The body of informed opinion in the construction industry however, appears to be that *British Eagle* has cast an invalidating spell on the post-liquidation effectiveness of direct payment facilities for subcontractors.

FORFEITURE CLAUSES

The detailed operation of the *pari passu* principle of insolvency distribution has also occasioned some controversy with respect to forfeiture clauses in building contracts.[29] An oft-cited case in this regard is *Re Harrison, ex parte Jay*.[30] Here a building contract contained a clause which provided that on the builder becoming bankrupt, all improvements, materials and effects on the land should become absolutely forfeited to the employer. The builder filed a bankruptcy petition and at this time there was a quantity of materials on the land placed there by the builder. It was held that the provision for forfeiture of the materials on the bankruptcy of the builder was void as being contrary to the policy of the bankruptcy legislation and that the materials on the land were the property of the trustee in bankruptcy. James L.J. said[31]:

> "a simple stipulation that, upon a man becoming bankrupt, that which was his property up to the date of the bankruptcy should go over to some one else and be taken away from his creditors, is void as being a violation to the policy of the bankrupt law."

---

[27] See Goode, *Principles of Corporate Insolvency Law* (1990), p. 62. See also Davis, *Construction Insolvency* (1991) pp. 155–157 and Lightman and Moss, *The Law of Receivers of Companies* (2nd ed., 1994), p. 278.

[28] In *British Eagle* [1975] A.C. Lord Cross said that the question in essence was whether what was called in argument the "mini liquidation" flowing from the clearing house arrangements is to yield to or prevail over the general liquidation. He did not doubt that on principle the rules of the general liquidation should prevail.

[29] For an impressive overview of this entire area, over and above building contracts see Oditah "Assets and the Treatment of Claims in Insolvency" (1992) 108 L.Q.R. 459.

[30] (1880) 14 Ch. D. 19.

[31] *ibid.* at 25.

This case is to be contrasted with *Re Garrud, ex parte Newitt*[32] where the factual matrix was broadly similar save for the fact that there was a forfeiture clause which could be activated in a number of situations, not including bankruptcy.[33] The builder filed a bankruptcy petition and on the same day the employer resumed possession of the works by reason of the forfeiture clause on the ground of failure to proceed regularly with the works. The conclusion of the court was that the property did not pass to the builder's trustee in bankruptcy. This time James L.J. said[34]:

> "To my mind it is immaterial at what particular moment the seizure was made. The broad general principle is that the trustee in bankruptcy takes all the bankrupt's property, but takes it subject to all the liabilities which affected it in the bankrupt's hands, unless the property which he takes as the legal representative of the bankrupt is added to by some express provision of the bankrupt law ... the building agreement provides, in effect, that in a certain event certain property of the builder may be taken by the landowner in full satisfaction of the agreement."

It has been argued that this case is not easily reconcilable with the House of Lords decision in the *British Eagle* case and highlights the uncertainty surrounding "equities" subject to which the liquidator takes.[35] Moreover, it was suggested that the distinction between *Re Garrud* and *Re Harrison* is an extremely narrow one. In one case we have a valid vesting clause that is good in insolvency whereas in the other there is an invalid forfeiture. The comment continues[36]:

> "It will take very little imagination to frame the clause as the first rather than the second and, to the extent that the draftsman is successful the assets available for the payment of unsecured claims will be correspondingly reduced."

Narrow distinctions in fact abound in this branch of the law. There are many cases involving the use of trusts which illustrate the same principles as *Re Harrison* and *Re Garrud* and also illuminate the differences between the outcomes in the respective cases. Simply, and baldly stated, a settlor cannot create in his own favour a trust until bankruptcy with remainders over in the event of bankruptcy. A case which demonstrates this proposition is *Re Burroughs-Fowler*.[37] The case involved an ante-nuptial settlement under which property belonging to one W.J. Fowler, the intended husband, were conveyed to trustees upon trust to sell and "to pay the rent profits and income thereof to the said W.J. Fowler or to permit him to receive the same during his life or until he shall be outlawed or be declared bankrupt..." after which event the income was to be paid to his wife. The husband was adjudicated bankrupt and the trustee in bankruptcy offered for sale the husband's life interest under the settlement. The intending purchaser objected that the husband's life interest remained defeasible if the debtor should

---

[32] (1880) 16 Ch. D. 522.
[33] *Re Garrud, ex parte Newitt* was referred to approvingly by Lord Morris in his dissenting judgment in *British Eagle v. Air France* [1975] 2 All E.R. 390. He cited the case as authority for the proposition that a trustee in bankruptcy stands in exactly the same position as the bankrupt himself stands in. In other words what was personally binding upon the debtor was also binding upon the trustee in bankruptcy.
[34] *ibid.* at 531.
[35] See Oditah (1992) 108 L.Q.R. 459 at 476 n. 111.
[36] *ibid.* at 476–477.
[37] [1916] 2 Ch. 251.

do or suffer any of the other specified acts of forfeiture. Peterson J. held that the limitation until the settlor was declared bankrupt was void against the trustee in bankruptcy. Therefore, so far as the trustee in bankruptcy was concerned, the provisions as to bankruptcy and insolvency must be treated as excluded from the settlement. On the other hand however, the provision as to bankruptcy and insolvency was not void as between the husband and the wife. This meant that the trustee in bankruptcy could dispose of more than was vested in the bankrupt himself. As far as the wife was concerned the forfeiture by reason of the bankruptcy has already taken place. Therefore it was no longer possible for the husband thereafter to do or suffer something which would determine his interest. Consequently the trustee in bankruptcy was now in possession of the life interest of the bankrupt and this was incapable of being affected by any subsequent forfeiture.

Re Burroughs-Fowler is to be contrasted with *Re Detmold*.[38] In this case under a marriage settlement of the settlor's own property, the income was payable to himself "during his life, or till he shall become bankrupt, or shall ... suffer something whereby [the income], or some part thereof, would ... by operation or process of law, if belonging absolutely to him, become vested in or payable to some other person". After the determination of the trust in favour of the husband, the trustees were to pay the income to the wife for her lifetime. An individual creditor of the husband obtained an order appointing himself receiver of the income due from the trust fund and subsequently the husband was adjudicated bankrupt. North J. put the matter succinctly when he said that the question was whether the life interest given by the settlement to the wife was now subsisting or whether it was invalid as against the trustee in bankruptcy of the husband. The judge held that the limitation of the life interest to the settlor was validly determined by the fact that, in consequence of the order appointing the receiver, he ceased to be entitled to receive the income. This took place before the commencement of the bankruptcy and therefore the forfeiture was valid as against the trustee in bankruptcy.[39]

To sum up a person cannot create in his favour an interest which is determinable upon his own bankruptcy but he may make it determinable upon any event other than bankruptcy. If a gift over is framed to take effect on any one of a number of events including bankruptcy, then the gift over, while void in the event of bankruptcy, is perfectly valid in the other situations. Moreover, if a settlor creates a trust in favour of a third party and imposes a condition that the trust property will not be subject to the claims of creditors, the condition will be void. The same result may however be achieved by a subtle change in terminology. An interest may be created by a settlor in favour of another person which is determinable upon that other person's bankruptcy. All this flexibility and possible avoidance of bankruptcy legislation is dependent on the creation of determinable rather than conditional interests. The distinction between determinable and conditional interests has been judicially described as little short of disgraceful to our jurisprudence and also as more a matter of words than anything else.[40] Nevertheless there are important practical consequences to

---

[38] (1889) 40 Ch.D. 585.
[39] (1889) 40 Ch.D. 585 at 588.
[40] By the Irish Judge Porter M.R. in *Re King's Trusts* (1892) 29 L.R. Ir. 401 at 410.

the distinction.[41] With a determinable interest the determining event is integral to the formulation of the duration of the interest whereas in the case of a conditional interest the condition is some superadded event which operates to cut short the interest before it reaches out to its natural duration. One commentator has likened the conceptual difference between conditional and determinable interests to the difference between giving someone a 12-inch ruler subject to being cut down to a six-inch ruler in certain conditions and giving someone a six-inch ruler in the first place.[42]

So a grantor when disposing of his property may qualify the interest of the grantee.[43] Page Wood V.C. explained in *Whitmore v. Mason*[44]:

"The distinction seems to be that the owner of property may, on alienation, qualify the interest of his alienee by a condition to take effect on bankruptcy; but cannot by contract or otherwise qualify his own interest by a like condition, determining or controlling it in the event of his own bankruptcy, to the disappointment or delay of his creditors."

PARI PASSU DISTRIBUTION AND DEBT SUBORDINATION AGREEMENTS

In essence the concept of debt subordination is a straightforward one.[45] One creditor (the senior creditor) agrees not to be paid until a particular other creditor (the junior creditor) or perhaps all other creditors are paid in full. Debt subordination agreements often take the form of a mere contractual arrangement between senior and junior creditor but sometimes the creation of a trust is involved. To be worth its salt a debt subordination agreement must survive the insolvency of the debtor. Here a possible conflict emerges with the *pari passu* principle of distribution of an insolvent debtor's estate, as applied by the House of Lords in the *British Eagle* case.[46] Another question arises as to whether a debt subordination agreement creates a registrable security interest.[47] These questions will be considered in the context of debt subordination trusts but first it is appropriate to say something about the use of debt subordination agreements in commercial practice.

REASONS FOR THE USE OF DEBT SUBORDINATION AGREEMENTS

For companies, subordinated debt is something of a hybrid form of finance that occupies an intermediate position between equity finance and debt finance, properly so called. From the debtor company's point of view a "capital base" is

---

[41] See generally Megarry and Wade *Law of Real Property* (5th ed., 1984), pp. 76–75; Glanville Williams (1943) 59 L.Q.R. 343.
[42] See Hayton and Marshall, *Cases and Commentary on the Law of Trusts* (9th ed., 1991 by D.J. Hayton) p. 260.
[43] *Re Walker, ex parte Barter, ex parte Black* (1884) 26 Ch. D. 510. Fry L.J. opined that a power upon bankruptcy to control the user, after bankruptcy, of property vested in the bankrupt was invalid.
[44] (1861) 2 J. & H. 204 at 209–210.
[45] See generally Wood, *The Law of Subordinated Debt* (Sweet & Maxwell, 1990); Johnston [1991] J.B.L. 225; Powell [1993] L.M.C.L.Q. 357 and Nolan [1994] J.B.L. 485. See also Johnston [1987] *Australian Business Law Review* 80 and Wood [1985] *International Financial Law Review* 11.
[46] [1975] 2 All E.R. 390.
[47] See generally on this point Goode *Commercial Law* (2nd ed., 1995), pp. 663–666.

provided from which the debtor can raise further funds through borrowing.[48] As one commentator states[49]:

> "[S]ubordinated debt exists largely to support further, and frequently less expensive borrowing beyond the amount that would be available with existing net worth."

Nevertheless, for taxation purposes the subordinated debt is treated alongside other forms of debt, so that payments of interest are deductible against profits for tax purposes, unlike dividend payments on shares. Moreover, the use of debt rather than equity avoids the legal problems attendant on a reduction of capital.[50]

LEGAL TECHNIQUES

While the basic idea behind debt subordination is a simple one the legal means by which it may be achieved is more complex. One writer explains[51]:

> "The manner and efficacy of subordinations depends upon the jurisdiction and in particular the local rules regarding the distribution of assets on liquidation, the assignment of claims, the recognition of trusts, the ability to grant the benefit of a contract to third parties and the registration of security interests."

With contractual debt subordination the junior creditor agrees that he will not be paid unless and until the senior creditor is paid in full. With a subordination trust, on the other hand, the senior creditor receives a double dividend. The junior creditor agrees to claim the junior debt when it matures or on liquidation and to hold the receipts on trust for the senior creditor. It is possible to envisage more intricate forms of arrangement. An example would be where the basic provision is that of contractual subordination and this is coupled with a covenant by the debtor or junior creditor not to amend the subordination provisions. The debtor or junior creditor then declares a trust over the benefit of that covenant in favour of the senior creditor.[52] In economic terms there is much to be said for the view that a subordination trust represents a charge over the junior debt or the proceeds of that debt in favour of the

---

[48] Johnston ([1987] *Australian Business Law Review*) argues that subordination increases the borrower's capacity to borrow from financial institutions on a senior creditor basis, as it is a support or "cushion" for the senior debt in much the same way as equity.

[49] See Johnson "Subordinated Debentures: Debt that serves as equity" (1955) 10 *Journal of Finance* 1 at 9 quoted in Johnston [1987] *Australian Business Law Review* 80 at 83.

[50] Geoffrey Fuller in *Corporate Borrowings: Law and Practice* (1995) pp. 73–75 refers to three main reasons why debt subordination is employed. Firstly, in the case of banks it is done to increase their capital base for regulatory purposes. He refers in this connection to the July 1988 Report on International Convergence of Capital Measurement and Capital Standards by the Basle Committee on Banking Regulations and Supervisory Practices. Second, the technique is used so that lenders on a senior basis will be more likely to lend greater amounts and finally so that external lenders can be sure that the proceeds of their loans are not used to repay debts to "insiders", such as a parent company or a major shareholder.

[51] See Wood, *Law and Practice of International Finance* (1980) p. 404.

[52] See generally on trusts of covenants *Fletcher v. Fletcher* (1844) 4 Hare 67; 67 E.R. 564. See also *Re Cook's Settlement Trusts* [1965] Ch. 902. For commentary see Elliott (1960) 76 L.Q.R. 100; Barton (1975) 91 L.Q.R. 236; Meagher and Lehane (1976) 92 L.Q.R. 427; Rickett (1979) 32 C.L.P. 1 and (1981) 34 C.L.P. 189; Goddard [1988] *Conveyancer and Property Lawyer* 19.

senior creditor.[53] If, in law, a subordination trust does entail the bringing into existence of a security interest the consequences are potentially profound. The issue is not one of enormous significance so long as the junior creditor remains solvent, except with respect to accounting requirements pertaining to the disclosure of security interests in the junior debtor's balance sheet.[54] Assume however, that the junior debtor is a company which has gone into liquidation. Part XII of the Companies Act 1985 requires the registration of certain charges created by a company for validity in the event of the company's liquidation.[55] Among the categories of registrable charge are charges created by a company over its book debts.[56] The view has been expressed that a subordination trust represents the creation by a junior debtor of a charge over its book debts. One leading commentator, Phillip Wood, proffers the following opinion[57]:

"The better view is that a properly drafted subordination trust of proceeds should not create a security interest under English law but the matter is undecided and, in light of the potentially disastrous consequences if this view is wrong, a doubt must be recorded."

Professor RM Goode is more dogmatic on the point but also approaches the matter from a slightly different perspective.[58] He suggests that it is necessary to distinguish between an undertaking to hand over recoveries prior to the debtor's liquidation and an undertaking as to proof and application of dividends in the winding up of the debtor. Outside the context of the liquidation of the debtor, where the undertaking to account creates a trust in favour of the senior creditor, it will create a charge on the junior creditor's book debts and will be void against the junior debtor's liquidator if not registered. This invalidity in the event of liquidation does not however affect the senior creditor's right to retain sums paid over by the junior creditor prior to the commencement of its liquidation. The Australian case *Re Row Dal Construction Pty Ltd*[59] may be cited in this connection. The case indicates that it is too late for a liquidator to

---

[53] See the observations by Wood *The Law of Subordinated Debt* (1990) at 38: "A subordination trust is in economic substance a collateral charge by the junior creditor over the junior creditor's debt or the proceeds of that debt to secure the senior debt, but without imposing any personal liability on the junior creditor to pay the senior debt himself. The question is whether the transfer of proceeds is in law a security interest."

[54] See Goode *Commercial Law* (1982) at 725.

[55] Part XII has been amended by Part IV Companies Act 1989 but these amendments have not been brought into force. The proposed(!) amendments are unlikely to be brought into force in their present form. In any event, they do not affect the point at issue. In November 1994 the DTI published a new consultation paper (URN94/635) on the reform of the law relating to registration of company charges. The document is very "green" however with no preferred option for change set out therein.

[56] s. 396(1)(e) of the Companies Act 1985.

[57] *The Law of Subordinated Debt* (1990), p. 39.

[58] *Commercial Law* (2nd ed.), pp. 664–666.

[59] [1966] V.R. 249. See also from an analagous context *Mace Builders (Glasgow) Ltd v. Lunn* [1987] Ch. 19 and see generally McCormack, *Registration of Company Charges* (Sweet & Maxwell, 1994) pp. 107–109.

intervene if an unregistered chargee has already been paid prior to liquidation.[60] The case concerned the loan of money by a ban to a company on the security of certain book debts which were assigned by the company to the bank. The book debtor duly paid the bank pursuant to the terms of the assignment, thereby discharging the company's indebtedness to the bank. This occurred before the company went into liquidation. Upon liquidation the liquidator sought recovery of the proceeds of the assignment on the basis that the assignment was invalid against him for non-registration. The claim failed as the debt had been paid prior to the liquidator's appointment.[61]

Goode also argues that the liquidation of the junior creditor does not have any effect on sums received from the debtor by the junior creditor before winding up and not yet paid over to the senior creditor. The argument proceeds on the basis that upon payment a book debt ceases to exist. Therefore the provision invalidating unregistered charges over book debts has no cutting edge in this instance. Insofar as an obligation undertaken by the junior creditor to hand over to the senior creditor dividends received in the debtor's winding up is concerned, Professor Goode contends that there is no question of a registrable charge being created. An entitlement to a dividend in a liquidation cannot be classified as a debt.[62] While a liquidator in a winding up has statutory duties to perform he is not a debtor in respect of dividends declared by him.[63]

Other commentators have argued that a subordination trust of debt proceeds does not create a charge on the basis that there is no equity of redemption involved in the transaction.[64] The existence of an equity of redemption in the chargor is an essential feature of the creation of a charge. If there is no equity of redemption there is no charge.[65] The use of absolute title as security is well

---

[60] To the same effect is *Saunderson & Co. v. Clark* (1913) 29 T.L.R. 579. This is a case where there was an unregistered charge over the debts of the company. Before winding up the debtor, pursuant to an instruction from the company, paid the secured creditor as assignee of the company. It was held by Lush J. that after the winding up the debtor was not liable to make the same payment once more to the liquidator nor could the liquidator recover the payment that was made from the assignee.

[61] Herring C.J. in the Supreme Court of Victoria said ([1966] V.R. 249 at 258): "Had liquidation in this case intervened before the payment of the £6,000 actually paid ... on 31 May, no doubt in that event there would have been a contest as to the destination of this sum, the liquidator claiming it as property of the company and relying upon non-registration of the assignment to defeat the bank's claim and the bank for its part claiming it as its property by reason of the absolute failure to register under s. 72 [of the Victorian Companies Act 1958]; when he was appointed on 6 July 1962 there was no property of the company upon which the bank claimed any security, and there was consequently no basis upon which he could call in aid s. 72 to defeat the bank's assignment. These considerations are in my opinion sufficient to dispose of this point."

[62] See the definition of book debts offered by Lord Esher M.R. in *Official Receiver v. Tailby* (1886) 18 Q.B.D. 25 at 29: "debts arising in a business ... which ought to be entered in the company's books." See generally on the definition of book debts McCormack, *Registration of Company Charges* (1994) pp. 40–51.

[63] See also on this point Wood, *The Law of Subordinated Debt* (1990), p. 38.

[64] For a development of this argument see Johnston [1987] *Australian Business Law Review* 80 at 133–135.

[65] See also J.R. Lingard, *Bank Security Documents* (3rd ed., 1993), p. 335 who argues that the primary reason why an agreement for postponement of a debt is not a charge is that it confers no right on the bank to sell or otherwise realise the subordinated debt nor is there any intention to create a charge. He cites the observations of Peter Gibson J. in *Carreras Rothmans Ltd v. Freeman Mathews Treasure Ltd* [1985] 1 All E.R. 155 that the rights to enforce a trust are wholly different from the rights of a chargee. A beneficiary under a trust did not have a power of sale nor was there any equity of redemption in the trust beneficiary.

established in certain commercial spheres. One might highlight in this connection finance leasing and the factoring of book debts. A practice that is not uncommon is the sale of goods or land followed by some sort of lease-back arrangement. Often it may be difficult to distinguish a genuine sale and lease back from the creation of a charge. The key differences were explained by Romer L.J. in *Re George Inglefield Ltd.*[66] He said *inter alia*[67]:

> "In a transaction of sale the vendor is not entitled to get back the subject-matter of the sale by returning to the purchaser the money that has passed between them. In the case of a mortgage or charge the mortgagor is entitled, until he has been foreclosed, to get back the subject-matter of the mortgage or charge by returning to the mortgagee the money that has passed between them."

Wood suggests that a trust of receipts by the junior creditor in favour of the senior creditor up to an amount equal to the senior debt leaves no equity of redemption since the junior creditor never transfers more than is required to pay the senior debt. In his view there is no surplus to swing back with the beneficial ownership in the proceeds split.[68] He draws an analogy with the tracing aspects of reservation of title clauses in sale of goods contracts. With such a provision the seller of goods retains title to goods until the goods have been paid for notwithstanding delivery of the goods to the buyer. The buyer is permitted to resell the goods in the ordinary course of business but the original seller lays claim to the resale proceeds up to the amount of the original contract debt. Is such a claim a legally viable one?[69] The answer would seem to be "no" on the basis of recent case law. This is where the Wood argument breaks down. From the reservation of title context one might cite *Compaq Computer Ltd v. Abercorn Group Ltd*[70] and *Modelboard Ltd v. Outer Box Ltd.*[71]

In the *Modelboard* case a supplier of cardboard sheets made claim to resale proceeds on the basis of a reservation of title clause which provided that the buyers were entitled to resell only as "agents and bailees, and on terms that the proceeds are held in trust for the [seller]". The judge took the view that the interest of the suppliers in the proceeds of sale was by way of charge. He used a hypothetical example to bolster this conclusion. Suppose that the buyer resold at a profit. In his opinion the supplier could have recourse to the resale price, so far as necessary to discharge the outstanding obligation of the buyer, subject to which the supplier must account to the buyer for the balance. That was in accord with commercial reality and meant that the suppliers' interest in resale proceeds was properly designated a charge. On the other hand, no charge was involved if the supplier was entitled to keep the whole resale price but with an obligation to refund the resale profit element if the buyer subsequently paid the

---

[66] [1933] Ch. 1.
[67] *ibid* at 26–27. Just to add a bit of spice to the distinction it was made clear by Chitty L.J. in *Durham Bros v. Robertson* [1898] 1 Q.B. 765 at 772 that once the security nature of a transaction is established equity will imply an equity of redemption. Oditah [1992] J.B.L. 541 at 546 argues that the speech of Romer L.J. in *Re George Inglefield Ltd* gives very little, if any, useful guidance.
[68] Wood *The Law of Subordinated Debt* (1990), pp. 39–40.
[69] See generally McCormack *Reservation of Title* (2nd ed., 1995) particularly at pp. 78–91.
[70] [1991] B.C.C. 484. See also *Pfeiffer Weinkellerei-Weineinkauf Gmbh & Co. v. Arbuthnot Factors Ltd* [1988] 1 W.L.R. 150; *Tatung (UK) Ltd v. Galex Telesure Ltd* (1989) 5 B.C.C. 325 and *Re Weldtech Ltd* [1991] B.C.C. 16.
[71] [1992] B.C.C. 945.

purchase price. The judge rejected the latter interpretation in favour of a charge construction. The non-charge approach in his opinion entailed devising an elaborate system of implied contractual obligations and this was felt to be beyond the bounds of judicial capabilities.

Having regard to the recent case law it is submitted that a debt subordination trust does create a charge or at least that there is sufficient doubt about the position to warrant registration *ex abundanti cautela*. A possible way around the registration difficulties has been outlined by Phillip Wood.[72] He states that a subordination trust may be constituted by a trust deed under which the junior debt is payable to a trustee who holds the recoveries for the benefit first of the senior creditor and then the junior creditor. The debtor may be authorised to pay the creditors direct until an event of default occurs in which event the debtor must pay the trustee. The proposition is that the trustee is not creating a charge because the trustee has no property of its own to charge. The junior creditor is not conveying any proprietary interest to the senior creditor but is merely taking a limited interest under the trust. As Wood himself recognises, the matter has not been decided and the same strictures levelled against debt subordination trusts *per se* might seem to apply. There is also an analogy that may be drawn with direct payment clauses in building contracts. The debtor is authorised to pay creditors direct until some default happens, at which time payment must thereafter be made to the trustee. The same objections that have been raised in relation to the construction contract equivalents of these clauses would have another outing here. There remains the larger question of the compatibility of debt subordination agreements with the principle of *pari passu* distribution of an insolvent's assets.

DEBT SUBORDINATION AND *PARI PASSU*

Do debt subordination agreements, in particular debt subordination trusts, fall foul of the *pari passu* principle as applied by the House of Lords in *British Eagle*.[73] Insofar as the English courts are concerned the answer seems to be no having regard to two first instance decisions of Vinelott J. namely *Re British & Commonwealth Holdings plc (No. 3)*[74] and *Re Maxwell Communications Corp plc (No. 2)*.[75] In the *British and Commonwealth* case the company and the trustee of various securities issued or guaranteed by the company entered into a trust deed governing the terms of issue of some £320 million of convertible subordinated unsecured loan stock. The trust deed provided that the claims of the holders of the stock were in the event of the winding up of the company subordinated in right of payment to the claims of all other creditors of the company. The company went into administration and Vinelott J., in effect, held that, for the purpose of the administration order procedure the debt subordination agreement should be treated as effective. The matter was investigated in more substantial detail in *Re Maxwell Communications Corp plc (No. 3)*—a case which was concerned with contractual subordination.

---

[72] *The Law of Subordinated Debt* (1990), pp. 39–40. See also Johnston [1987] *Australian Business Law Review* 80 at 135.

[73] *British Eagle International Airlines Ltd v. Cie Nationale Air France* [1975] 1 W.L.R. 758.

[74] [1992] 1 W.L.R. 672.

[75] [1994] 1 All E.R. 737. On this decision see Nolan [1994] J.B.L. 485.

In the *Maxwell* case a company, Maxwell Finance Jersey (MFJ), issued convertible bonds which were guaranteed by another company, MCC, under a guarantee which provided that MCC's liability to the bondholders was subordinated to MCC's liabilities to other unsecured creditors. In other words, if MCC became insolvent, the rights of the bondholders against MCC were subordinated to all other unsecured liabilities owed by MCC. The guarantee stipulated that payments under the guarantee were to be made to a Swiss bank, SBC, on behalf of the MFJ bondholders. The guarantee and the subordination agreement were expressed to be subject to Swiss law, which did not recognise trusts. Vinelott J. held that the subordination agreement was a valid contract. He took the view that since a creditor could waive his debt or decline to submit to proof, there was no reason why he should not, prior to any insolvency proceedings, agree to subordinate his claim to that of other creditors in the event of the debtor company's insolvency. On his analysis, the *pari passu* principle precluded a creditor from obtaining some advantage in the winding up of a company to which insolvency principles did not entitle him. Subordination however, did not undermine that principle in any way. The *British Eagle* decision was read restrictively. Essentially it was relegated to the realm of cases decided on its special facts. According to Vinelott J. the only real issues in the *British Eagle* case related to the construction and the proper analysis of the rights and obligations conferred and imposed by the agreement at issue. There was no argument as to the applicable principles of insolvency law.[76] The opinion expressed by Vinelott J. accords with the view of one commentator that all that the *British Eagle* case decided was that a creditor cannot, after the insolvency, walk into the insolvent's house and help himself to the furniture. This proposition is as ancient as the bankruptcy laws themselves.[77]

Reference was made by Vinelott J. in the *Maxwell* case to the decision of Southwell J. in the Australian case *Horne v. Chester & Fein Property Developments Pty Ltd*.[78] In the latter case the court held that the legislative provisions governing distribution of a company's assets on an insolvency did not require that in all cases a liquidator must distribute assets *pari passu* amongst creditors. The liquidator might distribute in accordance with an agreement between the parties where to do so could not adversely affect any creditor, not a party to the agreement. Southwell J. recognised that it was a general principle of insolvency law that the whole of a debtor's estate should be available for distribution to all creditors and that no one creditor or group of creditors could lawfully contract in such a manner as to defeat other creditors not parties to the contract. This principle was not contravened however where the performance of an agreement between various parties could not affect the entitlement of creditors who were not parties to the agreement.[79]

There is some support however for the proposition that *British Eagle* is authority for a wider proposition namely that[80]:

[76] [1994] 1 All E.R. 737 at 749.

[77] See Wood *The Law of Subordinated Debt* (1990) p. 25.

[78] [1987] V.R. 913; [1987] A.C.L.R. 245.

[79] See also the observations of Adams J. in the New Zealand Supreme Court case *Re Walker Construction Co. Ltd* [1960] N.Z.L.R. 523 at 536: "[A]s the statutory requirement of *pari passu* payment does not rest on considerations of public policy, but is a matter of private right to which the *maxim quilibet potest renunciare juri pro se introducto* (anyone may at his pleasure, renounce the benefit of a stipulation or other right introduced in his own favour) may properly be applied."

[80] *Carreras Rothmans Ltd v. Freemans Matthews Treasure Ltd* [1985] Ch. 207.

"... where the effect of a contract is that an asset which is actually owned by a company at the commencement of its liquidation would be dealt with in a way other than in accordance with [the *pari passu* principle], then to that extent the contract as a matter of public policy is avoided, whether or not the contract is entered into for consideration and for *bona fide* commercial reasons and whether or not the contractual provision affecting that asset is expressed to take effect only on insolvency."

This was the interpretation placed on *British Eagle* by Peter Gibson J. in *Carreras Rothmans Ltd v. Freemans Mathews Treasure Ltd.*[81] In my view it is too wide an interpretation and is open to the policy objections adverted to by Vinelott J. in the *Maxwell* case.[82] Nevertheless it is a pity that Vinelott J. did not consider these *dicta* of Peter Gibson J. Vinelott J. in *British Eagle* did consider the decision of the House of Lords in *National Westminster Bank Ltd v. Halesowen Presswork and Assemblies Ltd.*[83] In *Halesowen* the House of Lords held that the statutory regime of set-off applicable to insolvent companies was imperative. Persons who had dealings with an insolvent company could not validly contract out of the statutory set-off provisions. Vinelott J. distinguished this case on the basis that the rationale underlining the set-off regime was one of public policy rather than private rights. The judge drew attention to the inconvenience and potential unfairness to the liquidator, and so to other creditors, that might arise if a creditor was entitled either to exercise or, at his option, not to exercise the right of set-off. He said[84]:

"An agreement between the debtor and the creditor excluding the creditor's right of set-off, or the waiver by the creditor of his right of set-off, even after the commencement of the bankruptcy or winding up, might thus equally hinder the rapid, efficient and economical process of bankruptcy."

While the analysis by Vinelott J. of the *Halesowen* case been subjected to some criticism, it may derive some support, albeit silent support, from the recent decision of the House of Lords in *Stein v. Blake.*[85] In this case the House of Lords *per* Lord Hoffmann[86] endorsed the observations of Lord Simon in the *Halesowen* case[87] that bankruptcy set-off was part of a "code of procedure whereby bankrupts' estates ... are to be administered in a proper and orderly way". In other words, the statutory regime of set-off is based on considerations of public policy rather than on private rights which parties are competent to waive.

---

[81] [1985] Ch. 207.
[82] But see Nolan [1994] J.B.L. 485.
[83] [1972] A.C. 785. Note the following less than prophetic observations of R.M. Goode in *Legal Problems of Credit and Security* (2nd ed., 1988), pp. 96–97 on the Australian *Horne* decision: "English courts, however, will almost certainly consider that priority agreements are governed by the same principles as agreements excluding set-off and that they are bound by the House of Lords decisions to rule that such agreements must be disregarded by a trustee or liquidator in distributing the assets."
[84] [1994] 1 All E.R. 737 at 746.
[85] [1995] 2 All E.R. 961.
[86] [1995] 2 All E.R. 961 at 970.
[87] [1972] A.C. 785 at 809.

CONCLUSION

It is a fundamental principle of insolvency law that, in any formal insolvency procedure, an insolvent's assets should be divided equally (*pari passu*) between all creditors of the same class.[88] This principle has justly been described as fundamental but shallow largely because of the limitation that it only applies to creditors within the same class.[89] Moreover, the principle only applies to assets that are in the beneficial ownership of the insolvent at the time of the commencement of the insolvency procedure. If a trust has been established prior to such commencement, diverting assets away from the beneficial grasp of the insolvent involves no infraction of the *pari passu*. The establishment of the trust may generate questions of improper preference; these matters have been considered in the following chapter. With debt subordination through the vehicle of a trust there is also the question of the possible creation of a charge requiring registration. This issue has not been squarely resolved or indeed tackled by the courts so that it is only possible to provide guidance by way of analogy. A threat to the use of the trust as a means of circumventing the *pari passu* principle comes from a broad interpretation of the decision of the House of Lords in the *British Eagle* case. The courts however, in recent decisions appear to have been conscious of these dangers and interpreted *British Eagle* narrowly. Moroever, the legislature in the Companies Act 1989 has seen fit to claw back some of the tentacles of *British Eagle*; in other words to narrow the effect of the *pari passu* principle.

---

[88] See the comment by the Department of Trade Review Committee on Insolvency Law and Practice chaired by Sir Kenneth Cork (1982) Cmnd. 8558 at para. 1396: "it is a fundamental objective of the law of insolvency to achieve a rateable, that is to say *pari passu*, distribution of the uncharged assets of the insolvent among the unsecured creditors. In practice, however, this objective is seldom, if ever, attained. In the overwhelming majority of cases it is substantially frustrated by the existence of preferential debts. These are unsecured debts which, by force of statute, fall to be paid in bankruptcy or winding up in priority to all other unsecured debts ...."
[89] See *Oditah* (1992) 108 L.Q.R. 459 at 463.

CHAPTER THREE

Diminution of Trust Claims

While a trust claim against an insolvent company is, generally speaking, binding on the liquidator of that company there are a variety of ways in which the interest of a trust beneficiary interest may be diminished or even extinguished altogether. This chapter considers the circumstances in which such diminution or extinction may occur. Trust assets may have been lost or destroyed by the trustee. There may be a successful challenge to the validity of a trust on the ground say that it constitutes an improper preference contrary to section 239 of the Insolvency Act 1986. The interest of the trust beneficiary may have to yield in priority terms to a person with a charge or other security interest over the assets in respect of which the trust is alleged. Finally, an insolvency practitioner appointed to an insolvent company may have incurred expense in establishing the trust status of assets or in restoring the assets to the jurisdiction. The insolvency practitioner may wish to charge such expenses to the trust fund.

Broadly speaking these are all ways in which trust claims may be "reduced". The issues thrown up by these grounds of reduction are considered in this chapter in reverse order. The chapter therefore begins with a consideration of expenses claims.

REDUCTION OF TRUST ASSETS THROUGH EXPENSES CLAIMS

There may be complicated questions of law and fact to be resolved before the trust status of assets is finally determined. Court applications may be necessary before this issue is settled. Indeed trust assets held by a company as legal owner may have been hidden away by the company controller(s) in some secretive jurisdiction with stringent commercial and banking confidentiality laws. It may have taken prodigious efforts on the part of the liquidator/receiver/administrator/trustee in bankruptcy to restore these assets to the jurisdiction. Liquidators, etc., as qualified insolvency practitioners are normally members of recognised professional bodies such as chartered accountants. It is a truism to say that professional services do not come cheap. It is an equally trite comment that insolvency practitioners are not noted for their altruism. The question therefore arises whether insolvency practitioners can have their expenses met out of the trust assets or whether they must look exclusively for reimbursement to the assets of the company that are unencumbered by trust claims?[1]

The first thing to say on the point is that in the past the courts have displayed great diffidence in awarding remuneration to trustees where there has been no provision for remuneration in the trust instrument. This attitude has changed somewhat in recent times however with the professional trustee moving centre stage, and no plenitude of persons with the leisure and resources to take on unremunerated trusteeships.[2]

[1] See generally Anderson in McKendrick ed., *Commercial Aspects of Trusts and Fiduciary Obligations* (1992), 166 pp. 183–190.
[2] See the comment made by Fox L.J. in *Re Duke of Norfolk's Settlement Trusts* [1982] Ch. 61 at 79.

Among the more modern authorities one might cite *Re Masters, decd.*[3] Danckwerts J. there said that it was quite plain that there was an inherent jurisdiction in the court to authorise remuneration of a trustee, whether appointed by the court or not. *Re Freeman's Settlement Trusts*[4] and *Marshall v. Holloway*[5] were cited in support of this proposition. To the same effect is *Re Worthington decd.*[6] Here Upjohn J. observed that while the court had a jurisdiction to allow remuneration to trustees, that jurisdiction should only be exercised sparingly, and in exceptional cases.[7]

The authorities were reviewed by Walton J. in *Re Duke of Norfolk's Settlement Trusts.*[8] He concluded as follows[9]:

> "(i) The jurisdiction is a wholly exceptional one, to be exercised sparingly. (ii) Subject to (iii) below, the only ground upon which the court has ever acted, so far as the reported cases go, has been the necessity of obtaining the services either of some particular individual trustee, whose services were of special value to the trust, or of obtaining the services of some particular kind of trustee, such, for example as a trustee corporation: (iii) ... remuneration might be awarded if the circumstances of the case were such as to raise an implied promise to pay it on behalf of the beneficiaries ... (iv) There has never been a case in which a court has ever altered the general level of remuneration fixed by the trust instrument, since the trust has been unconditionally accepted ... (v) The court has always shown marked reluctance to award any remuneration unless the application has been made very promptly on assumption of office or where there has been a radical change in the circumstances."[10]

The Court of Appeal took a more liberal attitude than Walton J. to the jurisdiction to award remuneration to trustees.[11] Not only had the court the capacity to make provision for payments where none had been provided for under the trust instrument and also a jurisdiction to alter payment scales in the trust instrument *in futuro*, it also had the power, in cases of exceptional and unforseen work to increase payments for past work. Fox L.J. suggested that increasing the scales stipulated for in the trust instrument might entail a smaller interference with the terms of the instrument than inserting a payment provision where none existed before.[12] The rationale of the power to adjust payment scales was spelled out by Brightman L.J. He said[13]:

---

[3] [1953] 1 W.L.R. 81 at 83.
[4] (1887) 37 Ch. D. 148.
[5] (1820) 2 Swan 432.
[6] [1954] 1 W.L.R. 526 at 528.
[7] Reference was also made to the statement of Lord Cohen in *Dale v. Inland Revenue Commissioners* [1954] A.C. 11, 34.
[8] [1979] Ch. 37. See also *Re Jarvis* [1958] 1 W.L.R. 815 and *Re Barbours Settlement Trusts* [1974] 1 W.L.R. 1198.
[9] *ibid.* at 58.
[10] *Re Salmen* (1912) 107 L.T. 108 is often referred to in this connection.
[11] [1982] Ch. 61.
[12] *ibid.* at 78. He said at 79 that if the court decides "having regard to the nature of the trust, the experience and skill of a particular trustee and the amounts which he seeks to charge when compared with what other trustees might require to be paid for their services and to all the other circumstances of the case, that it would be in the interests of the beneficiaries to increase the remuneration then the court may properly do so."
[13] *ibid.* at 80. See also *Foster v. Spencer* [1996] 2 All E.R. 672 where *Re Duke of Norfolk's Settlement Trusts* was applied by Baker J. In *Foster v. Spencer* the judge added that the right of the trustee to remuneration for past services could not depend on the circumstance that at the time he seeks it, his services are further required so that he is in a position to demand remuneration for the past as a condition of continuing in office.

"If the court has an inherent power to authorise a prospective trustee to take remuneration for future services, and has a similar power in relation to an unpaid trustee who has already accepted office and embarked upon his fiduciary duties on a voluntary basis, I have some difficulty in appreciating the logic of the principle that the court has no power to increase or otherwise vary the future remuneration of a trustee who has already accepted office. It would mean that, if the remuneration specified in the trust instrument were lower than was acceptable to the incumbent trustee or any substitute who could be found, the court would have jurisdiction to authorise a substitute to charge an acceptable level of remuneration, but would have no jurisdiction to authorise the incumbent to charge precisely the same level of remuneration. Such a result appears to me bizarre, and to call in question the validity of the principle upon which it is supposedly based."

The general principle enunciated in *Re Duke of Norfolk's Settlement Trusts* was applied to the situation of a liquidator[14] by Edward Nugee Q.C. sitting as a Deputy High Court Judge in *Re Berkeley Applegate (Investment Consultants) Ltd (No. 2)*.[15] According to the judge the jurisdiction which was held to be exercisable in the *Duke of Norfolk* case was equally exercisable in other cases in which a person sought to enforce an interest in property to which he was entitled in equity. The principles on which a court of equity acted were not divided into watertight compartments but formed a seamless whole, however necessary it might be for the purposes of exposition to attempt to set them out under distinct headings.[16]

The principal business of the company concerned was to place funds on behalf of individual investors and to obtain mortgages over property with the money of the investors. Indivudual investors would pay the sum which they wished to invest to the company. The company would then lend the money it received to approved borrowers on mortgage, with the mortgage taken in the name of the company. The advance to any one borrower was generally derived from the investments of a number of individual investors. Before the making of the advance the money received from investors was held by the company in client accounts where it earned interest.

Edward Nugee Q.C. decided that the money in the client accounts and the benefit of the mortgages were held on trust for the investors. He pointed out that in recent years there appears to have been an increase in the number of companies going into liquidation which hold part of their assets on trust for their clients or customers. He added that in a significant number of these cases the free assets of the company were not sufficient to cover the costs of establishing and verifying the facts.[17] The question therefore arose whether any part of the

---

[14] In connection with the whole issue of an equitable allowance one might mention also *Boardman v. Phipps* [1967] A.C. 46. In this case the solicitor to a trust and one of the beneficiaries under a trust profited personally through information acquired by reason of their position with the trust. In effect the trustees assented to them taking up the profit making opportunity personally though this consent was defective in substance. The defendants were held liable to account to the trust for the profits made but an allowance had to be made for the expenditure which was necessary to enable the profit to be realised. Moreover, the defendants were remunerated generously for their labour and ability in procuring the profit for the trust. The reasoning was that it would be inequitable for the beneficiaries to step in and take the profit without paying for the skill and labour which produced it.
[15] [1989] Ch. 32.
[16] [1989] Ch. 32 at 51. The mixed metaphor is that of the judge.
[17] *ibid.* at 41.

liquidator's expenses or remuneration could be paid out of the trust assets. It was argued on behalf of the beneficiaries that what the liquidator had done[18] amounted to the officious conferment of a benefit and in the words of Bowen L.J. in *Falcke v. Scottish Imperial Insurance Co.*[19]: "Liabilities are not to be forced upon people behind their back any more than you can confer a benefit upon a man against his will." Edward Nugee Q.C. declined to accede to this line of reasoning. In his opinion, the allowance of fair compensation to the liquidator was a proper application of the rule that he who seeks equity must do equity. The authorities were said to establish the following general principle[20]:

> "where the person seeks to enforce a claim to an equitable interest in property, the court has a discretion to require as a condition of giving effect to that equitable interest that an allowance be made for costs incurred and for skill and labour expended in connection with the administration of the property."

The judge proceeded to enumerate relevant factors which would operate in favour of the discretion being exercised. These included the fact that if the work had not been done by the person to whom the allowance was sought to be made, it would have had to be done either by the person entitled to the equitable interest or by a receiver appointed by the court whose fees would have been borne by the trust property, and the fact that the work has been of substantial benefit to the trust property and to the persons interested in it in equity.[21]

There was in fact earlier authority in the shape of the decision of Vinelott J. in *Re Exchange Securities & Commodities Ltd*[22] that an equitable allowance could be made to a liquidator out of trust assets. The case concerned a number of companies which had taken deposits from the public for investment in commodities. The companies in question were ordered to be wound up with the Offical Receiver appointed as provisional liquidator. A special manager had also been appointed in all cases. Depositors claimed that their investment moneys were impressed with a trust and could be traced into the hands of various of the companies. Trying to determine the true beneficial ownership of the assets held by the companies was an especially complicated and costly business given the large number of inter-company transfers that had taken place. The Official Receiver therefore sought an order that his fees and expenses and those of the special manager be paid out of the assets ostensibly belonging to each company, even if it later transpired that those assets were beneficially

---

[18] The work undertaken by the liquidator on behalf of the trust beneficiaries was summarised by the judge under four heads: (1) preliminary investigation; (2) dealing with inquiries from investors and borrowers; (3) ascertainment of assets; (4) management of investments. About 12 times as much time was spent on matters relating to the investors' proprietary claims compared with general liquidation affairs.

[19] (1886) 34 Ch. D. 234 at 248. In furtherance of this line of reasoning counsel pointed out that a liquidator is not a trustee for anyone. He is a substitute for the board of directors. He is only the agent of the company and is more akin to the board than is a trustee in bankruptcy. Even a trustee in bankruptcy acquires no title to trust assets vested in the bankrupt.

[20] [1989] Ch. 32 at 50.

[21] *ibid.* at 50–51.

[22] [1985] B.C.L.C. 392. This case was in fact considered by Edward Nugee Q.C. in *Re Berkeley Applegate Ltd (No. 2)* [1989] Ch. 32. See also *Re Introductions Ltd (No. 2)* [1969] 1 W.L.R. 1359 where Stamp J. in a four line judgment said: "A labourer is worthy of his hire. It is quite plain that I must direct payment of the Official Receiver's costs, charges and expenses out of the assets, without prejudice as to how any of the costs, charges and expenses ought ultimately to be borne."

owned by depositors. Vinelott J. accepted the submission that the court had an inherent jurisdiction to direct payment to the Official Receiver of a just allowance for his services and the payment or reimbursement of all costs and expenses reasonably incurred by him in getting it, protecting and taking all steps necessary to ascertain the true ownership of assets held by each of the companies. In the circumstances however it was premature to try to prescribe the basis on which that allowance was to be calculated or to attempt to formulate the principles governing the manner in which it was to be apportioned as between the company and the trust assets.

In *Berkeley Applegate* an attempt was made to distinguish this authority on the basis that it was a case of compulsory winding up in which the official receiver, by virtue of his office, automatically becomes the liquidator until another liquidator is appointed. In *Berkeley Applegate* the company was in voluntary liquidation and the liquidator had an opportunity of considering his position before accepting office as liquidator. The distinction was rejected on the ground that it contravened the principle behind the maxim that he who seeks equity must do equity.[23]

The principle propounded by Edward Nugee Q.C. in *Berkeley Applegate* is sufficiently widely expressed to encompass office holders in other forms of insolvency proceedings as well as liquidators. The jursidiction to make an equitable allowance exists but whether or not it will be exercised in favour of the office holder is another question. Similar factors should obtain with respect to a trustee in bankruptcy as a liquidator. The position of an administrator also seems reasonably secure given the fact that he is under a statutory duty to take into his custody or under his control all the property to which the company is, or appears to be, entitled. Taking into account the presence in the legislation of the phrase "appears to be entitled" dealings by an administrator with trust assets can hardly be derided as officious interference. It has been argued that the position is different with respect to an administrative receiver and that there seems no reason why costs wrongly incurred intermeddling with assets which turn out to be trust assets should not simply constitute part of the costs of the receivership debited to the receivership fund.[24] The argument proceeds along the lines that a receiver is entitled to disregard assets covered by the security if he does not consider it in the interests of the debenture holder by whom he was appointed to pursue those assets. On the other hand if the receiver has conferred an advantage on the beneficial owners by his labours in administering the trust assets it seems inequitable that the beneficiaries should be able to enjoy the fruits of these labours without having to pay for the same. If remuneration and remimbursement of expenses for the receiver is off the agenda there is the very real risk that trust assets will be left unadministered and thereby placed in jeopardy.

CALCULATION OF REMUNERATION

The cases have established the existence of an inherent judicial discretion to award an office holder in insolvency proceedings an allowance for his work in

---

[23] [1989] Ch. 32 at 43–44.
[24] See Anderson, "The Treatment of Trust Assets in English Insolvency Law" in *Commercial Aspects of Trusts and Fiduciary Obligations* (McKendrick), pp. 166, 186.

connection with trust property. There remains the question of how this allowance is to be calculated. The issue of assessment arose in *Re Eastern Capital Futures Ltd*[25] Morritt J. decided that the liquidators should retain remuneration out of the trust fund equal to what they would have got if the trust moneys had been the company's own moneys. The trust moneys should be notionally aggregated with the company's assets and a prescribed scale then applied to the aggregate so as to calculate the total remuneration to which, on this hypothesis, the liquidators would be entitled. That proportion of the total remuneration which the trust assets bore to the combination of the company and trust assets, should be paid or retained as remuneration out of the trust assets.

Edward Nugee Q.C. did not have to decide questions of incidence of remuneration in *Re Berkeley Applegate Ltd (No. 2)*.[26] The matter returned to the court however, in *Re Berkeley Applegate Ltd (No. 3)*.[27] As we have seen, this was a case where a company received money from investors to lend out on mortgages. It went into voluntary liquidation at a time when there were £10.2 million in mortgages outstanding and £1.2 million in client accounts. There were two different classes of investor, namely those whose moneys could be traced into the outstanding mortgages and those whose investments were to be found in the client accounts. The company's free assets amounted to a sum in the region of £45,000–£80,000 while the total reimbursements and remuneration of the liquidator came to about £686,000, of which some £41,500 was estimated by the liquidator to represent expenses of the liquidation only, as distinct from expenses of administering the trust. How was the total bill to be apportioned?

In resolving this troublesome issue Peter Gibson J. firstly determined that the free assets of the company could not be used for meeting the costs of administering trust funds. Section 115 of the Insolvency Act 1986 stipulates that:

> "All expenses properly incurred in the winding up, including the remuneration of the liquidator, are payable out of the company's assets in priority to all other claims."

Trust administration expenses could not be regarded as winding up expenses for the purpose of the statutory provision. The section was simply dealing with the winding up of the company, involving as it did the getting in of the assets of the company, ascertaining its creditors, paying its liabilities in accordance with the statutory provisions and distributing any surplus. Expenses that arose in dealing with trust fund issues and in administering the trust fund fell outside the legislative conception of "expenses properly incurred in the winding up". There was no reason however, why investors whose trust assets had been depleted through administration expenses incurred by company liquidators should not be able to mount a claim alongside other unsecured creditors of the company to any surplus corporate assets after liquidation expenses had been taken care off.[28]

The issue of the apportionment of the remuneration and expenses between the two classes of investors was a matter of some complexity and demonstrates the attention to detail that is appropriate in this area. Peter Gibson J. accepted

---

[25] (1989) 5 B.C.C. 224.
[26] [1989] Ch. 32.
[27] (1989) 5 B.C.C. 803.
[28] *ibid.* at 805.

the submission of the liquidator that a somewhat rough and ready approach should be adopted towards apportionment. Save for an initial period when his work had been for the benefit of all investors, the liquidator's remuneration and unattributed expenses should be apportioned between all investors rateably, and that for the remaining period, 90 per cent of the expense should be borne pro rata by those who were still mortgage investors at the beginning of the later period, and 10 per cent divided between the rest.[29]

As well as suffering diminution through expenses claims the interests of the trust beneficiaries may also lose some of their value through competing claims over the asset that forms the subject-matter of the trust. A lender may have advanced money to the person with the legal title on the security of the asset in question. Such a lender may assert a charge or other security interest over the asset that enjoys priority to the claim of the trust beneficiary. The issue of priorities will now be investigated.

TRUST CLAIMS AND PRIORITIES

How are the claims of trust asset beneficiaries to be ranked *vis-à-vis* the position of unsecured creditors and fixed and floating charge holders? One thing is clear. A claimant under a properly constituted trust that is not challengeable as a transaction at an undervalue or a preference will come ahead of unsecured creditors. The trust claimant has a proprietary claim to the assets which the company holds as legal owner whereas the unsecured creditors are in no such position. The situation as regards secured creditors is somewhat more problematic. Take the case where the trust claim is indisputably first in time with the charge having been granted subsequently. If the debenture takes the form of a legal charge over land then the debenture holder should prevail as a matter of basic principle if he is a bona fide purchaser of the legal estate for value without notice of the prior equitable interest. Notice would encompass actual, constructive or imputed notice.[30] The fundamental common law rule still obtains in the case of unregistered land today; preserved by statute in the shape of section 199 of the Law of Property Act 1925 which talks about matters within a person's own knowledge or that would have come to his knowledge if such inquiries and inspections had been made as ought reasonably to have been made by him. Transaction with respect to unregistered land are by far the exception rather than the norm today.[31] In relation to registered land the operative principle is that something must be on the register to bind a purchaser. Section 59(6) of the Land Registration Act 1925 lays down that a purchaser acquiring title under a registered disposition shall not be concerned with any

---

[29] *ibid.* at 806–807. See also *Re Westdock Realisations Ltd* (1988) 4 B.C.C. 192; *Re Stetzel Thomson & Co. Ltd* (1988) 4 B.C.C. 74; *Acoma (Bilston) Ltd v. Comer & Ors* March 1, 1990, unreported, Micklem J. which is referred to by Anderson *op. cit.* at 187.

[30] A person has imputed notice according to s. 199(2) of the Law of Property Act 1925 if "in the same transaction with respect to which a question of notice to the purchaser arises, it has come to the knowledge of his counsel, as such, or of his solicitor or other agent, as such, or would have come to the knowledge of his solicitor or other agent, as such, if such inquiries and inspections had been made as ought reasonably to have been made by the solicitor or other agent."

[31] Under the Registration of Title Order 1989 (S.I. No. 1347) all conveyances on sale taking effect in England and Wales on or after December 1, 1990 must be recorded in the Land Register pursuant to the Land Registration Act 1925.

matter which is not protected by an entry on the register, "whether he has or has not notice thereof, express, implied or constructive."[32] The phrase "purchaser" is defined in section 3 of the Act as meaning a purchaser in good faith for valuable consideration. While notice is generally irrelevant in the registered land scenario there is a limited exception to the principle of indefeasibility of the register in situations of fraud. In one case *De Lusignan v. Jonhson*[33] Brightman J. distinguished sharply between "fraud" and mere "notice of the existence or possible existence" of unprotected rights. Only the former would operate to deny the claims of a purchaser of registered land. An example of fraud might be where a transfer of registered land had been brought about by a collateral representation made by the transferee that he would safeguard the unprotected rights of a third party.[34]

With respect to dealings in chattels it seems that it is only actual notice that will deprive a legal security interest holder of priority over an earlier equitable interest. The oft-cited dicta of Lindley L.J. in *Manchester Trust v. Furness*[35] spring to mind in this context. He said[36]:

> "The equitable doctrines of constructive notice are common enough in dealing with land and estates, with which the Court is familiar, but there have been repeated protests agsinst the introduction into commercial transactions of anything like an extension of those doctrines, and the protest is founded on perfect good sense. In dealing with estates in land title is everything, and it can be leisurely investigated; in commercial transactions possession is everything and there is not time to investigate title; and if we were to extend the doctrine of constructive notice to commercial transactions we should be doing infinite mischief and paralysing the trade of the country."

Reference was made to these dicta by Neill J. in *Feuer Leather Corporation v. Frank Johnstone & Sons*.[37] He took the view that a purchaser in a commercial transaction will not be affected by constructive notice.

Where the subsequent security interest is equitable in character the trust claimant should rank ahead on the basis of the principle that where the equities are equal the first in time prevails.[38] Moreover a floating charge deos not attach to any specific asset until the charge crystallises.[39] Therefore, a trust claim will come ahead of a floating charge even where the floating charge is already hovering over, in an uncrystallised form, the assets in respect of which the trust claim is generated at the time that this generation, so to speak, occurs. In the

---

[32] See also s. 20(1) of the Land Registraton Act 1925.

[33] (1973) 230 *Estates Gazette* 499; on which see M.P. Thompson [1985] C.L.J. 280. See generally K. Gray *Elements of Land Law* (2nd ed., 1993), pp. 186–197.

[34] See *Loke Yew v. Port Swettenham Rubber Co. Ltd* [1913] A.C. 491. Gray *Elements of Land Law* (2nd ed., 1993), p. 19, n. 8 provides a wealth of information on the background of the unprotected incumbrancer Loke Yew who was not the unwary innocent that one might suppose but rather the Carnegie of vice in Malaya.

[35] [1895] 2 Q.B. 539.

[36] *ibid.* at 545.

[37] [1981] Com L.R. 251.

[38] The Latin tag is *qui prior est tempore potior est jure*.

[39] See the remarks of Lord Macnaghten in *Illingworth v. Houldsworth* [1904] A.C. 355 at 358. Note too the comments of Buckley L.J. in *Evans v. Rival Granite Quarries Ltd* [1910] 2 K.B. 979 at 999: "A floating security is not a specific mortgage of the assets, plus a licence to the mortgagor to dispose of them in the course of his business but is a floating mortgage applying to every item until some event occurs or some act of the mortgagee is done which causes it to crystallise into a fixed security."

case of registered land however, the application of the old equitable maxim has been displaced by the statutory precedence accorded to registered interests over unregistered claims.[40]

The priority picture can get even more complicated. Say that the interest of the debenture holder has been created before the claim of "trust assets" can legitimately be made. The debenture may have included an after acquired property clause and the borrower later acquires additional property within the ambit of the clause. Say the subsequent acquisition is subject to a form of trust claim. The property may have been transferred under a mistake of fact. According to Goulding J. in the *Chase Manhattan Bank*[41] case the transferee in such a situation retains rights, of a kind recognised by equity, in the property. Superficially one might say that the debenture holder in this instance should win the priority battle by virtue of being first in time. An alternative anlysis is possible however. This draws on the analogy of what the Americans dub "the purchase money security interest" or PMSI.[42] Article 9–107 of the U.S. Uniform Commercial Code contains the following definition[43]:

> "A security interest is a purchase money security interest to the extent that it is
> (a) taken or retained by the seller of the collateral to secure all or part of its price; or
> (b) taken by a person who by making advances or incurring an obligation gives value to enable the debtor to acquire rights in or the use of collateral if such value is in fact so used."

In the United Kingdom the purchase money security interest has come before the courts in a situation where A makes an advance to the debtor on the security of its future property and the debtor subsequently acquires an asset with funds provided by B on the security of that asset.[44] A priority dispute arises between the interests of A and B. A case often cited in this connection is that of *Re Connolly Bros Ltd (No. 2)*.[45]

Here a company issued debentures subject to a condition that it would not create any other charge in priority to those debentures. A couple of years later when the company wished to purchase some premises but did not have enough money for that purpose, it "borrowed" £1,000 from a Mrs O'Reilly upon terms that should have a charge upon the premises when purchased. A memorandum

---

[40] ss. 59(6) and 20 of the Land Registration Act 1925.
[41] [1981] Ch. 105.
[42] This analysis was utilised in the context of the *Quistclose* trust by M.J. Bridge (1992) 12 O.J.L.S. 333 at 343–344.
[43] See generally on the purchase money security interest in U.S. law, Grant Gilmore *Security Interests in Personal Property* (1965), Chaps. 28–30. See also Kronman and Jackson (1979) 88 Yale L.J. 1143 at 1145. For an argument concerning the application of the concept of the purchase money security interest to fixtures in English law see Bennett and Davis (1994) 110 L.Q.R. 448.
[44] Even in the United States the doctrine of the purchase money security interest has a judicial parentage. According to the Supreme Court in *United States v. New Orleans Railroad* 79 U.S. 362: "A mortgage intended to cover after-acquired property can only attach itself to such property in the condition in which it comes into the mortgagor's hands. If the property is already subject to mortgages or other liens, the general mortgage does not displace them, though they may be junior to it in point of time. It only attaches to such interest as the mortgagor acquires; and if he purchases property and gives a mortgage for the purchase-money, the deed which he receives and the mortgage which he gives are regarded as one transaction, and no general lien impending over him ... can displace such mortgage for purchase-money."
[45] [1912] 2 Ch. 25.

of this equitable charge was duly executed. A contest arose as to whether the debenture holders had priority over Mrs O'Reilly's claim. It was held by the Court of Appeal that they did not. When the company purported to purchase the premises it in fact acquired only an equity of redemption in the property subject to the equitable charge of Mrs O'Reilly. The full ownership of the premises never formed part of the company's assets for the purpose of the floating charge in favour of the debenture holders. The money contributed by Mrs O'Reilly was therefore not so much a loan like the money lent by debenture holders but rather a part payment for the premises. She acquired an interest in the premises at the very moment when the company purported to purchase them.

Another case to the same effect is *Wilson v. Kelland*.[46] In this instance a vendor gave up his lien as unpaid seller over property he had agreed to sell for £5,350 in return for £2,350 and a contractual promise that he would be granted an equitable charge over the property of £3,000. The subsequently created charge was unregistered. However, it was held to prevail over a floating charge over all the assets, present or future of the company, which was duly registered and prior in point of time. The rationale of the decision was that the company had only acquired an equity of redemption in the property.

The same principle was applied by the Judicial Committee of the Privy Council in *Security Trust Co. v. Royal Bank of Canada*.[47] The difficulty with these decisions is that priority was determined by a matter largely divorced from the merits of the situation; namely the order in which the transactions take place. A person was relegated, priority-wise, if he does not bargain for his purchase-money security in advance but rather, without any prior binding agreement, takes it on completion of the purchase.[48] A case in point is *Church of England Building Society v. Piskor*.[49]

In *Piskor* the borrowers agreed to purchase premises. They were let into possession of the premises before completion and they then proceeded to let parts of the premises to other persons. Shortly thereafter, the purchase was completed and on the same day the borrowers charged the premises in favour of the plaintiff building society by way of legal mortgage. An advance of moneys from the society was necessary to enable the borrowers to complete the purchase of the property. It was held by the Court of Appeal that the purported tenants had acquired as against the borrowers a tenancy by estoppel. The subsequent acquisition of the legal estate by the borrowers fed the estoppel. The tenancy by estoppel was treated by the court as binding on the mortgagees because, according to the court, a moment of time necessarily elapsed between the acquisition of the property by the borrowers and the charge in favour of the building society. Evershed M.R. stated the matter thus[50]:

"It is no doubt true to say that in one sense the transaction was one transaction; but it is equally true to say that it consists necessarily of certain defined steps which must take place in a certain defined order if the result intended is eventually to be achieved.

---

[46] [1910] 2 Ch. 306.
[47] [1976] A.C. 503.
[48] See generally R.M. Goode, *Legal Problems of Credit and Security* (2nd ed., 1988), pp. 98–101.
[49] [1954] 1 Ch. 553.
[50] [1954] 1 Ch. 553 at 561.

That seems to me not an artificiality but a necessary result of the law and of the conveyancing practice which was involved."

In *Security Trust Co. v. Royal Bank of Canada*[51] Lord Cross sought to smooth a path through the thicket of competing case law. He attempted a reconciliation on the following lines[52]:

"[T]he basic difference between the two lines of cases is that in cases such as *Re Connolly Bros Ltd (No. 2)* and this case the charge under the debenture only bites on property which is already fettered by the agreement to give the other charge whereas on the the facts of *Church of England Building Society v. Piskor* the tenancy was created out of an interest which was then unfettered by any such agreement."

It may be argued that this is more the statement of a result rather than an explanation of why that particular result was reached.[53]

The following passage from Professor Goode's *Legal Problems of Credit and Security* demonstrated the absurdity of the situation[54]:

"[T]he courts have examined the sequence of operations with meticulous detail to find out whether the debtor's interest in the asset was encumbered at the outset by the purchase-money mortgage (in which case A's after acquired property clause can attach to the asset only in its encumbered form, so that B wins even if taking with notice of A's security interest) or whether on the other hand there was a moment of time (*scintilla temporis*) in which B was the unencumbered owner of the asset before granting the purchase money security interest, in which event A's after-acquired property flashes in to catch the asset seconds before the purchase money security takes effect."

Piskor has in fact been overruled by the House of Lords in *Abbey National Building Society v. Cann*.[55] There were two substantive judgments; those of Lords Oliver and Jauncey. Lord Oliver recognised that as a matter of legal theory, a person could not charge a legal estate that he did not have, so that there was an attractive legal logic in the *ratio* of *Piskor*. Nevertheless, his Lordship felt that it flew in the face of reality. The reality was that, in the huge majority of cases, acquisition of the legal estate and the charge were not only precisely simultaneous,

---

[51] [1976] A.C. 503.

[52] *ibid.* at 519.

[53] An unresolved question before *Abbey National Building Society v. Cann* [1991] 1 A.C. 56 was whether, for the purpose of securing his priority, it sufficed if the purchase money financier obtained an agreement for a charge before completion of the purchase or whether he had to go further and get it before exchange of contracts. The issue is addressed to a certain extent by both Lords Oliver and Jauncey in *Cann*. Lord Oliver said that the court in *Piskor* never grasped the nettle that the transaction necessarily involved an enforceable agreement for the grant of a charge at the stage when the money was advanced in order to enable the conveyance to take place. Lord Jauncey suggested that where the agreement to grant the mortgage preceded the granting of the tenancy, then when both equitable interests were clothed with the legal estate, the first equitable interest to be created would prevail.
Surely, however, the issue of priorities should depend on whether the agreement for the grant of the purchase money security interest precedes the exchange of contracts. If that occurs, then the debtor's equitable interest arising on exchange of contracts is fettered by the agreement to give the charge.

[54] (2nd ed., 1988), pp. 98–99.

[55] [1991] 1 A.C. 56 on which see Gregory (1990) 106 L.Q.R. 550. See also McCormack (1991) 12 Co. Law 11.

but indissolubly bound up together. The purchaser who relied on a loan for the completion of his purchase never in fact acquired anything but an equity of redemption, for the property was, from the very inception, charged with the amount of the loan without which it could never have been transferred at all and it had never been intended that it should be otherwise.[56]

Lord Jauncey expressed himself in similar terms. He said[57]:

> "a purchaser who can only complete the transaction by borrowing money for the security of which he is contractually bound to grant a mortgage to the lender *eo instanti* with the execution of the conveyance in his favour cannot in reality ever be said to have acquired even for a *scintilla temporis* the unencumbered fee simple or leasehold interest in land whereby he could grant interests having priority over the mortgage ..."

On the basis of *Cann* when can one say that, what may be described as a purchase money security interest holder, has priority? All is plain sailing where a purchaser needs a 100 per cent mortgage or a mortgage approaching that level. Here the reality clearly is that the advance is necessary for completion of the purchase. But what if the loan is in the nature of a top-up? Maybe, the purchaser has ample funds to complete out of his own resources but wishes to obtain a loan merely to smooth over potential financial difficulties. Does the purchase money financier prevail even in this case?[58] When may a purchaser be said to "rely" on a mortgage advance for finalisation of the acquisition? A further issue for future resolution involves consideration of the priority question when a short space of time undoubtedly elapses between completion of the purchase and execution of the mortgage or charge.[59]

Favourable treatment for purchase money security interests was suggested by the DTI commissioned report by Professor Aubrey Diamond on Security Interests in Property.[60] In the scheme of things envisaged by Professor Diamond such interests are to be afforded a priority over pre-existing security interests which include after-acquired property. The justification for this favouritism is that, whereas a security interest granted over property already owned may remove that property from the debtor's estate, a security interest over newly-acquired property to secure the price paid for that property is neutral in its effect. The debt in respect of the price is offset by the addition of the property. Moreover, if the new property helped the business of the debtor to earn extra profits, it would strengthen the position of existing creditors by swelling their

---

[56] [1991] 1 A.C. 56 at 92–93.

[57] *ibid.* at 102. It may be argued however that certain observations of Lord Browne-Wilkinson in *Westdeutsche Bank v. Islington L.B.C.* [1996] 2 W.L.R. 802 at 830 imply support for the *scintilla temporis* doctrine.

[58] In *Cann* no comment was passed on the judgment of Purchas L.J. in *Lloyds Bank plc v. Rosset* [1989] Ch. 350 at 407. Purchas L.J. pointed out that on the facts of *Rosset* the bank's participation in creating the charge was to secure an overdraft, the money from which was essentially to be used for the purposes of renovation and not for the acquisition of the property. In his view the bank's interest in securing the overdraft could not be said to be equivalent to the interest obtained by Mrs O'Reilly in the *Connolly* case [1912] 2 Ch. 25 or by the debenture holders in *Security Trust Co. v. Royal Bank of Canada* [1976] A.C. 503. The decision on the appeal in *Lloyds Bank plc v. Rosset* [1991] 1 A.C. was handed down by the House of Lords on the same day as that in *Cann*. The appeal in the *Rosset* case turned on the question however, of whether or not there was a beneficial interest in the first place. No attention was directed to the priorities question.

[59] A case in point is *Universal Permanent Building Society v. Cooke* [1952] 1 Ch. 95.

[60] (1989) at paras. 11.7.5–11.7.7.

security interest. In addition, if an earlier creditor could rely on an after-acquired property clause to the prejudice of a purchase money security interest holder, he would obtain a wholly unjustifed windfall at the expense of the later creditor, whose money enabled the additional property to be acquired.

These arguments for favourable treatment of the purchase money security interest have been expanded upon in the American academic literature.[61] The fundamental proposition is that the first creditor on the scene should not be permitted to obtain a security monopoly over the assets of the debtor. The effect of this would be to preclude the debtor from procuring further credit elsewhere or to force later creditors to contract on a riskier basis, having to settle for later ranking security or no security.[62]

While one must be wary of reading more into a judgment than is actually there it is submitted that the *Cann* case constitutes judicial recognition of the purchase money security interest in English law.[63] The arguments for prioritising a purchase money security could be applied also to the context under discussion. It is arguable therefore that a charge which was created earlier in point of time should rank after a trust claim to assets the acquisition of legal title to which by the company has been encumbered by the trust.

Apart from losing out in a priority battle another way in which the interest of a trust beneficiary may suffer a diminution is if the trust is vulnerable on some ground. The issue of avoidance of trusts will now be addressed.

AVOIDANCE OF TRUSTS

Trusts that operate to take property out of the assets of a company available for distribution to creditors are challengeable under a number of heads. One ground of complaint that is not available however is that of failure to comply with registration requirements. Part XII of the Companies Act 1985 imposes a requirement to register with the registrar of companies prescribed particulars of certain charges created by a company.[64] The expression charge is statutorily defined to include a mortgage.[65] Slade J. explained in *Re Bond Worth Ltd*[66] that the technical difference between a "mortgage" and a "charge" lies in the fact that a mortgage involves a conveyance of property subject to a right of redemption while a charge conveys nothing and merely invests the chargee with

[61] See generally Kronman and Jackson (1979) 88 Yale L.J. 1143 at 1167–1175 and see also Bennett and Davis (1994) 110 L.Q.R. 448.

[62] For an impassioned plea against according the purchase money security interest super priority status see Gough, *Company Charges* (2nd ed., 1996), pp. 434–439. Gough argues that the proposal for super-priority status artificially discriminates between one credit purpose and another. "It assumes that financial accommodation for the purpose of, for example, paying wages and salaries through cheques drawn on an overdraft account is less important than for the purchase of stocks or plant and equipment. This is not a real world distinction. Credit, as a matter of business need, is indivisible in the sense that all business inputs, including wages, overheads, equipment and supplies are all vital to an ongoing business."

[63] But for a somewhat restrictive reading of *Cann* in the reservation of title context see *Stroud Architectural Systems Ltd v. John Laing Construction Ltd* [1994] B.C.C. 18.

[64] Part IV of the Companies Act 1989 was intended to revamp Part XII of the 1985 Act but Part IV was never implemented and is unlikely to be implemented. For a full discussion of company charge registration see McCormack *Registration of Company Charges* (1994).

[65] s. 396(4) of the Companies Act 1985 as originally drafted.

[66] [1980] Ch. 228.

certain rights over the property as security for the loan.[67] So a mortgage entails the transfer of rights of ownership whereas a charge involves simply a right of recourse to the property for security purposes. A proprietary interest by way of trust is outside the concept of a charge. There is no security interest *stricto sensu* and so the registration of charge provisions are irrelevant. This was made clear by Peter Gibson J. in *Carreras Rothmans Ltd v. Freeman Mathews Treasure Ltd.*[68] It does not seem to matter that a single transaction can comprise both a loan and a trust.

Trust arrangements are at greater risk from the transactions at an undervalue provisions contained in sections 238–241 of the Insolvency Act.[69] Basically these sections invalidate gifts made by an insolvent company in the two year period prior to liquidation or administration or transactions in which the insolvent has received significantly less consideration than that given out.[70] In the case of transactions entered into for the purpose of defeating or prejudicing creditor claims the legislative regime is significantly tougher.[71] Proof of insolvency is not necessary nor are there any time limits.

The preference provisions are also relevant in this general area. The legislation strikes at acts or things done which have the effect of putting a creditor or surety in a better position than they would otherwise occupy in a bankruptcy or liquidation.[72] The act or thing done must have been at least partially influenced by the desire to put the creditor or surety in a better position. The statutory objective is to uphold the principle of *pari passu* distribution rather than to preserve the value of the assets that comprise the estate of an insolvent. The statutory provisions outlawing improper preferences have been argued upon most fiercely in connection with the so-called Quistclose trust[73] and detailed consideration of the issue will be postponed until Chapter 4.

Apart from invalidation of the trust on grounds set in this section trust fund beneficiaries may also lose through actions of their trustee. Their trustee may dissipate the trust assets leaving nothing in their place. This scenario will now be considered.

DISSIPATION OF TRUST ASSETS THROUGH ACTIONS OF THE TRUSTEE

Trust assets may become lost or dissipated as a result of dealings by the company which holds them as trustee. *Space Investments Ltd v. Canadian Imperial Bank of Commerce Trust Co. (Bahamas) Ltd*[74] supplies an example of this principle. This is a case where a bank acted as trustee and held certain funds in that capacity. It proceeded to deposit the trust funds with itself qua banker. This was perfectly lawful according to the terms of the trust instrument. Unfortunately, however, the bank became insolvent and went into liquidation. The question arose whether the trust fund beneficiaries should be paid in priority to the

---

[67] *ibid.* at 250.
[68] [1985] Ch. 207.
[69] These sections refer to corporate transactions. Ss. 339–342 of the Insolvency Act apply similar provisions to transactions involving individuals.
[70] The definition of "transaction" is contained in s. 436 of the Act.
[71] s. 423 of the Insolvency Act 1986 which applies to both individuals and companies.
[72] ss. 239 and 240.
[73] In particular major criticisms have been directed against *Re Kayford Ltd* [1975] 1 W.L.R. 279.
[74] [1986] 3 All E.R. 75.

unsecured creditors of the bank. The Privy Council answered this question in the negative. Lord Templeman who delivered the judgment of the Board said that equity protects beneficiaries against breaches of trust. The beneficiaries had a chose in action, namely an action against the trustee bank for damages for breach of trust and, in addition, they possessed the equitable remedy of tracing the trust money to any property into which it had been converted directly or indirectly. Equity however did not protect beneficiaries against the consequences of the exercise in good faith of powers conferred by the trust instrument.[75] This is in fact what happened in this case with the deposits having been lawfully made in accordance with an authorisation in the trust instrument. Where moneys were held by a bank on deposit the bank became simply a debtor, for it was a long established principle of banking law that the banker-customer relationship was a debtor-creditor one. The trust fund beneficiaries thus simply joined the list of unsecured creditors of the bank. The trustee quite lawfully just happened to deposit the trust money with itself in a different guise but this, while lawful, was improvident. With the benefit of hindsight it would have been far better off, at least for the sake of the beneficiaries, if the trustee had deposited the funds with a completely different bank.[76] The apparent harshness of the decision from the perspective of the beneficiaries stems from the dual capacity of the bank. The bank *qua* trustee and the bank *qua* banker were one and the same legal entity.[77]

CONCLUSION

This chapter has considered various ways in which the claims of trust beneficiaries may, in a broad sense, be reduced. The common thread linking the issues discussed in the chapter is diminution of trust claims; in other words, a reduction in the amount that would otherwise go to the trust beneficiaries. Expenses claims by insolvency practitioners who have administered trust assets, competing claims to trust assets by fixed and floating charge holders and challenges to the legal efficacy of trusts in an insolvency of the legal owner of the trust fund assets, all present obstacles to the practical utiliity of the trust claim. Such practical utility may also be undermined if the trustee has dissipated the trust funds. It may of course be that while the original trust assets themselves have been spent, there is some identifiable and traceable product. The issue of tracing is a different and difficult story that will be considered in Chapters 8 and 9.

[75] *ibid.* at 77. Some of what Lord Templeman said on tracing is in fact controversial and is considered in Chapter 8.
[76] Assuming of course that the latter bank did not itself become insolvent.
[77] See Anderson in *Commercial Aspects of Trusts and Fiduciary Obligations* (McKendrick ed., 1992), pp. 167, 181.

CHAPTER FOUR

Conditional Payments and Insolvency—
The *Quistclose* Trust

It is axiomatic that assets which form the subject-matter of a trust do not constitute part of the property of an insolvent available for distribution among the insolvent's creditors. Persons responsible for administering the affairs of insolvents take the property of the insolvent subject to equities. One such equity that must be recognised and upheld is the interests of beneficiaries under a trust where the insolvent holds the bare legal title. In this article the applicability of the doctrine of trusts in the realm of conditional payments will be considered. If a lender lends money on condition that it is used for a particular purpose and/or paid back out of a particular fund, or if a purchaser pays in advance on condition that the money is used to provide something he wants, to what extent can the lender or payer enforce the conditional agreement? There is something of an analogy with prepayments in sale of goods situations.[1] It is possible for a seller of goods to retain title to the goods notwithstanding delivery of the goods to the buyer until the goods have been paid for or some other condition has been fulfilled.[2] Conditional loans or payments are usually discussed under the rubric of the *Quistclose* trust and it is perhaps convenient to continue this classification.[3]

THE *QUISTCLOSE* TRUST

The *locus classicus* is *Barclays Bank Ltd v. Quistclose Investments Ltd.*[4] This is a case where Quistclose lent a company, Rolls Razor Ltd, some £210,000 to allow Rolls Razor to pay a dividend it had already declared. Rolls Razor sent the money to its bank, asking it to pay it into a separate dividend account and stating that the money was to be used only to pay the dividend. But before the dividend could be paid Rolls Razor went into voluntary liquidation, leaving Quistclose and the bank to dispute ownership of the £210,000. The company's bank claimed a right to set off the £210,000 credit against a debit balance in another account.

The claim failed. The money was held to be impressed with a trust in favour of Quistclose should the primary purpose of the payment fail. Lord Wilberforce said that the mutual intention of Quistclose and of Rolls Razor Ltd and the

---

[1] For a comprehensive examination of reservation of title clauses see McCormack, *Reservation of Title* (2nd ed., 1995).

[2] The link between reservation of title clauses in sales of goods and conditional loans or payments has not always been borne in mind when one or other of the two phenomena have been examined. However, the two are brought together in the excellent article by Goodhart and Jones, "The Infiltration of Equitable Doctrine into English Commercial Law" (1980) 43 M.L.R. 489. See also Priestley, "The Romalpa Trust and the Quistclose Trust" in *Equity in Commercial Relationships* (P.D. Finn ed.,1987); Milman and Durrant, *Corporate Insolvency Law and Practice* (2nd ed., 1994)) Chap. 8; M. Bridge (1992) 12 O.J.L.S. 333 and C.E.F. Rickett (1991) 107 L.Q.R. 608.

[3] Some would argue however that the *Re Kayford Ltd* [1975] 1 W.L.R. 279 line of authorites are not true examples of the *Quistclose* trust properly so called.

[4] [1970] A.C. 567.

essence of the bargain was that the sum advanced should not become part of the assets of Rolls Razor Ltd but should be used exclusively for payment of a particular class of its creditors, namely, those entitled to the dividend. This entailed the necessary consequence that if, for any reason, the dividend could not be paid, the money was to be returned to Quistclose. The word "only" was not capable of bearing any other effect.[5]

His Lordship was emphatic in his disavowal of the idea that a transaction giving rise to a legal action for debt could not also create a trust. He said[6]:

"There is surely no difficulty in recognising the co-existence in one transaction of legal and equitable rights and remedies; when the money is advanced, the lender acquires an equitable right to see that it is applied for the primary designated purpose . . .: when the purpose has been carried out (*i.e.* the debt paid) the lender has his remedy against the borrower in debt; if the primary purpose cannot be carried out, the question arises if a secondary purpose (*i.e.* repayment to the lender) has been agreed, expressly or by implication: if it has, the remedies of equity may be invoked to give effect to it, if it has not (and the money) is intended to fall within the general fund of the debtor's assets) then there is the appropriate remedy for recovery of a loan. I can appreciate no reason why the flexible interplay of law and equity cannot let in these practical arrangements, and other variations if desired; it would be to the discredit of both systems if they could not."

THE EARLY AUTHORITIES

In upholding the claim put forward by Quistclose, the House of Lords followed a long line of cases dating back to the beginning of the last century. According to Lord Wilberforce the fact that arrangements of this character for the payment of a person's creditors by a third person, give rise to a relationship of trust, in favour, as a primary trust, of the creditors, and secondarily, if the primary trust fails, of the third person, has been recognised in a series of cases over some 150 years. *Toovey v. Milne*[7] marks the *fons et origo* of this stream of authority. Abbott C.J. said[8]:

"I thought at the trial, and still think, that the fair inference from the facts proved was that this money was advanced for a specific purpose, and that being so clothed with a specific trust, no property in it passed to the assignee of the bankrupt. Then the purpose having failed, there is an implied stipulation that the money shall be repaid."

In *Toovey v. Milne*, A advanced money to his brother-in-law, B, for the purpose of B settling with his creditors.[9] That purpose failed and B was declared bankrupt. What was left of the money was repaid to A by the bankrupt. The court held that this repayment was protected and that the assignees in bankruptcy could not recover the money so repaid.

---

[5] *ibid.* at 580.
[6] *ibid.* at 581–582.
[7] (1819) 2 B. & Ald. 683. See also *Edwards v. Glynn* (1859) 2 E. & E. 29; *Gibert v. Gonard* (1884) 54 L.J. Ch. 439; *Re Rogers* (1891) 8 Morr. 243; *Re Drucker* [1902] 2 K.B. 237; *Re Watson* (1912) 107 L.T. 783 and *Re Hooley* [1915] 84 L.J. K.B. 181. See also the line of cases mentioned by Goode, *op cit.*, at 180–181 including *Re Pallitt* [1893] 1 Q.B. 455; *Re Mid-Kent Fruit Factory* [1896] 1 Ch. 567; *Re City Equitable Fire Insurance Co. Ltd (No. 2)* [1930] Ch. 293.
[8] (1819) 2 B. & Ald. at 684.
[9] *ibid.* The early cases are well analysed by Millett (1985) 101 L.Q.R. 269 at 270–274.

The principle enunciated in *Toovey v. Milne* was applied *sub silentio* as it were in *Gibert v. Gonard*[10] since the case is nowhere cited. *Gibert v. Gonard* is a case where A lent money to B for the purchase of a particular business. B in fact paid the money into his general bank account and drew against it to the extent of several hundred pounds for the purpose of meeting certain of his own personal liabilites unconnected with the business agreed to be purchased. B became bankrupt before the property acquisition could be completed and it was held that A was entitled to follow and recover the money in the bank account in the same manner as if it had been in terms a trust fund. According to North J. it was very well known law that if one person makes a payment to another for a certain purpose, and that person takes the money knowing that it is for that purpose, he must apply it to the purpose for which it was given. He may decline to take it if he likes but if he chooses to accept the money tendered for a particular purpose there was a legal obligation to apply it for that purpose.[11] In other words a duty was cast upon the borrower which placed him in the position of a trustee of the money advanced.

Re Rogers[12] is another authority, this time of the Court of Appeal, to the same effect. This is a case where A, a money-lender, lent money to B to enable pressing creditors to be paid. Some of that money was applied by B towards meeting the claim of C, a judgment creditor. B was adjudicated bankrupt and the question arose whether the trustee-in-bankruptcy could sue C to recover the money. The Court of Appeal declined to answer in the affirmative. The holding was that since the advance to B was for the special purpose of enabling his creditors to be paid, it was impressed with a trust for that purpose and never became the property of B. Lindley L.J. observed[13]:

> "I entertain no doubt that [A] could have obtained an injunction to restrain the bankrupt from using that money for any purpose except that of paying his pressing creditors. If this be so, the money never was the bankrupt's in any proper sense so as to vest in his trustee as part of his general assets."

Kay L.J. stated[14]:

> "The desire and intent of [A] ... was to prevent the bankruptcy of [B].... The true result of the evidence seems to me to be that the advance by [A] was for this special purpose, and the money was impressed with a trust, so that [A] could have prevented its being otherwise used."

As one commentator has pointed out one striking characteristic of these nineteenth-century cases is the immediacy of the debtor's need for outside sources of funding.[15] The party advancing the money is doing so on an emergency or rescue basis while the debtor serves merely as a conduit pipe through whom the money is channelled to the outside creditor. It can fairly be said that the debtor's possession of the money does not mislead. Nobody is

[10] (1884) 54 L.J. Ch. 439.
[11] *ibid.* at 440.
[12] (1891) 8 Morr. 243. Millett (1985) 101 L.Q.R. 269 at 273 describes it as the decision of a strong Court of Appeal. The court consisted of Lindley, Bowen and Kay L.JJ.
[13] *ibid.* at 248.
[14] *ibid.* at 249.
[15] See Bridge (1992) 12 O.J.L.S. 333.

induced into further dealings with him on the basis of a false assumption as to creditworthiness. Any benefit that might accrue to general creditors if the conduit pipe broke down would be pure windfall. Moreover the payer is not receving any special premium consequent on the transaction being characterised as a mere loan. Thus it does not seem unfair to general creditors if the payer is allowed to retain or recover the money as the case may be.

DOCTRINAL CRITICISMS OF *QUISTCLOSE*

The notion of the *Quistclose* trust has engendered some discussion and disquiet insofar as the finer points of the law of trusts are concerned.[16] Issues for debate include whether the trust is properly constituted, questions of enforcement, revocability and the identity of the beneficiary. Consideration of these questions will be postponed until later in the article but one might legitimately enquire here about why the primary purpose was deemed to have failed in *Quistclose*. Some observers have no doubts. For instance in *Re Northern Developments (Holdings) Ltd*[17] Sir Robert Megarry V.C. said:

> "[I]n the *Quistclose* case, the primary purpose was clear, simple and definite, both in its ambit and frustration. The purpose was to pay a particular debt due to particular creditors upon a particular date; and once the company [B] had decided to go into liquidation, that primary purpose plainly could never be accomplished. Once the voluntary winding up had commenced, the dividend could not be paid in competition with other creditors ... and so in the circumstances no trust for the payment of the dividend could be carried out."

There are some difficulties with this analysis however.[18] For a start the dividends had actually been declared before the loan was obtained. Case law establishes that the declaration of a dividend by resolution of the shareholders brings into being an immediate debt in their favour unless a later date for payment has been expressly specified. The argument therefore is that the trust to pay the dividends was complete. Subsequent liquidation of the company could not unravel that trust.[19] In his exposition Megarry V.C. relied on what is now section 74(2)(f) of the Insolvency Act 1986 which relegates shareholder claims for unpaid dividends behind debts due to external creditors. Clearly the statutory provision precludes debts based upon unpaid dividends being proved in competition with the claims of outside creditors. The legislative statement would not seem though to catch trusts of dividends.[20] As one judge writing extra-curially put the matter[21]: "It does not prevent a trustee from paying trust

---

[16] See in particular Millett (1985) 101 L.Q.R. 269 and Rickett (1985) 107 L.Q.R. 608.

[17] Unreported, October 6, 1978. Despite its unreported status the case has been referred to extensively by academic commentators and was also the subject of lengthy discussion in *Carreras Rothmans Ltd v. Freeman Mathews Ltd* [1985] Ch. 207.

[18] See generally H.A.J. Ford and W.A. Lee, *Principles of the Law of Trusts* (1990), p. 31; Millett (1985) 101 L.Q.R. 269 at 275–276; Rickett (1991) 107 L.Q.R. 608; Oditah (1992) 108 L.Q.R. 459 at 475.

[19] Millett, *op. cit.*, at 276 argues that there is no good reason why the right of the shareholders to the money should be affected by the subsequent liquidation of the company, B. The desire of B's liquidator to repay the loan to A rather than to pay the dividend is understandable though as the effect of paying the dividend would be to substitute A, an ordinary creditor, for C, a deferred creditor, to the detriment of the general body of creditors.

[20] See Oditah (1992) 108 L.Q.R. 459 at 475.

[21] See Millett (1985) 101 L.Q.R. 269 at 276.

money, which *ex hypothesi* does not belong to the company, to the persons beneficially entitled thereto."

The better view may be that the underlying purpose behind the conditional loan arrangements in Quistclose was not merely the payment of a dividend to shareholders but also the preservation of the company as a going concern.[22] In other words, the case is explicable with reference to a corporate salvage rationale.[23] A similar explanation may be proferred in respect of *Re E.V.T.R. Ltd.*[24] This is a case where the appellant, B, had the good fortune to win a big prize on the premium bonds. He was not in the business of lending money but was persuaded to lend £60,000 to a company, E.V.T.R. Ltd, that was experiencing financial difficulties. The company was run by a friend of his. B was advised by his accountant in no uncertain terms that he would be wasting his money if he simply lent it unconditionally to the company. What happened therefore was that B advanced to solicitors acting for E.V.T.R. the sum of £60,000 "for the sole purpose of buying new equipment". Unfortunately, E.V.T.R. did not have the balance necessary to buy the equipment outright and so a more complicated scheme was embarked upon with two other companies. The first company was the manufacturer of the equipment. E.V.T.R. contracted with this company for the supply of new equipment to be delivered within seven months and in the meantime to supply the company with temporary equipment. E.V.T.R. also entered into a contract with another company under which the second company agreed to take over E.V.T.R.'s obligations under the contract with the manufacturer by buying the new equipment and then leasing it to E.V.T.R. The contract involved E.V.T.R. paying a deposit of £60,000 plus 36 monthly instalments.

The bank who had financed E.V.T.R. appointed receivers to the company before the new equipment arrived and the two supplier companies returned the £60,000 less various agreed deductions. The question arose whether the refunded sum formed part of the general assets of E.V.T.R. available for distribution to its secured creditors or whether it was impressed with a trust in favour of B. This involved consideration of the point whether the original purpose of the transaction been accomplished. In other words had B been disappointed in his aim of making himself an unsecured creditor of E.V.T.R.?[25] The Court of Appeal answered in the affirmative. Dillon L.J. suggested that the purpose of B from which any trust was to be implied was, realistically, the purpose of E.V.T.R. acquiring new equipment and not the purpose of E.V.T.R. entering into an abortive contract for the lease/purchase of new equipment. Bingham L.J. opined that it would strike most people as very hard if B were in this situation to be confined to a claim as an unsecured creditor of the company.[26] Moreover, it must be pointed out that B was not a trade creditor conversant with credit risk and the bank's debenture had been granted some time before the injection of

---

[22] It might also be the case that there was a further condition attached to the payment to the effect that the money should be utilised for paying dividends only if Rolls Razor obtained further finance by a named date. On this point see [1968] Ch. 504 at 549–551.

[23] See R.P. Austin (1986) 6 O.J.L.S. 444 at 455.

[24] [1987] BCLC 646.

[25] To borrow the felicitous expression of Michael Bridge at (1992) 12 O.J.L.S. 333,

[26] *ibid.* at 652. The judge added that while it was literally true that the fund which the appellant B provided was applied to the stipulated purpose, the object of the payment was not achieved and that was why the balance was repaid.

credit by B. As once commentator perceptively observes[27]: "The bank would have been a windfall creditor if the Quistclose trust, and its failure of achievement, had not been recognised."

APPLICATION OF THE CONDITIONAL PAYMENT PRINCIPLE—SOME CONTROVERSIAL CASES

If the primary purpose of the payment had been carried out in *Quistclose* then the result achieved is one of credit substitution.[28] A, the payer, becomes a creditor of B, the person to whom the payment is made, instead of C, the third party creditors who are the ultimate intended recipients of the payment. Before the payment was made, there was no pre-existing relationship of debt between A and B. *Carreras Rothmans Ltd v. Freeman Mathews Treasure Ltd*[29] involves an extension of the *Quistclose principle* in that A stood in a relationship of debt to B prior to the time of making the payment. The facts of that case are as follows.

The plaintiff tobacco manufacturer arranged that the defendant advertising agency would place advertisements for it in newspapers, periodicals and by means of posters. The services of an agency were availed of for this purpose so as to secure deductions on advertisment fees. The advertising agency as principal thereby incurred debts to various media creditors. These debts it recharged to the plaintiff along with its own fees. The plaintiff became concerned about the solvency of the advertising agency. If the agency went into liquidation leaving media creditors unpaid the plaintiff's reputation would suffer. Alternatively, it would have to pay off the media creditors to avoid disruption of a major advertising campaign that it had launched. Therefore with the agreement of the defendant the plaintiff paid into a special account a sum equivalent to the money due to the third party creditors. The advertising agency went into insolvent liquidation but before the media creditors could be paid the liquidator froze the special account. The plaintiff, as had been feared was forced to discharge the sums due to the media people so as to maintain its advertising initiative. In return, it took an assignment of the debts due to the creditors. Thereupon it sought to recoup the moneys in the special account; a claim resisted by the defendant and its liquidator.

Peter Gibson J. acknowledged the factual differences between *Quistclose* and the present case.[30] In *Quistclose* the transaction was one of loan with no contractual obligation on the part of the lender to make payment prior to the agreement for the loan. In the present case there was no loan but there was an antecedent debt owed by the plaintiff. He held however that this factual difference was not legally material. The principle in all these cases is that equity fastens on the conscience of the person who receives from another property transferred for a specific purpose only and not therefore for the recipient's own purposes, so that such person would not be permitted to treat the property as his own or to use it for other than the stated purpose.[31]

---

[27] See Bridge (1992) 12 O.J.L.S. 333
[28] See Priestley, "The Romalpa Trust and the Quistclose Trust" in *Equity in Commercial Relationships* (P.D. Finn ed., 1987) p. 230 who points out that the attitude of other sources of finance might change if the credit substitution were known, but this is unlikely in the case of unsecured credit.
[29] [1985] Ch. 207.
[30] *ibid.* at 222.
[31] *ibid.*

Carreras Rothmans has attracted some criticism on the score that it ignores the possible application of the preference provisions in the Insolvency legislation.[32] Basically the legislation invalidates acts done by a company within six months prior to the commencement of winding up which have the effect of giving a creditor a preference over other creditors and which were influenced by a desire to achieve that result.[33] The relevant period is two years if the act is done in favour of a person connected with the company otherwise than by reason of his being its employee.[34] The material provisions are contained in sections 238–241 of the Insolvency Act which revamp the old law as embodied in section 615 of the Companies Act 1985 and preceding legislation. The previous statutory dispensation nullifed fraudulent preferences and these were judicially held to cover only acts done with the dominant intention to prefer.[35] A payment made under pressure however escaped invalidation as a fraudulent preference as the element of pressure was said to remove the dominant intention to prefer.[36] Thus the greater the pressure exerted by the debtor the greater the likelihood that any payment to him would not be stigmatised as a fraudulent preference.[37]

The relevance of cases on the old law in the new statutory context was however denied by Millett J. in *Re M.C. Bacon Ltd*[38] The new law strikes down acts that were influenced by a desire to put a creditor in a superior position *vis-à-vis* other creditors. The judge distinguished between desire and intention and intention. Intention was objective while desire was subjective. A person might have to choose between the lesser of two evils without desiring either. A payment could only be attacked if there was a positive wish to improve the creditor's position. Once the requisite desire was present however the payment would be condemned. The desire need not be the causative or decisive factor in the transaction. Something of a discordant note was struck by Robert Wright Q.C. in *Re Beacon Leisure Ltd*.[39] He said that in many cases the difference between the objective test of intention and the subjective test of desire might be small.[40]

---

[32] See Priestley *op. cit.*, at 235–236.

[33] ss. 238–241 of the Insolvency Act 1986. The relevant period is two years in the case of a payment made in favour of a person connected with the company otherwise than by reason only of being its employee. For the definition of connected person see s. 249 of the Act. Prior to the Insolvency Act reforms the law concerned itself only with fraudulent preferences as defined in s. 615 of the Companies Act 1985 re-enacting earlier legislation.

[34] For the definition of connected person see s. 249 of the Act.

[35] The judgment of Lord Tomlin in *Peat v. Gresham Trust Ltd* [1934] A.C. 252 is to this effect and his observations have been amplified in numerous other judicial decisions.

[36] See for instance *Re Eric Holmes Ltd* [1965] Ch. 1052. So if a creditor is paid off in response to a threat of legal action the intention of the company paying the debt is construed as being that of removing the threat rather than preferring the creditor.

[37] Opinions differ about whether this state of affairs has survived the new statutory regime. It may be argued however that giving a preference to a person can not be said to have been influenced by a desire to put the person in a preferential position if the preference would inevitably have been given whether or not the desire was present—in other words if there was an overwhelming reason for giving the preference rendering all other considerations superfluous. A majority on the Cork Committee favoured the retention of the old rule. Their contention was that a creditor who has taken active steps to obtain payment of his own debt should in principle be allowed to retain the fruits of his diligence (Cmnd. 8558 at para. 1256).

[38] [1990] B.C.L.C. 324.

[39] [1991] B.C.C. 213.

[40] See also on preferences *Weisgard v. Pilkington* [1995] B.C.C. 1108 and *Re Living Images Ltd* [1996] B.C.C. 112.

How does this exegesis apply in the present context? The argument goes something like this. *Carreras Rothmans* stands as authority for the proposition that the debtor of a company may discharge the debt by paying it to the company on terms which require the company to lay it aside and hold it on trust for payment only to creditors of the company who have been nominated by the debtor. The argument proceeds along the lines that the creditor negotiates away the right to receive the money beneficially in exchange for an arrangement under which one class of its unsecured creditors are satisfied from the sum paid. The consensual element in the payment is said to transform it into an act done by the recipient of the payment and and so attracting the invalidating effect of the preference provisions.[41] This conclusion is by no means inevitable. If the payment is made only on condition that it is applied for a specific purpose the recipient can hardly be said to have bargained away the right to receive the payment without strings attached. Moreover, the "influenced by a desire to" criterion may not be satisfied.[42]

There is another layer of complexity. If the primary purpose of the payment was carried through in Quistclose one category of unsecured debt is substituted for another. One unsecured creditor is paid off and another takes its place. Now to the "what if?" Say a loan secured by a charge over the company's assets is made on condition that the amount of the loan is used to discharge earlier unsecured indebtedness. How does this affect the picture? Generally floating charges granted by an insolvent company within the 12 month period prior to its liquidation are invalid except to the extent of any fresh advance.[43] Does the conditional loan count as a fresh advance?[44] The answer seems to be no, at least as a general proposition, though there is some discordance in the authorities.[45] The incongruity dates from *Re Matthew Ellis & Co. Ltd.*[46] In this case the Court of Appeal rejected the view advanced by Astbury J. in *Re Hayman, Christy & Lilly Ltd*[47] which exempted from the fresh advance exception cash payments made conditionally as to their mode of application.

Romer L.J. said that where a man advances money to a company on the security of a debenture on the terms that the money so advanced is to be applied by the company in discharge of one of its existing liabilities or in the acquisition of some asset which the company does not at the moment possess,

---

[41] It should be noted that Priestley's argument is made in the context of s. 122 of the Australian Bankruptcy Act which is worded differently than its U.K. counterpart.

[42] It could be said that the payment has been made as a result of pressure which negates any desire to prefer.

[43] The relevant provision is s. 245 of the Insolvency Act 1986. According to this provision a floating charge on the company's undertaking or property created at a relevant time is invalid except to the extent of the aggregate of—

(a) the value of so much of the consideration for the creation of the charge as consists of money paid, or goods or services supplied, to the company at the same time, or after, the creation of the charge,

(b) the value of so much of that consideration as consists of the discharge or reduction, at the same time as, or after, the creation of the charge, of any debt of the company, and

(c) the amount of such interest (if any) as is payable on the amount falling within paras (a) or (b) in pursuance of any agreement under which the money was so paid, the goods or services were so supplied or the debt was discharged or reduced.

[44] See generally Rajak, *Company Liquidations* (1988), pp. 286–287

[45] At least Kenny J. seemed to think so in the Irish case *Re Daniel Murphy Ltd* [1964] I.R. 1 at 15.

[46] [1933] Ch. 458.

[47] [1917] 1 Ch. 283, 285.

the money paid by the lender did not cease to be cash paid to the company merely by reason of the imposition of that condition.[48] The other members of the court comprising Lord Hanworth M.R. and Slesser L.J. were equally adamant about imposing the limitation that the fresh advance must not be applied in satisfaction of an antecedent debt. Something of a via media was suggested however by Lord Hanworth M.R. He said that the court had to have regard to transactions which might often be complicated and difficult. The task was to determine whether in substance the debenture sought to be invalidated had been issued for cash paid to the company.[49] If it had been, then, although the money might have been used by the company for the purpose of meeting a liability already incurred, the security stood good.

The facts of *Re Matthew Ellis & Co Ltd* do not indicate villainy and perhaps show why the section was given the interpretation that it was. The case concerned an insolvent company that was granted a loan by its chairman. The latter was also a partner in a firm which supplied the bulk of its stock of goods to the company. The chairman considered that an advance might save the company. Before advancing the money he was informed by his partners that they would only consent to continue to supply the company with goods on credit if the past debt to the firm was paid. The advance was made secured by a floating charge over the company's assets and out of this money a substantial sum was applied in discharging the past debt to the firm. It was held that the floating charge was good in respect of the entire sum advanced.

A more absolutist line on the section was taken by the Northern Ireland Court of Appeal in *Revere Trust Ltd v. Wellington Handkerchief Works Ltd.*[50] Here the court expressed approval for the dictum that cash payments to count as fresh advances must be absolute and uncontrolled.[51] Andrews L.J. drew a clear distinction between a cash payment to the company and the payment off of an existing liability of the company. The latter was not a cash payment to the company to do what it liked with as its own moneys.[52] While *Revere Trust Ltd v. Wellington Handkerchief Works Ltd* predates *Re Matthew Ellis & Co. Ltd* in point of time it is nowhere referred to in the latter case.

Re Matthew Ellis & Co. Ltd was considered but ultimately distinguished by Simonds J. in *Re Destone Fabrics Ltd.*[53] The judge suggested that the test in such cases may well be whether the transaction is to be regarded as one intended bona fide for the benefit of the company, or whether it is intended merely to provide certain moneys for the benefit of certain creditors of the company to the prejudice of other creditors of the company.[54]

This test was applied by Nourse J. in *Re G.T. Whyte & Co. Ltd.*[55] This is a case where a fresh secured loan was made by a wholly owned subsidiary of a secured creditor. The judge held that as a matter of substance the new advance was intended to secure the past indebtedness to the unsecured creditor and so the security was invalidated. So we are left with a "substance of the transaction"

---

[48] [1933] Ch. 458 at 477.
[49] *ibid.* at 474.
[50] [1931] N.I. 155.
[51] Thus applying the dictum of Astbury J. in *Re Hayman, Christy & Lilly Ltd* [1917] 1 Ch. 283, 285.
[52] *ibid.* at 155.
[53] [1941] Ch. 319.
[54] *ibid.* at 324–325.
[55] [1983] B.C.L.C. 311. See also *Re Fairway Magazines Ltd* [1993] B.C.L.C. 643.

test. Was the intention to provide a genuine commercial benefit for the company or merely to substitute secured for unsecured indebtedness?

It should be noted that all these cases were decided under old legislation which invalidated floating charges created within a certain period prior to the commencement of winding up except to the extent of "cash paid" to the company at the time of the creation of the charge, and in consideration for the charge. The wording has since been revised. The exception now covers the aggregate of

"(a) the value of so much of the consideration for the creation of the charge as consists of money paid, or goods or services supplied, to the company at the same time as, or after, the creation of the charge,
(b) the value of so much of that consideration as consists of the discharge or reduction, at the same time as, or after, the creation of the charge, of any debt of the company . . . ."

It is submitted that the new wording and in particular the introduction of paragraph (b) would make no difference to the result in the cases discussed. The contention is that the old debts are not in fact discharged as a matter of substance.[56] Support for this proposition may be derived from the decision of Mummery J. in *Re Fairway Magazines Ltd.*[57] In this case a company was indebted to its bank and the debt was personally guaranteed by one of its directors. This director lent sums of money to the company and, at his request, these moneys were paid directly into the company's overdrawn bank account. The director was granted a debenture by the company secured by a floating charge to support these advances. The effect of the payments into the company's bank account was to reduce the personal liability of the director under the guarantee. Mummery J. took the view that the payments by the director into the company's bank account were not in substance paid to the company for its benefit but rather for the director's benefit. In consequence the arrangment was caught by section 245 of the Insolvency Act since the payments were not "paid ... to the company" as required by section 245(1)(a). But the judge was at pains to point out that there was no dishonest or underhand conduct on the part of any of those involved. Such conduct however, was not a statutory prerequisite for the operation of the invalidating provisions.[58]

Failure to take account of the invalidating provisions of Insolvency legislation is also a criticism levelled at *Re Kayford Ltd.*[59] This case concerned a company which carried on a mail order business. The company was in financial difficulties and took advice on how best to protect customers. The customers were sending

---

[56] See *Gower's Principles of Modern Company Law* (5th ed, 1992), p. 424 but compare R. E. Pennington *Corporate Insolvency Law* (1991), pp. 221–222.

[57] [1993] B.C.L.C. 643.

[58] *Per* Nourse J. in *Re G.T. Whyte & Co. Ltd* [1983] B.C.L.C. 311 at 317. Mummery J. also referred to the general purpose of the provision as being to prevent a company, which was on its last legs, from creating a floating charge to secure past debts or to secure moneys which do not go to swell its assets and become more available for creditors. The judgment of Parker J. in *Re Orleans Motor Co. Ltd* [1911] 2 Ch. 41 at 49 was cited in this connection.

[59] [1975] 1 W.L.R. 279. It has been argued that *Kayford* and its direct derivatives are not examples of *Quistclose* type trusts. The contention is that in these cases recovery by the original "lenders" is by virtue of an express trust rather than a resulting trust. For a development of this argument see Rickett (1991) 107 L.Q.R. 608 at 609. In this chapter a broader commercial approach to conditional payments is taken and there is no doubt that *Re Kayford Ltd*, at least in the way that the judge saw the facts, involves an example of a conditional payment.

money to the company in anticipation of being supplied with goods. The company was advised by accountants to open a Customers Trust Deposit Account into which all further sums of money sent by customers for goods not yet delivered should be paid, so that should the company be forced into liquidation, these sums could be refunded to the customers who had sent them. The company largely accepted that advice but instead of opening a new account used a dormant deposit account in the company's name.

Megarry J. held that a trust in favour of the customers had been created. The whole object of what was done was to ensure that the moneys remained in the beneficial ownership of those who sent them and a trust was the obvious means of achieving this.[60] The sender could create a trust by using appropriate words when he sends the money or the company could do it by taking suitable steps on or before receiving the money. If either was done the obligations in respect of the money were transformed from contract to property, from debt to trust.

The judgment of Megarry J. is characterised by a concern for members of the consuming public some of whom, in his words,[61] "can ill afford to exchange their money for a claim to a dividend in the liquidation, and all of whom are likely to be anxious to avoid this." Some might think that this concern is misguided. For instance the Cork Committee on Insolvency Law and Practice[62] suggested that the customer who paid in advance for goods or services to be supplied later extends credit just as surely as the trade who supplies in advance goods or services to be paid for later. There was no essential difference. Each gave credit; and if the credit was misplaced each should bear the loss rateably. On the other hand, prepayment customers may not perceive themselves as providers of unsecured credit. There is much to be said for the view of the Office of Fair Trading that prepayment customers do not consciously become creditors, and that they have no means of securing the money which they advance.[63]

In Re Kayford Megarry J. said that no question of a fraudulent preference arose. One was concerned here not with the question of preferring creditors but

---

[60] ibid. at 282. He said that payment into a separate bank account was a useful (though by no means conclusive) indication of an intention to create a trust, but there was nothing to prevent the company from binding itself by a trust even if there were no effective banking arrangements.

[61] ibid. The judge added: "In cases concerning the public, it seems to me that where money in advance is paid to a company in return for the future supply of goods or services, it is an entirely proper and honourable thing for a company to do what this company did, on skilled advice, namely, to start to pay the money into a trust account as soon as there begin to be doubts as to the company s ability to fulfil its obliigations to deliver the goods or provide the services. I wish that, sitting in this court, I had heard of this occurring more frequently; and I can only hope that I shall hear more of it in the future."

[62] (1982) Cmnd. 8558 at para. 1052. The committee therefore rejected the idea of legislation that would generalise the protection afforded by a trust of the Re Kayford kind though there was one dissentient from their recommendations. The committee on the other hand welcomed "the sympathetic attitude to this [prepayment] problem shown by Megarry J. in Re Kayford". For details of legislative efforts in this sphere see [1994] J.B.L. 105.

[63] The Protection of Consumer Prepayments: A Discussion Paper (1984) at para 5.11. The OFT added: "Consumers cannot assess the risk fully, and the Office does not regard it as feasible that consumers should be expected to check on the financial standing of traders (e.g. by consulting company returns and accounts filed with the Department of Trade and Industry). Major creditors, particularly banks, can secure their loans, and other suppliers of credit have a certain security as a result of informal advice and information from their peers. They may also insure their risks through organisations such as Trade Indemnity. Consumers will always remain the least protected creditors, unless steps are taken to improve their position."

of preventing those who pay money from becoming creditors, by making them beneficiaries under a trust.[64]

This analysis has not been universally accepted. Attention may have been diverted from the question of who owned the moneys at the time that the company declared itself trustee of them. If the company owned the moneys at that time, then the declaration of trust had the effect of impermissibly altering the statutory order of priorities for payment of creditors.[65]

Despite all the criticisms *Re Kayford Ltd* was followed by the Court of Appeal in *Re Chelsea Cloisters Ltd.*[66] This was a case where the company which was the underlessee of a block of flats granted numerous tenancies. It took a deposit from individual tenants in respect of any sum which might be due from the tenant at the end of the tenancy for damage, breakages and compensation. Initially there were no special arrangements for dealing with the deposits of the tenants but when the company got into financial difficulties a chartered accountant was appointed to supervise the running of the company. This supervisor expressed a wish that the tenants deposits should be kept separate from other moneys of the company and so they were segregated from the company's general assets and paid into a Tenant's Deposit Account. The company went into liquidation and it was held that the deposits were held on trust for the tenants.

Lord Denning said that the deposits were not impressed with a trust from the very beginning.[67] The creation of the special arrangements, however, established a trust.[68] No issue of improper preference was raised.[69] According to Lord Denning the supervisor realised that the company was in a hopeless position: it had no money to pay anybody and there was a danger that these deposits might fall into the hands of the other creditors of the company, contrary to the justice of the case.[70] It must be pointed out however that the supervisor nowhere used explicit trust language; terminology that ought to have been familiar to a chartered accountant. The decision has been viewed as an exercise in discretionary justice. The company had gone into liquidation with total debts

[64] [1975] 1 W.L.R. 279 at 281. See also Goode, *Payment Obligations in Commercial and Financial Transactions* (1983), p. 18, n. 64.

[65] See Waters (1983) 21 *Alberta Law Review* 395 at 417. On the other hand it has been argued that if money is received in circumstances in which the court would hold the recipient accountable as a constructive trustee, then there will be no preference because the creation of the fund will not have put the customer in a better position than that customer would have enjoyed in an ensuing bankruptcy or liquidation. In other words there is no factual preference regardless of whether there was the requisite desire to produce that effect. For this argument see Hamish Anderson "The Treatment of Trust Assets in English Insolvency Law" in *Commercial Aspects of Trusts and Fiduciary Obligations* (Ewan McKendrick ed., 1992). The argument is developed *infra* in connection with the discussion of *Re Chelsea Cloisters Ltd* (1980) 41 P. & C.R. 98.

[66] (1981) 41 P. & C.R. 98. The case was approved in *Re Lewis's of Leicester Ltd* [1995] B.C.C. 514.

[67] *ibid.* at 101. He referred to *Potters v. Loppert* [1973] Ch. 399. See also Bridge L.J. at 102 and Oliver L.J. at 104 who were disinclined to express an opinion on this point.

[68] Referring to *Henry v. Hammond* [1913] 2 K.B. 515 and *Hughes v. Stubbs* (1842) 1 Hare 478 as well as *Re Kayford Ltd* [1975] 1 W.L.R. 279.

[69] Anderson, *op. cit.*, at 178 points out that the person responsible had acted in the belief that there was an obligation to protect the deposits thereby negativing the possibility of there being an improper preference. In *Re Vautin* [1900] 2 Q.B. 325 it was held with reference to the old statutory dispensation that a payment made under an honest and reasonable belief that there was a legally binding obligation to pay could not be struck down as an improper preference. See also on this point *Re Lewis's of Leicester Ltd* [1995] B.C.C. 514.

[70] (1981) 41 P. & C.R. 98 at 102.

approximating to £50 million whereas the sum of the tenants deposits was in the region of £20,000. Greater joy would be experienced by meeting the claims of the tenants in full rather than by spreading the piteously small sum of money almost invisibly across the general range of creditors.[71] It has been suggested that for the company to claim beneficial ownership of the deposit money would involve more than a taint of fraudulent trading. Under the legislation in force at the time Re Chelsea Cloisters Ltd was decided, where a company had gone into liquidation the court could direct particular payments to particular creditors who had been defrauded.[72] In 1986 a wider notion of wrongful trading was introduced in the Insolvency legislation[73] but the concept of fraudulent trading was retained to cover specific cases.[74] In situations of both fraudulent and wrongful trading however payments ordered to be made only go to swell the general assets of the company. Such payments cannot be earmarked by the court for specific creditors who may have been defrauded.

APPLICATION OF THE CONDITIONAL PAYMENT PRINCIPLE—SOME UNCONTROVERSIAL CASES

Re Kayford Ltd and Re Chelsea Clositers Ltd may be distinguished from Re Nanwa Gold Mines Ltd.[75] which seems safe from criticism. In Re Nanwa Gold Mines money was advanced on the faith of a promise to keep it in a separate account and Harman J. held that a trust had been created. He contrasted Moseley v. Cressey's Co.[76] where a simple statement that application moneys would be refunded was held not to bind moneys standing in a bank to the credit of the company, with a trust in favour of the depositor. The intent of the promise to keep in a separate account meant that the moneys would not be mixed with the company's moneys.[77]

Many of the great cases in the company law field involve speculative projects in far flung corners of the globe during the halcyon days of imperial expansion.[78] Such projects often involved great risk and to minimise the risk factor the trust arrangement was often employed. Financiers instead of advancing money directly to the company would advance it to intermediaries, trustees, who would release it to the company at various stages of the project. National Bolivian Navigation Co.

---

[71] See Bridge (1992) 12 O.J.L.S. 333.

[72] s. 332 of the Companies Act 1948 as interpreted by a majority (Lord Denning M.R. and Danckwerts L.J.) of the Court of Appeal in Re Cyona Distributors Ltd [1967] Ch. 889.

[73] s. 214 of the Insolvency Act 1986. Under this provision once a director or shadow director knows or ought to have concluded that there was no reasonable prospect that a company would avoid going into insolvent liquidation he must take every step with a view to minimising potential loss to company creditors. Otherwise the person may be declared liable to make such contribution (if any) to the company's assets as the court thinks proper.

[74] s. 213. This section applies to any liquidation whereas s. 214 is confined to cases of insolvent liquidation. Moreover, s. 213 covers any person who was knowingly party to the carrying on of the business in a fraudulent manner whereas s.214 is limited to directors and shadow directors.

[75] [1955] 3 All E.R. 219. See also National Bolivian Navigation Co. v. Wilson (1880) 5 App. Cas. 176. Elkins v. Capital Guarantee Society (1900) 16 T.L.R. 423; Re Independent Air Travel Ltd [1961] 1 Lloyd's Rep. 604 and Smith v. Liquidator of James Birrell Ltd [1968] S.L.T. 174.

[76] (1865) L.R. 1 Eq. 405.

[77] [1955] 3 All E.R. 219 at 223.

[78] One might instance in this connection some of the cases on promoters like Erlanger v. New Sombrero Phosphate Co. (1878) 3 App. Cas. 1218.

v. Wilson[79] involved such a project and arrangement. This is a case where money had been subscribed by investors for a particular purpose namely the construction of a railway linking Brazil and Bolivia. The money was placed in the hands of trustees for the investors and it was the duty of the trustees to pay portions of the money over to the company as portions of the intended railroad were constructed. The House of Lords held that if no such railroad nor any portion of it was constructed and its construction became impracticable, the bondholders were entitled to demand from the trustees repayment of what remained in their hands.[80]

Another area where the *Quistclose* principle has been uncontroversially applied lies in relation to employee claims for moneys in the hands of insolvent employers. A case in point is *Re Independent Air Travel Ltd.*[81] This is a case where a company insured the lives of its employees, three of whom later died in an air crash. It was a condition of employment that the company should insure the lives of the deceased employees for the latter's benefit. The insurers in fact paid over on foot of the insurance policies moneys for distribution to the families of the deceased but the company went into receivership before this task could be done. Plowman J. held that the moneys had been received on trust for the estate of the three deceased although no express words of trust had been employed.

A similar result was reached in the Scottish case *Smith v. Liquidator of James Birrell Ltd.*[82] This is a case where a company had paid into a special bank account moneys received from an insurance company representing different employee pension and insurance schemes which the company had decided to discontinue. The sum received was for the benefit of employees in the employment of the company at the date of discontinuance of the scheme. Lord Fraser in the Outer House of the Court of Session decided that this money did not form part of the general assets of the company. The money was clearly distinguishable and capable of being disentangled from the company's own funds and it ought to be paid to the former employees of the company entitled thereto.[83]

FORMALITIES FOR THE ESTABLISHMENT OF A TRUST

There remains to be considered the prerequisites for the creation of a valid express trust, namely the three certainties—certainty of intention, certainty of subject-matter and certainty of objects. Moreover, if the declaration of trust relates to land signed written evidence must be available before the trust can be enforced.[84]

CERTAINTY OF INTENTION

This issue was discussed in *Re Kayford Ltd* Megarry J. said that a trust can be

---

[79] (1880) 5 App. Cas. 176.
[80] According to Lord Blackburn the trust was created by the prospectus on the faith of which the bondholders, or those whom they represent, lent their money: see (1880) 5 App. Cas. 176 at 207.
[81] [1961] 1 Lloyds Rep. 604.
[82] 1968 S.L.T. 174.
[83] *ibid.* at 175.
[84] s. 53(1)(b) of the Law of Property Act 1925.

created without using the words "trust" or "confidence" or the like. The pertinent question was whether a sufficient intention to create a trust had been manifested.[85] Sufficiency of intention to create a trust was not manifested in *Swiss Bank Corporation v. Lloyds Bank Ltd.*[86]

The facts of the case are complicated but the nub of the issue was whether a lender of money, the Swiss Bank Corporation had obtained any kind of proprietary interest in securities which the borrower, as the lender knew, wished to use the loan in invest in.

The loan agreement did not actually confer such a proprietary interest, but in it the borrower did promise that it would observe all the conditions attached by the Bank of England to its consent for the loan. These conditions included the requirements that the loan was to be used exclusively for the purchase of certain foreign securities (F.I.B.I. securities) and that the interest on and capital of the loan were to be repaid to the Swiss Bank Corporation out of the F.I.B.I. securities or the proceeds of their sale. The borrower subsequently charged the F.I.B.I. securities to Lloyds Bank as security for a guarantee given in respect of a further loan from that bank. When the Swiss Bank Corporation sought repayment of the loan, it claimed to have a better interest in the securities than Lloyds Bank. Although the judge at first instance, Browne-Wilkinson J., held in the plaintiffs' favour both the Court of Appeal and the House of Lords held against them.

None of the appellate judges in the *Swiss Bank* case could see anything in the loan which specifically said that the borrowers would repay the loan out of the F.I.B.I. securities, nor would they imply any such promise. Both the Court of Appeal and the House of Lords judges were content to apply the law as stated by Lord Wrenbury in *Palmer v. Carey*[87]:

"An agreement for valuable consideration that a fund shall be applied in a particular way may found an injunction to restrain its application in another way. But if there be nothing more, such a stipulation will not amount to an equitable assignment. It is necessary to find further, that an obligation has been imposed in favour of the creditor to pay the debt out of the fund."

The requisite certainty of intention to create a trust was also held not to have been established in *Re Multi Guarantee Co. Ltd.*[88] This is a case where a company, MG, was incorporated to market warranties for domestic appliances which provided insurance after the manufacturer's guarantee expired. V was the owner of a chain of shops and it operated the MG scheme by collecting premiums from its customers and then paying them over to MG. V became concerned as a result of press reports that MG had not obtained proper insurance coverage for the scheme and it negotiated with MG so as to protect the interests of its customers by safeguarding the money in the relevant MG account. To stave off proceedings for a Mareva injunction or for an order for the interim preservation of property, MG agreed to transfer the money into a joint deposit account which could only be drawn on under the joint signatures of MG's and V's solicitors. There were however no detailed terms concerning the basis on which

---

[85] *Re Kayford* [1975] 1 W.L.R. 279 at 282.
[86] [1982] A.C. 584. See also *Re Multi Guarantee Co. Ltd.*
[87] [1926] A.C. 703 at 706–707.
[88] [1987] B.C.L.C. 257.

withdrawals might be made from this account. V succeeded in arranging its own insurance cover for the extended warranty protection, but before an agreement to release the money in the joint deposit account to V could be effectuated, MG went into liquidation. The question before the court was whether as V contended, MG had constituted itself a trustee of the money in the account and in this way divested itself of all beneficial interest therein.

The Court of Appeal held that MG had never displayed a sufficient intention to create a trust.[89] The necessary certainty of intention had not been shown and thus the premium moneys constituted part of the general assets of MG. The problem was that there were a number of possible destinations for the money joint account apart from being returned to V. For instance it could have been paid directly to any one or more of a number of possible insurers.

A *Quistclose* trust claim also failed in *Re Bank of Credit and Commerce International SA (No. 3)*[90] which case arose out of the well-publicised collapse of Bank of Credit and Commerce International (BCCI).[91] The bank failure has generated a torrent of litigation raising a multiplicity of points. In this specific case the question was whether the BCCI liquidators could recover the whole of loans outstanding from principal debtors where repayment of the loans was secured by purported charges over third party deposits with the bank. The depositors argued that the liquidators were only entitled to recover from the principal debtors so much of the outstanding loans that exceeded the amounts of the deposits purportedly charged by the depositors to secure those loans. The liquidators on the other hand, contended that they were entitled to recover the whole of the outstanding loans from the principal debtors, thus leaving the depositors to prove for their deposits in the liquidation of the bank.

An number of legal points were raised by the depositors, all of them unsuccessful. As very much a secondary submission *Quistclose* was invoked. It was submitted that that the deposits were provided to BCCI specifically for the purpose of discharging the indebtedness of the principal debtors and accordingly were held by the liquidators on trust to use them for that purpose. Rattee J took the view however, that this argument was not supported by the security documents which charged whatever credit balances might from time to time be standing to the credit of the depositors on accounts in the books of the bank. Neither in the security documents nor in the evidence of the depositors was there any suggestion of payments made to the bank for the specific purpose of discharging the indebtedness of the principal debtors.[92]

On the other hand *Re Multi Guarantee Co. Ltd* was distinguished and a trust held to have been established in *Re Lewis's of Leicester Ltd*.[93] This is a case where a number of licensees occupied "shop within a shop" concessions in a department store. The licensees included those who sold their own goods but put the takings in the company's tills on standard terms which provided for them to receive from the company a payment equivalent to gross takings less returns and

---

[89] See the statement by Nourse L.J. [1987] B.C.L.C. 257 at 268.

[90] [1994] 1 BCLC 758. See also *MS Fashions Ltd v. Bank of Credit and Commerce International S.A.* [1993] Ch. 425.

[91] *Re Multi Guarantee Co. Ltd* [1987] B.C.L.C. 257 was actually referred to in *Re Bank of Credit and Commerce International S.A. (No. 3)* but not in relation to this particular point.

[92] The decision of Rattee J. has been confirmed by the Court of Appeal [1996] 2 All E.R. 121. The *Quistclose* point is not referred to by the Court of Appeal.

[93] [1995] B.C.C. 514.

commissions. The financial position of the company became parlous and it took steps to ensure that future receipts of licensees' takings, mistakenly believed to be already subject to a trust under the standard form agreements, were kept separate and identifiable in segregated accounts. Did this mistaken assumption vitiate the intention to establish a trust on the basis that if a person believes that he is a trustee he cannot logically intend to create a trust for the first time? Robert Walker J. refused to accept this proposition. In his view there had been segregation of moneys and the incorrect assumption was *a fortiori* a reason for holding that a trust had been brought into being.[94]

A liberal attitude towards the existence of a *Quistclose* trust was also adopted by Hirst J. in *Guardian Ocean Cargoes Ltd v. Banco do Brasil SA*.[95] This case arose out of a complex financing arrangement for the construction of a ship. The plaintiff made three payments before the financing deal was put into place and when the deal broke down the question arose whether the payments were conditional on the deal being concluded. Hirst J. in fact held that the payments were contingent upon the conclusion of a deal. It was not intended that the payments should pass outright and irrevocably to the bank whatever the outcome of the financing negotiations. The plaintiffs were entitled to a judgment simpliciter for the return of their money. According to Hirst J. there was an alternative basis for the recovery of the money. Where, as here, money was paid for a special purpose which was not or could not be carried out, the payee held it on trust for the payer.[96]

CERTAINTY OF SUBJECT-MATTER

The property which is said to form the subject-matter of the alleged trust must be identifiable. A trust claim failed on this ground in *Re London Wine Co (Shippers) Ltd*.[97] This case involved a wine merchant who appropriated part of its general wine stock to a specific customer order only when the customer came in to collect the wine. The wine merchant went into receivership. Oliver J. held that the customers could not claim to be beneficiaries under a trust of the wine as the essential element of certainty of subject matter was absent.

---

[94] See also *Re Fleet Disposal Services Ltd* [1995] B.C.C. 605. In this case a now insolvent company sold motor vehicles as agent for Northern Telecom Europe Ltd ("Nortel") and the question for determination was whether the sale proceeds were held on trust for Nortel. Lightman J. answered the question in the affirmative. The judge recognised the general disinclination of the courts to see the intricacies and doctrines connected with trusts introduced into everyday commercial transactions. Nevertheless, in an agency relationship the court was particularly ready to infer a trust; it was not readily to be inferred that the agent was intended to be able to finance his business out of the proceeds of sale of his principal's property. In this particular case there were indications of a trust relationship, or at least language consistent with it. Moreover there was no unfair or undue consequences for the company or its unsecured creditors in acknowledging the existence of a trust.

[95] [1991] 2 Lloyd's Rep 68. See also *Tropical Capital Investment Ltd v. Stanlake Holdings Ltd* (unreported, May 24, 1991) where the purpose for which money was lent was not very specific in nature but nevertheless a *Quistclose* trust was held to come into existence. The case is analysed in detail by Rickett [1992] L.M.C.L.Q. 3.

[96] Somewhat surprisingly this trust was characterised by the judge as a constructive trust; [1991] 2 Lloyd's Rep 68 at 87.

[97] [1986] P.C.C. 121. The case was decided on November 7, 1975. See also *Export Credits Guarantee Dept. v. Turner* [1981] S.L.T. 286.

Re London Wine Co (Shippers) Ltd was distinguished in *Hunter v. Moss*.[98] In this case the defendant was the absolute beneficial owner of 950 shares in a company which had an issued share capital of 1,000 ordinary shares. He orally declared himself to be a trustee of 50 of these shares for the plaintiff. Was there the requisite certainty of subject matter for the trust to be effective? The Court of Appeal answered in the affirmative. In this particular case, since all the shares were of one class in one company and were of such a nature as to be indistinguishable from one another, they were all equally capable of satisfying the trust. Dillon L.J. said[99]:

> "Just as a person can give, by will, a specified number of his shares of a certain class in a certain company, so equally, in my judgment, he can declare himself trustee of 50 of his ordinary shares in ... whatever the company may be, and that is effective to give a beneficial proprietary interest to the beneficiary under the trust."

Re Clifford[1] and *Re Cheadle*[2] were cited as authority for the validity of such a testamentary bequest. It has been persuasively argued that the analogy is an inapt one.[3] For instance, Professor David Hayton has drawn attention to the fact that the intended beneficiaries under a will only have an equitable chose in action until the executor has completed the administration of the estate.[4] The whole estate of a testator passes to his executors. The latter have full ownership therein without regard to the distinction between legal and equitable interests but they come under fiduciary duties to administer the estate by paying debts, expenses and taxes, etc. Once that has been done, they are supposed to give effect to the executory trusts of the testator to the extent that sufficient property remains to satisfy such trusts. In other words, while there may be a superficial similarity between the functions of trustees properly so called and those of executors this masks an underlying dissimilarity. The *raison d'etre* of the rules of succession is to ensure the proper and efficient distribution of property whereas the function of the law of trusts is to regulate the retention of property.[5]

Moreover the decision in *Hunter v. Moss* resides somewhat uneasily with that of the Privy Council in *Re Goldcorp Exchange Ltd*.[6] In this case Lord Mustill said that it was in the very nature of things—*a priori* common sense—that legal title to goods could not pass until the goods had been ascertained. It made no difference what the parties intended if what they intended was impossible: as was the case with an immediate transfer of title to goods whose identity was not yet known.[7] Equitable title behaved no differently. According to Lord Mustill it was impossible to have a title to goods when nobody knows to which goods the title relates.

One point of distinction between *Re Goldcorp Exchange Ltd* and *Hunter v. Moss*

---

[98] [1994] 3 All E.R. 215. See also *Re Goldcorp Exchange Ltd* [1994] 2 All E.R. 806 and *Re Stapylton Fletcher Ltd* [1995] 1 All E.R. 192.
[99] [1994] 3 All E.R. 215 at 222.
[1] [1912] 1 Ch. 29.
[2] [1900] 2 Ch. 620.
[3] See the comment by Professor David Hayton (1994) 110 L.Q.R. 335–340.
[4] *Commissioner for Stamp Duties v. Livingston* [1965] A.C. 694.
[5] See Ockelton [1994] C.L.J. 448 at 449.
[6] [1994] 2 All E.R. 806.
[7] [1994] 2 All E.R. 806 at 814. Lord Mustill referred in this connection to the observations of Lord Blackburn in his *Treatise on the Effect of the Contract of Sale* (1st ed., 1845), pp. 122–123.

relates to the fact that *Goldcorp* is not an "ex-bulk" case. The goods that were intended to form the subject-matter of the contract of sale were not necessarily to come from a fixed and pre-determined source. Furthermore Lord Mustill appeared to recognise that the vendor of goods sold ex-bulk can effectively declare himself trustee of the bulk in favour of the buyer, so as to confer *pro tanto* an equitable title. In *Hunter v. Moss* there was obviously a fixed source from which the 50 shares were to come. It should be noted that the Sale of Goods (Amendment) Act 1995[8] has altered the law in respect of sales "ex-bulk". The Act allows a pre-paying buyer of goods sold "ex-bulk" to become a tenant in common of the bulk in the proportion that the goods purchased bears to the bulk as a whole.

CERTAINTY OF OBJECTS

Although the requirements of certainty of intention and certainty of subject matter are satisfied there cannot be a valid trust for beneficiaries or purposes if those beneficiaries or purposes are themselves insufficiently certain.[9] In such a situation of uncertainty the property is held on a resulting trust for the settlor. The word "resulting" is used in the sense of "springing back".[10] The beneficial interest is said to spring back to the grantor but in reality it never left him. In *Quistclose* itself the primary purpose of the payment was held to have failed so that the property was held on a resulting trust for the grantor.[11]

ENFORCEMENT RIGHTS

Controversy has dogged the *Quistclose* trust in relation to the right of the settlor, recognised in the *locus classicus* itself, to see that the property is applied for the primary stated purpose.[12] It has been suggested that the right is not the right of a beneficiary under the resulting trust, for if the primary purpose is fulfilled there is no resulting trust and the payer is a mere creditor. It is axiomatic that, as a general proposition, a grantor or settlor who retains no beneficial

---

[8] The Act follows the recommendations of the Law Commission in their report no. 215 (1993) *Sale of Goods forming Part of a Bulk*. On the Act see, *inter alia*, Burns (1996) 59 M.L.R. 260.

[9] Generally the only type of valid purpose trusts are charitable trusts because of the beneficiary principle, i.e. there must be beneficiaries who can apply to the court to enforce their rights. In the case of a charitable trust the Attorney General, as guardian of the public interest, may enforce. However, the courts have recognised a certain anomalous category of non-charitable trusts. See generally *Re Astor's Settlement Trusts* [1952] Ch. 534; *Leahy v. Attorney General for New South Wales* [1959] A.C. 457; *Re Denley's Trust Deed* [1969] 1 Ch. 373 and *Wicks v. Firth* [1983] A.C. 214.

[10] "Resulting" is derived from the Latin verb *resalire*.

[11] There has been some discussion as to the nature of this secondary trust. In the Australian High Court case *Australasian Conference Association Ltd v. Mainline Constructions Pty. Ltd* (1979) 141 C.L.R. 335 at 353 Gibbs A.C.J.conceived of *Quistclose* as standing for the proposition that where money is advanced by A to B with the mutual intention that it should not becompe part of the assets of B, but should be used exclusively for a specific purpose, there will be implied, at least in the absence of a contrary intention, a stipulation that if the purpose fails the money will be repaid. In *Quistclose*, on the other hand, Lord Wilberforce at one point seemed to see the secondary trust as resting on the lender's intention. It is submitted that the controversy is a somewhat sterile one with the differences in formulation being more a matter of terminology than of substance.

[12] See Heydon, Gummow and Austin, *op. cit.*, at 357; Millett, *op. cit.*, at 287.

interest cannot enforce the trust which he has created but the beneficiaries can.[13] This principle forms the basis of the rule against non-charitable purpose trusts and also is at the heart of the principle enunciated in *Saunders v. Vautier*.[14] Under this doctrine beneficiaries of full age and consent who are all ascertained and between them entitled to the entire beneficial interest in the trust property, may have the property transferred to themselves absolutely and bring the trust to an end.

Peter Millett Q.C., as he then was, has argued vehemently that *Quistclose* does not necessitate the recognition of a new *genus* of enforceable purpose trust which a settlor may enforce.[15] In his opinion the question of enforceability involves an examination of the payer's intention which is to be gleaned from the conduct of the parties, the language used and the circumstances of the case. Mr. Millett has suggested various guidelines by which the payer's intention may be ascertained.[16]

These guidelines were expressly adopted and applied by Hardie Boys J. speaking for the New Zealand Court of Appeal in *General Communications Ltd v. DFC New Zealand Ltd*.[17]

"1. If A's intention was to benefit C, or his object would be frustrated if he were to retain a power of revocation, the transaction will create an irrevocable trust in favour of C, enforceable by C, but not by A. The beneficial interest in the trust property will be in C.

2. If A's intention was to benefit B (though without vesting a beneficial interest in him), or to benefit himself by furthering some private or commercial interest of his own, and not (except incidentally) to benefit C, then the transaction will create a trust in favour of A alone, and B will hold the trust property in trust to comply with A's directions. The trust will be enforceable by A but not by C. The beneficial interest will remain in A.

3. Where A's object was to save B from bankruptcy by enabling him to pay his creditors, the prima facie inference is that set out in paragraph 2 above. Wherever that is the correct inference;

(i) Where A has an interest of his own, separate and distinct from any interest of B, in seeing that the money is applied for the stated purpose, B will be under a positive obligation, enforceable by A, to apply it for that purpose. Where A has no such interest, B will be regarded as having a power, but no duty, to apply it

---

[13] This principle forms the basis of the rule against non- charitable purpose trusts and also is at the heart of the doctrine enunciated in *Saunders v. Vautier* (1841) Cr. & Ph. 240. Under this doctrine beneficiaries of full age and consent who are all ascertained and between them entitled to the entire beneficial interest in the trust property, may have the property transferred to themselves absolutely and bring the trust to an end.

[14] (1841) Cr. & Ph. 240.

[15] *Op. cit.*, particularly at 290. Mr Millett is now a judge.

[16] *Ibid.* at 290. These guidelines were adopted by Hardie Boys J. speaking for the New Zealand Court of Appeal in *General Communications Ltd v. DFC New Zealand Ltd* [1990] 3 N.Z.L.R. 406. For criticial comment see Rickett (1991) 107 L.Q.R. 607 at 630 *et seq.* Other New Zealand cases include *Dines Construction Ltd v. Perry Dines Corp Ltd* (1989) 4 N.Z.C.L.C. 65, 298; *Re Securitibank Ltd* [1978] 1 N.Z.L.R. 97 and more recently *Lankshear v. ANZ* [1993] 2 N.Z.L.R. 481. Relevant Australian authority includes *Re Associated Securities Ltd* [1981] 1 N.S.W.L.R. 742; *Rose v. Rose* (1986) 7 N.S.W.L.R. 679; *Re Groom* (1977) 16 A.L.R. 278; *Re Miles* (1989) 85 A.L.R. 216 and *Re Australian Elizabethan Theatre Trust* (1991) 102 A.L.R. 681.

[17] [1990] 3 N.Z.L.R. 406 at 432–433. See also *Dines Construction Ltd v. Perry Dines Corp. Ltd* (1989) 4 NZ.C.L.C. 65, 298. The New Zealand cases are discussed by Rickett (1991) 107 L.Q.R. 608 at 630–646 and see also J.K. Maxton "Quistclose Developments in New Zealand" (1990) 9 Int. Banking Law 216.

for the stated purpose, and A's remedy will be confined to preventing the misapplication of the money.

(ii) Prima facie, A's directions will be regarded as revocable by him; but he may contract with B not to revoke them without B's consent.

(iii) Communication to C of the arrangements prior to A s revocation will effect an assignment of A's equitable interest to C, and convert A's revocable mandate into an irrevocable trust for C."

The New Zealand Court of Appeal entered one caveat. Mr Millett's formulation suggested that it was the lender's intention that was relevant whereas in *Quistclose* the emphasis was on mutual intention.[18] A reconciliation was suggested on the basis that intention had to be ascertained objectively.[19] What one party was objectively seen to have intended must *ex hypothesi* have been appreciated by the other and accepted by him when he participated in the arrangement.

General Communications involved in acute form the issue of the resolution of the following conundrum. A lender, A, lends money to B with the latter undertaking that the money shall be applied for the purpose of paying off his creditor, C. Is the creditor entitled to recover what he was given to understand was intended for him, but was not paid, having instead been reclaimed by the lender? The court said "yes" but only because of the peculiar circumstances of the case rather than by reason of the adoption of any general principle. While the guidelines propounded by Mr Millett were clearly accepted their manner of application is somewhat ambiguous. Stress was laid on the fact that the arrangements had been communicated to the creditor, C, making it clear that the latter need not rely on B alone for payment. This would indicate a category C(iii) case.[20] On the other hand, the court also said that as the purpose of the arrangement would be defeated by the lender A being able to revoke it at will, it had put the funds beyond its power of recall and had conferred a beneficial interest on each supplier as each contract of supply was fulfilled.[21] This exposition would seem to suggest a category one classification.

Mr Millett's analysis views the *Quistclose* trust as an example of what is sometimes called an "illusory trust."[22] Where a valid trust has been brought into being it cannot be revoked by the settlor unless the settlement itself contains a power of revocation. Where a debtor conveys property for the benefit of his creditors an exception to the principle of non-revocability is said to arise but the true view seems to be that the apparent beneficiaries never acquire any interest in the property at all. All we have is a trust to comply with the settlor's

---

[18] Lord Wilberforce said that the mutual intention of the respondents and of Rolls Razor Ltd, and the essence of the bargain, was that the sum advanced should not become part of the assets of Rolls Razor Ltd but should be used exclusively for payment of a particular class of its creditors, namely those entitled to the dividend: see [1970] A.C. 567 at 580.

[19] [1990] 3 N.Z.L.R. 407 at 433.

[20] [1990] 3 N.Z.L.R. 407 at 435.

[21] *ibid.* The court said that there was not the intention to confer a direct and immediate benefit that marked out *New, Prance & Garrard's Trustee v. Hunting* [1897] 2 Q.B. 19. The latter is a case where a trust was established to make good to their beneficiaries breaches of other trusts by the settlor, who intended to give them an absolute interest. Lord Esher M.R. said at p. 26 that it was "obvious that it could not be his intention to reserve to himself any right or possibility of undoing what he was doing, and that he intended that it should be irrevocable".

[22] (1985) 101 L.Q.R. 269 at 288–289.

directions.[23] According to one judge[24]: "A man who, without any communication with his creditors, puts property into the hands of his trustees for the purpose of paying his debts, proposes only a benefit to himself by the payment of his debts: his object is not to benefit his creditors."

According to James L.J. in *John v. James*[25]:

> "such a deed as this is to be construed as a mandate, the same sort of mandate that a man gives when he gives his servant money, with directions to pay it in a particular way: it does not create any legal or equitable right in favour of a particular creditor. The right to the direction of the money is the right of the person who has put the money in the hands of his agent or steward or whoever it may be."

ENGLISH UNORTHODOXY

The issue of enforceability of a *Quistclose* trust was considered in *Carreras Rothhmans Ltd v. Freeman Mathews Ltd*.[26] Peter Gibson J. pointed out that in none of the many reported cases in the *Quistclose* line of cases had any consideration been given to the question whether the person intended to benefit from the carrying out of the specific purpose which created the trust had enforceable rights. In this case he rejected the proposition that the third party creditors for the payment of whose debts the plaintiff had paid the moneys into the special account had no enforceable rights. He also said that the doctrine of illusory trusts had no application to the facts of the present case.[27] Copious reference was made in the case to the unreported decision of Sir Robert Megarry V.C. in *Re Northern Developments (Holdings) Ltd*.[28] This is a case where one company, Northern, was the parent company of a number of companies including one, Kelly, that was in financial difficulties. A consortium of banks agreed to put up a large sum of money in an attempt to rescue Kelly. This money was used to keep Kelly alive for a time but Kelly was then put into receivership at a time when more than half the fund was unexpended. The Vice Chancellor held that the fund was subject to a *Quistclose* type trust and this trust was enforceable by the bank as lenders, by Kelly for whose immediate benefit the fund was established, and by Kelly's creditors. The interests of creditors were described in the following fashion:

> "The fund was established not with the object of vesting the beneficial interest in them, but in order to confer a benefit on Kelly (and so, consequentially, on the rest of the group and the bankers) by ensuring that Kelly's creditors would be paid in an orderly manner. There is perhaps some parallel in the position of a beneficiary entitled to a share of residue under a will. What he has is not a beneficial interest in any asset

---

[23] See generally on illusory trusts Pettit, *Equity and the Law of Trusts* (7th ed., 1993), pp. 214–215.
[24] Pepys M.R. in *Bill v. Cureton* (1834) 2 My. & K. 503 at 511.
[25] (1878) 8 Ch. D. 744 at 749–750.
[26] [1985] Ch. 207.
[27] According to Peter Gibson J. the doctrine of illusory trusts applied where a debtor for his own convenience settled property in favour of his creditors, the court treating the trust as a revocable one. In the present case although the defendant agreed to the discharge of an asset, its book debts, by payment by its debtor, the plaintiff, in such a way that the moneys paid would be held on trust to pay its creditors, the defendant did not enter into the arrangement for its convenience but for good commercial reasons on the insistence of the plaintiff and the trust was not for its creditors generally but for a particular class of creditor.
[28] Unreported, October 6, 1978.

forming part of residue, but a right to compel the executor to administer the assets of the deceased properly. It seems to me that it is that sort of right which the creditors of Kelly had."

On this interpretation the beneficial interest is in suspense until the payment is made. Mr Millett argues that the right result was reached in *Re Northern Developments (Holdings) Ltd* but for the wrong reasons.[29] He relies on the fact that creditors of Kelly were aware of the existence of the fund and derived comfort from its existence. It seems that creditors of Kelly who applied for payment of their debts or who expressed concern were told of the existence, size and purpose of the fund, *i.e.* to stave off a liquidation of Kelly. In Mr Millett's view communication of the arrangements to the creditor, followed by forbearance by the creditor, raises an equity against the payer which prevents him from revoking the arrangements or otherwise intercepting payment to the creditor. Be that as it may, it is certainly not the way in which Megarry V.C. approached the case. It is submitted that the following statement by one commentator more truly reflects the principles expounded in the English cases on the *Quistclose* trust[30]:

"A variety of equitable rights and obligations arise in respect of the primary purpose trust:
  (i)   the transferor can enforce the trust, and it is suggested, restrain any breach of the trust on the part of the transferee;
  (ii)   the 'direct' or 'factual' beneficiaries can also enforce the trust, so as to acquire by the transfer of the money or property to them an absolute title, and, it is suggested, can also restrain any breach of the trust;
  (iii) certain other 'interested parties' might be treated as having standing also to enforce or restrain breaches, e.g., subsidiary companies where the transferee is the parent company and the transfer was made in the context of a corporate salvage plan.
While the primary purpose trust endures, the beneficial interest in the property remains in suspense."

CONCLUSION

Conditional payments made to a company that has subsequently become insolvent should escape the clutches of the liquidator. The devices through which this result is achieved are discussed in this article. The *Quistclose* trust is one such mechanism and the *Re Kayford* type trust is another. *Quistclose* involves a primary purpose/secondary purpose trust whereas the *Re Kayford* line of authorities entail more in the nature of an orthodox persons trust with specific and recognisable beneficiaries and no added complication of a secondary purpose. In this chapter both have been run together under the rubric of conditional payments since they serve the same commercial purpose. Both strain at the leash of conventional trust principles. With the *Quistclose* trust the difficulty lies with with the application of the beneficiary concept which is at the heart of trusts law. It is submitted however that the problems may be overcome if the relevant principles are interpreted flexibly and bearing in mind the overriding

---

[29] (1985) 101 L.Q.R. 269 at 278.
[30] See Rickett (1991) 107 L.Q.R. 608 at 619. The article by Rickett also contains an interesting account of the Australian cases *Re Groom* (1977) 16 A.L.R. 278; *Re Associated Securities Ltd* [1981] 1 N.S.W.L.R. 742; *Rose v. Rose* (1986) 7 N.S.W.L.R. 679 and *Re Miles* (1989) 85 A.L.R. 216.

commercial objective of conditional payment arrangements. The *Quistclose* trust is the functional equivalent of the purchase money security interest or acquisition mortgage and should be accorded recognition and priority as such.[31] With *Re Kayford* and associated cases the difficulties arise at an altogether more factual level. Sometimes the conditional element in the payment may seem like an exercise in *ex post facto* rationalisation and the decision approaches an application of discretionary justice. If that be the case then we are more in the realm of the so-called remedial constructive trust but that is another story. The remedial constructive trust is considered in Chapter 6.[32]

---

[31] For the use of the concept of the purchase money security interest in a different context see Bennett and Davis (1994) 110 L.Q.R. 448.
[32] An earlier version of this chapter appeared in the form of an article in [1994] *Denning Law Journal* 93–115.

CHAPTER FIVE

Fiduciaries, Bribes and Constructive Trusts

It is an unfortunate fact that fiduciaries, those in a relationship of trust and confidence to another, may break the terms of that confidence and make profits for which they are accountable to the principal. It is also the case that acting in the course of carrying out their duties, fiduciaries may receive bribes and secret commissions as an inducement to behave in a manner contrary to the interests of the principal. There is no doubting that the fiduciary is accountable to the principal for the bribes or secret commissions. What happens however if the fiduciary becomes insolvent and the principal is trying to claim in competition with the general creditors of the fiduciary? Is the principal to be treated as an unsecured creditor or has the principal a proprietary claim under a constructive trust that would afford priority over general creditors? These issues will be addressed in this chapter. Priority over general creditors is however only one reason why the existence of a fiduciary relationship may be alleged. Decided cases provide examples of other reasons why a fiduciary relationship and proprietary consequences are alleged to exist. These cases will be analysed in detail in this chapter but firstly the reasons why submissions based on the existence of a fiduciary relationship are presented to the court will be considered.

POLICY FACTORS UNDERLYING THE WOULD-BE ESTABLISHMENT OF A FIDUCIARY RELATIONSHIP

First and foremost, fiduciary duties are sometimes argued to exist by reason of the fact that a defendant would thereby become subject to stronger and more stringent duties than would otherwise be the case. Two Privy Council cases, *Clark Boyce v. Mouat*[1] and *Kelly v. Cooper*[2] may be cited in this connection though in both cases the defendants were undoubtedly fiduciaries. Claims for breach of fiduciary duty were prayed in aid to enlarge the scope of contractual duties. The Privy Council said that this was impermissable. In *Kelly v. Cooper*[3] Lord Browne-Wilkinson referred approvingly to the observations of Mason J. in the Australian case *Hospital Products Ltd v. United States Surgical Corporation*[4] on this subject. The latter said that a fiduciary relationship could not be superimposed upon the contract in such a way as to alter the operation which the contract was intended to have according to its true construction. Second, as we have seen, a plaintiff may endeavour to establish that the defendant is subject to fiduciary duties so as to gain precedence over other creditors of the defendant in the event of the defendant becoming insolvent. In *Re Goldcorp Exchange Ltd*[5]

---

[1] [1994] 1 A.C. 428.
[2] [1993] A.C. 205. See also *Bristol and West Building Society v. Mothew* [1996] E.G.C.S. 136; *The Times*, August 2, 1996.
[3] [1993] A.C. 205 at 215.
[4] (1984) 156 C.L.R. 41 at 97.
[5] [1994] 2 All E.R. 806.

this was the motivation behind the plaintiff arguing for the existence of a fiduciary relationship. Third, the fiduciary relationship argument may be a convenient way of circumventing legal and practical difficulties in the enforcement of a monetary judgment simpliciter, particularly if it is sought to enforce the judgment across international frontiers. This rationale provides a convincing explanation of why the fiduciary point was invoked in *Att.-Gen. for Hong Kong v. Reid.*[6] Fourth, a fiduciary relationship may be asserted so as to get around difficulties in the actual assessment of damages. In the Canadian case *Lac Minerals Ltd v. International Corona Resources Ltd*[7] proprietary relief founded on fiduciary duties was sought, partly at least, because of this factor. Fifth, and allied to the fourth point, the contention that the defendant is a fiduciary is sometimes advanced so as to obtain a form of consequential relief that would not be available in the absence of a fiduciary finding. *Westdeutsche Landesbank Girozentrale v. Islington L.B.C.*[8] is a case in point. In this case money was paid by the plaintiff to the defendant on foot of an *ultra vires* contract. The judge at first instance, Hobhouse J., and the Court of Appeal both held that personal and proprietary remedies were available for the recovery of the money. Why were the plaintiffs not content with a personal remedy? Well, if the defendants were deemed to be fiduciaries in respect of the receipt of the *ultra vires* payment, then, prima facie, they were liable to pay compound interest to the plaintiffs on the payment received. If they were not fiduciaries however, and came merely under a personal duty to repay, then there was only an obligation to pay simple interest.[9] The House of Lords took a different view of the law in *Westdeutsche*[10] holding that the receipt of money under an *ultra vires* contract did not generate any fiduciary duties in respect of the return of the money. While the recipient was under a personal restitutionary obligation to refund what had been received, both legal and equitable property in the money passed from the payer to the recipient. Sixth and finally, the state prosecution authorities may argue that a particular person is under fiduciary duties with a view to subjecting that person to criminal liability. *Att.-Gen.'s Reference (No. 1 of 1985)*[11] supplies an instance where it was endeavoured to establish fiduciary liability because of these considerations.

It is important to bear in mind the reaons why, in a particular case, the defendant allegedly comes under fiduciary obligations. In this chapter it is argued that proprietary relief should not be available automatically for breach of fiduciary duty but rather that the court should have a discretion to grant a proprietary remedy in appropriate circumstances. Different factors apply in different cases. It may be that the reasons why a plaintiff pleads fiduciary duties should influence the court in exercising its discretion to award appropriate relief.

---

[6] [1994] 1 All E.R. 1; [1994] 1 A.C. 324.
[7] (1989) 61 D.L.R. (4th) 14.
[8] [1994] 4 All E.R. 890.
[9] See the comment by Burrows on *Westdeutsche* in [1995] *Restitution Law Review* 15 at 27: "The consequence would appear to be that, even where the payee is solvent, it will always be in a payer's interests in seeking restitution to claim a ... trust in equity rather than bringing an action for money had and received, for the latter is confined to allowing recovery of the amount paid." Arguing for the existence of a fiduciary relationship/trust may also carry advantages for a plaintiff in terms of limitation periods, etc.
[10] [1996] 2 W.L.R. 802; [1996] 2 All E.R. 961.
[11] [1986] Q.B. 591; [1986] 2 All E.R. 219.

The remedy should be tailored to the precise circumstances of the case. Queue-jumping, so to speak, should not be tolerated, *i.e.* the plaintiff seeking to leapfrog other creditors in the defendant's insolvency. On the other hand, a proprietary remedy may be apposite if failure to grant such relief would deprive a judgment of the court of any force and effect.

Having looked at the reasons why fiduciary obligations are often relied upon it is necessary to examine what exactly is meant by the expression "fiduciary".[12] First however, it is useful to consider a couple of cases where the the "fiduciary" tag is simply used as a synonym for the separation of legal and equitable ownership.

SEPARATION OF LEGAL AND EQUITABLE OWNERSHIP

In some cases the expression "fiduciary relationship" is simply used, or misused, to denote a divide that exists between legal and equitable ownership in the particular case.[13] Employment of the term in this sense is particularly evident from the judgment of Hobhouse J. in *Westdeutsche Landesbank Girozentrale v. Islington LBC*.[14] This is a case where the plaintiff paid money to the defendant pursuant to an *ultra vires* contract and sought recovery of the same. The judge said[15]:

"The plaintiff is entitled to recover [the] sum either as money had and received by the defendant to the use of the plaintiff or as money which in equity belongs to the plaintiff and which it is entitled to trace in the hands of the defendant and have repaid to it out of the present assets of the defendant. The basis of the plaintiff's claim, whether at common law or in equity, is that the defendant has been unjustly enriched at the expense of the plaintiff and that in conscience the defendant must repay to the plaintiff, save in so far as it has already done so, the sum which it received from the plaintiff."

In essence, the equitable restitutionary claim was based on a trust. The plaintiff had physically parted with its money but retained equitable property in the money by virtue of the *ultra vires* of the contract under which it was purportedly paid. The whole language in which the judgment of Hobhouse J. is clothed is that of fiduciary relationship.[16] This in reality seems to mean the same thing as a trust though somewhat curiously at one point the judge denies

---

[12] In Consultation paper no. 124, *Fiduciary Duties and Regulatory Rules* (November 1995) at 1 the Law Commission described the nature of a fiduciary relationship as being "one in which a person undertakes to act on behalf of or for the benefit of another, often as an intermediary, with a discretion or power which affects the interests of the other who depends on the fiduciary for information and advice."

[13] See the observations of La Forest J. in *Lac Minerals Ltd v. International Corona Ltd* (1989) 61 D.L.R. (4th) 14 at 27. He said: "...[the] third usage of "fiduciary" stems, it seems, from a perception of remedial inflexibility in equity. Courts have resorted to fiduciary language because of the view that certain remedies, deemed appropriate in the circumstances, would not be available unless a fiduciary relationship was present. In this sense, the label "fiduciary" imposes no obligations, but is rather merely instrumental or facilitative in achieving what appears to be the appropriate result."

[14] [1994] 4 All E.R. 890. On the case see generally Cowan [1993] L.M.C.L.Q. 300; Swadling [1994] *Restitution Law Review* 73; Burrows (1993) 143 N.L.J. 480; Burrows [1995] *Restitution Law Review* 15; Birks (1993) 23 *University of Western Australia Law Review* 195.

[15] [1994] 4 All E.R. 890 at 955–956.

[16] See generally Burrows [1995] *Restitution Law Review* 15 at 25–26.

the existence of a trust saying[17]: "It is not alleged that the [defendants] received the money as trustees or as constructive trustees...".

Dillon L.J., in the Court of Appeal, was prepared however to embrace the notion of a trust. He said[18]:

> "The same result can be achieved on equitable, as opposed to common law, grounds. Since, contrary to the expectation of the parties, the swap transaction and contract are, and were from the outset, *ultra vires* and void, the purpose for which the £2.5 million was paid by the bank to the council has wholly failed, and the £2.5 million has, from the time the council received it, been held on a resulting trust for the bank".

The House of Lords in the case[19] said that there was no trust or fiduciary relationship. The payment of money or transfer of property on foot of an *ultra vires* contract vested legal and equitable title in the recipient. There was no separation of legal and equitable ownership so as to give rise to a trust or relationship of a fiduciary character. Another case that illustrates a broad usage of the expression "fiduciary" is *Chase Manhattan Bank NA v. Israel-British Bank (London) Ltd.*[20] In this case a sum of $2 million was mistakenly paid twice instead of once. Approximately one month after the mistaken second payment was made the defendant ceased to trade. The question before the court was whether the plaintiffs could trace the mistaken payment. Goulding J. answered the question in the affirmative. In his view a fiduciary relationship was necessary to support an equitable tracing claim of the kind advanced in this case. It was enough however, that the payment of money into the wrong hands gave rise to a fiduciary relationship. This approach may be criticised on the basis that it involves a manipulation of legal techniques to reach a particular desired result. A simpler route to the same conclusion would be to say that the circumstances of the mistaken payment were such that the payer retained equitable property in the payment made and that this was a sufficiently strong proprietary base to ground a tracing action.

Westdeutsche and the *Chase Manhattan Bank case* are cases that to a certain extent may be left to one side. The fiduciary notion is being used in a somewhat strained sense simply to signify a separation of legal and equitable ownership that was held to exist on the facts of the cases. The question still remains as to how the concept of "fiduciary" is employed more generally.

FIDUCIARIES

The first thing that one might say on this score is that the phrase "fiduciary" is not an expression of precision but basically it denotes the subsistence of a relationship of trust and confidence.[21] Professor Paul Finn has written widely on

---

[17] [1994] 4 All E.R. 890 at 916.
[18] [1994] 4 All E.R. 890 at 962. Reference was made to the speech of Viscount Haldane L.C. in *Sinclair v. Brougham* [1914] A.C. 398, 418, 420–421.
[19] [1996] 2 W.L.R. 802; [1996] 2 All E.R. 961
[20] [1981] Ch. 105.
[21] See generally on fiduciary relationships Paul Finn, *Fiduciary Obligations* (1977). See also Sealy "Fiduciary Relationships" [1962] C.L.J. 69; [1963] C.L.J. 119. Sealy explains how the the term "fiduciary" is a relative newcomer to the vocabulary of English law having only attained widespread usage in the law reports in the early to mid Victorian period. For a more contemporary account see Robert Flannigan (1988) 9 O.J.L.S. 285.

the subject of fiduciaries and has propounded the following test for determining when a person should be regarded as a fiduciary[22]:

"He is, simply, someone who undertakes to act for or on behalf of another in some particular matter or matters. That undertaking may be of a general character. It may be specific and limited. It is immaterial whether the undertaking is or is not in the form of a contract. It is immaterial that the undertaking is gratuious. And the undertaking may be officiously assumed without request."

Some fiduciary relationships are easily established and generally acknowledged.[23] The relationships of company and company director and trustee and beneficiary fall within this category. The question of fiduciary relationships was discussed to a certain extent by Lord Browne-Wilkinson in the recent case of *White v. Jones*.[24] This case involved a consideration of the question whether an intended beneficiary under a will is entitled to recover damages from the testator's solicitors by reason of whose negligence the testator's intention to benefit him under the will had failed to be effectuated. It was held that an intended beneficiary was entitled to damages in such circumstances.[25] In the course of his judgment Lord Browne-Wilkinson said[26]:

"The paradigm of the circumstances in which equity will find a fiduciary relationship is where one party, A, has assumed to act in relation to the property or affairs of another, B. A, having assumed responsibility, *pro tanto*, for B's affairs, is taken to have assumed certain duties in relation to the conduct of those affairs, including normally a duty of care. Thus, a trustee assumes responsibility for the management of the property of the beneficiary, a company director for the affairs of the company and an agent for those of his principal. By so assuming to act in B's affairs, A comes under fiduciary duties to B. Although the extent of those fiduciary duties (including duties of care) will vary from case to case, some duties (including a duty of care) arise in each case."

The courts however have fought shy of superimposing fiduciary duties where

---

[22] *ibid* at 201. Elsewhere in his book however Finn argues that it is meaningless to talk of fiduciary relationships as such. He suggests that it is pointless to describe a person as being a fiduciary unless at the same time it is said for the purposes of which particular rules and principles that description is being used. The rules, in his view, are everything while the description "fiduciary" is nothing (see p. 1).

[23] Occasionally the phrase "fiduciary" has been used as some sort of general umbrella expression. An example of this occurs in *Reading v. The Queen* [1951] A.C. 50. In this case a soldier who had obtained bribes by abuse of his position was held unable to recover the same from the Crown. He had been dispossessed of the bribe monies by the military authorities. Asquith L.J. delivering the judgment of the Court of Appeal ([1949] 2 K.B. at 236) appeared to hold that the soldier was a fiduciary. Lord Porter in the House of Lords however opined that Asquith L.J. had used the words "fiduciary relationship" in a wide and loose sense: see [1951] A.C. 507 at 516.

[24] [1995] 1 All E.R. 691.

[25] The House of Lords was divided 3–2. Lords Goff, Nolan and Browne-Wilkinson formed the majority while Lords Keith and Mustill dissented.

[26] [1995] 1 All E.R. 691 at 713. See also the speech of Lord Browne-Wilkinson in *Henderson v. Merrett Syndicates Ltd* [1994] 3 All E.R. 506.

parties have dealt with another at arm's length on the basis of a commercial contract. According to one Australian judge[27]:

> "It is usual—perhaps necessary—that in such a [fiduciary] relationship one party should repose substantial confidence in another in acting on his behalf or in his interest in some respect. But it is not in every case where that happens that there is a fiduciary relationship ... There is, however, the notion underlying all the cases of fiduciary obligation that inherent in the nature of the relationship itself is a position of disadvantage or vulnerability on the part of one of the parties which cause him to place reliance upon the other and requires the protection of equity acting upon the conscience of that other."

Recently, the Privy Council had occasion to pronounce on the signification of the phrase fiduciary in *Re Goldcorp Exchange Ltd.*[28] In this case the respondents were customers of a New Zealand company which dealt in gold and other precious metals. These customers purchased bullion for future delivery on the basis that they were acquiring "non-allocated" metal which would be stored and insured free of charge by the company. Each customer in this position was given a certificate of ownership and had the right to take physical delivery of the metal purchased on giving seven days' notice. The company explained that bullion purchased was not set aside as a customer's metal but that the stock of bullion held by the company from which customers could call for delivery if they so wished would always be sufficient to meet the company's obligations under all outstanding contracts of sale. The company became insolvent and a priority dispute arose between the customers and a bank which held a charge over the assets of the company.

A variety of arguments were advanced on behalf of the customers who were endeavouring to establish a proprietary interest over the bullion in the company's possession that took precedence to the bank's charge. It was contended *inter alia* that because the company held itself out as willing to vest bullion in the customer and to hold it in safe custody on his behalf in circumstances where he was totally dependent on the company, and trusted the company to do what it had promised without in practice there being any means of verification, the company was a fiduciary.[29] The argument continued along the lines that the company as fiduciary created an equity by inviting the customer to look on and treat stocks vested in it as his own and that the only appropriate way of recognising this equity was by treating the customer as entitled to a proprietary interest in the stock. Lord Mustill who spoke for the Privy Council was distinctly unimpressed

---

[27] Dawson J. in *Hospital Products Ltd v. United States Surgical Corporation* (1984) 156 C.L.R. 41. The judge also said that there are relationships which are ordinarily recognised as fiduciary, at least in some of their aspects, and little trouble is experienced with them. He observed that these were all relationships which were analogous to that which exists between a trustee and his beneficiary—the clearest of all fiduciary relationships. Obvious examples were the relationship between partners, between employer and employee, between agent and their principals, between solicitors and their clients, between directors and their companies and between wards and their guardians.

[28] [1994] 2 All E.R. 806.

[29] These arguments succeeded before the New Zealand Court of Appeal where the case is reported *sub nom Liggett v. Kensington* [1993] 1 N.Z.L.R. 257. For a defence of the decision in *Liggett v. Kensington* see S.R. Scott [1993] L.M.C.L.Q. 330.

by this submission based on a fiduciary relationship.[30] He said that to describe someone as a fiduciary without more was meaningless and quoted the observations of Frankfurter J. in *SEC v. Chenery Corp*[31]:

"To say that a man is a fiduciary only begins analysis; it gives direction to further inquiry. To whom is he a fiduciary? What obligations does he owe as a fiduciary? In what respect has he failed to discharge these obligations? And what are the consequences of his deviation from duty?"

In this particular case no fiduciary duties had been suggested beyond those which the company assumed under the contracts of sale read with the collateral promises. According to Lord Mustill the fact that one person was placed in a particular position *vis-à-vis* another through the medium of a contract did not necessarily mean that he did not also owe fiduciary duties to that other by virtue of being in that position.[32] The essence of a fiduciary relationship was that it created obligations of a different character from those deriving from the contract itself. Many commercial relationships involved reliance by one party on the other and to invest such relationships with a fiduciary character would have undesirable and far-reaching consequences. While the customers had high expectations that their contracts would be fulfilled this did not result in equitable remedies.[33]

The reluctance of the Privy Council, manifested in *Re Goldcorp Exchange Ltd* to find a fiduciary relationship in a particular commercial context, was also displayed by the High Court of Australia in *Hospital Products International v. United States Surgical Corp.*[34] This case will now be examined along with another Australian High Court decision.

FIDUCIARY DUTIES AND COMMERCIAL RELATIONSHIPS IN AUSTRALIA

This is a case where the plaintiff granted to the defendant the exclusive Australian distributorship rights of certain surgical products manufactured by the plaintiff. The defendant however aimed to establish itself in direct competition with the plaintiff. What it did was to put off the satisfaction of orders for the plaintiff's products and once it had brought to an end the relationship with the plaintiff it met the orders that had built up for the plaintiff's products with goods of its own manufacture. According to the plaintiff the defendant was not only

---

[30] Even S.R. Scott [1993] L.M.C.L.Q. 330 at 335–336 who defends vigorously the New Zealand Court of Appeal decision in *Liggett v. Kensington* has argued that Cooke P. and Gault J. in that case took a wide view of the facts so as to find a fiduciary relationship, thereby providing a traditional jurisprudential basis for the imposition of the constructive trust.

[31] (1943) 318 U.S. 80 at 85–86. Lord Mustill was in fact using the reference to the case in Goff and Jones *The Law of Restitution* (4th ed., 1993), p. 644.

[32] [1994] 2 All E.R. 806 at 821–822.

[33] See also the statement of Lord Jauncey in *Clark Boyce v. Mouat* [1994] 1 A.C. 428 at 434 that fiduciary duties could not be "prayed in aid to enlarge the scope of contractual duties." Note too *Kelly v. Cooper* [1993] A.C. 205.

[34] (1984) 156 C.L.R. 41. The case is examined by the distinguished Equity commentator J.R. Lehane in *Essays in Equity* (P.D. Finn ed., Sydney 1985), p. 95. Lehane argues that not academics only, but practitioners and their clients also, have some cause for disappointment, for despite promising beginnings the case is not a landmark. In his view no clear principle emerges to guide those who have to grappled in practice with this notoriously difficult area of the law. For an analysis of the Australian cases see Oakley [1995] C.L.J. 377 at 389–397.

liable for breach of contract but also that it held its business on a constructive trust for the plaintiff on the basis that the relationship between the parties was a fiduciary one. The constructive trust claim carried in its wake the prospect of greater monetary recovery and also priority over the defendant's creditors in the event of the latter becoming insolvency.

A majority of the High Court of Australia took the view that the contractual nexus between plaintiff and defendant did not entail any fiduciary obligations. Consequently the defendant could not be regarded as a constructive trustee and was merely contractually liable in damages. The gravamen of the majority conclusion was that the parties had dealt with each other in a commercial footing on an arm's length basis.[35] Moreover, the whole object of the transaction from the defendant's perspective had been profit-making. Mason J. (as he then was) dissented. He took the view that there was a limited fiduciary duty that arose out of the exclusive responsibility of the defendant with respect to the Australian marketing of the plaintiff's products and the manner in which these products were to be promoted. These circumstances rendered it incumbent on the defendant not to make a profit by virtue of its position.[36]

Mason J. later became the Chief Justice of Australia and he has commented extra-judicially on the *Hospital Products* case in the *Law Quarterly Review*.[37] In his view the problem which proved intractable in that case was in establishing that the alleged fiduciary was bound to act in the interests of the principal or in the joint interests of the parties in relation to product goodwill and not solely in his own interests. He spoke of a natural reluctance to impose upon parties in a commercial relationship who are in a relatively equal position of strength the higher standards of conduct which equity prescribes.[38] Elsewhere in the article however the learned judge describes the fiduciary relationship as the spearhead of equity's incursions into the area of commerce.[39] This spearhead is thrown

---

[35] Gibbs C.J., Wilson and Dawson JJ. formed the majority. Mason J. thought that there was a limited fiduciary relationship between the parties. Deane J. thought, in line with the majority, that there was no fiduciary relationship but said that the defendant was liable to account as a constructive trustee "in accordance with the principles under which a constructive trust may be imposed as the appropriate form of equitable relief in circumstances where a person could not in good conscience retain for himself a benefit, or the proceeds of a benefit, which he has appropriated to himself in breach of his contractual or other legal or equitable obligations to another. " The judge deferred until some subsequent occasion a more precise identification of the principles governing the imposition of a constructive trust in such circumstances. Oakley [1995] C.L.J. 377 at 391 has expressed the hope that this reticence continues indefinitely.

[36] (1984) 156 C.L.R. 41 at 101–102. Mason J. added that fiduciary relationships range from the trustee to the errand boy and that the scope of the fiduciary duty must be moulded accoring to the nature of the relationship and the facts of the case. He said that the rigorous standards appropriate to a trustee will not apply to a fiduciary who is permitted by contract to pursue his own interests in some respects.

[37] (1994) 110 L.Q.R. 238 at 245–248.

[38] The Australian Chief Justice also said that the absence of a clear definition has enabled the courts to classify as fiduciaries persons who would not have been so regarded at an earlier time. In his view the reason why the classification has been more extensive is that courts, reflecting higher community standards or values, perceive in a wide variety of relationships that one party has a legitimate expectation that the other party will act in the interests of the first party or at least in the joint interests of the parties and not solely self-interestedly: see (1994) 110 L.Q.R. 238 at 246.

[39] (1994) 110 L.Q.R. 238 at 245. The judge also however is mindful of the dangers pointed out by Professor Birks of over-extending the concept of "fiduciary", particularly if the motive is to achieve a proprietary remedy: see Birks, "Restitutionary Damages for Breach of Contract" [1987] L.M.C.L.Q. 421 at 438–439 and Finn, "The Fiduciary Principle" *Equity, Fiduciaries and Trusts* (in Tim Youdan ed., 1989), p. 56.

sharply into focus in another Australian High Court decision *United Dominions Corp. v. Brian.*[40]

This case concerned three commercial undertakings dealing on an arm's length basis who entered into a joint venture arrangement. This arrangement was treated as analogous to a partnership. The question in the case was whether prior to the execution of the formal documents the parties owed fiduciary duties to one another so as to preclude the obtaining of collateral advantages without the informed consent of other participants. The High Court answered in the affirmative. It was stressed that a fiduciary relationship with attendant fiduciary obligations would ordinarily exist between prospective partners who had embarked upon the conduct of the partnership business or venture before the precise terms of any partnership agreement had been settled. In such a situation the mutual confidence and trust which underlay most consensual fiduciary relationships was likely to be more readily apparent than in the case where mutual rights and obligations had been expressly defined in some formal agreement.[41]

THE FIDUCIARY PRINCIPLE IN CANADA

The Supreme Court of Canada has also had occasion to consider the troublesome conundrum of when a person may be deemed to be a fiduciary.[42] In *Guerin v. The Queen*[43] Dickson J., who spoke for a majority of the court, referred favourably to the proposition advanced by Professor Ernest Weinrib to the effect that the hallmark of a fiduciary relationship was that the relative legal positions were such that one party was at the mercy of the other's discretion.[44] In the Professor's view a fiduciary relationship meant that the interests of the principal could be affected by, and were therefore dependent on, the manner in which the fiduciary used the discretion which had been delegated to him. The fiduciary obligation was the blunt tool in the armoury of the law for the control of this discretion.[45] Dickson J. added[46]:

---

[40] (1985) 157 C.L.R. 1.

[41] (1985) 157 C.L.R. 1 at 12 *per* Mason, Brennan and Deane JJ.

[42] See also *Norberg v. Wynrib* (1992) 92 D.L.R. (4th) 449 where some members of the Supreme Court took the view that the doctor-patient relationship was, at least in part, fiduciary. McLachlin J. observed that imbalance of power was a necessary but not sufficient condition to establish a fiduciary relationship. She opined that there must also be potential for interference with a legal interest or a non-legal interest of vital and substantial practical interest as well as an assumption or undertaking to look after the interest of the beneficiary exclusively for the good of the beneficiary.

[43] (1984) 13 D.L.R. (4th) 321 at 339–341.

[44] See also on the existence of fiduciary relationships another Canadian case *Frame v. Smith* (1987) 42 D.L.R. (4th) 81 at 98–99 where Wilson J. said: "... there are common features discernible in the contexts in which fiduciary duties have been found to exist and these common features do provide a rough and ready guide to whether or not the imposition of a fiduciary obligaton on a new relationship would be appropriate and consistent. Relationships in which a fiduciary obligation have been imposed seem to possess three general characteristics:
(1) The fiduciary has scope for the exercise of some discretion or power.
(2) The fiduciary can unilaterally exercise that power or discretion so as to affect the beneficiary's legal or practical interests.
(3) The beneficiary is peculiarly vulnerable to or at least at the mercy of the fiduciary holding the discretion or power.

[45] (1975) 25 *University of Toronto Law Journal* 1 at 4.

[46] (1984) 13 D.L.R. (4th) 321 at 340.

"I make no comment upon whether this description is broad enough to embrace all fiduciary obligations. I do agree, however, that were by statute, agreement, or perhaps by unilateral undertaking, one party has an obligation to act for the benefit of another, and that obligation carries with it a discretionary power, the party thus empowered becomes a fiduciary. Equity will then supervise the relationship by holding him to the fiduciary's strict standard of conduct."

More recently, the Canadian Supreme Court has been sharply divided on the existence of fiduciary obligations in the commercial context. This division is exemplified by two cases— *LAC Minerals Ltd v. International Corona Resources Ltd*[47] and *Hodgkinson v. Simms*.[48] Interestingly, the main judgments in both cases were delivered by the same judges. La Forest J. in *LAC Minerals* found that a fiduciary relationship existed whereas Sopinka J., who spoke for the majority of the court, did not. Roles were reversed in *Hodgkinson v. Simms*. La Forest J., this time voicing the opinion of the majority of the court, again was prepared to discern a fiduciary relationship on the facts whereas Sopinka J., who delivered a joint judgment with McLachlin J., did not. It is possible nevertheless to distinguish the cases on the facts. *LAC Minerals* essentially involved a commercial relationship at arm's length whereas what was being considered in *Hodgkinson v. Simms* was a commercial advisory relationship. *LAC Minerals* will be examined in detail later on in this chapter for its consideration of the discretion of the court to award proprietary relief. It is appropriate however to subject *Hodgkinson v. Simms* to some scrutiny at this juncture.

HODGKINSON V. SIMMS

In this case the plaintiff was a stockbroker whose income had increased enormously in recent times. He approached the defendant accountant for advise on tax planning and prudential investments. The defendant suggested investment in certain types of residential dwellings (MURBs) that offered tax advantages but failed to disclose to the plaintiff his relationship with the property developer which meant that he earned commission on investments in the dwellings. It was found as a fact that the plaintiff would not have made the investment had he known of the defendant's relationship with the developers. The advice was financially sound at the time that it was given but the plaintiff later lost heavily on the investments when there was a general downturn in the property market. He sued the defendant so as to recoup these losses alleging, *inter alia*, that the defendant had broken fiduciary duties owed to him by failing to reveal the connection with the developers.

In finding in favour of the existence of a fiduciary relationship La Forest J. said that, outside the established categories, what is required is evidence of a mutual understanding that one party has relinquished its own self-interest and agreed to act solely on behalf of the other party.[49] The existence of a fiduciary

---

[47] (1989) 61 D.L.R. (4th) 14.

[48] (1994) 117 D.L.R. (4th) 161. For an analysis of this decision see Ogilvie [1995] J.B.L. 638.

[49] (1994) 117 D.L.R. (4th) 161 at 176–177. According to La Forest J. this idea was well-stated in the Amercian case of *Dolton v. Capitol Federal Savings and Loan Association* (1982) 642 P. 2d 21 at 23–24, in the banker-customer context, to be a state of affairs "which impels or induces one party "to relax the care and vigilance it would and should have ordinarily exercised in dealing with a stranger.". . . [and] . . . has been found to exist where there is a repose of trust by the customer along with an acceptance or invitation of such trust on the part of the lending institution."

duty in a given case depended on the reasonable expectations of the parties and these turned on such factors as trust, confidence, complexity of subject matter, and community or industry standards. Relationships characterised by a unilateral discretion that was capable of harming others and hence designated as "fiduciary" were merely species of a broader family of "power-dependency" fiduciary relationships. The judge added[50]:

> "Further, the relative 'degree of vulnerability' . . . does not depend on some hypothetical ability to protect one's self from harm, but rather on the nature of the parties' reasonable expectations. Obviously, a party who expects the other party to a relationship to act in the former's best interests is more vulnerable to an abuse of power than a party who should be expected to know that he or she should take protective measures."

The judge drew a sharp distinction between arm's length commercial relationships which were characterised by self-interest and professional advisory relationships whose essence was precisely trust, confidence and independence.[51] La Forest J. pointed out that courts exercising equitable jurisdiction have repeatedly affirmed that clients in a professional advisory relationship have a right to expect that their professional advisors will act in their best interests, to the exclusion of all other interests, unless the contrary was disclosed. By enforcing duties of honesty and good faith, courts were able to regulate an activity that was of great value to commerce and society generally. The law recognised that not all relationships were characterised by a dynamic of mutual autonomy and that the marketplace cannot always set the rules. Moreover, in many advisory relationships norms of loyalty and good faith were suggested by the codes of professional responsibility and behaviour established by the relevant self-regulatory body.[52] The rationale underlying such codes was the protection of parties in situations where they could not, despite their best efforts, protect themselves, due to the nature of the relationship.

There was a powerful dissenting judgment in the case from Sopinka and McLachlin JJ. who suggested that the distinguishing characteristic between advice simpliciter and advice giving rise to a fiduciary duty was the ceding by one party of effective power to the other.[53] They focussed on the concept of "vulnerability" which involved a relationship of dependency. Complete reliance was necessary for a fiduciary relationship to exist in their view because of the draconian consequences which its imposition entailed. The minority judges refused to countenance a distinction between professional advisors and other commercial interactions saying[54]:

[50] (1994) 117 D.L.R. (4th) 161 at 179.
[51] La Forest J. also said that the precise legal or equitable duties the law will enforce in any given relationship are tailored to the legal and practical incidents of a particular relationship. Reference was made to the observations of Lord Scarman in *National Westminster Bank plc v. Morgan* [1985] 1 All E.R. 821 at 831 that "[t]here is no substitute in this branch of the law for a meticulous examination of the facts".
[52] The judge said at (1994) 117 D.L.R. (4th) 161 at 188: "With respect to the accounting profession, the relevant rules and standards evinced a clear instruction that all real and apparent conflicts of interest be fully disclosed to clients, particularly in the area of tax-related investment advice. The basis of this requirement is the maintenance of the independence and honesty which is the linchpin of the profession's credibility with the public. It would be surprising indeed if the courts held the professional advisor to a lower standard of responsibility than that deemed necessary by the self-regulating body of the profession itself."
[53] (1994) 117 D.L.R. (4th) 161 at 218–219.
[54] *ibid.* at 220.

"It cannot be assumed that the latter are always based on self-interest and the former are not. Moreover, as far as social utility is concerned, it could be debated whether advice as to how to add to one's personal wealth while paying the least amount of tax is to be preferred over business dealings which may lead to the development of a mine providing employment to many Canadians."

THE ENGLISH EXPERIENCE

What lessons may be drawn from Canadian experience for the future development of English jurisprudence in the sphere of fiduciary law? The first thing to say is that not all Canadian decisions in the broad realm of equity and constructive trusts are congruent with English judicial thinking. One may cite *Peter v. Beblow*[55] on the award of a beneficial interest in the family home to a stay-at-home cohabitant in this connection. Having said that there is considerable support in traditional English jurisprudence for the distinction drawn by the majority in *Hodgkinson v. Simms* between professional advisory relationships and other commercial dealings.[56] Morevoer, the sentiments voiced by the minority judges in *Hodgkinson v. Simms* that professional advisory relationships may not have great social utility in terms of job creation and hence do not necessarily merit judicial protection are not the kinds of opinions that have traditionally cut much ice with English judges. It is submitted that judges in England are more likely to be influenced by codes created for the regulation of professional advisors by self-regulatory bodies to the extent that these codes lay down duties of loyalty and good faith.

Of course the mere fact that a particular person may be deemed a fiduciary does not necessarily entail the consequence that all assets held by that person are held on trust. This axiom is evidenced in an Australian High Court decision *Daly v. Sydney Stock Exchange*.[57] This is a case where an investor sought the advice of a firm of stockbrokers about shares in which he might invest. An employee of the stockbrokers told the investor that it was not a good time to buy shares and that he should put the money on deposit with the firm until circumstances changed. The investor lent the money to the stockbrokers at interest. Subsequently however the firm became insolvent and was unable to repay the loan. The investor claimed compensation from a fidelity fund established under a statutory scheme for the regulation of the securities industry. Entitlement to compensation was conditional on him establishing a proprietary interest in the moneys deposited. The High Court denied the proposition that the investor had any beneficial stake in the sums advanced. According to Gibbs C.J. recognition of a constructive trust was unnecessary to protect the legitimate rights of the lender and could lead to consequences that were unjust both to the creditors of

---

[55] (1993) 101 D.L.R. (4th) 621.

[56] One might also refer in this connection to the judgments of Lord Browne-Wilkinson in *Henderson v. Merrett Syndicates Ltd* [1994] 3 All E.R. 506 and *White v. Jones* [1995] 1 All E.R. 691.

[57] (1986) 160 C.L.R. See also the comments of Sir Peter Millett in "Bribes and Secret Commissions" [1993] *Restitution Law Review* 7 at 23 which were referred to approvingly by Laddie J. in *Nelson v. Rye* [1996] 2 All E.R. 186 at 199; "Every agent is a fiduciary; he may or may not be a trustee. Often he holds no money or property for his principal. If he receives goods from his principal, he may be a bailee only. Where, however, he receives property from a third party intended for his principal, his obligation will almost invariably be to transfer it *in specie* to his principal and, if so, he will be treated as holding it as trustee for his principal. He cannot assert a beneficial title to property which was never intended to be his own."

the borrower and to the borrower itself.[58] He also pointed out that the loan was not made for any specified purpose and there was no agreement, express or implied, that the moneys lent should not form part of the borrower's general assets.[59]

Brennan J., who delivered a concurring judgment, took a slightly different tack. In his opinion the stockbrokers were in breach of their fiduciary duty to the investor. Equity intervened to prevent a fiduciary from retaining property acquired under a contract entered into in breach of his fiduciary obligation. So too did it intercede to prevent him from retaining money acquired in similar circumstances. The lender however could not assert an equitable title to the money lent until he elected to avoid the contract of loan. In a case where, like the present, the borrower acquired title to money paid to him pursuant to a contract of loan, he could not be made a trustee of the money without his consent so long as the contract still stood.[60] In this particular case the contracts of loan had not been avoided.[61]

AMBIT OF FIDUCIARY DUTIES

Whatever about the circumstances in which a person is deemed to be a fiduciary, questions also arise concerning the nature and extent of fiduciary obligations. When talking about the content of fiduciary duties it is possible to particularise and individualise to the nth degree. Usually however fiduciary obligations are subsumed under two heads namely the "no-profit" rule and the "no-conflict" rule. This delineation of duty is encapsulated in the following observations of Lord Herschell in *Bray v. Ford*[62]:

> "it is an inflexible rule of a Court of Equity that a person in a fiduciary position ... is not, unless otherwise expressly provided, entitled to make a profit; he is not allowed to put himself in a position where his interest and duty conflict. It does not appear to me that this rule is, as has been said, founded upon principles of morality. I regard it rather as based on the consideration that, human nature being what it is, there is danger, in such circumstances, of the person holding a fiduciary position being swayed by interest, rather than by duty, and thus prejudicing those whom he was bound to protect."

Fiduciaries are not allowed to make a secret profit or in other words a profit that is not sanctioned by the instrument from which they derive their authority.[63] This would be the documents establishing a trust in the case of a trustee or the memorandum and articles of association of a company in the case of a company director. Moreover fiduciaries are required not to enter into a situation of actual

---

[58] *ibid* at 380.
[59] Thus bringing into existence a trust on the basis of the principles enunciated by the House of Lords in *Quistclose Investments Ltd v. Rolls Razor Ltd* [1970] A.C. 567.
[60] (1986) 160 C.L.R. 371 at 389–390.
[61] The judgment of Brennan J. was referred to favourably by Millett J in *El Ajou v. Dollar Land Holdings plc* [1993] 3 All E.R. 717. He held that persons who had been induced to purchase worthless shares by false and fraudulent misrepresentations were entitled to rescind the transaction and revest the equitable title to the purchase money in themselves at least to the extent necessary to support an equitable tracing claim.
[62] [1896] A.C. 44 at 51–52.
[63] Se *Regal (Hastings) Ltd v. Gulliver* [1942] 1 All E.R. 378 and *Boardman v. Phipps* [1967] 2 A.C. 46.

or potential conflict between their self-interest and their duties to the principal. The latter proposition is well illustrated by reference to the well known company law case of *Aberdeen Railway Co. v. Blaikie Bros.*[64]

This is a case where the respondents had agreed to manufacture iron chairs for the company but the company was held not to be bound by the contract because, at the time when it was made, the chairman of its board of directors was a member of the respondent partnership. According to Lord Cranworth a body corporate can only act by agents and it was the duty of those agents so to act so as to promote the interests of the corporation whose affairs they were conducting. It was a rule of universal application that no one, having such duties to discharge should be allowed to enter into engagements in which he has, or can have, a personal interest conflicting, or which may conflict, with the interests of those whom he was bound to protect. This principle was adhered to so strictly that no question could be raised as to the fairness of the contract entered into.[65]

The "no-profit" rule is exemplified by the decision of the House of Lords in *Cook v. Deeks.*[66] This is a case where three out of four directors of a Canadian railway company diverted a contract in which the company was interested to another company which they had formed. It was held by the Privy Council that the contract was one which in equity belonged to the company and which the directors had acquired for themselves while ostensibly acting on behalf of the company. The Lord Chancellor, Lord Buckmaster, who gave the advice of the Privy Council, spelled out the factual position. He said that the defendants, while still retaining their position as directors and with their duties to the company in which the plaintiff was a shareholder entirely unchanged, proceeded to negotiate for a new contract. In reality they acted on their own behalf but did so in exactly the same manner as they had always acted for the company and doubtless with their claims backed up by the expeditious manner in which they, while acting for the company, had caused the last contract to be carried through. Lord Buckmaster added that men who assume the complete control of a company's business must remember that they are not at liberty to sacrifice the interests which they are bound to protect and while ostensibly acting for the company to divert in their own favour business which should properly belong to the company which they represent.[67] Directors holding a majority of votes in a company were not permitted to make a present of company property to themselves. In the same way, if directors had acquired for themselves property or rights which they must be regarded as holding on behalf of the company, a resolution that the rights of the company should be disregarded in the matter would amount to forfeiting the interest and property of the minority of shareholders in favour of the majority, and that by the votes of those who were

---

[64] (1854) 1 Macq 461; [1843–1860] All E.R. Rep 249.
[65] In *Boardman v. Phipps* [1967] 2 A.C. 46 at 124 Lord Upjohn said: "The phrase "possibly may conflict" requires consideration. In my view it means that the reasonable man looking at the relevant facts and circumstances of the particular case would think that there was a real sensible possibility of conflict; not that you could imagine some situation arising which might, in some conceivable possibility in events not contemplated as real sensible possibilities, by any reasonable person, result in a conflict.", These observations, while made in a dissenting speech, were taken as accurately representing the law by the Privy Council in *Queensland Mines Ltd v. Hudson* (1978) 52 A.L.J.R. 399.
[66] [1916] 1 A.C. 554.
[67] [1916] A.C. 554 at 563.

interested in securing the property for themselves. Such a use of voting power had never been sanctioned by the courts.

The leading House of Lords authority on the fiduciary duties of company directors must be that in *Regal (Hastings) Ltd v. Gulliver*.[68] In this case the plaintiff company had formed a subsidiary company which was to take up a lease of two cinemas. The owner of the cinemas however insisted that the subsidiary should have a paid-up capital which, in the honest opinion of the plaintiffs board, was greater than the plaintiff could afford to subscribe. The directors of the plaintiff company accordingly subscribed themselves at the par value for part of the balance of the shares in the subsidiary company. The whole transaction had been carried out with a view to the sale of the two cinemas together with another cinema which the plaintiff company itself owned. Ultimately however, the transaction was carried out in a different form with all the shares of the plaintiff and of the subsidiary purchased at a price substantially above par. Thus the directors had made a handsome profit on their investment in shares in the subsidiary. The plaintiff company, which was of course in new hands, sued the directors for an account of their profits. It was found that the directors had all acted honestly throughout but nevertheless they were held liable to account to the plaintiffs.

Lord Russell said that the rule of equity which insists on those, who by use of a fiduciary position, make a profit, being liable to account for that profit, in no way depends on fraud, or absence of bona fides, or upon such questions or considerations as to whether the profit would or should otherwise have gone to the plaintiff or whether the profiteer was under a duty to obtain the source of the profit for the plaintiff, or whether the plaintiff had in fact been damaged or benefited by his action. The liability arose from the mere fact of a profit having, in the stated circumstances, been made. The profiteer, however honest and well-intentioned, could not escape the risk of being called upon to account.[69]

According to Lord Macmillan the plaintiff company had to establish two things as a condition of liability. Firstly that what the directors did was so related to the affairs of the company that it could properly be said in the course of their management and in utilisation of their opportunities and special knowledge as directors. The second requirement was that what they did resulted in a profit to themselves.[70]

The principles enunciated by the House of Lords in *Regal (Hastings) Ltd v. Gulliver* have been criticised for rigidity and excessive strictness. The decision of the Supreme Court of Canada in *Canadian Aero Services Ltd v. O'Malley*[71] signals a more flexible approach and this approach seems to have carried over into English law[72]. In *O'Malley* the plaintiff company offered mapping and geophysical exploration services. The two defendants had been directors of the plaintiff company and had been involved in carrying out preparatory work for the plaintiff in connection with a project in Guyana. This project was sponsored by the Canadian government as part of its overseas aid programme. The Canadian

---

[68] [1942] 1 All E.R. 378; [1967] 2 A.C. 134n.
[69] [1967] 2 A.C. 134 at 144–145. Lord Russell also said at 147 that the directors' profit was made "by reason, and only by reason of the fact that they were directors of Regal, and in the course of their execution of that office."
[70] [1967] 2 A.C. 134 at 153.
[71] (1971) 23 D.L.R. (3d) 632.
[72] [1986] B.C.L.C. 460.

government later invited the plaintiff company and others to submit tenders for the project. At this time, the defendants resigned their offices with the plaintiff company and formed their own surveying company which sought, and was awarded the contract. The defendants were held liable to the plaintiff company for loss of the contract. According to Laskin J., who spoke for the court, a director or senior corporate officer was precluded from usurping for himself or diverting to another person or company with whom or with which he was associated, a maturing business opportunity which his company was actively pursuing.[73] He was also precluded from so acting even after his resignation where the resignation may fairly be said to have been prompted or influenced by a wish to acquire for himself the opportunity sought by the company, or where it was his position with the company rather than a fresh initiative that led him to the opportunity which he later acquired.[74]

The court laid down that the general standards of loyalty, good faith and avoidance of a conflict of duty and self-interest must be tested by a number of factors which it would be reckless to attempt to enumerate exhaustively. Factors would include the office or position held, the nature of the corporate opportunity, its ripeness, its specific nature and the director's relationship to it, the amount of knowledge possessed, the circumstances in which it was obtained and whether it was special or even private information. Laskin J. said that the test of accountability for profits acquired by reason only of being directors and in the course of execution of office referred to by Lord Russell in *Regal* should not be regarded as an exclusive touchstone of liability.

The more flexible formula employed by the Canadian court in *O'Malley*[75] found favour with Hutchinson J. in *Island Export Finance v. Umunna*.[76] The judge uttered the truism that directors, no less than employees, acquire a general fund of knowledge and expertise in the course of their work, and it was plainly in the public interest that they should be free to exploit it in a new position.

While it may be true to say that *Regal (Hastings) Ltd v. Gulliver* has undergone a certain trimming at the edges at the hands of the judiciary recently, it was principal authority relied upon by the House of Lords in *Boardman v. Phipps*[77] when discussing the fiduciary duties of trustees. To summarise greatly that case held the trustees liable to account but the precise nature of the liability imposed upon the trustees is a matter of some debate. It is unclear whether one is talking about personal accountability or constructive trusteeship properly so called. Perhaps the best approach is to detail the facts of the case and then to focus on the orders made. Basically a testator had established a trust for the benefit of his widow and children. The trust assets included a 27 per cent minority shareholding in a private company. Boardman who was the solicitor to the trust became concerned about the value of the investment and considered that something must be done to improve its performance. Boardman and one of the beneficiaries under the trust, P, went along to the annual general meeting of

---

[73] (1971) 23 D.L.R. (3d) 632.
[74] In *Island Export Finance Ltd v. Umunna* [1986] B.C.L.C. 460 at 481 Hutchinson J. approved of the proposition formulated by Laskin J. except insofar as it "could justify holding former directors accountable for profits wherever information acquired by them as such led them to the source from which they subsequently, perhaps as the result of prolonged fresh initiative, acquired business."
[75] The *O'Malley* decision is analysed by D.D. Prentice (1974) 37 M.L.R. 464.
[76] [1986] B.C.L.C. 460.
[77] [1967] 2 A.C. 46.

the company as representatives of the trust. They attempted unsuccessfully to have P elected to the board of directors of the company. Shortly after this meeting Boardman and P decided to try to obtain control of the company by themselves purchasing shares. They acted with the knowledge of two of the trustees. The third trustee was senile. The trustees had no power to invest trust monies in shares of the company. An application to the court for permission would be necessary to do so. The negotiations for the acquisition of the shares were somewhat prolonged. In the course of these negotiations Boardman purported to represent the trust and thereby acquired information about the affairs of the company that would be unavailable to members of the general public. Boardman and P bought the shares and were instrumental in having carried through a corporate reorganisation that resulted in capital distributions to shareholders which did not impact adversely on the value of the shares. In this way the trust benefited to the tune of £47,000 whereas Boardman and P made a profit of around £75,000. Could they retain this profit?

The House of Lords by a three-to-two majority and confirming the decision of the lower courts said not.[78] This conclusion was reached despite the fact that the good faith of Boardman and his colleague was never questioned. Boardman and P, who was to be treated as a co-adventurer in the whole affair, had placed themselves in a fiduciary relationship by acting as representatives of the trust for a number of years. Arising from this fiduciary relationship they had obtained the opportunity to make a profit and the knowledge that there was a profit to be made. Some commentators have criticised the actual decision in the case on the basis that the standards it imposes are too stringent.[79] In other words, the argument is that equitable principles have been carried to an inequitable conclusion. Be that as it may, the exact nature of the relief granted by the House of Lords is clouded in ambiguity and obscurity. The reasoning in the case is framed in the language of constructive trusteeship with the obvious proprietary overtones but maybe this is just a reflection of the way in which the case was argued. The Privy Council in *Att.-Gen. for Hong Kong v. Reid*[80] however thought that there was greater significance attached to the expressions of constructive trusteeship. According to Lord Templeman the solictor was held to be a constructive trustee by a majority of the House of Lords in *Boardman v. Phipps* because the solicitor obtained the information which satisfied him that the purchase of the shares in the take-over company would be a good investment and the opportunity of acquiring the shares as a result of acting for certain purposes on behalf of the trustees.[81] The Privy Council in *Reid* said that if a fiduciary acting honestly and in good faith and making a profit which his principal could not make for himself becomes a constructive trustee of that profit, then *a fortiori* a fiduciary acting dishonestly and criminally who accepts a bribe and thereby causes loss and damage to his principal must also be a constructive trustee.

While this explanation of *Boardman v. Phipps* is certainly a plausible one it is

[78] Lords Guest, Hodson and Cohen formed the majority while Viscount Dilhorne and Lord Upjohn dissented.
[79] See for example the articles by Professor Gareth Jones (1968) 84 L.Q.R. 472 and (1970) 86 L.Q.R. 463.
[80] [1994] 1 All E.R. 1.
[81] [1994] 1 All E.R. 1 at 11. Reference was made to certain observations of Lord Cohen in *Boarmdan v. Phipps* [1967] 2 A.C. 46 at 103.

not completely convincing.[82] The writ in the action claimed that the defendants held the shares as constructive trustees for the plaintiff and secondly an account of the profits made by the defendants out of the shares. The *Weekly Law Reports* records the conclusions of Wilberforce J. as follows[83]:

> "Declaration that the first and second defendants were accountable: directions that an account be taken and enquiry held as to the allowances to which they were entitled. Plaintiff to have costs. Further consideration of order to transfer the shares held by the defendants and payment of any profit found on the taking of the account adjourned."

There is no reference to a declaration of constructive trusteeship nor it appears was there any order for the transfer of shares. It must be conceded however that the judgment has not been consistently reported.[84]

Lords Cohen, Hodson and Guest formed the majority in the House of Lords. Lord Cohen talked about accountability. He said that the defendants were accountable to the plaintiff for his share of the net profits which they derived from the transaction. Both Lord Hodson and Lord Guest adopted an "information is property" analysis and consequently imposed liability on that basis.[85] It is only in the judgment of Lord Guest however that the issue of constructive trusteeship is addressed. He said that the defendants held the shares as constructive trustees and were bound to account to the plaintiff.[86] One point that must be stressed is that the defendants were solvent and indeed wealthy. The issue of priority in the event of insolvency was simply irrelevant in the case.[87]

The same comment applies with respect to *Industrial Development Consultants v. Cooley*.[88] In this case the defendant was managing director of the plaintiff company. He failed in an attempt to obtain on behalf of the company a valuable contract with the local gas board. The Gas Board subsequently approached him

---

[82] While not directly in point, the comments of Gibbs J. in the Australian case *Consul Development Pty Ltd v. D.P.C. Estates Pty. Ltd* (1975) 5 A.L.R. 231 at 249 illustrate the general situation. He said: "The question whether the remedy which the person to whom the duty is owed may obtain against the person who has violated the duty is proprietary or personal may sometimes be one of some difficulty. In some cases the fiduciary has been declared a trustee of the property which he has gained by his breach; in others he has been called upon to account for his profits and sometimes the distinction between the two remedies has not ... been kept clearly in mind."

[83] [1964] 1 W.L.R. 993 at 1018.

[84] The *All England Reports* record a declaration of constructive trusteeship: see [1964] 2 All E.R. 187.

[85] Dr. Paul Finn has said that perhaps the most sterile of the debates which have arisen around the subject of information received in confidence is whether or not such information should be classified as property—see *Fiduciary Obligations* (1977), p. 131. For an overview of this whole area see Palmer and Kohler "Information as Property" in *Interests in Goods* (Palmer and McKendrick eds., 1993), Chap. 7.

[86] [1967] 2 A.C. 46 at 117.

[87] See the comment by Hayton (1990) 106 L.Q.R. 87 at 102: "The plaintiff beneficiary was happy to seek an order making the wealthy defendant personally liable to account for his profit less the allowance, and thus the judges concentrated on this, rather than the form of order claimed by the plaintiff, which, as a preliminary, declared a constructive trust of the relevant shareholding... It seems that, despite the form of the court order, the case should be interpreted only as authority for personal liability and not as one involving a proprietary constructive trust, expecially when three of the five members of the House of Lords emphasised that the information exploited by the defendant was incapable of protection by an injunction, and was not to be regarded as trust property." See also Crilley [1994] *Restitution Law Review* 57.

[88] [1972] 1 W.L.R. 443.

with an offer to take up the contract in his personal capacity and it intimated that it was still not interested in letting the company have the contract. The defendant concealed the offer from the company, and by misrepresenting that he was in poor health, procured the company to release him from service contract, so that he was free to take up the gas board contract himself. It was held by Roskill J. that he was liable to account to the company for the profit which he obtained from performing the contract, on the footing that he should have informed the company of the gas board's offer to him and that, after the offer was made, he embarked on a deliberate policy and course of conduct which put his personal interest as a potential contracting party with the gas board in direct conflict with his pre-existing and continuing duty as managing director of the company. The judgment does not distinguish between personal accountability and constructive trusteeship and in this respect mirrors *Boardman*.[89] Making the distinction was not necessary to the resolution of the case.

PROPRIETY OF PROPRIETARY RELIEF

The question of the appropriateness or otherwise of granting proprietary relief for breaches of fiduciary duty has engendered considerable academic debate which obviously has profound practical consequences.[90] An elaborate exercise in classification has been attempted by Professor R.M.Goode.[91] He distinguishes four basic situations as follows:

Class 1: Enrichment by subtraction where the claim of the plaintiff has a proprietary base.
Class 2: Enrichment by an equitable wrong producing deemed agency gains.
Class 3: Enrichment by an equitable wrong producing wrongs other than deemed agency gains.
Class 4: Enrichment by a wrong producing gains not resulting from breach of equitable obligation.

In the scheme of things envisaged by the good professor Class 1 claims would give rise to a constructive trust that was automatic in its application. Class 2 situations would generate a constructive trust of the remedial variety with the court tailoring the relief granted so as to safeguard the position of secured and unsecured creditors. The other categories of case would simply result in a money judgment with no proprietary consequences. Criticisms that might be levelled against the scheme are those of over-elaboration and the difficulties experienced in ascribing concrete cases to one category or another. For instance, take the facts of *Cook v. Deeks*.[92] Is this a category one case or not? Professor Goode says

---

[89] The judgment was issued *ex tempore* and records that "an order for an account will be issued because the defendant made and will make his profit as a result of having allowed his interest and his duty to conflict".

[90] It is impossible to do justice to the literature but for something of a non-English perspective see Emily Sherwin [1989] 2 *University of Illinois Law Review* 297; David Paciocco (1989) 68 *Canadian Bar Review* 315 and W.M.C. Gummow in *Essays on Restitution* (Paul Finn ed., 1990) at 47.

[91] See generally Goode "Property and Unjust Enrichment" in *Essays on the Law of Restitution* (A.S. Burrows ed., 1991) at 215–247 and see also Goode "The Recovery of a Director's Improper Gains: Proprietary Remedies for Infringement of Non-proprietary Rights" in *Commercial Aspects of Trusts and Fiduciary Obligations* (McKendrick ed., 1992).

[92] [1916] A.C. 554.

not. In his conception there are three cases which suffice to constitute a proprietary base.[93] There are as follows:

(1) An asset was transferred by the plaintiff to the defendant in circumstances such that the defendant never had, or had lost, the right to the asset.
(2) The asset can be identified under the tracing rules as the proceeds or product of another asset so transferred.
(3) The defendant has intercepted money or property to which the plaintiff had a direct right *vis-à-vis* the transferor.

The restitutionary terminology of Professor Peter Birks has proved popular in this area and the three examples serve as instances of what Professor Birks has described as subtractive enrichment.[94] They do not encompass however the whole field of interceptive subtraction. In particular one important case of interceptive subtraction highlighted by *Cook v. Deeks* is left out.[95] The reference is to a situation where but for intervention by the defendant an asset such as a contract would have reached the hands of the plaintiff from a third party. According to Professor Goode any constructive trust in such a case is of a remedial character. In his view, fairness to the general creditors of the defendant requires that any costs of acquisition incurred by the defendant which the plaintiff did not have to meet should be reimbursed as a condition of the court making a proprietary award.[96] Other commentators would treat the *Cooks v. Deeks* type as a straightforward case that justifies automatic proprietary relief. The following passage comes from Professor Birks[97]:

> "[I]t is possible for the subtraction sense of ["at the expense of"] to reach receipt from a third party, and in principle it is easy to say in what circumstance it can do so. If the wealth in question would certainly have arrived in the plaintiff if it had not been intercepted by the defendant en route from the third party, it is true to say that the plaintiff has lost by the defendant s gain....[T]he conclusion is not artifical. The certainty that the plaintiff would have obtained the wealth in question does genuinely indicate that he became poorer by the sum in which the defendant was enriched."

It is submitted that provided the acquisition costs of the asset in question are met by the plaintiff there is no good reason for denying him an entitlement to a proprietary remedy.

The treatment by Professor Goode of so-called deemed agency gains is also somewhat controversial in terms of existing English law. Deemed agency gains refer to situations where it was the duty of the defendant to obtain an asset if he obtained it at all not for himself but for the plaintiff. At the moment English

---

[93] In Burrows ed., *Essays on the Law of Restitution* (1991), pp. 215, 225.

[94] Professor Birks has written extensively on this whole area. For a flavour of his writing see *An Introduction to the Law of Restitution* (1985), pp. 133 *et seq.*

[95] According to Professor Goode case 3 represents only the first of the two forms of interceptive subtraction—see Goode *op. cit.* at 225.

[96] *ibid.* at 226. He argues that if this is done, such creditors have no ground for complaint even if the value of the asset exceeds the acquisition costs, for the effect in either case is to put the defendant's estates back into the position in which it would have been if the defendant had not acted in breach of duty to the plaintiff in the first place.

[97] *An Introduction to the Law of Restitution* (1985), pp. 133–134. Professor Birks admits however that there is some difficulty about the circumstances in which you can say that the plaintiff would certainly have received the money if the defendant had not.

seems to veer towards acceptance of the proposition that such situations generate proprietary remedies for the plaintiff. Of course the issue of insolvency has not been squarely addressed in cases like *Boardman v. Phipps*.[98] Professor Goode argues for a discretionary approach towards the grant of proprietary relief. This kind of analysis commended itself to the Supreme Court of Canada in *Lac Minerals Ltd v. International Corona Resources Ltd*[99] but so far has not found judicial adherents on this side of the Atlantic. The merits of the competing views will be assessed later on in this chapter. First however, it is appropriate to look at the third category of case considered by Professor Goode. This encompasses all instances in which the gain received by the defendant in breach of his equitable duty is not of a kind that he should have procured it for the defendant. Examples would be gains derived from an activity that is unconnected with any existing or prospective line of business of the plaintiff and also bribes.[1] In these situations Goode argues, there should be personal accountability but no proprietary remedy. Insofar as bribes were concerned, this analysis had the support of the old Court of Appeal decision in *Lister v. Stubbs*[2] but the Privy Council has recently adopted a radically different perspective in *Att.-Gen. for Hong Kong v. Reid*.[3] So emphatic was the rejection of *Lister v. Stubbs* that it would be a brave lawyer indeed who would contend that it still represents the law in England.[4] Nevertheless the decision deserves an examination for the context it lends the discussion.

LISTER V. STUBBS

In this case the defendant Stubbs was authorised by the plaintiff company to purchase materials for use in their business as silk-spinners, dyers and manu-facturers. In the course of his duties, Stubbs improperly received from trade customers large sums by way of secret commission. These payments were made so as to induce him to place orders with the customers. A large part of the secret commissions had been invested in land and the plaintiffs sought an injunction to restrain Stubbs from dealing with the land and also an order directing him to bring the remaining cash and other investments into court. The application failed. It was held that the plaintiffs were not the owners of the money wrongly taken nor of the investments purchased. The relationship between the parties was merely that of debtor and creditor. Lindley L.J. put the matter thus[5]:

---

[98] [1967] 2 A.C. 46.
[99] (1989) 61 D.L.R. (4th) 14 on which see J.D. Davies [1990] L.M.C.L.Q. 4 and Birks [1990] L.M.C.L.Q. 460. See also the Australian High Court case *Warman International v. Dwyer* (1995) 128 A.L.R. 201.
[1] See Goode in A.S. Burrows ed., *Essays on the Law of Restitution* (1991), pp. 230–231.
[2] (1890) 45 Ch.D. 1.
[3] [1994] 1 All E.R. 1.
[4] See the comment by Nolan (1994) 15 Co. Law 3 at 5. Others have contended that *Lister v. Stubbs* should not be consigned to the footnotes of English legal history; see Crilley [1994] *Restitution Law Review* 57 at 72. It is noteworthy that *Lister v. Stubbs* was still referred to, notwithstanding *Reid*, by Peter Gibson L.J. speaking for the Court of Appeal in *Halifax Building Society v. Thomas* [1995] 4 All E.R. 673 at 681.
[5] (1890) 45 Ch.D 1 at 15. Lindley L.J. also spoke about the dangers of confounding ownership and obligation. See also Cotton L.J. at p. 12: "... this is not the money of the plaintiffs, so as to make the defendant a trustee of it for them, but it is money acquired in such a way that, according to all the rules applicable to such a case, the plaintiffs, when they bring the action to a hearing, can get

"I apprehend that [the defendant] is liable to account for it the moment that he gets it. It is an obligation to pay and account to Messrs Lister & Co, with or without interest, as the case may be. I say nothing at all about that. But the relation between them is that of debtor and creditor; it is not that of trustee and cestui que trust. We are asked to hold that it is—which would involve consequences which, I confess, startle me. One consequence, of course would be that, if Stubbs were to become bankrupt, this property acquired by him with the money paid to him by Messrs. Varley would be withdrawn from the mass of his creditors and be handed over bodily to Lister & Co. Can that be right? Another consequence would be that, if the Appellants are right, Lister & Co could compel Stubbs to account to them, not only for the money with interest, but for all the profits which he might have made by embarking in trade with it. Can that be right?"

Some people would answer yes to the last rhetorical question. Be that as it may, it is well to remember, leaving aside *Reid*, that the actual decision in *Lister v. Stubbs* may be different today. The case involved an application for an injunction to restrain disposal of assets by the defendant before the trial of the action. The action was dismissed on the basis that the plaintiff was not the owner of the assets in question. In those days ownership was a condition of success in the action. The advent of the *Mareva* injunction breaks the nexus with ownership.[6] The plaintiffs would now be able to obtain their injunction if their was a strong likelihood that the defendant would be able to frustrate any judgment against him by moving assets out of the jurisdiction or by dissipating them within the jurisdiction. The goal posts have shifted but that does not of itself affect the ownership issue addressed in *Lister v. Stubbs*.[7]

The *Lister* decision follows that in *Metropolitan Bank v. Heiron*[8] though the latter case has often been marginalised as one concerned with the effect of the limitation statutes which decisions are said to be peculiarly unreliable outside their particular context.[9] Basically the company instituted proceedings against a director in respect of the receipt of a bribe more than seven years before. It was held that the action was statute barred notwithstanding the fact that the Statute of Limitations did not impinge upon actions against defaulting trustees. One interpretation of the decision is that the exception is confined to express trustees and so does not encompass constructive trustees.[10] There is another strand to

---

an order against the defendant for the payment of that money to them. That is to say, there is a debt due from the defendant to the plaintiffs in consequence of the corrupt bargain ..."

[6] See the comments by Birks [1988] L.M.C.L.Q. 128 at 135. and also the remarks of Megarry V.C. in *Barclay-Johnston v. Yuill* [1980] 1 W.L.R. 1259 at 1263–1266.

[7] See the comments of Ackner L.J. in *A.J. Bekhor & Co Ltd v. Bilton* [1981] Q.B. 923 at 945–946: "[I]t must be borne in mind that the foundation of the jurisdiction is the need to prevent judgments of the court from being rendered ineffective by the removal of the defendant's assets from the jurisdiction ... The *Mareva* injunction was not intended to rewrite the English law of insolvency ... The purpose of the *Mareva* was not to improve the position of claimants in an insolvency but simply to prevent the injustice of a defendant removing his assets from the jurisdiction which might otherwise have been available to satisfy a judgment. It is not a form of pre-trial attachment but a relief *in personam* which prohibits certain acts in relation to the assets in question."

[8] (1880) 5 EX D 319.

[9] In *Att.-Gen. for Hong Kong v. Reid* [1994] 1 All E.R. 1 Lord Templeman opined that the same result in the case could have been achieved by denying an equitable remedy on the grounds of delay or ratification.

[10] See generally T.G. Youdan "The Fiduciary Principle: The Applicability of Proprietary Remedies" in *Equity, Fiduciaries and Trusts* (Youdan ed., 1989), p. 98.

the case however with various dicta supporting the proposition that the action was over a simple debt. Cotton L.J. for example said[11]:

"Here the money sought to be recovered was in no sense the money of the company.... It is very different from the case of *a cestui que* trust seeking to recover money which was his own before any act wrongfully done by the trustee."

The principle enunciated in *Lister v. Stubbs* appeared to be a deeply entrenched one with many cases following the lead given.[12]

Lister v. Stubbs was followed by Leggatt J. in the civil context in *Islamic Republic of Iran Shipping Lines v. Denby.*[13] In this case a solicitor received a bribe from an opposing litigant to compromise a case. He was held to be accountable for the amount of the bribe but no proprietary consequences ensued. It must be said however that *Lister v. Stubbs* was followed without any great criticism.[14] It is also true to say that *Lister v. Stubbs* has been subjected to a considerable volume of criticism.[15] A lot of the criticism centres around the apparent disparity in treatment between the honest fiduciary exemplified in *Boardman v. Phipps*[16] and the corrupt fiduciary as typified by *Lister v. Stubbs.* The honest fiduciary is deemed to be a constructive trustee whereas personal accountability is the order of the day insofar as his dishonest counterpart is concerned. At first blush, this strikes one as distinctly odd. One's instinct would be to say that the roles should be reversed.[17] Of course if one reads *Boardman v. Phipps* in a different way as it is possible to do and say that all it was concerned about was personal accountability, the adverse comment is substantially undermined.

Certain commentators have contended that *Lister v. Stubbs* is seriously deficient in terms of precedent, principle and policy.[18] It is argued that the reliance placed in the case on *Metropolitan Bank v. Heiron* was flawed in that *Heiron* is inextricably bound up with a consideration of the statute of limitations and decisions thereon are of limited general application.[19] The objection in terms of principle centres on the fact that the Court of Appeal in *Lister* seemed to think that restitutionary remedies were exclusively personal in nature.[20] The possible proprietary dimensions of restitutionary claims were simply not appreciated in the case. Goff and Jones contend[21]:

[11] (1880) 5 Ex D 319 at 325. James L.J. also expressed the view that the liability of the director was that of a debtor.

[12] See *Powell & Thomas v. Evan Jones & Co* [1905] 1 K.B. 11 and see also the comments of Gibbs C.J. in *Daly v. Sydney Stock Exchange* (1986) 160 C.L.R. 371 at 379–380.

[13] [1987] 1 Lloyd's Rep 367; on which see Birks [1988] L.M.C.L.Q. 128.

[14] Leggatt J. spoke of the temptation to hold that a proprietary remedy was available for the defendant's breach of his fiduciary duties: see [1987] 1 Lloyd's Rep 367 at 371.

[15] For just some of the criticism see Sir Peter Millett [1993] *Restitution Law Review* 7; Sir Anthony Mason in *Essays in Equity* (Paul Finn ed., 1985) at 246; Underhill and Hayton, *Law Relating to Trusts and Trustees* (14th ed., 1987) p. 305; Paul Finn, *Fiduciary Obligations* (1977) at para 513; Meagher, Gummow & Lehane, *Equity Doctrine and Remedies* (3rd ed. 1992), pp. 152–157; A.J. Oakley, *Constructive Trusts* (2nd ed., 1987), p. 56.

[16] [1967] 2 A.C. 46.

[17] See Gareth Jones (1968) 84 L.Q.R. 463 at 502.

[18] See Youdan "The Fiduciary Principle; The Applicability of Proprietary Remedies" in *Equity, Fiduciaries and Trusts* (Youdan ed., 1989), p. 98.

[19] See Donovan Waters, *The Constructive Trust* (1964), p. 296.

[20] See Youdan, *op. cit.*, at 98.

[21] (3rd ed., 1986), p. 657.

"If it is accepted that a constructive trust may be a remedy to prevent unjust enrichment and to give the plaintiff the additional benefits which flow from the creation and imposition of such a trust, the reasoning in *Lister v. Stubbs* ceases to be persuasive."

In terms of policy the Court of Appeal in *Lister v. Stubbs* questioned the justice of allowing the principal of a bribed agent to enjoy priority over the general creditors of the agent.[22] Others have disputed the assumption underlying the judgment of the Court of Appeal[23]:

"[I]t would seem to be right and proper [that the employer should have priority over the employee's general creditors;] more proper than that those general creditors, whose conduct has not been in any way affected by Stubbs' apparent wealth, should take advantage of a windfall which should never have belonged to Stubbs.... As between the plaintiffs and Stubbs, and as between the plaintiffs and Stubbs creditors, it is submitted that the plaintiffs had the better right."

The argument is that the agent should never have received the bribe monies in the first place. To allow the general creditors to participate in this accretion to the wealth of the agent would be to provide them with a windfall at the expense of the principal to whom the corrupt agent is accountable.[24]

Has the agent profited at the expense of his principal? In other words are we talking about a case of subtractive enrichment and in particular the subhead of interceptive subtraction.[25] The words of Romer L.J. in *Hovenden and Sons v. Millhoff*[26] are worth quoting in this context. He said[27]:

"First, the court will not inquire into the donor's motive in giving the bribe, nor allow evidence to be gone into as to the motive. Secondly, the court will presume in favour of the principal and as against the briber and the agent bribed, that the agent was influenced by the bribe; and this presumption is irrebuttable. Thirdly, if the agent be a confidential buyer of goods for his principal from the briber, the court will assume as against the briber that the true price of the goods as between him and the purchaser must be taken to be less than the price paid to, or charged by, the vendor, by at any rate, the amount or value of the bribe. If the purchaser alleges loss or damage beyond this, he must prove it."

In cases like *Lister v. Stubbs* and *Islamic Republic of Iran Shipping Lines v. Denby* it is easy to say that the agent has been enriched at the expense of the principal. If a person is prepared to pay somebody representing the other party to the transaction a secret commission then it logical to suppose that the person is willing to pay the opposing party that bit more. One commentator argues that there is an incontrovertible assumption that the bribe has been taken at the

---

[22] (1890) 45 Ch.D. 1 at 15 *per* Lindley L.J.

[23] See Ronald Maudsley (1959) 75 L.Q.R. 234 at 244–245.

[24] But see the counter-argument advanced by Professor R.M. Goode (1987) 103 L.Q.R. 433 at 444: "To accord the plaintiff a proprietary right to the benefit obtained by the defendant, and to any profits or gains resulting from it, at the expense of the defendant's unsecured bankruptcy creditors seems completely wrong, both in principle and policy, because the wrong done to the plaintiff by the defendant's improper receipt is no different in kind from that done to creditors who have supplied goods and services without receiving the bargained-for payment, so that the debtor's default has swelled his assets at their expense."

[25] This argument is developed by Youdan *op. cit.*

[26] (1900) 83 L.T. 41.

[27] *ibid* at 43.

expense of the victim who will have lost property of a value at least equal to the bribe received by the fiduciary, so that the bribe may justifiably be regarded as representing the victim's property.[28] It is submitted that acceptance of this proposition is stretching things too far. It fails to bring into the reckoning cases like *Att.-Gen. for Hong Kong v. Reid*. One cannot buy immunity from successful prosecution which the corrupt fiduciary was in effect selling in that case. It is proposed now to subject *Reid* to detailed analysis.

ATT.-GEN. FOR HONG KONG V. REID[29]

The facts of the case fall within a short compass. Reid was a national of New Zealand who happened to be in the employ of the Hong Kong government where he held the prominent position of director of the Commercial Crime Unit in the Colony. Unfortunately Reid grossly abused the trust reposed in him by the Hong Kong government and accepted large amounts to obstruct the prosecution of criminals. Eventually the day of judgment dawned. Reid was convicted of bribery, sentenced to imprisonment and ordered to pay HK$12.4 million under the Prevention of Bribery Ordinance. This judgment remained unsatisfied. No payment on foot of the judgment was ever received from him. Some of the monies received as bribes, Reid had invested in properties in New Zealand. It was claimed by the Attorney-General for Hong Kong that these properties were held on a constructive trust for the Crown and an order was sought that would inhibit dealings by Reid with the properties. The Crown was only entitled to this relief if it was entitled to a proprietary claim on the assets in question.

ADVANTAGES OF PROPRIETARY RELIEF IN THE CASE

Essentially the Crown were making a proprietary claim in the case to circumvent the difficulties inherent in enforcing judgments across international frontiers. The motives of Reid in opposing the applicant while failing to satisfy the outstanding judgment against him seem equally stark. According to Lord Templeman who delivered the judgment of the Privy Council in the case the course of action followed by Reid must have reflected the hope that the properties in the absence of an appropriate order, could be sold and the proceeds "whisked away to some Shangri-La which hides bribes and other corrupt moneys in numbered bank accounts."[30] One might say that there must be something wrong with the process of enforcing judgments if an order made in 1990 can

---

[28] See Youdan, *op. cit.*, at 98: "Even if there is not an irrebuttable presumption that the receipt of a bribe by a buying agent from a vendor causes the principal to lose a discount in an amount corresponding to the value of the bribe, it will ordinarily be easy for the principal to prove that such a loss in fact occurred."

[29] [1994] 1 All E.R. 1; [1994] A.C. 324. The *Reid* decision has generated an enormous welter of articles and comment. For just some of the literature see Birks [1988] L.M.C.L.Q. 128 and [1993] L.M.C.L.Q. 30; Millett [1993] *Restitution Law Review* 7; Crilley [1994] *Restitution Law Review* 57; J.C. Smith (1994) 110 L.Q.R. 180; Nolan (1994) 15 Co. Law 3; Pearce [1994] L.M.C.L.Q. 189; Allen (1995) 58 M.L.R. 87: Cowan, Edmunds and Lowry [1996] J.B.L. 22.

[30] [1994] 1 All E.R. 1 at 12.

remain completely unsatisfied in 1993.[31] It is a truism to say that the execution in one jurisdiction of an order made in another is laborious and productive of difficulty. There is also the problem concerning characterisation of the confiscation order made in Hong Kong. If it was regarded as a criminal sanction then one has to confront squarely the principle that criminal penalties imposed in one jurisdiction are generally not directly enforceable in another.[32] The constructive trust approach adopted by the Privy Council shortcircuits these potential obstacles to effective enforcement. It may be that it was these practicalities that Lord Templeman had in mind when he talked about the proceeds of the properties being whisked away to some Shangri-La which hides bribes and other corrupt moneys in numbered bank accounts.

Authority was used by Lord Templeman to undermine the foundations of the principle propounded in *Lister v. Stubbs*.[33] In his view the decisions of the Court of Appeal in *Metropolitan Bank v. Heiron*[34] and *Lister v. Stubbs* were inconsistent with earlier authorities which were not cited in those cases. None of these so-called prior inconsistent authorities are conclusive however.

In *Fawcett v. Whitehouse*[35] and *Sugden v. Crossland*[36] the language of trusteeship is used but nothing necessarily turns on the point. There was no talk of priority for the principal over general creditors in the event of the agent's insolvency. Proprietary relief as such is not an issue. The authorities indeed support the subtle distinction drawn by Professor Goode between rights in *rem* (proprietary rights) and rights *ad rem*.[37] In his framework an *ad rem* right is a personal right to the transfer or delivery of an asset or to a charge or lien on it. It may be characterised as a right to the asset rather than a right in or over it. An order to transfer a specific asset would not of itself change the ownership or protect the plaintiff from the consequences of the defendant's insolvency. The plaintiff would acquire a real right in the asset only through enforcement of the order or the defendant's compliance with it prior to bankrupty.[38] This analysis explains the well known case of *Keech v. Sandford*[39] where the trustee of leasehold property took a renewal of the lease for his own benefit after the landlord refused to grant a renewal for the benefit of the infant beneficiary. The orders made by Lord King that the lease be assigned and that the trustee account to the infant for any profit made are perfectly explicable on a right *ad rem* analysis. Particular reliance was placed by Lord Templeman on the observations of Jessel M.R. in *Re Caerphilly Colliery Co.*[40] In this case the Master of the Rolls said *a propos* the bribed fiduciary[41]:

---

[31] As Pearce ([1994] L.M.C.L.Q. 189 at 193) points out the same problem affects anyone with an unsatisfied judgment. He asks: "Should the employer of a corrupt employee be more favourably treated in this respect than the person injured in a road accident who has obtained an unsatisfied order for damages? . . . It is not desirable to confer a proprietary interest on a claimant for no better reason than it would aid the enforceability of the judgment."

[32] See generally Nolan (1994) 15 Co. Law 3 at 4.

[33] (1890) 45 Ch.D. 1.

[34] (1880) 5 ExD 319.

[35] (1829) 1 Russ. & M. 132; 39 E.R. 51.

[36] (1856) 3 Sm. & G. 192; 65 E.R. 620.

[37] See his essay "Property and Unjust Enrichment" in *Essays on the Law of Restitution* (A.S. Burrows ed., 1991), p. 215.

[38] See Goode, *op. cit.*, at 221–222.

[39] (1726) Sel. Cas. Ch. 61.

[40] Pearson's Case (1877) 5 Ch D 336.

[41] *ibid* at 341.

"He must be deemed to have obtained [the bribe] under circumstances which made him liable, at the option of the cestuis que trust, to account either for the value at the time of the present he was receiving or to account for the thing itself and its proceeds if it had increased in value."

According to Lord Templeman this was an emphatic pronouncement by the most distinguished equity judge of his generation that the recipient of a bribe holds the bribe and the property representing the bribe in trust for the injured person.[42] It is submitted, with respect, that it is no such thing. In my view, the remarks suggest an account of profits rather than a constructive trust properly so called. It is submitted also that the faith place by Lord Templeman in the maxim, "Equity considers as done that which ought to have been done" is somewhat misplaced. It was said that as soon as the bribe was received, whether in cash or in kind, the false fiduciary holds the bribe on a constructive trust for the person injured. If this maxim is applied across the board in the way signposted by Lord Templeman then the whole field of personal obligations in equity has been eviscerated. Personal rights automatically have proprietary consequences. One is immediately repelled by the far reaching consequences of the proposition. There is also the view that application of the maxim in the context under discussion only produces the proposition that an account owed is treated as an account given. The matter is addressed by Professor Birks[43]:

"If there was only a duty to account, and no other explanation as to why an asset in the hands of the accountant already belonged to the plaintiff, the maxim could only yield the quaint result that an account due was an account given. If that meant anything at all, it meant only that a sum of money which the taking of the account would find to be owing should be regarded as owing even before the figure was acertained. There might be some contexts in which that could have a practical bearing, but it certainly could not be made to produce a proprietary interest in any specific thing."

What about the antiquity of *Lister v. Stubbs*? Was this a reason for not overruling it? Lord Templeman commented that while over one hundred years had passed since *Lister v. Stubbs* was decided, no one could be allowed to say that he had ordered his affairs in reliance on the two decisions of the Court of Appeal. What about third parties? Have they not been left out of the equation? The court said that the unsecured creditors could not be in a better position than their debtor. Lord Templeman observed:[44]

"The authorities show that property acquired by a trustee innocently but in breach of trust and the property from time to time representing the same belong in equity to the cestui que trust and not to the trustee personally whether he is solvent or insolvent. Property acquired by a trustee as a result of a criminal breach of trust and the property from time to time representing the same must also belong in equity to his *cestui que* trust and not to the trustee whether he is solvent or insolvent"

Some might argue that the authorities show no such thing. At best they are equivocal. Some commentators have contended that Lord Templeman seriously

---

[42] [1994] 1 All E.R. 1 at 7.
[43] [1993] L.M.C.L.Q. 30 at 32.
[44] [1994] 1 All E.R. 1 at 5.

downplayed the position of third party creditors. The following comment, although predating Lord Templeman's judgment, seems appropriate[45]:

"the wrong done to the plaintiff by the defendant's improper receipt is not different in kind from that done to creditors who have supplied goods and services without receiving the bargained-for payment, so that the debtor's fault has swelled his assets at their expense. Indeed, it is strongly arguable that they should be in a better position, for they have parted with property against a promised payment, whereas our plaintiff has not parted with anything and may not have lost anything."

The argument is why should an equitable wrong like breach of a fiduciary obligation be treated any differently in terms of insolvency consequences from a common law wrong like defamation.[46] The retort might be that in many cases the amount of the bribe paid to the corrupt would have gone to the principal in the form of enhanced payment for the goods or services in question.[47] So the case is one of subtractive enrichment rather than merely an equitable wrong. Even in cases like *Reid* where this is not strictly so the principal has in some sense suffered a diminution by the act of bribery. Lord Templeman waxed lyrical on this particular topic describing bribery as an evil practice which threatens the foundations of any civilised society. He continued[48]:

"Where bribes are accepted by a trustee, servant, agent or other fiduciary, loss and damage are caused to the beneficiaries, master or principal whose interests have been betrayed. The amount of loss or damage resulting from the acceptance of a bribe may or may not be quantifiable."

In concluding the discussion on *Reid* one might say that the arguments for and against granting a proprietary remedy are more evenly balanced than is apparent from the judgment of the Privy Council. The considerations are more evenly balanced. Be that as it may, there is some merit in awarding proprietary relief. It has been argued that the bribery cases represent a situation where the courts should have discretion to impose a remedial constructive trust where it appears just to do so.[49] This would have the advantage of achieving justice in the case at hand, while leaving the courts free to do justice to creditors as the need may arise in future cases. Moreover, the proposition advanced in *Reid* that

---

[45] See R.M. Goode "Ownership and Obligation in Commercial Transactions" (1987) 103 L.Q.R. 433 at 444–445. Professor Goode adds that the court should exercise particular care before recognising a proprietary claim in proceedings potentially affecting unsecured bankruptcy creditors whose interests are not represented in the litigation.

[46] See Pearce [1994] L.M.C.L.Q. 189 at 195.

[47] The words of Romer L.J. in *Hovenden and Sons v. Milhoff* (1900) 83 L.T. 41 at 43 are worth repeating in this context. He said: "First, the court will not inquire into the donor's motive in giving the bribe, nor allow evidence to be gone into as to the motive. Secondly, the court will presume in favour of the principal and as against the briber and the agent bribed, that the agent was influenced by the bribe; and that this presumption is irrebuttable. Thirdly, if the agent be a confidential buyer of goods for his principal from the briber, the court will assume as against the briber that the true price of the goods as between him and the purchaser must be taken to be less than the price paid to, or charged by, the vendor by, at any rate, the amount or value of the bribe. If the purchaser alleges loss or damage beyond this, he must prove it."

The point is developed by Tim Youdan "The Fiduciary Principle: The Applicability of Proprietary Remedies" in *Equity, Fiduciaries and Trusts* (Youdan ed., Carswell Toronto, 1989) pp. 92 *et seq.*

[48] [1994] 1 All E.R. 1 at 4.

[49] See Allen (1995) 58 M.L.R. 87 at 94.

bribe monies received by a corrupted agent are invariably held on a constructive trust for the principal has far reaching implications in the criminal sphere.[50] The Privy Council in *Reid* appears to have brought about a major *sub silentio* change in the criminal law by their attitude towards the recognition of proprietary claims. The criminal law consequences of *Reid* will now be discussed.

REID AND THE CRIMINAL LAW

The *Lister v. Stubbs* principle was applied in the criminal context in *Powell v. MacRae*.[51] This is a case where the defendant was employed as a turnstile operator at Wembley Stadium and was paid £2 to admit somebody who had not got a ticket to an event at the stadium. He was charged and convicted of stealing £2 cash, the property of his employers, contrary to section one of the Theft Act 1968. The defendant successfully appealed against conviction on the basis that the definition of theft in section one of the 1968 Act had not been satisfied. According to the court while he was the recipient of a bribe, by no stretch of language could it be said that the money "belonged to" the employers.

To the same effect is the decision of the House of Lords in *Tarling v. Singapore Republic Government*.[52] In this case the court, by a majority, took the view that an agreement by company directors to acquire and retain a secret profit for which they were accountable to the shareholders was not evidence of an agreement to defraud. Lord Wilberforce opined that "the making of a secret profit is no criminal offence, whatever other epithet may be appropriate".[53] He also said that breach of fiduciary duty, exorbitant profit-making, secrecy and failure to comply with the law as to company accounts was one thing whereas theft and fraud were different.

The same result obtained in cases decided prior to the introduction of the Theft Act 1968.[54] One might cite *R. v. Cullum*[55] in this connection. In this case the captain of a barge, contrary to instructions from the barge owner, carried a particular cargo and pocketed the resultant freight charge. Was he guilty of embezzling the barge owner's money? The court said not. Bramwell B. in the archaic terminology of the day observed that the servant undoubtedly did not receive the money "for" his master, nor "on account of" his master, nor "in the name" of his master.[56] Blackburn J. asked during the course of the argument, expecting a negative response, "Suppose a private coachman used his master's carriage without leave and earned half a crown, would the money be received for the master, so as to become the property of the latter?"[57] The result reached in the case was obviously to the liking of the Criminal Law Revision Committee

---

[50] See generally J.C. Smith (1994) 110 L.Q.R. 180 at 185.
[51] [1977] Crim L.R. 571.
[52] (1977) 70 Cr. App. R. 77.
[53] *ibid.* at 111.
[54] See generally on this whole area A.T.H. Smith, "Constructive Trusts in the Law of Theft" [1977] Crim. L.R. 395.
[55] (1873) L.R. 2 C.C.R. 28.
[56] (1873) L.R. 2 C.C.R. 28 at 32.
[57] *ibid.* at 30.

who, despite academic prompting,[58] decided to recommend no change in the law. The Committee observed[59]:

"although the conduct when it occurs is reprehensible enough to deserve punishment, it does not seem to us that it occurs often enough to involve a substantial problem or to require the creation of a new criminal offence."

The general issue of potential criminal liability in this sphere was considered in *Att.-Gen.'s Reference (No. 1 of 1985)*[60] where *R. v. Cullum* was favourably mentioned. In the view of Lord Lane C.J. section 5(3) of the Theft Act 1968 was intended to reproduce the result in that case.[61] The subsection provides:

"Where a person receives property from or on account of another, and is under an obligation to the other to retain and deal with that property or its proceeds in a particular way, the property or proceeds shall be regarded (as against him) as belonging to the other."

Re Att.-Gen.'s Reference (No. 1 of 1985) is a case where a brewery employee, the manager of a tied public house, made a secret profit by selling, in breach of contract, his own beer rather than that supplied by his employer. Was the employee guilty of theft in respect of the profit element on the beer sales? The Court of Appeal said not. The employee was accountable to the employer for the element of profit on the beer sales but the latter had no proprietary rights in this profit element so as to render the employee guilty of theft. According to the court there was a clear and important difference between a person misappropriating specific property with which he had been entrusted, and on the other hand a person in a fiduciary position who uses that position to make a secret profit for which he will be held accountable.[62] Lord Lane C.J. added that the draftsmen of the Theft Act 1968 must have had the decision in *Lister v. Stubbs* in mind when considering the wording of section 5.[63]

If the *Reid* decision represents the law in England then, as one distinguished commentator has pointed out, it has a profound effect on the law of theft, making a substantial extension of the crime which the Criminal Law Revision Committee expressly declined to recommend and which it must be assumed Parliament, having considered the Committee's report, did not intend to make.[64] Moreover, it is an extension which goes far beyond the modest reform proposal which the Committee considered and rejected. Quite apart from a possible comment about judicial usurpation of the legislative function, one might argue that the constructive trust is an insecure foundation for criminal liability given the complexity of the concept. As Lord Lane said notably in *Att.-Gen.'s Reference (No. 1 of 1985)* there are topics of conversation more popular in public houses than the finer points of the law relating to constructive trusts.

[58] By J.C. Smith (1956) 19 M.L.R. 39 who argued that the criminal law should be broadened to encompass the case of an employee who earns secret profits by unauthorised use of his employer's property.
[59] Cmnd. 2977 at para. 57(iii) (8th Report 1966).
[60] [1986] Q.B. 591; [1986] 2 All E.R. 219.
[61] [1986] 2 All E.R. 219 at 222.
[62] *ibid.* at 223.
[63] *ibid.* at 225. The Lord Chief Justice said that had they intended to bring within the ambit of the 1968 Act a whole new area of behaviour which had previously not been considered to be criminal, they would have used much more explicit words than those which are to be found in s. 5.
[64] (1994) 110 L.Q.R. 180 at 183.

One might take the view that *Reid* was correctly decided on its facts yet still surmount the pitfalls presented by retrospective criminalisation of conduct previously considered free of penal associations. This view would mean adopting the position that the court has a discretion to impose a constructive trust in cases of bribe-taking. This discretion should not however be exercised so as to impose criminal liability in the *Att.-Gen.'s Reference (No. 1 of 1985)* type situation or in cases of possible prejudice to creditors of the bribe recipient.

CURRENT STATE OF THE LAW

At the moment the position in English law seems to be that all breaches of fiduciary obligations, whether they be honest or dishonest generate proprietary remedies in favour of the wronged principal. There is the authority of *Att.-Gen. for Hong Kong v. Reid* in respect of corrupt breaches of duty.[64a] *Boardman v. Phipps* is taken as establishing the same principle for innocent breaches of trust though the point is not directly addressed in the case. Is there a case for differentiating between honest and dishonest fiduciaries?[65] The case for a distinction has been pressed by Professor Gareth Jones[66]:

"[T]he principal should be allowed a proprietary claim only if the court considers it appropriate that he should be granted the additional benefits which naturally flow from such a grant. The honest fiduciary who is deemed to have breached his duty of loyalty but has not been unjustly enriched and whose principal has suffered no loss should only be liable to account for his profits. On the other hand, a fiduciary who is dishonest or has otherwise manifestly disregarded his principal's interest should be held to be a constructive trustee of the benefits obtained at his principal's expense."

This preoccupation with honesty and probity may be questioned. While it may have some bearing on the situation *vis-à-vis* principal and agent third parties are affected in the same way irrespective of whether the fiduciary has been honest or dishonest. In both cases if a proprietary remedy is made available to the principal, the estate of the insolvent agent will suffer a diminution thus reducing the amount that may be distributed to them.

There is Canadian support in the shape of *Lac Mineral Ltd v. International Corona Resources Ltd*[67] for a discretionary approach towards the grant of proprietary remedies where wrongdoing but basically honest fiduciaries are concerned. This decision will now be analysed.

[64a] But see the Statement of Scott V.C. in *Att.-Gen. v. Blake* [1996] 3 All E.R. 903 at 912 that the disapproval by the Privy Council in *Reid* or *Lister v. Stubbs* did not relieve him from the obligation as a first instance judge in the English jurisdiction of accepting its authority.
[65] See also the decision of the House of Lords in *Att.-Gen. v. Guardian Newspapers (No. 2)* [1990] 1 A.C. 109 (the *Spycatcher* case). In this case it was held that members of the Security Services owed a lifelong duty of confidentiality, surviving retirement, to the Crown. While the matter is not fully discussed there are suggestions in some of the judgments that the copyright in books written in circumstances that contravene this duty of confidentiality are held on a constructive trust for the Crown. See Lords Keith, Griffiths and Goff in the House of Lords at 262–263, 275 and 288 respectively. The issue is also ventilated by Dillon L.J. in the Court of Appeal at 211 and by Scott J. at first instance who says at 161 that the profit made through the use of confidential information "in equity, belongs to the owner of the information." See also *Att.-Gen. v. Blake* [1966] All E.R. particularly at 912 *per* Scott V.C.
[66] (1968) 84 L.Q.R. 463 at 502.
[67] (1989) 61 D.L.R. (4th) 14; on which see Davies [1990] L.M.C.L.Q. 4; Birks [1990] L.M.C.L.Q. 460.

DISCRETION IN CANADA—*LAC MINERALS LTD V. INTERNATIONAL CORONA RESOURCES LTD*

The facts of this case, shortly stated, are as follows. The plaintiff, Corona, was a recently formed mining company that had mining rights to certain land in Northern Ontario on which it was conducting exploratory drilling. The tests revealed the fact that land immediately adjacent to its property was probably gold bearing. Corona approached LAC, a better established and financed mining company, with a view to forming a joint venture so as to develop the adjacent land. In the course of these discussions Corona revealed the results of the drilling which was obviously significant information known only to itself. Corona attempted to acquire the mining rights to the adjacent property only to lose out to a competing bid put in by LAC. LAC proceeded to develop a mine on the adjacent property for its own account. The Supreme Court of Canada held that in so doing it was in breach of a duty not to misuse confidential information. The court differed about whether there was incumbent upon LAC a fiduciary obligation not to misuse the information. La Forest and Wilson JJ. thought that there was such a duty. A majority of the court made up of Sopinka, McIntyre and Lamer JJ. disagreed. Sopinka and McIntyre JJ. also took the view that the appropriate remedy for the wronged party was damages rather than the award of a constructive trust. Lamer J. in effect was the "swing" judge adopting the line that there was no fiduciary relationship but nevertheless the most suitable outcome in the circumstances of the case was the declaration of a constructive trust rather than the award of monetary damages.

It seems clear however that the majority of members of the court believed that they had a choice as to remedy.[68] Once liability had been shown the remedy did not come neatly pre-packaged. The court had a deliberate choice to exercise about awarding damages or creating a constructive trust. This is clear for instance from the judgment of Wilson J. She suggested that the remedy of constructive trust was available for breach of confidence as well as for breach of fiduciary duty.[69] The distinction between the two causes of action as they arose on the facts of this particular case was a very fine one. Inherent in both causes of action were concepts of good conscience and vulnerability. She thought that it would be strange if the law accorded them widely disparate remedies. In her view, the only sure way in which Corona could be fully compensated for the breach of duty in this case was by the imposition of a constructive trust on LAC in favour of Corona with respect to the property. Full compensation might or might not be achieved through an award of damages depending upon the accuracy of valuation techniques. It could certainly be achieved through the award of a proprietary remedy. La Forest J., with whom Lamer J. concurred on the remedy aspect, also adverted to the difficulties in making an accurate assessment of loss given the unique nature of the property in question.[70] In his

---

[68] McIntyre and Sopinka JJ. thought that a constructive trust should only be awarded in the most exceptional circumstances in cases of breach of confidence. The remedial flexibility of the majority judges has been applauded by J.D. Davies who says ([1990] L.M.C.L.Q. 4 at 5): "There is much to be said for the majority view that, if a ground of liability is established, then the remedy that follows should be the one that is most appropriate on the facts of the case rather than one derived from history or over-categorisation."

[69] (1989) 61 D.L.R. (4th) 14 at 17.

[70] See generally (1989) 61 D.L.R. (4th) 14 at 44–52.

view this strongly suggested the appropriateness of a proprietary remedy. He endorsed the following observations in the court below[71]:

"... there is no question but that gold properties of significance are unique and rare. There are almost insurmountable difficulties in assessing the value of such a property in the open market. The actual damage which has been sustained by Corona is virtually impossible to determine with any degree of accuracy. The profitability of the mine, and accordingly its value, will depend on the ore reserves of the mine, the future price of gold from time to time, which in turn depends on the rate of exchange between the U.S. dollar and Canadian dollar, inflationary trends, together with myriad other matters, all of which are virtually impossible to predict."

La Forest J. was also of the opinion that to adopt the approach of awarding damages would have the effect not of encouraging bargaining in good faith but of encouraging the contrary. He said that if by breaching an obligation of confidence one party is able to acquire an asset entirely for itself, at a risk of only having to compensate the other for what the other would have received if a formal relationship between them were concluded, the former would be given a strong incentive to breach the obligation and acquire the asset. The insolvency issue was directly addressed. La Forest J. thought it fair that Corona should have priority over other creditors in the event of LAC going into liquidation. Essentially this was so because the judge believed that the case was one of "interceptive subtraction". LAC intercepted the plaintiff and thereby frustrated its efforts to obtain a specific and unique property that the courts below held would otherwise have been acquired. The recognition of a constructive trust simply redirects the title of the property to its original course.[72]

The judge also focussed on the moral quality of the defendants act but he did not place so much emphasis on this factor. La Forest J. said[73]:

"Allowing the defendant to retain a specific asset when it was obtained through conscious wrongdoing may so offend a court that it would deny to the defendant the right to retain the property. This situation will be more rare, since the focus of the inquiry should be upon the reasons for recognising a right of property in the plaintiff, not on the reasons for denying it to the defendant."

Sopinka J., with whom McIntyre J. agreed, dissented as to the appropriateness of the particular remedy. He thought that there was no fiduciary relationship between the parties and moreover that a declaration of a constructive trust was not apposite in cases of breach of confidence. He pointed out that the conventional remedies for breach of confidence are an accounting of profits or damages. An injunction might be coupled with either of these remedies in appropriate circumstances. A restitutionary remedy was appropriate in cases involving fiduciaries because they were required to disgorge any benefits derived from the breach of trust. In a breach of confidence case, the focus was on the loss to the plaintiff and, as in tort actions, the particular position of the plaintiff must be examined. The object was to restore the plaintiff momentarily to the

[71] *ibid.* 49. La Forest J. added that to award only a monetary remedy in such circumstances when an alternative remedy was both available and appropriate would be unfair and unjust.
[72] *ibid.* at 51.
[73] *ibid.* at 51–52.

position he would have been in if no wrong had been committed.[74]

It should be noted that one of the other judges in the case, Wilson J. eschewed any strict divide between fiduciary wrongs and other types of wrongdoing. She adopted the following rhetorical question of Professor John D. McCamus[75]:

> "Would it not be anomalous to allow more sophisticated forms of relief for breach of fiduciary duty than for those forms of wrongdoing recognised by the law of torts, some of which, at least, would commonly be more offensive from the point of view of either public policy or our moral sensibilities than some breaches of fiduciary duty?"

THE AUSTRALIAN APPROACH

The High Court of Australia seemed to think however that it clearly had a discretion to award a constructive trust remedy for breaches of fiduciary duty in *Warman International v. Dwyer.*[76] This is a case where the plaintiff were agents for the distribution of Italian gearboxes in Australia. The gearbox manufacturers suggested to them a joint venture arrangement for the assembly of its products in Australia but the plaintiffs were unreceptive to this proposal. The manufacturers then terminated the agency agreement with the plaintiffs and proceeded to form a joint venture with the defendant. The latter was the employee of the plaintiffs most intimately associated with the distributorship. He had not however been consulted about the plaintiffs' decision to reject the manufacturers' proposal. The turn of events incensed the plaintiffs who sought a declaration that the goodwill of the joint venture was held on trust for them and an account of profits to date. The statement of claim also talked about a declaration that the defendant held his shares in the joint venture company in trust but this argument was not pressed forward.[77] The High Court held that there had been a breach of fiduciary duty and imposed a personal liability to account for certain profits of the joint venture. With respect to the appropriateness of a proprietary remedy the court observed[78]:

> "The outcome in cases of this kind will depend on a number of factors. They include the nature of the property, the relevant powers and obligations of the fiduciary and the relationship between the profit made and the powers and obligations of the fiduciary. Thus, according to the rule in *Keech v. Sandford*, a trustee of a tenancy who obtains for himself the renewal of a lease holds the new lease as a constructive trustee even though the landlord is unwilling to grant it to the trust. But the 'rule depends partly on the nature of leasehold property' and partly on the position which the trustee occupies. A similar approach will be adopted in a case in which a fiduciary acquires for himself a specific asset which falls within the scope and ambit of his fiduciary responsibilities, even if the asset was acquired by means of the skill and expertise of the fiduciary and would not otherwise have been available to the person to whom the fiduciary duty is owed.

---

[74] *ibid.* at 76–77.

[75] (1989) 61 D.L.R. (4th) 14 at 17. The quote comes from "The Role of Proprietary Relief in the Modern Law of Restitution" *Cambridge Lectures 1987* 141 at 150. See also Birks [1990] L.M.C.L.Q. 460 at 462 who argues that the historical origin in equity of the wrong of breach of confidence should not entitle it to a divergent remedial regime.

[76] (1995) 182 C.L.R. 544; (1995) 128 A.L.R. 201.

[77] See the statement in the joint judgment of Mason C.J., Brennan, Deane, Dawson and Gaudron JJ.; (1995) 128 A.L.R. 201 at 213.

[78] (1995) 128 A.L.R. 201 at 211–212.

But a distinction should be drawn between cases in which a specific asset is acquired and cases in which a business is acquired and operated . . ."

CONCLUSION

At the moment, following from *Reid*, one can interpret the English position as saying that proprietary relief is available as a matter of right in all cases of breach of fiduciary duty.[79] In this chapter the case for a more discretionary approach is advanced. I would suggest that proprietary relief is appropriate where the defendant has misappropriated the plaintiff's property or where the defendant has intercepted assets that would otherwise have gone to the plaintiff. Such relief may also be justified where there are acute difficulties in assessing damages or where there would be considerable difficulties in enforcing a money judgment. In these cases however the position of general creditors of the defendant has to be borne in mind and the order of the court may have to be structured so as to avoid prejudice to their interests.[80] The honesty or otherwise of the defendant's conduct should not normally be a pertinent consideration since as has been presciently observed the "focus of the inquiry should be upon the reasons for recognising a right of property in the plaintiff, not on the reasons for denying it to the defendant."[81]

The foregoing analysis begs the question as to why fiduciary wrongs should be treated differently from other wrongs? In other words why should the victims of fiduciary wrongs be more favourably treated in the sense of being accorded the possibility of proprietary remedies, compared with the victims of common law wrongs? As an answer, albeit not a wholly convincing answer, one might refer to historical precedents. Claims arising out of the abuse of a relationship of trust and confidence, have traditionally been treated differently from common law claims. Moreover, the facts of *Cook v. Deeks*[82] adverted to already, demonstrate the difficulty in distinguishing between a straightforward misappropriation of property and a simple fiduciary wrong with no property deprivation. If proprietary relief is available automatically in the first instance, then there should at least be the possibility of this form of relief in the second. There are comments by Lord Browne-Wilkinson in *Westdeutsche Bank v. Islington L.B.C.*[83] which suggest that a discretionary approach towards the award of proprietary remedies is not completely excluded in this particular instance in England. He talked about proprietary relief constituting a suitable road forward and added;[84]

"The Court by way of remedy might impose a constructive trust on a defendant who

---

[79] But see the statement of Laddie J. in *Nelson v. Rye* [1996] 2 All E.R. 186 at 199 that not all breaches of fiduciary duty give rise to constructive trusts. It may be argued, however, that this case is not a strong authority since, it is concerned in reality with an express trust arising by virtue of an agency relationship rather than a constructive trust.

[80] While this Chapter does not follow the line advocated by Professor R.M. Goode in his essay "Property and Unjust Enrichment" in *Essays on the Law of Restitution* (A.S. Burrows ed., 1991), p. 215 this essay at p. 240 *et seq.* provides valuable guidance as to the form such orders might take and the considerations that have to be borne in mind.

[81] The quote comes from La Forest J. in *LAC Minerals v. International Corona Resources* (1989) 61 D.L.R. 14 at 52.

[82] [1916] A.C. 554.

[83] [1996] 2 W.L.R. 801; [1996] 2 All E.R. 961

[84] [1996] 2 W.L.R. 802 at 839. Compare *Halifax Building Society v Thomas* [1995] 4 All E.R. 673 in the English Court of Appeal; on which see Birks [1996] *Trust Law International* 2.

knowingly retains property of which the plaintiff has been unjustly deprived. Since the remedy can be tailored to the circumstances of the particular case, innocent third parties would not be prejudiced and restitutionary defences, such as change of position, are capable of being given effect. However, whether English law should follow the United States and Canada by adopting the remedial constructive trust will have to be decided in some future case when the point is directly in issue."

Be that as it may, it is true to say that the judgment of Lord Browne-Wilkinson in *Westdeutsche* contains a number of general pronouncements not securely grounded on a detailed analysis of the case law or competing principles. This appears to have attracted the ire of Lord Goff who made a number of what can only be described as pointed comments: Lord Goff said it was not the function of the House of Lords to rewrite the agenda for the law of restitution, nor even identify the role of proprietary claims in that part of the law.[85] In his view, the judicial process was neither designed for, nor properly directed towards, such objectives. Taking into account the subtle nuances of judicial expression, I think that it is possible to read into his observations some piercing criticism directed in particular at Lord Browne-Wilkinson. Lord Goff said[86]

"I regard it as particularly desirable that your Lordships should, so far as possible, restrict the inquiry to the actual questions at issue in this appeal, and not be tempted into formulating principles of a broader nature. If restitution lawyers are hoping to find in your Lordships' speeches broad statements of principle which may definitively establish the future shape of this part of the Law, I fear that they may be disappointed. I also regard it as important that your Lordships should, in the traditional manner, pay particular regard to the practical consequences which may flow from the decision of the House."

[85] Lords Browne-Wilkinson, Slynn and Lloyd formed the majority, Lords Goff and Woolf dissented from the actual conclusion in the case.
[86] [1996] 2 W.L.R. 802 at 810.

CHAPTER SIX

Proprietary Restitutionary Remedies— the Remedial Constructive Trust

In many cases it is argued before the courts that they should award priority to a particular person in the event of insolvency by declaring that that person is a beneficiary under a remedial constructive trust. In this chapter the doctrine of the constructive trust will be considered and a distinction drawn between family and commercial cases but first it is useful to say something about the nature and classification of constructive trusts in general.

THE CONSTRUCTIVE TRUST

Constructive trusts arise independently of the intention of the parties.[1] In certain circumstances equity deems the legal owner of property to be constructive trustee for another.[2] The famous American jurist, Cardozo J., put the matter eloquently when he said in *Beatty v. Guggenheim Exploration Co.*[3]:

"A constructive trust is the formula through which the conscience of equity finds expression. When property has been acquired in such circumstances that the holder of the legal title may not in good conscience retain the beneficial interest, equity converts him into a trustee."

As a generalisation it is fair to say that broad statements of general principle have never appealed much to English judges. An obvious exception is the former Master of the Rolls, Lord Denning. In a number of sweeping judgments in the early 1970's Lord Denning attempted to import into English law the constructive trust on the American model. Evidence of these efforts is demonstrated in *Hussey v. Palmer*.[4] In this case the Master of the Rolls suggested that a constructive trust "is a trust imposed by law whenever justice and good conscience require it . . . it is an equitable remedy by which the court can enable an aggrieved party to obtain restitution."[5]

In furtherance of this objective he made somewhat selective use of certain observations of Lord Diplock in *Gissing v. Gissing*.[6] In that case Lord Diplock declared[7]:

---

[1] See generally A.J. Oakley, *Constructive Trusts* (2nd ed., 1987). See also D.W.M. Waters, *The Constructive Trust: The Case for a New Approach in English Law* (1964) and for a more theoretical analysis G. Elias, *Explaining Constructive Trusts* (1990).
[2] See also the statement by the distinguished American academic Professor Austin Scott (1955) 71 L.Q.R. 39 at 41L: "The court does not give relief because a constructive trust has been created; but the court gives relief because otherwise the defendant would be unjustly enriched; and because the court gives this relief it declares that the defendant is chargeable as a constructive trustee"
[3] 225 N.Y. 380 at 386 (1919).
[4] [1972] 1 W.L.R. 1286.
[5] *ibid.* at 1289–1290.
[6] [1971] A.C. 886.
[7] *ibid.* at 905.

"A resulting, implied or constructive trust—and it is unnnecessary for present purposes to distinguish between these three classes of trust—is created by a transaction between the trustee and the *cestui que* trust in connection with the acquisition by the trustee of a legal estate in the land, whenever the trustee has so conducted himself that it would be inequitable to allow him to deny to the *cestui que* trust a beneficial interest in the land acquired. And he will be held so to have conducted himself if by his words or conduct he has induced the *cestui* trust to act to his own detriment in the reasonable belief that by so acting he was acquiring a beneficial interest in the land."

Lord Diplock in *Gissing* did not draw any distinction between a resulting and a contrustive trust. Lord Denning was guilty of the same vice, if one might call it that, in *Hussey v. Palmer*. In that case Lord Denning pointed out that the plaintiff had argued for the existence of a resulting trust whereas he thought it was more in the nature of a constructive trust. At the end of the day the Master of the Rolls thought that this was more a matter of words than anything else. The two ran together.

STATUTORY FORMALITY REQUIREMENTS

The legislation however appears to draw a clear distinction between resulting and constructive trusts. The relevant provision is found in section 53(2) of the Law of Property Act 1925 which is concerned with formality requirements. The subsection states that the documentary demands imposed in relation to trusts by section 53(1) do not affect the "creation or operation of resulting, implied or constructive trusts". The statutory terminology seemingly suggests a four-fold classification of trusts with express trusts on the one hand ranged against resulting, implied and constructive trusts on the other. It is more usual however to view the phrase "implied trusts" as an umbrella expression encompassing both resulting and constructive trusts.[8] That leaves a division with express trusts on one side of the line and resulting/constructive trusts on the other hand. Resulting trusts are commonly said to be based on the presumed intention of the parties whereas constructive trusts arise by operation of law and come into being independently of the parties intention. Resulting trusts arise in certain stereotypical situations where the legal owner of property is assumed to have intended that the property should be held for the benefit of another.[9] A typical example would be where a conveyance is taken in the name of A alone whereas the purchase price has been put up by B. In such a situation A holds the property on a resulting trust for B unless there is positive evidence of a donative intention on the part of A.[10]

CLASSIFYING CONSTRUCTIVE TRUSTS

Mapping out the prototype of the constructive trust is no easy matter. One view conceives of the constructive trust as some sort of legal dustbin or as one commentator opines "a vague dust-heap for the reception of relationships which

---

[8] See generally A.J. Oakley, *Constructive Trusts* (2nd ed., 1987).
[9] See generally Kevin Gray *Elements of Land Law* (2nd ed., 1993), pp. 382–384.
[10] The word "resulting" comes from the Latin "resultare" or "resalire" "to spring back".

are difficult to classify or which are unwanted in other branches of the law."[11] Be that as it may, there is some sort of murky consensus about the categories of relationships that come within the compass of the constructive trust. Most observers would say that a constructive trust arises in the following situations[12]:

(1) where a fiduciary has profited in one form or another from a breach of his duty of loyalty;
(2) under the *Barnes v. Addy*[13] principle where there has been a disposition of property in breach of trust and either knowing receipt of the trust property or knowing assistance in the breach of trust.
(3) where there has been fraudulent or unconscionable conduct and a person has profited thereby;
(4) where a mortgagee has exercised the power of sale a constructive trust is said to arise with regard to the moneys generated by the sale;
(5) secret trusts and mutual wills.

This process of categorisation is not free from controversy and some judges and commentators would reject the designation of constructive trust being applied to secret trusts.[14] Moreover the categories are susceptible of subdivision. The class of constructive trust that arises wherever a person has obtained an advantage through fraudulent or unconscionable conduct particularly lends itself to this operation. For instance there is the general principle that no criminal may benefit from his crime[15] and also the proposition that equity will not allow a statute to be used as an instrument of fraud.[16] An example of a case within the first subhead would be where a beneficiary under a will murders the testator. This circumstance prevents the beneficiary from benefiting under the will and the constructive trust is the mechanism by which such preclusion is achieved. The policy rationale underlying this doctrine was stated with clarity by Fry L.J. in *Cleaver v. Mutual Reserve Fund Life Association*.[17] He said[18]:

"It appears to me that no system of jurisprudence can with reason include among the

---

[11] See generally Sykes "The Doctrine of Constructive Trust" (1941) 15 Aust. L.J. 171, 175 quoted by D.W.M. Waters in "The Remedial Constructive Trust" in *The Frontiers of Liability: Volume 2* (Birks ed., 1994).

[12] See generally A.J. Oakley, *Constructive Trusts* (2nd ed., 1987). See also the classification adopted by R.P. Austin "Constructive Trusts" in *Essays in Equity* (P.D. Finn ed., Sydney 1985).

[13] (1874) 9 Ch. App. 244.

[14] There is a distinction between fully secret and half-secret trusts. With a half-secret trust the existence of the trust is apparent on the face of the will but the identity of the beneficiaries are unknown. In the case of the fully secret trust on the other hand there is no reference to the trust from the terms of the will.

[15] *Ex turpi causa non oritur ius.*

[16] The doctrine of part performance which developed so as to render enforceable a contract for the sale of an interest in land notwithstanding the absence of written evidence is a manifestation of this principle.

[17] [1892] 1 Q.B. 147.

[18] *ibid.* at 156. These observations were quoted with approval by Lord Atkin in *Beresford v. Royal Insurance Co. Ltd* [1938] A.C. 586 at 596. The forfeiture rule is now defined for the purpose of the Forfeiture Act 1982 as "the rule of public policy which in certain circumstances precludes a person who has unlawfully killed another from acquiring a benefit in consequence of the killing."

rights which it enforces rights directly resulting to the person asserting them from the crime of that person."[19]

The classic manifestation of the other subhead occurs where reliance is placed on statutory formality requirements such as those appertaining to land contained in the Law of Property Act 1925 to deny a claim of beneficial entitlement. A constructive trust is employed to correct the injustice that would otherwise be occasioned. Lindley L.J observed in *Rochefoucauld v. Boustead*[20]:

> "It is fraud on the part of a person to whom land is conveyed as a trustee and who knows it is so conveyed to deny the trust and to claim the land for himself. Consequently, notwithstanding the statute, it is competent for a person claiming land conveyed to another to prove by parol evidence that it was so conveyed upon trust for the claimant, and that the grantee, knowing the facts, is denying the trust and relying upon the form of conveyance and the statute to keep the land himself."[21]

While the boundaries are not marked out with exact precision the circumstances in which a constructive trust arises are generally well established. In that sense the constructive trust might be described as a substantive institution rather than a general free-wheeling remedy invoked on a more discretionary basis by judges who may feel that personal rather than proprietary remedies are inappropriate or inadequate in a particular case.[22] In *Westdeutsche Bank v. Islington L.B.C.*[22a] Lord Browne-Wilkinson offered some interesting views on the nature of the constructive trust and in doing so distinguished between the institutional trust and the remedial constructive trust. He said[22b]:

> "Under an institutional constructive trust, the trust arises by operation of law as from the date of the circumstances which give rise to it: the function of the Court is merely to declare that such trust has arisen in the past. The consequences that flow from such trust having arisen (including the possibly unfair consequences to third parties who in the interim have received the trust property) are also determined by rules of law, not under a discretion. A remedial constructive trust ... is different. It is a judicial remedy giving rise to an enforceable equitable obligation: the extent to which it operates retrospectively, to the prejudice of third parties lies in the discretion of the Court."

---

[19] The court is sanctioned by s. 2 of the Forfeiture Act 1982 to modify the operation of the rule if having regard to the conduct of the offender and of the deceased and other material circumstances, the justice of the case requires the effect of the rule to be so modified. On the exercise of the discretion conferred by the section see *Re K* [1986] Ch. 180.

[20] [1897] 1 Ch. 196 at 206.

[21] For an application of the principle enunciated by Lindley L.J. see *Bannister v. Bannister* [1948] 2 All E.R. 133. See also *Binions v. Evans* [1972] Ch. 359 and *Ungurian v. Lesnoff* [1990] Ch. 206.

[22] In the New Zealand case, *Dickie v. Torbay Pharmacy (1986) Ltd* [1995] 3 N.Z.L.R. 429, Hammond J. attempted to sum up the substantive institution versus remedial device controversy. His comments, while illuminating, do not however accurately represent the current English judicial position. He said (at p. 441): "As to the nature of a constructive trust, there has been a great deal of juristic debate as to whether such is a substantive institution, or a remedial device. And is such declaratory of something that always existed—and hence is more like an express trust? Or, is it "constituted", and hence essentially a remedial vehicle? Or, is there more than one kind of constructive trust? My own view is that, functionally, constructive trusts can (and do) serve a variety of purposes and whether such should be decreed must turn less on abstract theory than on the facts of a given case; the nature of the "wrong" committed; whether proprietary relief is appropriate; and the variety of discretionary considerations which routinely attend an exercise of this kind."

[22a] [1996] 2 W.L.R. 802; [1996] 2 All E.R. 961.

[22b] [1996] 2 W.L.R. 802 at 837.

The relative doctrinal rigidity has been the source of some tension when it comes up against changed patterns of living and increased cohabitation outside marriage. Typically in these cases we have got a situation where one party, normally a man, is sole legal owner while his estranged former cohabitee is claiming a proprietary interest in the property through the vehicle of the resulting or constructive trust. The non-legal owning party, to use an ungainly expression, may have contributued directly towards the acquisition of the property by paying all or part of the initial deposit or by meeting mortgage instalments. In other cases she may have assisted indirectly in the acquisition of the property by paying general household expenses or indeed by her house-keeping or by work within the home by tending to the needs of children. Where married spouses divorce there is a jurisdiction in the courts to reallocate property irrespective of strict legal entitlements.[23] A whole gamut of discretionary considerations may enter the equation in the judicial resolution of the property division issue. With unmarried cohabitation there is no such competence in the courts to reassign property on a discretionary basis following the breakdown of the relationship.[24] Other legislatures follow a different path and legislation has been enacted according the courts the capacity to reallocate property on the breakdown of a relationship. One might cite the New South Wales *De Facto Relationships Act 1984* in this connection. Under the Act a court has the power to[25]:

"make such order adjusting the interests of the partners in the property as to it seems just and equitable having regard to-
(a) the financial and non-financial contributions made directly or indirectly by or on

---

[23] The same obtains throughout most of Western Europe. Mary Ann Glendon has stated the matter thus in *The Transformation of Family Law* (1989) at 234: "Most divorces involve relatively young couples with minor children. Such couples typically have few assets other than the family dwelling, which may be leased, mortgaged, or owned. One way or another, courts everywhere, with more or less aid from legislation, endeavour to preserve the marital home or its use for the needed period of time for the custodial spouse and children. Thus, in terms of the outcomes of a very large group of cases, one can say that a new marital property regime has emerged—one which applies in the majority of divorces—and that its basic features are similar everywhere. Only Sweden has cast it in statutory form: possession of the home and its contents are to be awarded to the spouse "who needs it most".
For an excellent analysis of imputed trusts and family breakdown in England see Moffat, *Trusts Law: Text and Materials* (1994), Chap. 12 by John Dewar.

[24] It seems now that there is a jurisdiction in respect of the family home in cohabitation cases that involves in the same way as divorce cases. The jurisdiction was conferred by s. 12 of the Family Law Reform Act 1987 which inserted a provision into the Guardianship of Minors Act 1971. The provision has been re-enacted in amended form in para. 1 of the First Schedule to the Children Act 1989:
"1. (1) On an application made by either parent of a child, ... the court may—(a) in the case of an application to the High Court or a county court, make one or more of the orders mentioned in sub-paragraph (2);....
(2) The orders referred to in sub-paragraph (1) are ...(e) an order requiring either or both parents of a child (i) to transfer to the applicant, for the benefit of the child, or (ii) to transfer to the child himself, such property to which the parent is, or the parents are, entitled (either in possession or reversion) as may be specified in the order."
In *K. v. K. (minors: property transfer)* [1992] 2 All E.R. 727 it was held by the Court of Appeal that the court could make an order under this section that the father transfer to the mother his interest in the joint tenancy of the family home. See generally John Eekelaar "Non-marital property" in *The Frontiers of Liability; Volume 2* (Peter Birks ed., 1994), pp. 210–211.

[25] s. 20. On the New South Wales provision see generally Moffat, *Trusts Law: Text and Materials* (2nd ed., 1994), pp. 479–480

behalf of the *de facto* partners to the acquisition, conservation or improvement of any of the property of the partners or either of them or to the financial resources of the partners or either of them; and

(b)   the contributions, including any contributions made in the capacity of homemaker or parent, made by either of the *de facto* partners to the welfare of the other *de facto* partner or to the welfare of the family constituted by the partners and one or more of the following, namely-

(i)   a child of the partners;

(ii)   a child accepted by the partners or either of them into the household of the partners, whether or not the child is a child of either of the partners."

One of the difficulties with legislation of this kind is that there will always be troublesome cases that fall just outside the thresholds for consideration under the Act. In these cases the courts must fall back on common law and equitable principles. As well as the pragmatic there is an ideological perspective. One commentator has pointed to the proposition that the sanctity of property and its immunity to discretionary adjustment is deeply rooted in legal thought.[26] In his view such a state of affairs is dictated by respect for the individual and individual preferences and by the fear of prejudicing third parties.

The interests of third parties have often intruded in cases of quasi-matrimonial property. Often the property has been mortgaged to a bank or building society and the latter is endeavouring to enforce its security. The next stage is for the non-legal owner who is party to the cohabitation to assert a proprietary interest which binds the the chargee usually because her consent to the secured transaction was not obtained or because the creditor had notice of her claim.[27] Sometimes the couple are at one in supporting a benefical entitlement for the non legal owner and the chargee has the difficult task of adducing evidence to undermine the claim. Such was the situation in *McHardy and Sons v. Warren.*[28]

In this case husband and wife were living in amity together. The plaintiff trade creditors were grantees of a charge executed by the husband solely. They sought to enforce their security and repudiated the suggestion by husband and wife that the wife was a co-owner of the property in equity. Dillon L.J. who spoke for the Court of Appeal affirmed that the wife had a beneficial interest though the principles under which such a beneficial interest arose were not discussed at any length. In this case recognition of a beneficial interest clearly works to the manifest detriment of a third party creditor who has trusted appearances and dealt with the legal owner.[29]

In Australia, and more particularly in Canada, the courts have moulded the concept of the remedial constructive trust as a wide ranging and overrarching device that is capable of redressing perceived injustices in the resolution of

---

[26] See generally Professor Peter Birks "Proprietary Rights as Remedies" in *The Frontiers of Liability: Volume 2* (Peter Birks ed., 1994).

[27] A distinction has to be drawn between registered and unregistered land. With registered land there will be an overiding interest binding the land without registration of the interest if the claimant has a proprietary right and is in actual occupation of the land: see s. 70(1)(g) of the Land Registration Act 1925. In the case of unregistered land on the other hand, a beneficial proprietary interest binds all all those who take an interest in the property except a *bona fide* purchaser of a legal estate for value without notice of the prior equitable interest in the property.

[28] [1994] 2 F.L.R. 338.

[29] Lest one go overboard in sympathy for the trade creditor it must be pointed that they did not take the precaution another bank in the same case took of seeking the wife's concurrence to the charge and agreement to postpone her interest: see [1994] 2 F.L.R. 338 at 340.

matrimonial and quasi-matrimonial property disputes. Generally the judges have trod more warily in the commercial context but there are signs of the invocation of the constructive trust outside established categories. In considering the issue of the remedial constructive trust perhaps the best approach is to look at judicial handling of matrimonial/quasi-matrimonial property disputes in this jurisdiction, followed by an examination of some overseas comparisons and then to analyse whether there has been some "spillover" of more discretionary principles onto the commercial plane.

THE CONSTRUCTIVE TRUST AND THE RESOLUTION OF DOMESTIC PROPERTY DISPUTES

The starting point for the consideration of this issue must now be the judgment of Lord Bridge in *Lloyds Bank plc v. Rosset*[30] which was concurred in by all his brethren. According to Lord Bridge the first and fundamental question which must always be resolved is whether, independently of any inference to be drawn from the conduct of the parties in the course of sharing the house as their home and managing their joint affairs, there has at any time prior to acquisition, or exceptionally at some later date, been any agreement, arrangement or understanding reached between them that the property is to be shared beneficially. He continued[31]:

> "The finding of an agreement or arrangement to share in this sense can only, I think, be based on evidence of express discussions between the partners, however imperfectly remembered and however imprecise their terms may have been. Once a finding to this effect is made it will only be necessary for the partner asserting a claim to a beneficial interest against the partner entitled to the legal estate to show that he or she acted to her detriment or significantly altered his or her position in reliance on the agreement in order to give rise to a constructive trust or proprietary estoppel."

Lord Bridge distinguished between this situation and what he called the very different one where there was no evidence to support a finding of an agreement or arrangement to share, however reasonable it might have been for the parties to reach such an arrangement if they had applied their minds to the question. In the latter instance the court had to rely entirely on the conduct of the parties both as the basis from which to infer a common intention to share the property beneficially and as the conduct relied on to give rise to a constructive trust. In this situation Lord Bridge observed that direct contributions to the purchase price by the partner who was not the legal owner, whether initially or by payment of mortgage instalments, would readily justify the inference necessary to the creation of a constructive trust. His Lordship went on to say on the basis of a restrictive reading of the authorities which has been much criticised that it was extremely doubtful whether anything less than that would do.[32]

The exposition by Lord Bridge has considerable explanatory force and has

---

[30] [1991] 1 A.C. 107.
[31] *ibid.* at 132.
[32] [1991] 1 A.C. 107 at 133. For criticism see, *e.g.* Gray, *Elements of Land Law* (2nd ed., 1993) pp. 430–431.

the merits of clarity and ease of presentation. It does however mark something of a departure, at least on a linguistic level, from the existing case law. Fitting the cases into the framework envisaged by Lord Bridge smacks somewhat of *ex post facto* rationalisation though two cases could easily succomb to his analysis. Both of these cases, namely *Eves v. Eves*[33] and *Grant v. Edwards*[34] are indicative of the arrangement or understanding plus detriment scenario.[35] In *Eves v. Eves*[36] the male had intimated to the female that the only reason why the property was to be acquired in his name alone was because she was under the age of majority. But for her age he said that he would put the property into their joint names though he admitted in evidence that this was merely an "excuse".

Grant v. Edwards[37] involves a similar factual backdrop. Here the female partner was told by the male partner that the only reason for not acquiring the property in joint names was because she was involved in divorce proceedings. The explanation or excuse was that if the property was acquired jointly this might prejudice her in those proceedings. According to Lord Bridge the subsequent conduct of the female partner in each of these cases, which the court rightly held sufficient to generate a beneficial interest, fell measurably short of such conduct as would by itself have supported the claim in the absence of an express representation by the male partner that she was to have such an interest.

A case similar to *Lloyds Bank plc v. Rosset* that nestles in to the *Grant v. Edwards* and *Eves v. Eves* mould is *Hammond v. Mitchell*.[38] The case is also illustrative of the practial difficulties that are encountered when it comes to the application of the *Rosset* formula. Waite J. describes vividly the commencement of the relationship out of which the litigation sprang. He said[39]:

> "In the summer of 1977 Mr. Tom Hammond, a married man of 40 separated from his wife, was setting off for a ride in Epping Forest, when he had a chance encounter with Miss Vicky Mitchell, a 21-year-old girl who had stopped her car to ask the way. Their conversation led to further meetings and within a very short time they were living together."

The relationship endured for 11 years and the net value of the assets which the parties enjoyed at the time of their parting and were now in dispute approached £450,000. This dispute occupied 19 days of High Court time and cost the parties more than £125,000 between them in legal fees. A major part of the dispute concerned a large bungalow in Essex in which the parties

---

[33] [1975] 1 W.L.R. 1338.

[34] [1986] Ch. 638.

[35] In *Eves v. Eves* the woman did a great deal of work on the house and garden including the use of a sledgehammer. According to Brightman J.: "I find it difficult to suppose that she would have been the one wielding the 14-pound sledgehammer, breaking up the large area of concrete, filling the skip and doing the other things which were carried out when they moved it, except in pursuance of some expressed or implied arrangement and on the understanding that she was helping to improve a house in which she was to all practical intents and purposes promised that she had an interest."

[36] [1975] 1 W.L.R. 1338. According to Lord Denning the man never intended to put the property in joint names but always determined to have it in his own name. He should be judged however by what he told her -by what he led her to believe—and not by his own intent which he kept to himself.

[37] [1986] Ch. 638. See also *Midland Bank plc v. Dobson* [1986] 1 F.L.R. 171.

[38] [1991] 1 W.L.R. 1127; [1992] 2 All E.R. 109.

[39] [1992] 2 All E.R. 109 at 111.

cohabited. Waite J. after a detailed consideration of the factual matrix decided that that there had been express discussions which, although not precisely directed to the parties proprietary interests, were sufficient to amount to an understanding that the bungalow and the successive additions to it would be shared beneficially. The main evidence for this finding appears to be a conversation in which Hammond allegedly said[40]:

> "I'll have to put the house in my name because I have tax problems due to the fact that my wife burnt all my account books and my caravan was burnt down with all the records of my car sales in it. The tax man would be interested, and if I could prove my money had gone back into a property I'd be safeguarded."

It was further held that Miss Mitchell had acted to her detriment by her wholehearted participation in the commercial activities based at the bungalow which had they been unsuccessful would have involved the sale of the property to repay the bank.

A TERMINOLOGICAL CONUNDRUM

Some adverse comment has been made about the use by Lord Bridge of the terminology of the constructive trust throughout his judgment.[41] It is believed by many that reference to a resulting trust would have been more appropriate when one is assessing the degree to which contributions towards the acquisition of property might generate a beneficial interest. On the other hand, it is possible to reconcile the observations of Lord Diplock in *Rosset* with orthodox doctrine.[42] On this conception of things resulting trusts are confined to those arising on purchase because of the provision of resources towards the purchase and any trust that arises later is deemed to be a constructive trust. Contributions towards the payment of mortgage instalments would necessarily generate a constructive trust. For a resulting trust to come into being the beneficial interests should be fixed at the time of completion with the levels of contribution finalised at that time. Agreements reached about beneficial ownership only after completion and variations in the amount of contributions call forth a constructive trust.

INDIRECT CONTRIBUTIONS

Leaving matters of terminology aside, it is in relation to indirect contributions that the pronouncements of Lord Bridge are particularly controversial. Consideration of this question involves reference back to the twin peaks of *Pettitt v. Pettitt*[43] and *Gissing v. Gissing*.[44] In *Gissing* Lord Denning in the Court of Appeal applied the principle that any substantial contribution to general family expenses will invest the contributor with a share of the beneficial ownership in the family dwelling. *Gissing* involved a claim by a wife to part of the equity in the family

---

[40] [1992] 2 All E.R. 109 at 113.
[41] See, *e.g.* Gray, *Elements of Land Law* (2nd ed., 1993), pp. 430–431. According to Gray the ruling underlines the intense preoccupation with money payments whic dominates so much of the law of trusts. He suggests that the ruling is both confusing and severely restrictive.
[42] See generally Sparkes (1991) 11 O.J.L.S. 39 at 44–45.
[43] [1970] A.C. 777.
[44] [1971] A.C. 886.

dwelling grounded on the fact that she had paid for *inter alia*, furnishings and the laying of a lawn out of her earnings. The House of Lords overturned the Court of Appeal and unanimously rejected the claim. There were five judgments delivered and it is no easy matter to work out common strands of principle. Three of their Lordships seemed to think that "indirect" contributions would generate a beneficial interest in certain circumstances. Lord Pearson suggested that contributing to household expenses as part of an arrangement would count if they enabled the other party to pay off the mortgage. Lords Reid and Diplock envisaged as qualifying expenditure the payment of any household expenses that the other spouse would otherwise have to bear. For Lord Diplock there was an additional element. There had to be some referability between the acquisition of the property and the contribution by the claimant.[45]

In a series of cases led by Lord Denning the Court of Appeal removed the requirement of referability. One such cases is *Hazell v. Hazell*.[46] Here Lord Denning used language that was strongly reminiscent of the so-called "family assets" doctrine that was thoroughly rejected by the House of Lords in both *Pettitt* and *Gissing*. He said[47]:

> "It is sufficient if the contributions made by the [claimant] wife are such as to relieve the husband from expenditure which he would otherwise have had to bear. By so doing the wife helps him indirectly with the mortgage instalments because he has more money in his pocket with which to pay them. It may be that he does not strictly need her help—he may have enough money of his own without it—but if he accepts it (and thus is enabled to save more of his own money), she becomes entitled to a share."

Megaw L.J. took a similar tack. He said *a propos* referability[48]:

> "it would involve investigation of such questions, really reducing the proposition to an absurdity, as whether the husband, if the wife had not made this contribution to the housekeeping, would have cut down his smoking or drinking, or could have sold his car so as to incur less expenses in that way in order to provide the money which the wife in fact provided by her contribution."

The sweeping pronouncements of the Court of Appeal in *Hazell v. Hazell* were not to every judicial taste. The Northern Ireland Court of Appeal refused to recognise indirect contributions as generating a beneficial interest on the

---

[45] [1971] A.C.. 886 at 909. See also the comments of Lord Diplock in *Pettitt v. Pettitt* [1970] A.C. 777 at 826: "It is common enough nowadays for husband and wives to decorate and to make improvements in the family home themselves, with no other intention than to indulge in what is now a popular hobby, and to make the home pleasanter for their common use and enjoyment. If the husband likes to occupy his leisure by laying a new lawn in the garden or building a fitted wardrobe in the bedroom while the wife does the shopping, cooks the family dinner or bathes the children, I, for my part, find it quite impossible to impute to them as reasonable husband and wife any common intention that these domestic activities or any of them are to have any effect upon the existing proprietary rights in the family home on which they are undertaken. It is only in the bitterness engendered by the break-up of the marriage that so bizarre a notion would enter their heads."

[46] [1972] 1 W.L.R. 301, see also *Muetzel v. Muetzel* [1970] 1 W.L.R. 188; *Falconer v. Falconer* [1970] 1 W.L.R. 1333; *Davies v. Vale* [1971] 1 W.L.R. 1022; *Finch v. Finch* (1975) 119 S.J. 793; *Hall v. Hall* (1982) 3 F.L.R. 379.

[47] *ibid.* at 304.

[48] *ibid.* at 306.

particular facts of *McFarlane v. McFarlane*.[49] The judgment of Lord MacDermott L.C.J. in the case was praised by Lord Bridge in *Rosset* for its incisiveness. In it Lord MacDermott suggested that there was a relevant distinction between direct and indirect contributions and that an indirect contribution must be the subject of an agreement or arrangment between the spouses if it was to earn a beneficial interest.[50] In his view the distinction was too well marked to be disregarded. Indirect contributions were not to be put on the same plane as direct contributions in ascertaining beneficial interests for this would constitute, in the absence of any agreement or arrangement between the spouses, the application of the discredited doctrine of "family assets".

The retirement of Lord Denning brought about a stricter approach towards indirect contributions in England. This more orthodox approach manifested itself in *Burns v. Burns*.[51] Fox L.J. opined that if a payment could not be said to be, in a real sense, referable to the acquisition of the house, it was difficult to see how it could base a claim for an interest in the house. In the logic that appeals to the hard-nosed property lawyer, a woman who pays the food and electricty bills with her own money acquires lots of rights in the food and electricity but does not obtain any interest in the house which her partner has in the meantime managed to purchase with his own money.[52]

While *Burns v. Burns* was not explicitly endorsed by the House of Lords in *Rosset* the observations of Lord Diplock clearly sanction a limited, if not non-existent, role for indirect contribution claims. There have been differing views expressed in the Court of Appeal post *Rosset* about the potential of indirect contributions in generating a beneficial interest. In *Ivin v. Blake*[53] the Court of Appeal led by Glidewell L.J. adopted the strict line towards the recognition of indirect contributions advocated by Lord Bridge in *Rosset* and by the Northern Ireland Court of Appeal in *McFarlane*. On the other hand, in *Midland Bank plc v. Cooke*[54] the Court of Appeal, in a judgment authored by Waite L.J., ruled that positive evidence that the parties neither discussed nor intended any agreement as to the proportions of their beneficial interest did not preclude the court, on general equitable principles, from inferring one. This view seems flatly inconsistent with *Rosset*. It may be however, that it is only the House the Lords that is capable of resolving the disagreements at lower court level. The reticence in the acknowledgment of the role of indirect contributions manifested in *Rosset* is at variance with the approach adoped by the highest courts in Canada and Australia. The developments in these Commonwealth jurisdictions will now be considered.

---

[49] [1972] N.I. 59.
[50] *ibid.* at 70. See also the comments of Lowry J. at 75–76.
[51] [1984] Ch. 317.
[52] *ibid.* at 329.
[53] [1995] F.L.R. 70. See also *Springette v. Defoe* [1992] 2 F.L.R. 388.
[54] [1995] 4 All E.R. 562. According to Waite L.J. (at 575) it would be anomalous, against that background, to create a range of home-buyers who were beyond the pale of equity's assistance in formulating a fair presumed basis for the sharing of beneficial title, simply because they had been honest enough to admit that they never gave ownership a thought or reached any agreement about it.

THE CONSTRUCTIVE TRUST IN THE COMMONWEALTH

It is in Canada among commonwealth countries that the greatest departure from the traditional conception of the constructive trust has taken place.[55] The process was a gradual one. It began in the Supreme Court of Canada with the dissent of Laskin J. in *Murdoch v. Murdoch*[56] whereas the majority in that case were content to apply orthodoxy as articulated by the House of Lords in *Pettitt* and *Gissing*.[57] The development attained its full flowering in *Pettkus v. Becker*.[58] In that case Dickson J. who enjoyed the supported of his brethren observed[59]:

> "The principle of unjust enrichment lies at the heart of the constructive trust . . . . The great advantage of ancient principles of equity is their flexibility: the judiciary is thus able to shape these malleable principles so as to accommodate the changing needs and mores of society, in order to achieve justice. The constructive trust has proven to be a useful tool in the judicial armoury."

So the the imposition of the constructive trust was a means of redressing unjust enrichment. For the principle to succeed there were three constitutive elements; namely an enrichment, a corresponding deprivation, and the absence of any juristic reason—such as a contract or a disposition of law—for the enrichment. In *Sorochan v. Sorochan*[60] Dickson C.J.C. said that the constructive trust constituted one important judicial means of remedying unjust enrichment. Other remedies, such as monetary damages, might also be available to rectify situations of unjust enrichment. The court had to ask whether and under what circumstances it was appropriate for it to impose a constructive trust.

McLachlin J. spoke for the majority of the Supreme Court of Canada in the landmark case *Peter v. Beblow*.[61] While there were some differences of approach between her judgment and that of Cory J. who wrote for the minority in the case, the court was at one in upholding the proposition that homemaking and child care services generated a beneficial interest in property. McLachlin J. argued that the notion that household and child care services were not worthy of recognition by the court failed to recognise that these services were of great

---

[55] See generally D.W.M. Waters, "The Remedial Constructive Trust" in *The Frontiers of Liability: Volume 2* (Birks ed., 1994). See also M. Welstead, "Domestic Contribution and Constructive Trusts: the Canadian Perspective" [1987] Denning L.J. 151.

[56] (1974) 41 D.L.R. (3d) 367. See also *Degelman v. Guaranty Trust Co. of Canada* [1954] S.C.R. 725.

[57] In *Rathwell v. Rathwell* (1978) 83 D.L.R. (3d) 289 Dickson J. declared: "The constructive trust amounts to a third head of obligation, quite distinct from contract and tort, in which the court subjects "a person holding title to property . . . to an equitable duty to convey it to another on the ground that he would be unjustly enriched if he were permitted to retain." Dickson J. was in a minority in that case. The majority in the Supreme Court of Canada resolved the issues on the basis of the doctrine of the resulting trust.

[58] (1981) 117 D.L.R. (3d) 257. See also *Rawluk v. Rawluk* (1990) 65 D.L.R. (4th) 161. Here a majority of the Supreme Court of Canada took the view that if the court was requested to declare a constructive trust and determined that such a remedy was warranted, then the proprietary interest awarded is deemed to have arisen when the unjust enrichment first occurred. In other words, there is an automatic retroactive impact but this does not detract from the discretionary character of the constructive trust since the court has a discretion about whether to award the remedy in the first place. Reference was made in this connection to a passage from Scott, *Law of Trusts*, (Boston, 4th ed., 1989), vol. 5, pp. 323–324. See generally on this point Birks, *The Frontiers of Liability: Volume 2* (1994) p. 218.

[59] *ibid.* at 273.

[60] (1986) 29 D.L.R. (4th) 1.

[61] (1993) 101 D.L.R. (4th) 621.

value, not only to the family but to the other spouse.[62] She quoted the words of Lord Simon: "The cock-bird can feather his nest precisely because he is not required to spend most of his time sitting on it."[63] She added that furthermore the notion was pernicious in that it systematically devalues the contributions which women tend to make to the family economy.

The court had two options when it came to redressing the unjust enrichment that was found to have occurred; namely the award of monetary compensation or the imposition of a constructive trust. In this case the personal remedy was inadequate as an order for the payment of monetary compensation was unlikely to be enforceable easily.[64] This was a precondition for the establishment of a constructive trust. McLachlin J. also opined that there should be no divorce between family and commercial cases and that for a constructive trust to be found there must be a link between the services rendered and the property in which the trust is claimed.[65] In her view, the concern for clarity and doctrinal integrity with which the court had long been preoccupied in this area mandated that the basic principles governing the rights and remedies for unjust enrichment should remain the same in all cases.[66] She suggested that to dispense with the link between the services rendered and the property which was claimed to be subject to the trust would be inconsistent with the proprietary nature of the notion of constructive trust. The value of the trust should be assessed with reference to the actual value of the remaining property of the union. In other words, a "value survived" rather than a "value received" approach should be adopted. An approach based on "value survived" best accorded with the expectations of most parties. It was more likely that a couple expected to share in the wealth generated from their partnership, rather than to receive compensation for the services performed during the relationship.

The "value survived" idea was also judged doctrinally sounder. In *Pettkus v. Becker*[67] it was laid down that that extent of the interest must be proportionate to the contribution to the property. In determining the contribution one started by defining the property and then went to assess what portion of that property could be ascribed to efforts by the claimant. For a monetary award on the other hand, the "value received" approach was appropriate and the value conferred on the property irrelevant.[68]

[62] (1993) 101 D.L.R. (4th) 621 at 646–647.
[63] "With All My Wordly Goods" Holdsworth Lecture University of Birmingham, March 20, 1964, at p. 32.
[64] Cory J. at 640 referred to Hovious and Youdan, *Law of Family Property* (1991), p. 147 for the following list of factors which he thought were helpful in determining that a monetary distribution might be more appropriate than a constructive trust:
"(a) is the "plaintiff's entitlement ... relatively small compared to the value of the whole property in question",
(b) is the "defendant ...able to satisfy the plaintiff's claim without a sale of the property" in question;
(c) does "the plaintiff [have any] special attachment to the property in question",
(d) what "hardship might be caused to the defendant if the plaintiff obtained the rights flowing from [the award] of an interest in the property"."
[65] (1993) 101 D.L.R. (4th) 621 at 650.
[66] Reference was made to the observations of Wilson J. in *Hunter Engineering Co. v. Syncrude Canada Ltd* (1989) 57 D.L.R. (4th) 321 at 383.
[67] (1980) 117 D.L.R. (3d) 257 at 277.
[68] It should be noted that Cory J. in his minority judgment thought that in a family relationship the work, services and contributions provided by one of the parties need not be clearly and directly linked with specific property in order for a constructive trust to be imposed. He also considered that either the value surviving or the value received approach might be utilised to quantify the value of the constructive trust.

In Australia the concept of the remedial constructive trust has not been blessed with as much judicial favour as in Canada. In *Muschinski v. Dodds*[69] the High Court was at one in repudiating the idea of a wide-ranging remedial constructive trust. Gibbs C.J. talked about the ill-defined limits of the rules relating to constructive trusts.[70] Brennan J. said that there was no jurisdiction in an Australian Court of equity to declare an owner of property to be a trustee of that property for another merely on the ground that, having regard to all the circumstances, it would be fair so to declare. He added that the flexible remedy of the constructive trust was not so formless as to place proprietary rights in the discretionary disposition of a court acting in accordance with vague notions of what is fair.[71] Deane J. stated that the constructive trust could properly be described as a remedial institution which equity imposed regardless of actual or presumed agreement or intention to preclude the retention or assertion of beneficial ownership of property to the extent that such retention or assertion would be contrary to equitable principle. He was adamant however that there was no place in the law for notion of a constructive trust of a new model which was imposed whenever justice and good conscience (in the sense of "fairness" or what "was fair") required it. Proprietary rights fell to be governed by principles of law and not by some mix of judicial discretion, subjective view about which party ought to win and the formless void of individual moral opinion.[72]

In *Baumgartner v. Baumgartner*[73] the High Court of Australia shifted the goalposts somewhat and moved in the direction of recognising unconscionable conduct as the basis for equitable intervention. In this case the parties to a *de facto* relationship pooled their incomes for living expenses. First of all, they lived in a flat owned by the man. This flat was later sold and the net proceeds of sale used to assist in the purchase of a house in his name which was bought with the additional aid of a mortgage, also in his name. The parties separated and the man asserted that the land was his sole property. The court held that the man held the house on trust for the parties in the proportions in which they had contributed their earnings to its acquisition, subject to a charge in favour of the man for the net sale proceeds of the flat. In the opinion of the court the assertion by the man after the relationship had broken down that the property which had been financed in part through the pooled funds was his to the exclusion of any interest on the part of the woman amounted to unconscionable conduct. This attracted the intervention of equity and the imposition of a constructive trust. Mason C.J., Deane and Wilson JJ., in a joint judgment set their face against idiosyncratic notions of what is just and fair but acknowledged that general notions of fairness and justice were relevant to the traditional concept of unconscionable conduct. The latter concept underlay fundamental

---

[69] (1986) 16) C.L.R. 583. See also *Caverley v. Green* (1984) 155 C.L.R. 242.

[70] *ibid.* at 595.

[71] *ibid.* at 608.

[72] *ibid.* at 615–616. The judgment of Deane J. contains a quite extensive discussion on the role of the constructive trust as an institution.

[73] (1987) 164 C.L.R. 137. See generally for an analysis of the Australian position Neave "The new unconscionability principle—property disputes between *de facto* partners" (1991) 5 *Australian Journal of Family Law* 185. See also Moffat, *Trusts Law: Text and Materials* (1994), pp. 473–474.

equitable doctrines including the constructive trust.[74] One might comment that being opposed to idiosyncracy but supporting fairness and justice is a bit like being against sin but for virtue.

ASSESSMENT OF THE APPROACHES ADOPTED IN THE COMMONWEALTH AND THEIR POSSIBLE APPLICATION IN COMMERCIAL SITUATIONS

In England powerful academic as well as judicial voices have spoken against the discretionary adjustment of property rights entailed in the remedial constructive trust. Professor Peter Birks points to the tradition of the law as being against powerful discretions to adjust property rights.[75] He quotes the words of Lord Nottingham that otherwise the way would be "opened to the Lord Chancellor to construe or presume any man in England out of his estate".[76] He also criticises the way in which in his view unjust enrichment has been illegitimately enlisted to the business of fulfilling expectations.[77] A court, like the Canadian courts, which splits the ground of liability from the remedy, thus affirming that once an unjust enrichment has been established the possible responses are at large, will wrongly believe itself free to do things for which no case has been made.[78] Methinks that the commentator doth protest too much. It is questionable whether the judicial approach in England towards the resolution of property disputes consequent on unmarried divorce leads to any greater certainty or predictability than that in Canada. The point becomes clearer when one recalls that Lord Bridge in *Rosset*[79] talked about a common intention founded on imprecisely remembered or imperfectly understood discussions. The evidentiary difficulties involved in unearthing such a common intention are profound. One wonders whether the straightforward approach towards fulfilling reasonable expectations that is prevalent in Canada is not more consonant with certainty. It may also be more securely grounded on the factual realities.

---

[74] *ibid.* at 148. For the New Zealand approach in this area see *Gillies v. Keogh* [1989] 2 N.Z.L.R. 327. In this case the New Zealand Court of Appeal tried to draw the various strands represented in the different Commonwealth jurisdictions together and formulated an analysis based on the fulfilment of reasonable expectations. Cooke P. said at 330: "Normally it makes no practical difference in the result whether one talks of constructive trust, unjust enrichment, imputed common intention or estoppel. In deciding whether any of these are established it is necessary to take into account the same factors."

[75] See paper "Proprietary Rights as Remedies" in *The Frontiers of Liability: Volume 2* (Peter Birks ed., 1994).

[76] *Cook v. Fountain* (1676) 3 Swanston App. 585 at 586.

[77] A New Zealand judge, Hammond J. in *Brown v. Pourau* [1995] 1 N.Z.L.R. 352 at 368 has compared English and Commonwealth approaches as follows: "Essentially, English legal theory and practice on remedies is monastic. That is, right and remedy are perceived to be congruent. But, in the United States, and increasingly in Canada and New Zealand, our courts proceed on a dualistic basis. The court first makes enquiries as to the obligation the court is asked to uphold; it then (and only then) makes a context-specific evaluation of that remedy which will best support or advance that obligation."

[78] *ibid.* at 222: "In *Sorochan v. Sorochan* (1986) 29 D.L.R. (4th) 1 an unmarried couple had lived together for 42 years. The woman had done all the labour that a farmer's wife could conceivably be expected to do. She successfully established a beneficial interest under a constructive trust in a severed one third of the farm and a personal entitlement to a substantial sum of money. Nobody would quarrel with the substance of that result. But it was reached on the basis of the man's unjust enrichment even though it is virtually impossible to explain as restitution strictly of his gain at her expense."

[79] [1991] 1 A.C. 107 at 132.

Searching for an elusive common intention founded on vague, imprecise discussions of yesteryear appears a curiously difficult and backward looking step.[80] Moreover, reference to the views of Lord Nottingham seems somewhat quaint. Certainly, his Lordship would not be au fait with contemporary societal trends or changing patterns of family arrangement. Another justification put forward by Birks for agnosticism if not downright atheisim a propos belief in the remedial constructive trust is couched in the following terms[81]:

> "A judgment for the surrender of items of property inflicts loss, as does a money judgment, but, unlike a money judgment, also entangles itself in the complexities both of unwanted consequences for third parties and of individual economic priorities. The latter point is important and often neglected. Taking money from people makes them worse off and narrows their options, taking specific things is a more erratic instrument of justice, because of their subjective value: the same 'adjustment' will cause vastly different degrees of pain, depending on the sentiments and tastes of the loser."

In response to this it might be said that McLachlin J. speaking for the majority of the Canadian Supreme Court in *Peter v. Beblow*[82] insisted on a link between the services rendered and the property in respect of which the trust is claimed. Awarding a cohabitee a beneficial interest in the property in which she resides or resided may well cause pain to her erstwhile partner but this pain may well pale into insignificance compared with the other pain of the relationship.

It is submitted that the comments of Professor Birks and the more general complaint about the existence of a discretion to vary property rights have more force when applied to the commercial context. In England even today in the family context the courts routinely postpone the rights of beneficial owners to third party creditors by imputing to the beneficial owners an intention that their rights should be secondary to those of the creditors.[83] The benefical owners, the courts say, must have intended this because otherwise the property could never have been acquired. With a more discretionary approach in the sphere of unmarried divorce the postponement of beneficial rights to the claims of third parties would sit more easily. At the moment there is a degree of fiction about the element of imputed intention. The courts ascribe an intention to a party because the courts feel that that is the way that the party ought to have thought.[84] It is submitted that "ought" and "is" are not kept rigidly distinct in this area.

There has been some judicial pleading for doctrinal consistency between the

---

[80] For recent academic writing on the subject of family property disputes see Gardner (1993) 109 L.Q. R. 263. See also Ferguson (1993) 109 L.Q.R. 114 and Hayton [1990] Conv. 370. The Ferguson paper looks at *inter alia* the role of proprietary estoppel in this area. This doctrine may allow more leeway for a judicial approach that works towards the fulfilment of reasonable expectations.

[81] See Birks, *The Frontiers of Liability: Volume 2* (1994), p. 218.

[82] (1993) 101 D.L.R. (4th) 621.

[83] See *Equity & Law Home Loans v. Prestidge* [1992] 1 W.L.R. 137. See also *Paddington Building Society v. Mendelsohn* (1985) 50 P. & C.R. 244 and *Bristol and West Building Society v. Henning* [1985] 1 W.L.R. 778.

[84] See in particular *Equity & Law Home Loans v. Prestidge* [1992] 1 W.L.R. 137. In this case Mustill L.J. said that the beneficial interest of the wife was one which from the outset had carved out of it by anticipation a recognition of the rights of the mortgagees whose finance was intended to bring the purchase into being.

family and commercial contexts. According to McLachlin J. in *Peter v. Beblow*[85] the creation of special rules for special situations might have an adverse effect on the development of this emerging area of equity. In *Hunter Engineering Co. v. Syncrude Canada Ltd*[86] Wilson J. cautioned against confining constructive trust remedies to family law cases and said that to do would be to impede the growth and impair the flexibility crucial to the development of equitable principles.

It is submitted however that there is a demonstrated need for diversity. One commentator claims with some force that the reasons for this distinction are compelling. He states[87]:

> "In spousal cases a general policy of division of property upon marriage dissolution had developed, both statutorily and through judicial initiative. Consistent with that policy, courts had been awarding specific relief for some time by employing a discreditable resulting trust analysis. The remedial constructive trust was alopted in an effort to legitimise that process.... The spousal cases must be understood in this historical setting for which there is no parallel in the commercial sphere. Indeed, in commercial cases there has been for some time a healthy tendency among courts to be sceptical of the efforts of parties to employ equitable doctrines to secure priority over other creditors, where that priority had not previously been negotiated."

The argument is that family relationships are characterised by a lack of formality with little real negotiation about how property is to be divided in the event of dissolution. Fair and equitable treatment of parties to such relationship and the preservation to the hilt of shared future expectation have broader implications in terms of social policy than the normal gamut of commercial considerations. In the commercial context the expectation is that the parties will protect their interests contractually. If proprietary rights are anticipated as an outcome of the commercial nexus the expectation is that this will be provided for specifically.[88] Constructive trusts in family cases typically involve two party situations, *i.e.* the erstwhile couple are at loggerheads over property allocation. Where the interests of third parties obtrude commonly the latter take precedence.[89] In commercial cases, on the other hand, the *raison d'etre* of the constructive trust is priority over third parties. The name of the game insofar as a party arguing for the establishment of a constructive trust is concerned may be to obtain ascendancy over the rights of third parties. These third parties may have advanced credit on the assumption that they would achieve priority. If this assumption proves to be unfounded the source of loans may dry up to the detriment of the mainsprings of commerical life. Alternatively, the rate of interest chargeable on loans may be increased and again this may have a deleterious effect on commercial activity. If the third party has contracted with the company on an unsecured basis the question arises why should another unsecured creditor

---

[85] (1993) 101 D.L.R. (4th) 621.

[86] (1989) 57 D.L.R. (4th) 321 at 383.. See also La Forest J. in *Lac Minerals Ltd v. International Corona Resources Ltd* (1989) 61 D.L.R. (4th) 14.

[87] See Paciocco "The Remedial Constructive Trust: A Principled Basis for Priorities over Creditors" (1989) 68 *Canadian Bar Review* 315 at 326.

[88] See generally Paciocco, *op. cit.* See also S.R. Scott "The remedial constructive trust in commercial transactions" [1993] L.M.C.L.Q. 330.

[89] See, *e.g. Equity & Law Home Loans v. Prestidge* [1992] 1 W.L.R. 137 and see generally D.J. Hayton (1993) 109 L.Q.R. 485.

be able to leapfrog over him through invocation of a constructive trust claim. Equality of treatment between unsecured creditors is the statutory norm even if this turns out to be equality of misery. Statute decrees an established order by which claims are met out of the estate of an insolvent. Where the legislature has spoken the courts should hesitate to tread. There seems little rhyme nor reason in the courts upsetting the statutory applecart except perhaps by strict analogy with existing categories of claim. While there has been some extension in the classes of claim recognised as having equitable proprietary status most notably in the areas of bribes[90] and insurance recoveries[91] this has been done by way of extension or recognition of categories rather than by the courts arrogating to themselves a general discretionary jurisdiction. There remains the question of course, about whether these class extensions are themselves desirable. But that is a somewhat different question which will be considered later on.

EQUITABLE PROPRIETARY CLAIMS IN COMMERCIAL CASES—METHODS OF VINDICATION—CONSTRUCTIVE TRUSTS AND EQUITABLE LIENS

The recognition of equitable proprietary claims leads in consequence to a diminution of a debtor's estate available for distribution to general creditors. Such claims are sometimes vindicated through the vehicle of the constructive trust and other times by means of the creation of an equitable lien.

If a constructive trust is held to exist the beneficiary becomes an owner in equity of the property that forms the subject matter of the trust. Commonly in cases where a constructive trust arises the constructive trust beneficiary will have the entire beneficial interest in the property to the exclusion of anybody else. In such circumstances the beneficiary is entitled to call for a transfer of the property in question together with any income that the property produced since the constructive trust first came into being. Where there are other parties with beneficial interests in the property that forms the subject matter of the constructive trust the constructive trust beneficary will have rights commensurate with the beneficial interest that he has.[92] To sum it up a constructive trust equals partial or total ownership of the the property in equity. The equitable lien, on the other hand, is a different kettle of fish. It equals a right of recourse against the property to ensure the payment of money. Essentially it may be described as an equitable security right arising by operation of law. It differs from an equitable charge in that it is non-consensual in nature rather than being dependent on the agreement of the parties as is the case with an equitable charge. Slade J. said as much in *Re Bond Worth*[93]:

"... although the word lien is sometimes used in practice to describe a right which arises by way of express contractual agreement of the interested parties, it is more commonly used, in a narrower sense, to refer to a right arising by operation of law. Liens in this narrow sense may arise by virtue of statute, common law or equity."

It is usual to draw a distinction between a common law lien and an equitable

---

[90] *Att.-Gen. for Hong Kong v. Reid* [1994] 1 A.C. 324.
[91] *Lord Napier and Ettrick v. Hunter* [1993] 2 W.L.R. 42.
[92] See generally A.J. Oakley ed. Parker and Mellows: *The Modern Law of Trusts* (6th ed., 1994), pp. 209–221.
[93] [1980] 1 Ch. 228 at 250.

lien. The difference has been elaborated upon in the following terms[94]:

> "An equitable lien differs from a common law lien in that a common law lien is founded on possession and, except as modified by statute, merely confers a right to detain until payment, whereas an equitable lien, which exists quite irrespective of possession, confers on the holder the right to a judicial sale."

In *Tappenden v. Artus*[95] Diplock L.J. compared the common law remedy of a possessory lien with other "primitive remedies" such as abatement of nuisance, self-defence or ejection of trespassers to land. Common law liens arise in situations where the right has been established by a process of historical development. As one commentator has noted the modern law is content to leave the existence of a common law lien to legal history without making any real attempt to rationalise its existence in contemporary conditions.[96] It is difficult to conceive of judicial extensions of the categories of common law liens though statute has sometimes brought into existence what might be described as lien-type creatures. An example is served by the litigation in *Bristol Airport plc v. Powdrill*.[97] At issue in that case was section 88 of the Civil Aviation Act 1982 which gave airport authorities a right to detain aircraft to force payment of unpaid airport charges. The Court of Appeal took the view that the statutory right of detention was a "lien or security" over property within the meaning of section 248 of the Insolvency Act 1986.

POSSIBLE FLEXIBILITY IN THE CREATION OF EQUITABLE LIENS

Equitable liens, as distinct from common law liens, are somewhat more expansive in nature. One might compare them with an unruly dog and say that if not securely chained to their kennel they are apt to wander into places where they ought not to be and to upset the whole principle of *pari passu* distribution in the law of insolvency.[98] One critic has even suggested that "the equitable lien is a dangerous and elusive enemy of the law of preference" and that as "applied to some bankruptcy cases, it seems as well named as the Holy Roman Empire, for it is neither equitable nor a lien."[99] A leading contemporary case on equitable liens is the decision of the High Court of Australia in *Hewett v. Court*[1] where there is much discussion on the subject. Deane J. referred to an equitable lien as a right against property which arises automatically by implication of equity to secure the discharge of an actual or potential indebtedness.[2]

---

[94] *Halsbury's Laws of England* (4th ed., 1973) Vol. 28, para. 551.
[95] [1964] 2 Q.B. 185.
[96] See Bridge, *Personal Property Law* (1993), p. 133. Professor Bridge points to general confluence between the conferment of a lien and the exercise of a common calling. See also A.P. Bell, *Modern Law of Personal Property in England and Ireland* (1989), pp. 138–139.
[97] [1990] Ch. 744.
[98] Adopting the words of Lord Mersey in *Kreglinger v. New Patagonia Meat and Cold Storage Co. Ltd* [1914] A.C. 25 at 46.
[99] M. McLaughlin [1927] Harv. L. Rev. 341 at 389 referred to by Phillips in Chap. 25 of N.E. Palmer and E. McKendrick ed., *Interests in Goods* (1993), pp. 653–654.
[1] (1983) 57 A.L.J.R. 211. The case is extensively discussed by Hardingham "Equitable Liens for the Recovery of Purchase Money" (1985) 15 *Melbourne University Law Review* 65.
[2] *ibid.* at 220. Reference was made *inter alia* in this connection to *Re Bernstein* [1925] 12 at 17–18 and *Re Bond Worth Ltd* [1980] Ch. 228 at 251.

Possible Flexibility in the Creation of Equitable Liens

The best known equitable liens are the vendor's lien for unpaid purchase money and the purchaser's lien. The existence of these liens was rationalised by Gibbs C.J. in *Hewett v. Court* as follows[3]:

> "A vendor's lien for unpaid purchase money has been said to be founded on the principle that 'a person, having got the estate of another, shall not, as between them, keep it, and not pay the consideration'. *Mackreth v. Symmons* (1808) 15 Ves. 329 at p. 340; 33 E.R. 778 at p. 782. The lien of a purchaser for the purchase money that he has paid to the vendor on a sale that has gone off through no fault of the purchaser may perhaps rest on the converse principle that he who has agreed to convey property in return for a purchase price will not be allowed to keep the price if he fails to make the conveyance. At all events, the rule has been said to be founded on 'solid and substantial justice': *Rose v. Watson* (1864) 10 H.L.C. at 672 at p. 684; 11 E.R. 187 at p. 1192."

The question arises whether the categories of equitable liens are closed. Perhaps one might respond by adopting the statement of Bagnall J. in *Cowcher v. Cowcher*[4] and saying that equity is not beyond childbearing in this particular area. Its progeny however, must be legitimate; by precedent out of principle. The procreational qualities of equitable liens will be discussed in the context of two leading cases, one Irish and the other Australian, namely *Re Barrett Apartments Ltd*[5] and *Hewett v. Court.*[6]

In *Re Barrett Apartments Ltd* Barrett Apartments Ltd owned a site on which it proposed to build a block of flats. "Booking deposits" were paid by prospective purchasers of the flats and a further sum was to be paid on the execution of a building agreement. Building agreements were signed in only a couple of cases. A receiver was appointed to the company and the question arose whether the depositors had secured claims against the company. A distinction was drawn between depositors who had, and those who had not, signed a legally enforceable contract for the purchase of premises. The liquidator paid off the two who had signed such agreements. He rejected however, all other claims. The Irish Supreme Court said that he was right in so doing.

Henchy J. said that the rationale behind allowing a purchaser a lien on the purchased property in respect of a deposit paid to the vendor was that by paying the deposit in pursuance of the contract, the purchaser acquired an equitable estate or interest in the property.[7] Therefore he should be allowed to follow that estate or interest by being accorded a lien on it.[8] Where no contract of purchase was entered into by the depositor, the payment of the booking deposit did not give the payer any estate or interest, legal or equitable, in the property—as

---

[3] (1983) 57 A.L.J.R. 211 at 213.
[4] [1972] 1 W.L.R. 425 at 430. Somewhat more controversially Bagnall J. also said that in determining rights, particularly property rights, the only justice that can be attained by mortals, who are fallible and not omniscient was justice according to law, namely the justice which flowed from the application of sure and settled principles to proved or admitted facts. But one need not necessarily take on board this baggage.
[5] [1985] I.R. 350 on which see McCormack (1986) 7 Co. Law 113; Coughlan (1988) 10 *Dublin University Law Journal* 90. See also McCormack, *Reservation of Title* (2nd ed., 1995) at pp. 29–30.
[6] (1983) 57 A.L.J.R. 211.
[7] [1985] I.R. 350 at 357–358. Reference was made to *Rose v. Watson* (1864) 10 H.L.C. 672 and *Tempany v. Hynes* [1976] I.R. 101.
[8] It has been argued that this view is at odds with the accepted learning that equitable charges are not dependent on possession or ownership, either at law or equity. See Coughlan *op. cit.* at p. 96.

131

would have been the case if a written contract had been entered into and the booking deposit had been converted into a deposit paid on foot of the contract.

The judge added that depositors as a class did not have an equity to be treated as secured creditors, while other creditors, whose debts could be more deserving of payment and no less closely connected with the property, were left to languish as unsecured creditors without hope of payment at the tail-end of the queue of creditors.[9]

Re Barrett Apartments Ltd may be looked at from the point of view of a judicial reaction to the multiplicity of arguments for secured status in corporate insolvency. The Irish Supreme Court viewed rateable allocation of available resources as a principle of overriding weight and importance. Any suggested departure from this *desideratum* was treated with considerable caution. The court conceived the case almost entirely in terms of policy. What was fair or just for the judges to decide? Even-handed distribution of corporate assets appears to have been taken as a touchstone of justice. Some would say however that the decision gives monied might priority over social justice.[10] Certainly the majority of the High Court of Australia took a more expansive view of equitable liens in *Hewett v. Court*.[11] Firstly, they decided that the availability of specific performance to a purchaser was not essential in deciding upon an equitable lien.[12] Specific performance results in fulfilment of the contract whereas an equitable lien came about in the event of the contract not being performed. Logically the two were quite distinct. A decree of specific performance might be withheld from an innocent purchaser on grounds which had nothing to do with the question whether the purchaser should be accorded security for the return of the purchase money[13].

The facts of *Hewett v. Court* are that a company agreed with purchasers to construct a transportable house according to agreed plans and specifications and to transport it to the site of the purchasers and place it in position on blocks there. Property in the home, it was agreed, was to remain with the company until the contract price had been paid in full. The price was payable in stages, a deposit on entry into the contract followed by instalments at various stages of the operations. The company went into liquidation however before the stage of completion but it was held that the purchasers had an equitable lien

---

[9] [1985] I.R. 350 at 358–359. For an argument supporting a more individuated claim to a lien see Coughlan *op. cit.* at pp. 104–106.

[10] To use a turn of phrase associated with Lord Denning in *Williams & Glyn Bank v. Boland* [1979] Ch. 312 at 333. The decision was affirmed by the House of Lords [1981] A.C. 487 where Lord Scarman said at p. 510 that the court should not be perturbed by supposed difficulties as a result of the decision in the banking or conveyancing sectors. Bankers and solicitors existed to provide the services which the public needed. They could adjust their practice if it was socially required. Some might say that at the end of the day the consumer loses because the banks will pass on the losses associated with judicial rejection of their claims in the form of increased charges.

[11] (1983) 57 A.L.J.R. 211.

[12] The issue is most fully considered by Deane J. at pp. 221-223. Gibbs C.J. opined at p. 215 that specific enforceability was not relevant in adjudicating upon a purchaser's lien but did not conclusively rule out the proposition that specific enforcement was a prerequisite to an unpaid vendor's lien. Deane J. took the view that specific enforceability was irrelevant to equitable liens generally and Murphy J. appears to have been of a similar opinion.

[13] In *Re Barrett Apartments Ltd* [1985] I.R. 350 Keane J. in the Irish High Court took the view that the availability of the remedy of specific performance was not a precondition for the existence of an unpaid purchaser's lien. The Supreme Court however adopted no view on the matter.

over the buildings for the purchase money paid when the company become insolvent.

The whole court held that the contract in the instant case for the supply of a house was one for the provision of work and materials and not one for the sale of goods. In this respect it was not to be distinguished from a contract to construct a house on land as its permanent site. The court differed on the availability or otherwise of an equitable lien. Gibbs C.J., Murphy and Deane JJ. were in the majority. The Chief Justice opined that the fact that there was no authority precisely in point did not mean that in the present circumstances no lien could arise. The rules of equity were not so rigid and inflexible that it was necessary to discover precise authority in favour of the existence of a lien before one could be held to have been created. The present case was analogous to that of a purchaser's lien. Technically, the contract was not one of sale and purchase but the doctrines of equity attached more importance to substance than to technicalities in a succinct judgment.[14]

Murphy J. confronted "head-on" the questions of policy involved. He said an equitable lien such as this will often be necessary to protect consumers, who, unlike traders, cannot be expected to enquire into the solvency of the person with whom they are dealing. He noted however that as so often happens in commercial and conveyancing cases, the court was not assisted by any "commercial impact statement" of what would be the effect in commerce generally of equitable liens arising in such circumstances.[15]

Deane J. adopted a more traditional case-based analysis. He outlined a number of factors which were sufficient for the implication, independently of agreement, of an equitable lien between contracting parties. These criteria were satisfied in the present case. The factors are as follows[16]:

(a) an actual or potential indebtedness by the owner of the property the subject of the contract to the other party arising from a payment or promise thereof of consideration in relation to the acquisition of the property or of an expense incurred in relation to it;

(b) the property is specifically identified and appropriated to the performance of the contract and

(c) the relationship between the indebtedness and the property is such that it would be unconscientious or unfair for the owner to dispose of the property without the consent of the other party or discharge of the liability.

It has been argued that the concepts of unconscientiousness and appropriation are too opaque so as to make it difficult to determine whether in any particular case an equitable lien will be held to have arisen. It may be that given the difficulties that the tests engender the appropriate approach to adopt would be that of Gibbs C.J., *i.e.* of reasoning by reference to established categories of liens. One must also bear in mind however, that any further recognition of

[14] *ibid.* at p. 215.
[15] *ibid.*
[16] *ibid.* at 223. John Phillips in *Interests in Goods* (N.E. Palmer and E. McKendrick ed., 1993), Chap. 25 has persuasively argued (at p. 651) that the principles expounded by Deane J. based as they are on the concepts of appropriation and unconscientious dealing, make it difficult to determine in any given factual situation whether or not a lien will arise.

equitable proprietary claims leads to a diminution in the amount of the insolvent's estate avaliable for distribution to general creditors. If however the tests are applied to the facts of *Re Barrett Apartments* it seems clear that no lien would have arisen. An apartment could not be said to have been appropriated to the performance of a contract unless a contract for the purchase of the same had been signed.[17]

UNITED KINGDOM RECOGNITION OF EQUITABLE PROPRIETARY CLAIMS

As has been stressed in this chapter and indeed throughout the book when one considers the question whether a payment should be impressed with a trust or a claim to an equitable lien upheld, it must always be remembered that the real contest may not be between payer and recipient but between the payer and the recipient's creditors.[18] A constructive trust claim was recognised however in *Neste Oy v. Lloyds Bank PLC*.[19] This was a case where a principal made various payments to its agent, a company called P.S.L. At the time that the last payment was made, the directors of P.S.L. had resolved to discontinue trading and to seek the appointment of a receiver.

Bingham J. decided that this last payment was subject to a constructive trust for P.S.L. could not in good conscience, at the time of receipt of the payment, retain it. It would have seemed little short of sharp practice for them to take any advantage from the payment. Moreover, it would be contrary to any ordinary notion of fairness, according to the learned judge, that the general body of creditors should profit from the accident of a payment at a time when there was bound to be a total failure of consideration.[20] There are certain difficulties with the decision however. It may be that in receiving the payment the company was carrying on business in a fraudulent manner and the directors who were parties to the carrying on of the business in this manner were guilty of fraudulent trading. At the time that the decision was handed down under the fraudulent trading legislation then in force the court could direct that particular payments be made to particular creditors who had been defrauded.[21] The statutory regime has now been supplanted by sections 213 and 214 of the Insolvency Act 1986. Section 213 is a fraudulent trading provision whereas section 214 introduces the wider notion of wrongful trading. Under this section once a director or shadow director knows or ought to have concluded that there

---

[17] It should be noted that an equitable lien may be qualified or negatived by agreement between the parties. The issue of express or implied ouster of the intervention of equity as it were has arisen particularly in the context of vendors' liens and subrogation to vendors' liens. See generally on this question *Burston Finance Ltd v. Speirway Ltd* [1974] 1 W.L.R. 1648 and *Orakpo v. Manson Investments* [1978] A.C. 95.

[18] See generally Goode, "Ownership and Obligation in Commercial Transactions" (1987) 103 L.Q.R. 433.

[19] [1983] 2 Lloyd's Rep. 658. See also *Re Irish Shipping Ltd* [1986] I.L.R.M. 518.

[20] *ibid*. 666. Bridge (1992) 12 O.J.L.S. 333 at 360 suggests a very close link between an imposed trust liability and fraudulent and wrongful trading. He says that the following proposition would seem to be justifed. "When a company's circumstances plainly show that to accept payment would give rise to at least wrongful trading liability, a constructive trust will extend to the payment received. If the circumstances do not speak quite so plainly, but the company is concerned enough about its potential liability in this area to use effective trust language, its actions will not be seen as an unlawful preference."

[21] *Re Cyona Distributors Ltd* [1967] Ch. 889.

was no reasonable prospect that a company would avoid going into insolvent liquidation, he must take every step with a view to minimising potential loss to company creditors. Unless such steps are taken the person runs the risk of being forced to make such contribution to the assets of the company as the court thinks proper. It should be noted that under both this section and the preceding section any contribution order made goes to swell the assets of the company available for distribution to general creditors. The courts have no jurisdiction to direct that the contributions to the assets of the company should be made over to creditors who have suffered loss during the periods of fraudulent and wrongful trading. Recognising and upholding a constructive trust in favour of an individual creditor in such a situation would seem to contradict the underlying legislative policy.

As I have already said the courts in England have generally proceeded by way of recognising a new category of proprietary claims. The issue of class extensions, so to speak, will now be considered. In view of the decision of the House of Lords in *Lord Napier and Ettrick v. Hunter*[22] particular attention will be paid to the question of insurance recoveries. The *Lord Napier* case may usefully be compared with that of the Privy Council in *Re Goldcorp Exchange Ltd*[23] which case will also be considered.

LORD NAPIER AND ETTRICK V. HUNTER[24]

The House of Lords were prepared to recognise an equitable proprietary claim on the facts of *Lord Napier and Ettrick v. Hunter*. The factual backdrop to the case is the financial woes afflicting the insurance market at Lloyds. The plaintiffs in the case were Lloyds names and members of the Outhwaite syndicate. The names suffered large losses but fortunately had secured stop-loss insurance cover and were able to make successful claims under the stop-loss insurance policies. Subsequently the plaintiffs had instituted proceedings against the managing agent of the Outhwaite syndicate contending that the large losses had been sustained as a result of negligence and breach of duty on the part of the managing agent. These proceedings were settled on payment to solicitors acting for the names of the sum of £116 million. The stop-loss insurers claimed an equitable proprietary interest in this sum. Obviously establishment of such a claim would short-circuit the whole recovery process insofar as the stop-loss insurers were concerned. The alternative for them was distinctly less appealing. If the damages were paid over to the names the stop-loss insurers would have to make a demand to the names for payment. If such payment was not forthcoming separate proceedings for money had and received would have to be launched against all 246 of the names and if perchance any of the names was insolvent the stop-loss insurers would only rank as an unsecured creditor with little hope of full recovery. There was the additional complication that some of the names were resident overseas including the U.S. Lord Templeman painted a picture of the U.S. as a country that constituted a veritable hell on earth for insurers. In particular civil litigation was confined to the tender mercies

[22] [1993] 2 W.L.R. 42; [1993] 1 All E.R. 385.
[23] [1994] 2 All E.R. 806.
[24] [1993] 2 W.L.R. 42; [1993] 1 All E.R. 385; on which see *inter alia* Jones [1993] Conv. 391.

of juries who were not noted for their sympathy towards insurers.[25]

Against this rendering of the facts it is hardly surprising that their Lordships recognised an equitable proprietary interest in the insurers. In reaching this conclusion the decisions of Saville J. at first instance and the Court of Appeal were overturned. The lower courts placed heavy emphasis on various judicial pronouncements by Lord Diplock.[26] The latter had conceived of the doctrine of subrogation as it applied to insurance as a common law doctrine based on the implied terms of the contract of insurance. The role of equity was limited to assisting the common law right of recovery by compelling the assured to permit the insurers to sue third parties in the name of the assured. He said that if the assured, after payment of the loss by the insurer, had received a sum of money from a third party in reduction of the loss, the insurer could capture the amount of the reduction as money had and received. Given its common law origins the right of subrogation enjoyed by insurers was unlikely to generate equitable proprietary interests according to the Court of Appeal in *Lord Napier and Ettrick v. Hunter*.[27]

The House of Lords begged to differ. In their view a series of decisions from 1748 onwards demonstrated the fact that courts of equity were themselves enforcing rights of subrogation against the assured and also that both equity and common law courts referred to the assured as holding benefits received from a third party as "trustee" for the insurers or subject to a lien in favour of the insurers. Reference was made to *Randal v. Cockran*[28] from 1748. Here Lord Hardwicke L.C. said: "as to the goods themselves, if restored in specie, or compensation made for them, the assured stands as a trustee for the insurer, in proportion for what he paid . . ."

The authority of *White v. Dobinson*[29] was also invoked. In this case an injunction was granted to restrain the insured person from receiving and the wrongdoer from paying a sum in respect of damages without first paying or providing for the sum in respect of which the insurers were entitled to be subrogated. The court rejected the proposition that the only remedy of the insurer was an action for money had and received.

Lord Goff could see no justification for sweeping the line of equity cases under the carpet as though they did not exist.[30] Morevoer he failed to discern any inconsistency between the equitable proprietary right recognised by courts of equity in these cases and the personal rights and obligations embodied in the contract of insurance itself. Moneys received by an assured from a third party in reduction of a loss paid by an insurer should not be treated as available for the assured's normal cash flow. The rights of the insurer to such money were sufficiently strong to entitle the insurer to priority in the event of the assured's bankruptcy.[31] The judgment of Wynn-Parry J. in *Re Miller Gibb & Co. Ltd*[32] was

---

[25] [1993] 1 All E.R. 385.
[26] See his comments as Diplock J. in *Yorkshire Insurance Co Ltd v. Nisbet Shipping Co. Ltd* [1962] 2 Q.B. 330 and in the House of Lords in *Hobbs v. Marlowe* [1978] A.C. 16.
[27] *The Times* July 17, 1992.
[28] (1748) 1 Ves Sen 99, 27 E.R. 916. See also *Blauwpot v. Da Costa* (1758) 1 Eden 130, 28 E.R. 633; *Mason v. Sainsbury* (1782) 3 Doug 61, 99 E.R. 538; *Yates v. White* (1838) 1 Arn 85.
[29] (1845) 5 L.T.O.S. 233 affirming (1844) 14 Sim 273, 60 E.R. 363.
[30] [1993] 1 All E.R. 385 at 401–402. Lord Templeman said that he was not prepared to treat authorities which span over two centuries in a cavalier fashion: see [1993] 1 All E.R. 385 at 397.
[31] [1993] 1 All E.R. 385 at 402.
[32] [1957] 1 W.L.R. 703; [1957] 2 All E.R. 266.

cited in support of this proposition. Here the Board of Trade issued a company with a policy of insurance that covered 90 per cent of the loss sustained in respect of goods sold to Brazil if local regulations precluded payment of the purchase price of the goods. Transfer of payment was in fact prevented by Brazilian currency exchange regulations and the Board of Trade accordingly met its liabilities under the policy. The company went into compulsory liquidation. Subsequently a bank who was acting as agent for the company received full payment from Brazil. Wynn-Parry J. made an order directing the liquidator of the company to execute all such documents and to do all such things necesssay to enable the insurer to obtain 90 per cent of the amount that had been received by the bank.

According to Lord Templeman where an insured person had been paid policy moneys by the insurer for a loss in respect of which the insured person recovers damages from a wrongdoer the insured person is guilty of unconscionable conduct if he does not procure and direct that the sum due to the insurer shall by way of subrogation be paid out of the damages.[33] In his view if the stop-loss insurers have no equitable remedy in connection with their rights and if a name beceomes bankrupt then subrogation was a mockery. If the argument on behalf of the names was correct, the unsecured creditors of the insured name would benefit by double payment. The stop-loss insurers would be in a worse position than an unsecured creditor because the insurers could resist payment under the policy whereas an unsecured creditor may choose whether to advance moneys or not. Lord Templeman was clearly influenced by the fact that by the time that litigation had been brought to a successful conclusion the names might no longer be in a position to meet an award of damages. Although Lord Browne-Wilkinson did not specifically address the insolvency issue the whole tenor of his judgment is to the effect that the insurer would have priority over general creditors. He said explicitly that an insurer who has paid over the insurance moneys does have a proprietary interest in moneys subsequently recovered by an assured from a third party wrongdoer.[34]

There has been some criticism voiced at the awarding of a proprietary remedy in *Lord Napier and Ettrick v. Hunter*.[35] The argument is that since the insurer's payment was under a contract it could not be said to have been involuntary. Unlike a person who pays money under mistake or duress he has to some extent taken the risk of the assured's insolvency. The insurer could be said to have taken the risk of bankruptcy by not having contracted for security. It is submitted however that these criticisms are not well founded. An insured should not be benefiting from double recovery in the same way as a person should not profit from mistaken payments or payments made under duress. There was never any intention that an insured should be paid twice as it were. On the other hand where a customer has paid in advance for goods the expectation of the parties clearly is that the payee should have the money beneficially and be able to use it, perhaps by obtaining supplies of the goods in question himself. The insurer contracts to indemnify the insured against loss but where there is no loss there is no reason for indemnification and no reason for payment. Consequently it is

[33] [1993] 1 All E.R. 385 at 397.
[34] [1993] 1 All E.R. 385 at 409.
[35] [1993] Conv. 391 at 399–400.

suggested that the situation is analogous to that of mistaken payments.[36]

EQUITABLE LIEN OR CONSTRUCTIVE TRUST

The lower courts in *Lord Napier and Ettrick v. Hunter* were of the view that the only method of vindicating an equitable proprietary claim on the part of the insurers was by the creation of a constructive trust. In other words there would have to be a trust fund held in trust by trustees for different beneficiaries in different shares, the trustees being burdened with administrative and investment duties, the trustees being liable for all the duties imposed on trustees but being free from liability if the trust fund was lost without negligence. Lord Templeman agreed that if this were the only method of protecting the rights of an insurer the practical disadvantages would be fearsome.[37] But he said that equity was not so inflexible or powerless. The appropriate avenue of redress was to declare that the damages payable by the wrongdoer to the insured person were subject to an equitable lien or charge in favour of the insurer. Lord Goff agreed that the constitution of the assured as trustee of such money may impose upon him obligations of too onerous a character. He suggested that a lien was the more appropriate form of proprietary right in circumstances where, as here, its function was to protect the interest of the insurer in an asset only to the extent that its retention by the assured would have the effect that he was more than indemnified under the policy of insurance.[38]

Lord Goff's analysis calls to mind an argument that was advanced by himself extra-judicially, along with his co-author, Professor Gareth Jones. In their seminal textbook on the *Law of Restitution*[39] there is a discussion of constructive trusts, liens and subrogation as equitable remedies created and imposed by the courts. There is a treatment of the situation that arises where the defendant knows the facts which from the basis of the plaintiff's restitutionary claim and is insolvent. It is pointed that the contest is in reality between the plaintiff and the defendant's general creditors. They contend that even though the defendant may have been guilty of wrongdoing, the plaintiff should be granted a lien over identifiable assets, but only to secure a sum which represents the value, at the date of its receipt, of the benefits conferred.[40] It is submitted that to grant a proprietary remedy such as a constructive trust over an asset whose value was now greater than the cost of its acquisition would be to confer a windfall at the expense of the defendant's general creditors. This assessment mirrors the approach that found favour with all the Law Lords in *Lord Napier and Ettrick v. Hunter*. Lord Browne-Wilkinson for instance said that the proprietary interest was adequately satisfied in the circumstances of subrogation under an insurance contract by granting the insurers' a lien over the moneys recovered by the assured from the third party.[41]

---

[36] One question that the House of Lords in *Lord Napier and Ettrick v. Hunter* [1993] 1 All E.R. 385 did not resolve was whether the insurer once he had indemnified the assured had a proprietary interest in the right of action against the wrongdoer. Their Lordships hesitated to express a final view on the issue.

[37] [1993] 1 All E.R. 385 at 397.

[38] *ibid.* at 402–403.

[39] 4th ed. 1993.

[40] *ibid.* at 97–98.

[41] [1993] 1 All E.R. 385 at 409.

THE REMEDIAL CONSTRUCTIVE TRUST IN THE PRIVY COUNCIL—RE GOLDCORP EXCHANGE LTD

The Privy Council, on appeal from New Zealand, had occasion to pronounce on the doctrine of constructive trust in *Re Goldcorp Exchange Ltd.*[42] There is a very full and careful consideration of the issue in the judgment of the Board which was handed down by Lord Mustill. In the case a bank holding a debenture had appointed receivers over the assets of a company. Some of the claimants had purchased gold bullion for future delivery but at the date when the receivers were appointed there had not been any appropriation of specific and segregated parcels of bullion to the individual purchase contracts. At first blush this would seem to suggest that the bullion was swallowed up as it were by the bank's charge but the claimants invoked a number of arguments including that of the constructive trust. The claimants received a certificate of ownership from the company stating that they were purchasing non-allocated metal and had the right on giving seven days notice to take physical delivery of the metal purchased. It was represented by and on behalf of the company that bullion purchased was not set aside as a customer's metal but was instead stored in safe-keeping as part of the company's overall stock of bullion and was insured by the company and that the stock of bullion held by the company from which customers could call for delivery if they so wished would always be sufficient to meet the company's obligations under all outstanding contracts of sale. Did property in the bullion pass to the claimants upon the conclusion of the contract of sale? The Privy Council said not because the contract was one for the sale of unascertained goods and a buyer could not acquire title until it was known to what goods the title related. According to Lord Mustill this was no arid legal technicality but was dictated by *a priori* common sense.[43] In this case the seller had perfect freedom to decide for himself how and from what source he would obtain goods answering the contractual description.[44] Consequently the cases on sales "ex-bulk" were irrelevant to the decision.[45]

Having failed on the pure Sale of Goods point the claimants adduced a number of additional arguments to sustain the claim to a proprietary interest. They claimed that Goldcorp held the bullion in trust for the claimants, that Goldcorp were estopped from denying that title had passed, that title had passed when Goldcorp had subsequently purchased bullion, that Goldcorp were fiduciaries and finally that the court should declare a remedial constructive trust over the bullion that remained in the vaults of Goldcorp. None of these propositions cut much ice with the Privy Council.

Lord Mustill did not doubt that the vendor of goods sold ex-bulk could effectively declare himself trustee of the bulk in favour of the purchaser, so as to confer *pro tanto* an equitable title. The present transaction however was not

---

[42] [1994] 2 All E.R. 806; on which see McKendrick (1994) 110 L.Q.R. 509.

[43] *ibid.* at 814. Reference was made in this connection to observations by Lord Blackburn at pp. 122–123 of his *Treatise on the Effect of the Contract of Sale* (1st ed. 1845).

[44] The Law Commission has recommended that property should be able to pass where the bulk has been identified but the individual parts have not been set aside for any particular claimant: see Law Com. No. 215 (1993). The Law Commission recommendations have been implemented in the Sale of Goods (Amendment) Act 1995.

[45] Cases such as *Re Wait* [1927] 1 Ch. 606 and *Carlos Federspiel & Co SA v. Charles Twigg & Co. Ltd* [1957] 1 Lloyd's Rep. 240.

of this type. The company did not intend to create an interest in its general stock of gold which would have inhibited any dealings with it otherwise than for the purpose of delivery under the non-allocated sale contracts.[46] The estoppel argument posited that the company, having represented to its customers that they had title to bullion held in the vaults could not be heard to say that they did not. The simple answer to this submission was that an estoppel gave no title to that which was the subject-matter of the estoppel. An estoppel was effective *inter partes* but could not bind third parties who were strangers to the arrangement.[47] In other words an estoppel might operate as between the claimants and the company Goldcorp but did not impinge upon the rights of the bank.

The argument founded on acquisition of title to after-acquired bullion was equally unsuccessful. Old cases relied upon like *Holroyd v. Marshall*[48] were concerned with situations where the goods upon acquisition could be unequivocally identified with individual contracts. Reference was made to the observations of Lord Hanworth M.R. in *Re Wait*[49] that the reasoning in these cases could not be transferred to a situation like the present where there was no means of knowing to which, if any of the non-allocated sales a particular purchase by the company was related. Similarly there was nothing in the fiduciary point. Certainly the customers had put faith in the company and this trust had not been repaid. But high expectations did not necessarily lead to equitable remedies. Goldcorp were obliged honestly and conscientiously to perform its contractual duties but so were a lot of contracting parties

Nor was there in the Privy Council any judicial support for the proposition that the court should create in favour of the non- allocated claimants a remedial restitutionary right superior to the security created by the charge. Lord Mustill pointed out that the bank relied on the floating charge to protect its assets whereas the customers relied on the company to deliver the bullion. The fact that the claimants were private citizens whereas their opponent was a commercial bank could not justify the court in simply disapplying the bank's valid security. That would be to stretch a nascent doctrine beyond breaking point.[50] The judgment of the Privy Council involved overturning the decision of the New Zealand Court of Appeal where the case is reported *sub nom. Liggett v. Kensington.*[51] In New Zealand the argument that Goldcorp had assumed the position of fiduciaries *vis-à-vis* the non-allocated claimants had found favour with a majority of the Court of Appeal. But as we have seen the Privy Council were wary of the tag "fiduciary" being applied to the commercial relationship between the contracting parties considering it to be a mere label on which to hang a result

---

[46] [1994] 2 All E.R. 806 at 815.
[47] Reference was made in this connection to *Knights v. Wiffen* (1870) L.R. 5 Q.B. 660 and *Simms v. Anglo-Amercian Telegrah Co.* (1879) 5 Q.B.D. 188.
[48] (1862) 10 H.L. Cas. 191. See also *Benjamin's Sale of Goods* (3rd ed. 1987), pp. 80, 218–219.
[49] [1927] 1 Ch. 606.
[50] There was a group of claimants—the Walker & Hall claimants who were able to demonstrate sufficient appropriation to establish a shared interest in the pooled bullion. On a conventional tracing analysis however, their claim was limited to the lowest balance of metal held by Goldcorp between the accrual of their rights and the commencement of receivership. They attempted to circumvent this limitation by arguing for the existence of a general equitable lien on the basis of *Space Investments Ltd v. Canadian Imperial Bank of Commerce Trust Co. (Bahamas) Ltd* [1986] 1 W.L.R. 1072 but Lord Mustill refused to declare such a lien on the grounds that it would be inequitable in the particular circumstances of the case: [1994] 2 All E.R. 806 at 831–832.
[51] [1993] 1 N.Z.L.R. 257.

already reached on other grounds. There is an argument that it would have been "just" for a remedial constructive trust to have been imposed over the bullion stocks in favour of the non-allocated claimants.[52] The argument proceeds along the lines that the unallocated purchasers did not perceive that they were assuming the position of unsecured creditors. They were totally reliant upon Goldcorp, they paid their money for a specific purpose and thought that specific property (*i.e.* the bullion) was theirs. On this view the trust should only extend over the bullion and not over the general assets of Goldcorp. Believing that they were the owners of the bullion, the unallocated purchasers could be presumed to have taken the risk that something could happen to it.

It is suggested that this argument is not completely convincing. False assumptions as to the state of one's legal rights do not generally found legal rights. Persons who pay for goods in advance generally believe that they will receive what they bargained for. High hopes and even expectations do not necessarily entail equitable proprietary remedies. Is there are any reason to prefer somebody who wrongly believes something over another person who takes care to ascertain the correct legal position and adjusts his behaviour accordingly?

So the "big bad man" emerged victorious. It must be remembered however that banks who lose do not bear the loss themselves but will pass on the cost to customers in the form of higher charges. One commentator has questioned the justice of privileging a plaintiff like Mr Liggett who has the odd US$732, 000 to invest in gold bullion over the ordinary bank customer.[53]

THE REMEDIAL CONSTRUCTIVE TRUST IN THE ENGLISH COURT OF APPEAL—*HALIFAX BUILDING SOCIETY V. THOMAS*

While *Re Goldcorp Exchange Ltd* was not referred to in the judgments, the restrictive approach towards the recognition of equitable proprietary claims witnessed in *Goldcorp* was also manifested in *Halifax Building Society v. Thomas.*[54] In this case the first defendant advanced a 100 per cent mortgage loan from the plaintiff building society so as to acquire a flat. The granting of the loan had been induced by fraudulent misrepresentations on the part of the defendant. In fact he had assumed the identity of another for the purpose of the loan application. The first defendant defaulted on his repayment obligations despite a rising property market. The building society repossessed the flat and exercised its power of sale over the property. The flat was actually sold at a sum that was more than sufficient to repay the total debt owed to the society. A dispute arose over entitlement to the surplus. Who could claim it? The Crown Prosecution Service made to a claim thereto pursuant to the powers conferred on it by Part VI of the Criminal Justice Act.[55] Essentially the CPS were saying that the surplus represented the proceeds of criminal conduct which it could confiscate under the statutory scheme. The building society however contended that it was entitled to retain the surplus for its own benefit on the basis of a constructive trust.

---

[52] See S.R. Scott [1993] L.M.C.L.Q. 330.
[53] See McKendrick (1994) 110 L.Q.R. 509 at 513.
[54] [1995] 4 All E.R. 673. For an analysis of the case, see Birks [1996] *Trust Law International* 2.
[55] The powers to confiscate the proceeds of criminal conduct have been strengthened by the Criminal Justice Act 1993.

The Court of Appeal refused to entertain this constructive trust claim. Peter Gibson L.J. could not accept that the wrongdoing of the mortgagor could translate the mortgagee into the owner of the entire beneficial in the property when the mortgage had not been set aside. There was no fiduciary relationship between the borrower and the society in respect of the mortgage but merely that of debtor and secured creditor. The judge pointed out that English law had not followed other jurisdictions where the constructive trust had become a remedy for unjust enrichment. Reference was made in this connection to the following passage from *Snell's Equity*[56]:

> "In England the constructive trust has in general remained essentially a substantive institution; ownership must not be confused with obligation, nor must the relationship of debtor and creditor be converted into that of trustee and *cestui que* trust."

The legislative provisions were addressed by the judge. He suggested that Parliament had acted in the shape of Part VI of the Criminal Justice Act 1988 on the footing that without statutory intervention the criminal might keep the benefit of his crime. Moreover, the legislation had given the courts the power in specific circumstances to confiscate the benefit rather than reward the person against who the crime had been committed.[57] Glidewell L.J., in a concurring judgment, also stated that the readiness of Parliament to address the problem by legislation weakened the case for providing a solution by judicial creativity.

A number of comments about the *Thomas* judgment seem appropriate. First, one wonders whether the court would have been so happy in reaching the conclusion that it did in the absence of legislation to deprive a criminal of the fruits of his crime. The legislative intervention provided a convenient solution to the difficulties that might otherwise have arisen. Secondly, it was something surprising to see *Lister & Co. v. Stubbs*[58] stage a judicial comeback notwithstanding its disapproval by the Privy Council in *Att.-Gen. for Hong Kong v. Reid*.[59] Peter Gibson L.J. appeared to think that the *Lister* case was "impeccable when applied to the case in which the person claiming the money has simply made an outright loan to the defendant."[60] Thirdly, Lord Browne-Wilkinson seemed more favourably disposed to the possibility of a remedial constructive trust in *Westdeutsche Bank v. Islington L.B.C.*[61] He said:[62] "The court by way of remedy might impose a constructive trust on a defendant who knowingly retains property of which the plaintiff has been unjustly deprived. Since the remedy can be tailored to the circumstances of the particular case, innocent third parties would not be prejudiced and restitutionary defences, such as change of position, are capable of being given effect. However, whether English law should follow the United States and Canada by adopting the remedial constructive trust will have to be decided in some future case when the point is directly in issue." While

---

[56] (29th ed. 1990) at p. 197.
[57] He referred to the words of Hoffmann J. in *Chief Constable of Leicestershire v. M* [1988] 3 All E.R. 1015 at 1018: "The recent and detailed interventions of Parliament in this field suggest that the courts should not indulge in parallel creativity by the extension of general common law principles."
[58] (1890) 45 Ch.D. 1.
[59] [1994] 1 All E.R. 1; [1994] 1 A.C. 324.
[60] Quoting the words of Gibbs C.J. in *Daly v. Sydney Stock Exchange Ltd* (1986) 160 C.L.R. 371 at 379.
[61] [1996] 2 W.L.R. 802; [1996] 2 All E.R. 961.
[62] [1996] 2 W.L.R. 802 at 839.

the judgment of Lord Browne-Wilkinson traverses a wide area he does not engage directly with many of the leading cases. There is an inclination in his observations towards the incautious generalisation. While some commentators might see his free-wheeling and broad-ranging comments as a welcome breath of fresh air, others may be tempted to view them as potentially destabilising particular aspects of the law pertaining to proprietory claims. Certainly, Lord Goff seemed to be of that view.[63] He said that the court should restrict the inquiry to the actual questions at issue, and should not be tempted into formulating principles of a broader nature. It was not the function of the House of Lords in the particular case to identify the role of equitable proprietory claims in the law of restitution.

CONCLUSION

As a general proposition it is submitted that the doctrine of the remedial constructive trust should be kept within narrow bounds. There is a dichotomony which must be observed between family and commercial cases. The remedial constructive trust should be confined to the family sphere. Application of a more discretionary approach in this sphere would be in line with the expectation of the parties and productive of no greater uncertainty than the lengthy and detailed search for an elusive if not wholly fictitious common intention. Third parties need not be prejudiced as the remedy may be tailored to take account of the particular circumstances of the case. This process already occurs to a certain extent at the moment. In commercial cases however the very rationale of a constructive trust claim in most situations is to obtain priority over other creditors. The reason that a constructive trust is invoked is to achieve this preference. A discretionary approach towards the recogniton of equitable proprietary remedies would work to the detriment of third parties and also is potentially disruptive of commercial life. It is submitted that a proprietary remedy should only be granted by strict analogy with established categories and always bearing in mind the overriding fact that the real contest may be between the claimant and other creditors.

---

[63] *ibid.* at 810–811.

CHAPTER SEVEN

Mistaken Payments, Proprietary Claims and Insolvency

It is something of a paradox that modern technology may have increased rather than decreased the possibility of mistaken payments being made.[1] The policy of the law is to grant restitution in situations where the mistake causes the payment to be made though a change of position defence is available to the payee which may in particular circumstances restrict recovery in whole or in part.[2] This position has however only recently been arrived at in England. One matter on which there has been little authority and with which this chapter is concerned relates to the proprietary aspects of such mistaken payments. Do such payments generate a proprietary claim on the part of the payer so that in the event of the payee becoming insolvent the payer will have priority over the payee's general creditors? This chapter focusses on the issue. What is said also has implications with respect to the proprietary dimensions of payments made under a mistake of law. The traditional view of English law is that mistaken payments are not recoverable merely by virtue of being made under a mistake of law. This preclusive principle may not survive scrutiny at the House of Lords[3] but the proprietary consequences of such payments remains an unexplored issue.[4] The proprietary effect of mistaken payments has, to a certain extent, been addressed by the House of Lords recently in *Westdeutsche Bank v. Islington*.[4a] This case will be looked at in detail. It must be remembered, however, that consideration of the proprietary dimensions of mistaken payments was not necessary to the actual decision in the case. All judicial observations must be read *secundam subjectam materiam*. Moreover, Lord Goff said that if restitution lawyers were hoping to find from the House of Lords judgments broad statements of principle which might definitively establish the future shape of this part of the law, then they were likely to be disappointed.[4b]

RECOVERY OF MISTAKEN PAYMENTS BY PERSONAL ACTION

Prior to the decision of Robert Goff J. in *Barclays Bank v. W.J. Simms Ltd*[5] the generally understood view was that recovery of mistaken payments was confined to cases of "supposed liability" mistakes. The authority for this limitation on

[1] In *Barclays Bank v. W.J. Simms Ltd* [1980] 2 W.L.R. 218 Robert Goff J. made this comment specifically directed to the case of a bank overlooking its customer's instructions to stop payment of a cheque.
[2] This comment is made with respect to mistakes of fact. Below the level of the House of Lords there appears to be a general bar to recovery in cases of mistakes of law. For proposals for reform of this principle see the Law Commission paper No. 227 *Restitution: Mistakes of Law and Ultra Vires Public Authority Receipts and Payments* (Cm 2731) November 1994.
[3] The rule of non-recovery is generally taken to originate in *Bilbie v. Lumley* (1802) 2 East 469; 102 E.R. 448 and see also *Brisbane v. Dacres* (1813) 5 Taunt 143; 128 E.R. 641.
[4] See *Woolwich Equitable Building Society v. I.R.C.* [1993] A.C. 70.
[4a] [1996] 2 W.L.R. 802; [1996] 2 All E.R. 961.
[4b] [1996] 2 W.L.R. 802 at 810–811.
[5] [1980] 2 W.L.R. 218.

recovery was said to derive partly from the judgment of Parke B. in *Kelly v. Solari*.[6] The case involved an action by the plaintiff insurance company to recover money which they had paid out on foot of an insurance policy forgetting that the policy had lapsed by reason of the deceased failing to pay a premium. Parke B. said[7]:

> "I think that where money is paid to another under the influence of a mistake, that is, upon the supposition that a specific fact is true, which would entitle the other to the money, but which fact is untrue, and the money would not have been paid if it had been known to the payer that the fact was untrue, an action will lie to recover it back, and it is against conscience to retain it ..."

These observations of Parke B. were usually coupled with dicta of Bramwell B. in *Aiken v. Short*[8] to constitute cornerstones of the "supposed liability" confinement of recovery. Bramwell B.'s remarks are as follows[9]:

> "In order to entitle a person to recover back money paid under a mistake of fact, the mistake must be as to a fact which, if true, would make the person paying liable to pay the money; not where, if true, it would merely make it desirable that he should pay the money."

There were however dotted through the body of precedents statements and cases which supported a wider principle of recovery. For instance in *Kleninwort, Sons & Co. v. Dunlop Rubber Co.*[10] Lord Loreburn L.C. made a very broad statement about the principles governing recovery. He said that if money is paid under a mistake of fact and is redemanded from the person who received it before his position has been altered to his disadvantage, the money must be repaid in whatever character it was received. Some of these decisions could be rationalised on the basis of an extended view of liability mistakes. For example in *Jones Ltd v. Waring & Gillow Ltd*[11] a payment was recovered where the payer was acting under the mistaken belief that he was under a legal liability to a third party to make the payment. Other cases are explicable on the ground that the payer was acting under the belief that a state of affairs existed which brought into being a moral duty to make the payment.[12] These extensions in the categories of "supposed liability" mistakes have attracted criticism. It has been argued that if the test is framed so as to encompass moral as well as legal obligations this deprives it of the doctrinal advantages of objectivity and certainty.[13] Moreover, from the point of view of economic analysis the introduction of moral considerations into the equation is at odds with the formulation

---

[6] (1841) 9 M & W 54; 152 E.R. 24.
[7] (1841) 9 M & W 54 at 58.
[8] (1856) 1 H & N 210;
[9] (1856) 1 H & N 210 at 215.
[10] (1907) 97 L.T. 263 at 264. See also *Colonial Bank v. Exchange Bank of Yarmouth, Nova Scotia* (1886) 11 App. Cas. 84.
[11] [1926] A.C. 670 and see also *Kerrison v. Glyn, Mills, Currie & Co* (1911) 81 L.J.K.B. 465.
[12] *Larner v. London County Council* [1949] 2 K.B. 683.
[13] See generally Essay No. 6 "Mistaken Payments in the Law of Restitution" in *The Use and Abuse of Unjust Enrichment* (Jack Beatson ed.), p. 154. This essay was originally co-authored with W. Bishop and published in (1986) 36 *University of Toronto Law Journal* 149. See also *Royal Bank v. R* [1931] 2 D.L.R. 685.

of a rule which identifies mistakes that have lower avoidance costs.[14] Furthermore, in the case of a supposed moral obligation the payer is less likely to have the means of knowing whether or not the payer is in fact mistaken.

More fundamentally there is the point that these enlargements of the conception of "supposed liability" mistakes do not adequately explain all the case law. Some decisions are not reconcilable on the basis of any notion of "supposed liability". This point was brought home by Robert Goff J. in *Barclays Bank v. W.J. Simms Ltd*[15] who conducted a masterly review of the authorities before reaching certain conclusions. These conclusions are as follows[16]:

> "(1) If a person pays money to another under a mistake of fact which causes him to make the payment, he is prima facie entitled to recover it as money paid under a mistake of fact. (2) His claim may however fail if (a) the payer intends that the payee shall have the money at all events, whether the fact be true or false, or is deemed in law so to intend; or (b) the payment is made for good consideration, in particular if the money is paid to discharge, and does discharge, a debt owed to the payee (or a principal on whose behalf he is authorised to receive the payment) by the payer or by a third party by whom he is authorised to discharge the debt; or (c) the payee has changed his position in good faith, or is deemed in law to have done so."

The move from a "supposed liability" to a purely causative test has met with general approbation among commentators, not least for its open acknowledgement of the restitutionary basis of liability.[17] Moreover, in *Barclays Bank v. W.J. Simms Ltd* there is some incidental reference to the proprietary consequences of mistaken payments.[18] Before delving deeply into this issue it is appropriate to say something about the distinction between mistake and motive and also the policy rationale underpinning recovery of mistaken payments.[19]

WHY ALLOW RESTITUTION?

On grounds of economic analysis it has been argued that a restitutionary

---

[14] See Beatson *op cit.* at 154.

[15] [1980] 1 Q.B. 677. It has been argued that *Barclays Bank Ltd v. W.J. Simms Ltd* could have been decided by simply extending the meaning of supposed liability on the basis that the bank paid the money to the defendant under the mistaken belief that it was bound to do so under a legal liability to its customer. For this argument see Burrows, *The Law of Restitution* (1993) p. 100.

[16] *ibid* at 697.

[17] See generally on mistakes of fact Goff and Jones, *The Law of Restitution* (4th ed., 1993), pp. 107–141.

[18] At one point in his judgment Robert Goff J. said that where an action is brought to recover money paid under a mistake of fact, property will almost invariably have passed to the defendant.

[19] The limitations on recovery spelled out by Robert Goff J. have also attracted some debate and discussion. In particular controversy has centred on the question of recovery of payments made in submission to an honest claim. In *Kelly v. Solari* Parke B. said that a claim may fail if "the payer intends that the payee shall have the money at all events whether the fact be true or false ...". For further discussion on this issue see Andrews [1989] L.M.C.L.Q. 431; Arrowsmith, essay 2 in *Essays on the Law of Restitution* (Burrows ed., 1991). Arrowsmith argues that restitution should normally be refused whenever the payer had doubts on the issue on which he claims to be mistaken at the time he paid. The payer may be said to have waived his right to recover in such circumstances, since he ought not to pay unless the payee agrees to accept a payment which is conditional. She contends that it is preferable to refer to the doctrine of *Kelly v. Solari* as one of "waiver" than as one of "submission to an honest claim".

right is appropriate to avoid wasted expenditure on wasted avoidance.[20] Moreover, mistakes diminish the payer's property and augments the recipient's property. The consequence of permitting recipients to retain mistaken payments is the economic equivalent of levying a small tax on those who create valuable assets and then making random distributions of the proceeds of this tax to all members of the community irrespective of need or the extent to which they have contributed to the generation of wealth. Only those who have accumulated property can lose it whereas corresponding gains are completely random.

On the other hand there is something to be said with respect to the dangers of too much restitution. The policy of sanctity of title or quieting a person's possession is a feature of many areas of the law.[21] With this objective in view the security of receipts should not readily be undermined. This consideration partly explains traditional judicial reluctance to countenance wide grounds of recovery. The factor no doubt influenced the following observations of Sir Wilfred Greene M.R. in *Morgan v. Ashcroft*[22]:

"If a father, believing that his son has suffered a financial loss, gives him a sum of money, he surely could not claim repayment if he afterwards discovered that no such loss had occurred."

The distinction between mistake, motive and misprediction is not a very clearcut one.[23] Nevertheless the following example does have some explanatory power. Suppose that X pays Y a sum of money thinking that Y will support X's point of view in some coming contest.[24] This may be described as a misprediction or indeed the motive for the payment and does not found a claim for restitution. On the other hand while the law should not encourage second thoughts amongst donors there seems no reason why mistaken gifts should not be recoverable in appropriate circumstances. If a donor can prove that a particular gift was made under a misapprehension as to fact then as a general proposition restitution should be made. After all the recipient of the gift is a mere volunteer. Provided that he is "afforded some protection for his reliance or change of position as a result of the gift, there is little to be said for allowing him to keep the property."[25]

MISTAKES OF LAW[26]

In *Sawyer and Vincent v. Window Brace Ltd*[27] Croom-Johnson J. observed:

---

[20] See Beatson, *The Use and Abuse of Unjust Enrichment* (1991), pp. 138–139.
[21] One may highlight the statute of limitations and the law of adverse possession.
[22] [1938] 1 K.B. 49 at 66. The Master of the Rolls added that to hold the contrary would almost amount to saying that motive not mistake was the decisive factor.
[23] According to Goff and Jones, *The Law of Restitution* (4th ed., 1993), p. 121 the line is a thin one. They give the example of a father who gives his son £1,000 in the belief, not induced by his son's misrepresentation, that his son has achieved straight A's in his mock examination. When the school reports arrive on the door step he discovers that his son has got straight D's.
[24] The example comes from Birks, *An Introduction to the Law of Restitution* (1985), p. 147.
[25] Goff and Jones, *op cit.*, at 121. They quote from an article by Parker (1959) 58 Mich. L. Rev. 90 at 92.
[26] See generally Law Commission Report No 227 *Restitution: Mistakes of Law and Ultra Vires Public Receipts and Payments* (Cm 2731 November 1994).
[27] [1943] 1 K.B. 32 at 34. See also *R v. Tower Hamlets London Brough Council, ex p. Chetnik Developments Ltd* [1988] A.C. 858.

"That a voluntary payment made under a mistake of law cannot be recovered is, I should have thought, beyond argument at this period in our legal history."

The *fons et origo* of the rule precluding recovery for mistakes of law is usually taken to be the judgment of Lord Ellenborough C.J. in *Bilbie v. Lumley*.[28] This is a case where the plaintiff underwriters had paid out on foot of an insurance policy not realising that they were not liable to pay by reason of the fact that the assured had failed to disclose a material fact. Recovery was not permitted because the money had been paid under a mistake of law. Lord Ellenborough succinctly stated[29]:

"Every man must be taken to be cognisant of the law; otherwise there is no saying to what extent the excuse of ignorance might not be carried."

It has been argued that this judgment should only be taken to rule out recovery of money which was paid in settlement of an honest claim.[30] The implication of this approach would be to say that any other payment made under a mistake of law should be recoverable if it would be recoverable had the mistake been one of fact.[31] While there is a lot to be said for this approach as a matter of policy, the law excluding recovery seems securely settled at least below the level of the House of Lords.[32] In *Woolwich Building Society v. I.R.C.* Lord Goff pointed out that the principle had been the subject of forceful criticism.[33] While it had originally been adopted throughout the Commonwealth the preclusive principle had now been abrogated in many jurisdictions either by statute or by judicial action.[34] Other Law Lords seemed equally sceptical of the merits of the rule. Lord Jauncey doubted whether the distinction between mistake of fact and of law could be justified any longer.[35] Lord Slynn opined that the mistake of law rule was open to review by the House of Lords.[36] Lord Keith sounded something of a dissentient note. He thought that the rule was too deeply embedded in English jurisprudence to be uprooted judicially.[37]

As was remarked by Lord Goff however, such judicial upheavals have occurred in other jurisdictions. In this connection one might instance the judgment of the High Court of Australia in *David Securities Pty. Ltd v. Commonwealth Bank of*

---

[28] (1802) 2 East 469; 102 E.R. 448. See also *Brisbane v. Dacres* (1813) 5 Taunt 143; 128 E.R. 641.
[29] (1802) 2 East 469 at 472.
[30] Goff and Jones *op cit.* at 143. There is a full discussion of the issue in Chap. 4 of the treatise by Goff and Jones and see also Burrows, *The Law of Restitution* (1993), pp. 109–120.
[31] According to McCamus (1983) 17 U.B.C.L.R. 233 it would be difficult to identify another private law doctrine which has been so universally condemned or another reform which enjoys such widespread support. For a full discussion of the issue see Law Commission Report No. 227.
[32] *Westdeutsche Landesbank Girozentrale v. Islington L.B.C.* [1994] 1 W.L.R. 938.
[33] [1993] A.C. 70 at 192. He did not think that the principle of recovery should be inapplicable simply because the citizen has paid the money under a mistake of law.
[34] For judicial decisions see *Air Canada v. British Columbia* [1989] 1 S.C.R. 1161 (Supreme Court of Canada); *David Securities Pty Ltd v. Commonwealth Bank of Australia* (1992) 66 A.L.J.R. 768 (High Court of Australia); *Willis Faber Enthoven (Pty) Ltd v. Receiver of Revenue* (South African Appellate Division). For Scotland see now *Morgan Guaranty Trust Co. of New York v. Lothian Regional Council* 1995 S.L.T. 299. The case is commented upon by Andrew [1995] C.L.J. 246 and also by Gretton [1996] J.B.L. 327.
[35] [1993] A.C. 70 at 192.
[36] *ibid* at 199.
[37] [1993] A.C. 70 at 154.

Australia.[38] There the court under the leadership of Mason C.J. took the view that the principle that money paid under a mistake of law was irrecoverable was too broad and more restrictive than was necessary. According to the court, a narrower principle, founded firmly on the policy that the law wishes to uphold bargains and enforce compromises entered into, would be more equitable. The majority judges took the view that the identification and acceptance of such a narrow principle was strongly supported by the difficulty and artificiality of seeking to draw a rigid distinction between cases of mistake of law and mistake of fact.[39] The judges added that the criticism voiced of the preclusive principle gained added impetus in Australia by virtue of the judicial recognition in *Pavey & Matthews Pty. Ltd v. Paul*[40] of the unifying legal concept of unjust enrichment. Once a doctrine of unjust enrichment was recognised, the distinction as to mistake of law and mistake of fact became simply meaningless.[41]

PROPRIETARY CLAIMS AND POINTS OF COMPARISON AND DIFFERENTIATION

Clearly mistaken payments are recoverable in certain circumstances by personal action. The question arises whether such payments may also form the subject of a proprietary claim. The *locus classicus* is *Chase Manhattan Bank N.A. v. Israel-British Bank (London) Ltd*[42] which answers the question in the affirmative. Before delving deeply in this decision it is necessary to discuss a number of preliminary points. These points have not always been separated out in the cases. A disentangling process is however useful to appreciate the variety of considerations that may arise. Firstly, there is the question of the law/equity divide. It may be that title to a mistaken payment has passed to the recipient at law but that the payer retains an equitable proprietary interest. This was the analysis adopted in *Chase Manhattan.* On the other hand there is a certain body of authority for the proposition that, at least with respect to particular types of mistakes, no title, whether at law or in equity, passes to the recipient of the money or property being transferred.[43] The question arises whether there is any significance in the distinction. Another issue relates to the existence of a contract between payor and payee. What is the significance of this factor?[44] How does it impact on the passing of property? This question needs to be considered but first I propose to look at the law/equity divide.

---

[38] (1992) 66 A.L.J.R. 768.
[39] Mason C.J. along with Deane, Toohey, Gaudron and McHugh JJ. formed the majority. Brennan J. delivered a separate judgment.
[40] (1987) 162 C.L.R. 221.
[41] Reference was made in this connection to the observations of Dickson J. in *Electric Commission of Nepean v. Ontario Hydro* (1982) 132 D.L.R. (3d) 193. The Australian High Court said that if the ground for ordering recovery is that the defendant has been unjustly enriched there was no justification for drawing distinctions on the basis of how the enrichment was gained, except in so far as the manner of gaining the enrichment bears upon the justice of the case.
[42] [1981] Ch. 105. Recently applied in New Zealand in *Hong Kong and Shanghai Banking Corp. v. Fortex Group Ltd* (1995) 5 N. 2. B.L.C. 103, 869.
[43] *Cundy v. Lindsay* (1878) 3 App. Cas. 459.
[44] See generally Worthington [1995] *Trust Law International* 113.

THE LAW/EQUITY DIVIDE IN MISTAKE CASES

Judges have not always satisfactorily divided between the passage of property at law or in equity. There has been a degree of terminological confusion. In certain cases it has been held that the mistake made was sufficiently fundamental to prevent the passing of property even at law. One might cite in this connection the judgment of Lord Wright, speaking for the Privy Council, in *Norwich Union Fire Insurance Society v. W.H. Price Ltd.*[45] While on the passing of property point the judgment is somewhat obscure nevertheless the judge seems to say that the effect of a mistake may be to negative altogether the transmission of title from payer to recipient. He said[46]:

"The mistake being of the character that it was, prevented there being that intention which the common law regards as essential to the making of an agreement or of the transfer of money or property.... It is, however, essential that the mistake relied on should be of such a nature that it can be properly described as a mistake in respect of the underlying assumption of the contract or transaction or as being fundamental or basic."

In some other cases, the judges have simply said that the mistake made was sufficient to prevent the passing of property but without distinguishing between legal and equitable title. In the final category of cases, exemplified by the decision of Goulding J. in the *Chase Manhattan* case, it has been held that while legal title passes to the recipient of a payment, the payer, because of the nature of the mistake made, keeps ownership of the property in equity. In other words the recipient has legal title and the payer equitable. A trust relationship has been created with the recipient constituted as a trustee and the payer the trust beneficiary. What are the implications of the establishment of a trust? In particular are all the onerous consequences of being a trustee case on the recipient of a mistaken payment, namely investment duties and potential liabilities for breach of trust? There are suggestions from the judgment of Lord Browne-Wilkinson in *Target Holdings v. Redferns*[47] that this is in fact not the case. While the *Target Holdings* case is specifically concerned with the issue of assessing the amount of compensation payable to trust beneficiaries for breach of trust the approach taken by the House of Lords is strongly hostile to a blanket uniformity being applied across all types of trusts. Different considerations and different principles may apply to different types of trusts. Lord Browne-Wilkinson said[48]:

"But in my judgment it is in any event wrong to lift wholesale the detailed rules developed in the context of traditional trusts and then seek to apply them to trusts of quite a different kind. In the modern world the trust has become a valuable device in commercial and financial dealings. The fundamental principles of equity apply as much to such trusts as they do to the traditional trusts in relation to which those principles were originally formulated. But in my judgment it is important, if the trust is not to be rendered commercially useless, to distinguish between the basic principles of trust law and those specialist rules developed in relation to traditional trusts which

---

[45] [1934] A.C. 455.
[46] *ibid* at 463.
[47] [1995] 3 All E.R. 785.
[48] *ibid* at 795.

are applicable only to such trusts and the rationale of which has no application to trusts of quite a different kind."

If these observations are borne in mind in the present context then there should be no practical differences between mistake cases where legal title is retained and those where equitable title is retained. The differences only exist at the terminological level. It must be said however, that the differences, while they may be simply ones of verbal fomulation, serve to cloud understanding. There is a strong argument for the removal of such differences.

DIFFERENT KINDS OF MISTAKE

This chapter has already differentiated to a certain extent between different kinds of mistake. As we have seen there was a body of authority restricting restitutionary recovery to supposed liability mistakes but this limitation has now been swept away. Some mistaken payments involve gifts made under a mistake of fact. In other cases, a contract exists between payer and payee so that there is a contractual background to the payment. But the contractual characterisation conflates a number of sets of circumstance. There may been a mistaken double payment, *i.e.* the same debt is paid twice over. A sum may have been paid to satisfy a contractual claim but due to some miscalculation the amount paid is more than sufficient to satisfy the debt. Alternatively there may be a contract in existence between payer and payee but, at the time that the payment is made, there is no contractual obligation to make any payment where the payer mistakenly thinks that there is. It is submitted that in terms of restitutionary proprietary implications these cases are governed by the same principles as mistaken gifts. With the possible exception of cases where an overpayment is made in purported settlement of a debt the case law does not support any differentiation between the various kinds of mistake. Slightly different is the situation where a payment has been made on foot of a purported contract but the contract is subsequently adjudged to be void at common law or voidable in equity. The latter scenarios merit a degree of individual attention.

CONTRACTS WHICH ARE VOID OR VOIDABLE ON GROUNDS OF MISTAKE

There is a view that if a contract is void on grounds of mistake then this has the effect of automatically invalidating any transfer of property that might physically have taken place.[49] This view derives some support from the decision of the House of Lords in *Cundy v. Lindsay*.[50]

Cundy v. Lindsay is a well known case where a rogue called Blenkarn wrote to the plaintiffs and offered to buy certain goods. He masked his signature so as to resemble that of Blenkiron & Co, a substantial undertaking carrying on business in the same street and with whom the plaintiffs had previously dealt. The plaintiffs forwarded the goods under the assumption that they were dealing with Blenkiron & Co. The goods eventually came into the possession of the defendant, an innocent purchaser. The House of Lords held that the contract between the plaintiffs and Blenkiron was void for mistake. No property in the

---

[49] See generally on this question Watts [1995] *Restitution Law Review* 49.
[50] (1878) 3 App. Cas. 459.

goods passed and the plaintiff was entitled to recover them. Lord Cairns L.C. said[51]:

> "If the property in the goods in question passed it could only pass by way of contract; there is nothing else which could have passed the property."

The same view was expressed by a New Zealand judge, Gresson P., in *Fawcett v. Star Car Sales Ltd*[52] where he said:

> "The acquisition of title to a chattel (save in certain special cases) must be pursuant to a contract of sale. In a sale of goods the essential thing about which the parties are contracting is the property in the chattel which is the subject of the transaction. But it is equally essential that the sale be supported by a valid contract. The passing of property is not something quite independent of the contract; the property passes only if there is a contract pursuant to which the property passes."

On the other hand, it must be borne in mind that passing of title questions were not investigated to any extent in *Cundy v. Lindsay*. Moreover, the judgment of Gresson P. in the New Zealand case was a dissenting one. The majority judges were of the opinion that the intention to transfer title plus physical delivery would mean that title passed. Cleary J. said that the question whether any property in goods passed depended primarily on the vendor's intention.[53] *Cundy v. Lindsay* was explained on the basis that the vendors' only intention was to make a sale to Blenkiron & Co. This negatived any intention to make a sale to Blenkarn. This seems to be a plausible explanation of the case. Be that as it may there is much to be said, on the basis of fundamental legal principle for the proposition advanced by one commentator that the matter of whether title has passed is to be determined independently of the validity of the contract[54]:

> "The primary question is whether, despite the failure of the contract, title was intended to pass; a mere mistaken assumption as to the validity of the contract not acting to prevent the passage of title."

So one is left with the conclusion that the the invalidity of the contract does not automatically exclude the passing of property.[55] But of course the same factors that operate to render a contract invalid on grounds of mistake may prevent property from passing. If a mistake under which both parties are labouring is sufficiently large to make the contract void then, it may be, that no property passes, but there is no necessary connection between this conclusion and the invalidity of the contract.

Contracts that are voidable in equity on grounds of mistake are a different

---

[51] *ibid.* at 464.

[52] [1960] N.Z.L.R. 406 at 424.

[53] [1960] N.Z.L.R. 406 at 430.

[54] Watts [1995] *Restitution Law Review* 49 at 53. Watts refers to Roman and modern German law on which see Nicholas, *Introduction to Roman Law* (1962), pp. 115–120, 231–232; Evan-Jones and MacCormack in "Iusta Causa Traditionis" of *New Perspectives in the Roman Law of Property* (Peter Birks ed., 1989), Chap. 7 and Zweigert & Kotz, *An Introduction to Comparative Law* (2nd revised ed., 1987) translated by Tony Weir at pp. 580–582.

[55] A different view is taken in R.M. Goode, *Commercial Law* (2nd ed., 1995, pp. 82–83 but *cf.* Goode *op cit.* at p. 55.

story. First of all, to the jurisdiction of the courts. Basically equity gives assistance where the common law does not, providing relief in a wider category of cases.[56] At the risk of gross over-simplification, a mistake does not have to be so "fundamental" to ground a case for relief in equity. The contract however is valid until set aside (rescinded) by the courts. Therefore property passes though the recipient may be divested of title through a subsequent exercise of judicial discretion. The question then arises whether or not the possibility of rescission is enough to support a claim to trace the property through changes in form. There is recent judicial support for the proposition that it is, notably from Millett J. in *El Ajou v. Dollar Land Holdings*[57] though the point is by no means an uncontroversial one. There is detailed consideration of the issue in Chapter 8. Passing of property issues were considered to a certain degree by the House of Lords in *Westdeutsche Bank v. Islington London Borough Council*.[58] Not all the relevant authorities were opened to the court. Argument by counsel before the House of Lords was confined to the comparatively narrow point of the jurisdiction of the court to award compound interest and even then the argument was somewhat truncated. Counsel for the local authority informed the House that because of the costs which the local authority was incurring on the appeal, he was required by his clients to curtail his presentation. Be that as it may, sufficient was said on the point of proprietary claims in *Westdeutsche* to warrant according the case extended treatment.

WESTDEUTSCHE BANK V. ISLINGTON L.B.C.

The *Westdeutsche* case arose out of the interest rate swap contracts[59] entered into by local authorities in the 1980s to circumvent central government controls on borrowing.[60] These swaps were held to be *ultra vires* the local authorities by Dillon J. in *Hazell v. Hammersmith and Fulham London Borough Council*[61] which decision was subsequently confirmed on final appeal to the House of Lords.[62] In many instances banks had made upfront payments to the local authorities pursuant to these interest rate swap contracts. For instance in the *Westdeutsche* case itself a payment of £2.5 million had been made by the bank and the local

---

[56] *Solle v. Butcher* [1950] 1 K.B. 671.
[57] [1993] 3 All E.R. 717 at 734. See also *Lonrho plc v. Fayed (No 2)* [1992] 1 W.L.R. 1 at 11–12; *Brady v. Stapelton* (1952) 88 C.L.R. 322; *Daly v. Sydney Stock Exchange Ltd* (1986) 160 C.L.R. 371 at 387–390 *per* Brennan J.
[58] [1996] 2 W.L.R. 802; [1996] 2 All E.R. 961
[59] An interest rate swap contract was described by Lord Templeman in *Hazell v. Hammersmith and Fulham London Borough Council* [1992] 2 A.C. 1 at 24 as follows: "an agreement between two parties by which each agrees to pay the other on a specified date or dates an amount calculated by reference to the interest which would have accrued over a given period on the same notional principal sum assuming different rates of interest are payable in each case. For example, one rate may be fixed at 10 per cent and the other rate may be equivalent to the six-month London InterBank Offered Rate (LIBOR). If the LIBOR rate over the period of the swap is higher than 10 per cent then the party agreeing to receive 'interest' in accordance with LIBOR will receive more than the party entitled to receive the 10 per cent. Normally, neither party will in fact pay the sums which it has agreed to pay over the period of the swap but instead will make a settlement on a 'net payment basis' under which the party owing the greater amount on any day simply pays the difference between the two amounts due to the other."
[60] See the comments of Lord Goff in *Westdeutsche* [1996] 2 W.L.R. 802 at 805.
[61] [1990] 2 Q.B. 697.
[62] [1992] 2 A.C. 1.

authority had only repaid some £1 million leaving an outstanding balance of over £1 million when the invalidity of the contract became clear as a result of the *Hazell* decision. Proceedings were brought to recover this sum which proceedings were successful at first instance and in the Court of Appeal notwithstanding the fact that on first impressions there appeared to be substantial legal obstacles to recovery.[63] The local authority did not appeal on the substantive issue to the House of Lords. One suspects this was the case because, despite the fact that the decisions of the lower courts had been subjected to forceful doctrinal criticism, the merits were overwhelmingly in favour of the banks and it was surmised that the legal impediments inhibiting recovery would be brushed aside by the House of Lords.[64] The local authority did however appeal on the question whether simple interest or compound interest was payable on the amount found to be due. In the event the House of Lords, by a 3–2 majority, held that simple interest only was payable.[65] In resolving this issue it was necessary however, to investigate to a certain extent the proprietary effect of payments made on foot of an *ultra vires* contract. While their Lordships eschewed a general discussion of the role of proprietary claims within the law of restitution and the impact of insolvency principles some of the judgments range more broadly than the narrow point specifically at issue. This is particularly true of that of Lord Browne-Wilkinson.

The balance of the upfront payment was held to be recoverable on foot of a personal restitutionary claim by the bank. At first instance and in the Court of Appeal it was also held that the *ultra vires* nature of the payment constituted the local authority a trustee in respect of the receipt of the money. There was a separation of legal and equitable ownership with the local authority holding the money in a fiduciary capacity as a trustee.[66] This brought into play an equitable jurisdiction to award compound interest against the local authority. The House of Lords took the view that payments made pursuant to an *ultra vires* contract did not give rise to any relationship of trust between payer and recipient. In other words the payee obtained full legal and equitable ownership. All that the payer had was a personal restitutionary right of action to recover the *ultra vires* payment. There was no equitable proprietary claim available. Consequently the grounds for awarding compound interest advanced by the Court of Appeal fell away. Moreover, the House of Lords, in a 3–2 majority decision, felt unable to award compound interest in supplementation of the personal right of recovery. There was no power in equity to remedy the supposed defects of the common law.

Lord Browne-Wilkinson summarised the principal argument of the bank as being that, since the contract was void, title did not pass at the date of payment either at law or in equity. The effect of the mixing of the money with other

---

[63] See generally Swadling [1994] *Restitution Law Review* 73; Burrows (1993) 143 N.L.J. 480; Burrows [1995] *Restitution Law Review* 15; Birks (1993) 23 *University of Western Australia Law Review* 195.

[64] See the comments by Burrows [1995] *Restitution Law Review* 15: "The high rate of out-of-court settlements reflects a widely-shared view at the Bar, as I perceive it, that whichever party makes a gain from a void swap contract at the expense of the other party is, subject to defences, unjustly enriched and should make restitution; and that any barriers which the present law puts against that conclusion would be removed, if a case gets there, by the House of Lords."

[65] Lord Browne-Wilkinson, Slynn and Lloyd formed the majority. Lords Goff and Woolf dissented.

[66] Strangely enough Hobhouse J., at first instance, spoke exclusively of fiduciary relationships and seemed to deny the possibility of a trust: "It is not alleged that the councils received the money as trustees or as constructive trustees ..." [1994] 4 All E.R. 890 at 916.

moneys in a running account however, was to extinguish the legal title of the bank thereto. The bank nevertheless retained an equitable proprietary interest. This submission was supported by two main planks. First, the decision of the House of Lords in *Sinclair v. Brougham*[67] and secondly the academic writings of Professor Peter Birks.[68]

First, *Sinclair v. Brougham*. This case has long baffled judges and commentators. In *Re Diplock*[69] Lord Greene said that the court would be lacking in candour if it did not confess that it found the speeches in *Sinclair v. Brougham* difficult if not impossible to understand. Similar feelings of incomprehension beset Lord Browne-Wilkinson who spoke with the concurrence of Lords Slynn and Lloyd. He said *Sinclair v. Brougham* was a bewildering authority in that no single *ratio decidendi* could be detected and all the reasoning was open to serious objection. His Lordship suggested that *Sinclair v. Brougham* should be overruled and the law developed in accordance with principle and commercial common sense. He said[70]:

"[A] claimant for restitution of moneys paid under an *ultra vires*, and therefore void, contract has a personal action at law to recover the moneys paid as on a total failure of consideration; he will not have an equitable proprietary claim which gives him either rights against third parties or priority in an insolvency; nor will he have a personal claim in equity, since the recipient is not a trustee."

While Lord Browne-Wilkinson spoke for the majority on the issue of overruling *Sinclair v. Brougham* his brother judge, Lord Goff, was not prepared to confine the case solely to the realms of legal history. He thought that the case should stand as an assertion that those who are caught in the trap of advancing money under *ultra vires* borrowing contracts will not be denied appropriate relief.[71]

Professor Peter Birks has argued that the plaintiff should have a proprietary remedy on the basis of a resulting trust whenever he has transferred value under a mistake or under a contract the consideration for which wholly fails.[72] The proposition advanced by Birks was adopted by counsel on behalf of the bank in *Westdeutsche*. Both Lords Browne-Wilkinson and Goff seemed to think that this submission was incompatible with basic principles of the law of trusts, *i.e.* that the conscience of the trustee is affected. Lord Browne-Wilkinson said[73]:

"Unless and until the trustee is aware of the factors which give rise to the supposed trust, there is nothing which can affect his conscience. Thus neither in the case of a subsequent failure of consideration nor in the case of a payment under a contract subsequently found to be void for mistake or failure of condition will there be circumstances, at the date of receipt, which can impinge on the conscience of the recipient, thereby making him a trustee."

---

[67] [1914] A.C. 398, *Sinclair v. Brougham* is a case where a building society carried on an *ultra vires* banking business. The House of Lords held that persons who had made deposits to the society in connection with the *ultra vires* banking business could trace into the assets of the now insolvent society.

[68] In particular the paper "Restitution and Resulting Trusts" in *Equity: Contemporary Legal Developments* (S. Goldstein ed. 1992), p. 335. As Lord Goff noted at [1996] 2 W.L.R. 802 at 814, Professor Birks' thesis is avowedly experimental having been written to test the temperature of the water.

[69] [1948] Ch. 465.

[70] [1996] 2 W.L.R. 802 at 836–837.

[71] [1996] 2 W.L.R. 802 at 813.

[72] "Restitution and Resulting Trusts" in *Equity and Contemporary Legal Developments* (S. Goldstein ed. 1992), p. 335.

[73] [1996] 2 W.L.R. 802 at 832.

Lord Browne-Wilkinson said that Professor Birks had to impose on his wider view an arbitrary and admittedly unprincipled modification so as to ensure that a resulting trust did not arise when there had only been a failure to perform a contract, as opposed to total failure of consideration. Such an arbitrary exclusion,[74] while designed to preserve the rights of creditors in the insolvency of the recipient, cast doubt on the validity of the entire concept. In rejecting the bank's arguments based on the existence of a resulting trust Lord Browne-Wilkinson also has regard to what he deemed to be commercial commonsense. He said[75]:

> "If the bank's arguments are correct, a businessman who has entered into transactions relating to or dependent upon property rights could find that assets which apparently belong to one person in fact belong to another; that these are 'off balance sheet' liabilities of which he cannot be aware; that these property rights and liabilities arise from circumstances unknown not only to himself but also to anyone else who has been involved in the transactions. A new area of unmanageable risk will be introduced into commercial dealings."

So the bottom line from Lord Browne-Wilkinson seems to be that property passes to the recipient, both at law and in equity, in cases of *ultra vires* contracts. Is the position any different where a contract is void on grounds of mistake? The general tenor of Lord Browne-Wilkinson's judgment is to the effect that the recipient of property transferred pursuant to a void contract should have full legal and equitable title thereto. The judge stressed that the creation of an equitable proprietary interest in moneys received under a void contract was capable of having adverse effects quite apart from insolvency. Such a proprietary interest would be enforceable against any recipient of the property other than the purchaser for value of a legal interest without notice. Lord Browne-Wilkinson provided examples to illustrate his point and concluded by saying that he could see no moral or legal justification for according priority to the right of the transferor to obtain restitution over third parties who had not themselves been enriched, in any real sense, at the transferor's expense and indeed have had no dealings with the transferor.[76] If the contract had been valid the transferor would have had purely personal rights against the recipient of the property. He should not be any better off because the contract was void.

Lord Browne-Wilkinson went on to consider the decision of Goulding J. in *Chase Manhattan Bank N.A. v. Israel-British Bank (London) Ltd.*[77] In the *Chase Manhattan Bank* case it was held that the receipt of money paid under a mistake of fact constituted the recipient a trustee. The payer retained an equitable proprietary interest in it and the conscience of the recipient was subjected to a fiduciary duty to respect this proprietary right. Lord Browne-Wilkinson was unimpressed by this reasoning saying that the recipient's "conscience" could not be affected at a time when he was not aware of any mistake. He thought however, that the result in the case could be supported on other grounds. Within two days of the mistaken payment having been made, the defendant learned of the situation and either knew that it was a mistake, or was put fully on inquiry by facts that

---

[74] See Birks "Restitution and Resulting Trusts" at pp. 356–359 and 362.
[75] [1996] 2 W.L.R. 802 at 828.
[76] [1996] 2 W.L.R. 802 at 827–828.
[77] [1981] Ch. 105.

should have indicated it might be a mistake.[78] While Goulding J. thought that this was irrelevant,[79] Lord Browne-Wilkinson considered it to be highly relevant. The latter said that the mere receipt of the moneys, in ignorance of the mistake, gave rise to no trust, the retention of the moneys after the recipient bank learned of the mistake might well have given rise to a constructive trust.

Does this mean that the actual result in *Westdeutsche* would have been different had the recipient local authority been aware of the potentially *ultra vires* nature of the interest rate swap contract shortly after the up-front payment was made by the bank? With respect, it may be said that this rationalisation is difficult to reconcile with other parts of Lord Browne-Wilkinson's judgment. Surely knowledge on the part of the recipient of a mistaken/*ultra vires* payment is irrelevant as far as third parties are concerned. They are still exposed to the risk of losing priority irrespective of whether or not the initial recipient knows of the mistaken/*ultra vires* nature of the payment. What about the dangers of hidden trusts and off-balance sheet liabilities on which Lord Browne-Wilkinson waxed lyrical? Lord Goff was altogether more tentative on this issue. He did not find it necessary to review the decision of Goulding J. in the *Chase Manhattan Bank* case.[80] However, he found it difficult to escape the conclusion that, generally speaking, the beneficial interest in money paid under a void contract passes to the payee. He added[81]:

> "This must certainly be the case where the consideration for the payment fails after the payment is made, as in cases of frustration or breach of contract; and there appears to be no good reason why the same should not apply in cases where, as in the present case, the contract under which the payment is made is void *ab initio* and the consideration for the payment therefore fails at the time of payment."

Lord Goff seemed to think that property may not have passed where a fundamental mistake of fact, as distinct from one of law, was made but no authorities on this question were examined. In fact the authorities are in a state of considerable confusion on this issue. Nothing was resolved in *Westdeutsche* on the subject of the proprietary effect of mistaken payments. If anything the decision has had something of a destabilising effect throwing into doubt established authorities like the *Chase Manhattan Bank* case. Given the lack of any clear guidance provided in *Westdeutsche* the soundest course seems to be to examine in detail *Chase Manhattan* and the other cases concerned with the proprietary consequences of mistakes.

PROPRIETARY CLAIMS: *CHASE MANHATTAN*

In this case the plaintiff, a New York bank, was instructed to pay over $US2 million to M Ltd, another New York bank, for the account of the defendant, a bank in England. The plaintiff duly made the payment through the New York clearing house system. Due to a clerical error later that day it made a second payment of the same amount through the clearing house system to M Ltd for the account of the defendant. Within a month of the mistaken payment the

---

[78] [1996] 2 W.L.R. 802 at 837.
[79] [1981] Ch. 105 at 114.
[80] See [1996] 2 W.L.R. 802 at 815.
[81] *ibid.* at 813.

defendant petitioned the English High Court to be wound up compulsorily on the ground of insolvency and subsequently a winding up order was made. The question at issue was whether the plaintiff was entitled to trace and recover the mistaken payment notwithstanding the insolvency of the defendant. The parties agreed that the legal effects of the mistaken payment had in the first instance to be determined in accordance with the law of the State of New York as the *lex causae* but that the procedural rights and remedies had to be ascertained by the law of England as the *lex fori*.

Goulding J. held that under English law a person who paid money to another under a mistake of fact retained an equitable property in it and the conscience of the payee was subjected to a fiduciary duty to respect that continuing proprietary interest. He also said that on the basis of the expert evidence submitted to him that the plaintiff had a similar right which was also founded on a continuing proprietary interest under New York law. Consequently, under whatever system of law the plaintiff's title was founded, the assets, if any, in the defendant's hands properly representing the plaintiff's money at the initiation of the winding up procedure did not belong to the defendant beneficially. The judge referred to the absence of direct English authority in point but invoked a U.S. case—*Re Berry*[82]—to support his conclusion. In this case it was held that mistaken payments were impressed with a trust. Had insolvency not supervened there was no question but that the money was recoverable. The general creditors of the bankrupt could not acquire any better title. There was no injustice to the general creditors for the money in dispute never belonged to the bankrupt. The creditors, upon broad principles of equity, had no more right to it than if the transaction in error had never taken place. Creditors could not be said to have extended credit on the basis that the assets of the borrower would be swollen by mistaken payments.

PASSING OF PROPERTY IN CRIMINAL CASES

The *Chase Manhattan Bank* case was applied in the criminal context by the Court of Appeal in *R. v. Shadrokh-Cigari*.[83] In this case the appellant was convicted of four counts of theft. He acted as guardian to his nephew whose father in Iran arranged for money to be paid to the child's bank account from the U.S. The U.S. bank made a factual error and $286,000 was credited to the account instead of $286. As a result of a suggestion made by the appellant the child signed an authority for the issue of four banker's drafts drawn in favour of the appellant for various sums. The appellant paid two drafts into his own bank account and used the others to open other accounts in his own name. By the time that the appellant was arrested about a month later only a fairly small sum remained in these accounts. He was convicted and appealed on the basis that the drafts did not belong to the bank but were the property of the appellant and so there was no question of him appropriating property belonging to another.

According to the court who dismissed the appeal the error in the submissions lay in the assumption that the entire proprietary interest in the drafts existed and vested in the appellant leaving the bank with no rights at all. The court

---

[82] (1906) 147 F 208.
[83] [1988] Crim. L.R. 465.

concluded that the drafts had been drawn under a mistake of fact. An action was available to recover money paid under a mistake of fact and following the decision in *Chase Manhattan* the payer retained an equitable proprietary interest.[84]

Despite this endorsement at Court of Appeal level the point is by no means a closed one and there are a number of dicta and cases which suggest a different analysis. First to *Barclays Bank v. W.J. Simms Ltd*.[85] This is the case where a bank mistakenly ignored a stop instruction on a cheque. The payee had gone into receivership and Robert Goff J. held that the money having been paid under a mistake of fact was prima facie recoverable. The parties agreed that since the action was intended to be in the nature of a test case to ascertain whether money paid in the given circumstances was recoverable, the bank's action should not fail for want of parties. It was agreed that upon the bank not proceeding further against the receiver, the receiver would procure payment of any sum found due by the judgment. However at one stage in his judgment, Robert Goff J. said that where an action was brought to recover money paid under a mistake of fact, property will almost invariably have passed to the defendant. The effect of the action, if successful, would simply be to impose on the defendant a personal obligation to repay the money. Reference was made in this connection to *Chambers v. Miller*.[86] In this case the plaintiff was a clerk who presented for payment at the defendant's bank a cheque held by his employers which was drawn on the bank by one of their customers. The cashier, having overlooked the fact that the customer's account was insufficient to meet the cheque, received the cheque and placed the amount in cash on the counter. After a short interval the cashier realised his mistake and said that the cheque could not be paid. The plaintiff placed the money in his pocket whereupon he was detained by the cashier under the threat of being taken into custody on a charge of theft. The plaintiff brought an action for assault and false imprisonment and the crucial question in the context of the case was whether the property in the money had passed to the bearer of the cheque. The court answered that question in the affirmative. The mistake made by the cashier did not prevent the property in the money from passing.

Many of the decided cases have arisen in connection with the law of theft.[87] The basic definition of theft is contained in section 1(1) of the Theft Act 1968 which provides as follows:

> "A person is guilty of theft if he dishonestly appropriates property belonging to another with the intention of permanently depriving the other of it . . ."

---

[84] *R v. Shadrockh-Cigari* is discussed along with *R v. Davis* [1988] Crim. L.R. 762 by J.C. Smith in *The Law of Theft* (7th ed., 1993) at pp. 42–47.

[85] [1980] Q.B. 677.

[86] (1862) 13 C.B.N.S. 125.

[87] Insofar as the law of theft is concerned the cases referred to in the following s. must be read in conjunction with the controversial decision of the House of Lords in *R v. Gomez* [1993] A.C. 442 1. In this case it was held that a person could be guilty of theft, contrary to s. 1 (1) of the Theft Act 1968, by dishonestly appropriating goods belong to another if the owner of the goods was induced by fraud, deception or a false representation to consent to or authorise the taking of the goods. There could be an appropriation for the purposes of the section even if the taking was consented to, where this consent was procured by fraud, deception or misrepresentation. It may be argued that this approach towards "appropriation" renders s. 5(3) of the Theft Act largely unnecessary. See also on this area *Lawrence v. Commissioner of Police for the Metropolis* [1972] A.C. 626 and *R. v. Morris* [1984] A.C. 320.

Section 5(4) of the 1968 Act also merits attention. It lays down:

"Where a person gets property by another's mistake, and is under an obligation to make restoration (in whole or in part) of the property or its proceeds or of the value thereof, then to the extent of that obligation the property or proceeds shall be regarded (as against him) as belonging to the person entitled to restoration, and an intention not to make restoration shall be regarded accordingly as an intention to deprive that person of the property or proceeds."

It seems that section 5(4) was inserted in the legislation for the purpose of reversing the decision in *Moynes v. Coopper*.[88] This is a case where a wages clerk put more money into the pay packet of an employee than was due to the employee. The mistake arose because the employee had already received an advance on his wages but the wages clerk had failed to realise this fact. At the time when he received the pay packet the employee did not know that it contained more than was due to him. It was only later at home that the employee realised that he had been overpaid. He held on to the excess and was charged with stealing contrary to section 2 of the Larceny Act 1916. The Divisional Court upheld his acquittal on the basis that to constitute the offence of larceny the taker must have the requisite *mens rea* at the time when he took the property. Since at the time when he took the packet the employee did not know of the mistake on the part of the wages clerk, the mental element necessary to constitute the offence was not present.

At Quarter Sessions the defendant was acquitted on the more fundamental ground that the wages clerk had authority to pass the property in the wages packet and its contents. He intended to pass the property therein to the defendant and he handed the packet to the defendant without making any mistake as to the identity of the packet or its contents or of the recipient. Thus property passed to the defendant who could not therefore be guilty of the offence of larceny. This issue of the passing of property is not expressly adverted to by Lord Goddard C.J. who delivered the majority judgment of the Divisional Court.[89]

Moynes v. Coopper was not fully considered and it is submitted distinguished on not very satisfactory grounds in *R. v. Gilks*.[90] The latter is a case where the defendant placed bets on several horses in a betting shop. His winnings amounted to £10.62. The bookmaker believed that the defendant had backed a certain successful horse when he had not and handed him £117.25. The defendant was aware of the bookmaker's mistake but decided to accept the money and keep it. He was charged with stealing the overpayment from the bookmaker contrary to section 1 of the Theft Act 1968. Could not the defendant have been convicted by virtue of section 5(4) of the Theft Act on the basis that he was under a restitutionary obligation to refund the surplus payment. The Court of Appeal said not because of the impact of the Gaming Act 1845. The expression

---

[88] [1956] 1 Q.B. 439.
[89] He referred to *R. v. Middleton* (1873) L.R. 2 C.C.R. 38 and said; "[T]he taker must have animus furandi at the time when he takes the property. In *Middleton's case* the wrong amount of money was paid by the post office clerk before the prisoner, who picked it up knowing of the clerk's mistake and so took it *animo furandi*. In the present case it is found that the defendant did not know of the mistake when he took the money, so the taking was not *animo furandi*. We prefer to base our decision on this ground, namely, that there was no taking here within the section."
[90] [1972] 1 W.L.R. 1341.

"obligation" in section 5(4) signified a legal obligation only. The bookmaker would not be entitled to recover the money by action because that would involve taking an account of gaming transactions which were void under the Gaming Act. However, and somewhat strangely in the light of *Moynes v. Coopper*, section 1(1) of the Theft Act was held to apply on the basis that the property in the excess payment had never passed to the punter. The mistake made was sufficient to prevent property from passing.

The only civil case mentioned in *R. v. Gilks* is *Morgan v. Ashcroft.*[91] In the latter case the plaintiff bookmaker mistakenly paid the defendant punter twice on a bet. It was held by the Court of Appeal that an action to recover the money was not maintainable. The kernel of the decision seems to lie in the proposition that as the court could determine the amount of overpayment only by examining accounts of gaming transactions, which it was forbidden to do by the Gaming Act 1845, the action could not be entertained. On the other hand one might say that the mistake was pretty similar to that made in *R. v. Gilks*. If a mistake is sufficient to prevent property from passing then it could be argued that moneys paid by virtue of the mistake should be recoverable in a restitutionary action.

An endemic feature of this whole area is the fact that all the relevant authorities are not often cited. A case that is open to this criticism and which comes down, at least inferentially, on the "property does not pass" side of the argument is *R. v. Davis*.[92] Basically in this case the appellant was mistakenly sent cheques in respect of housing benefit by a local authority. The prosecution counsel did not suggest that the appellant could have been convicted in the absence of section 5(4) of the Theft Act. The court thought that counsel was probably right to take this course though there was no reference to the *Chase Manhattan* case. That case which of course was applied in the criminal context in *R. v. Shadrokh-Cigari*[93] adopted the stance that a payer who makes a mistake of fact retains an equitable proprietary interest in the assets physically transferred. This approach would mean that reliance on section 5(4) was unnecessary.

THEORIES ON THE PASSING OF PROPERTY IN MISTAKE CASES

In the absence of consistent judicial guidance on the subject of the passing of property in mistake cases it is perhaps appropriate to turn to the views of academic commentators for enlightenment. Professor Glanville Williams in an influential but now somewhat dated article on mistake in the law of theft writes on the assumption that it is only mistakes which may be deemed "fundamental" preclude property from passing.[94] In his view a mistake is fundamental if and only if its existence makes it reasonable to say that there is in fact no consent (intention, agreement) on the part of the transferor to transfer this property to this person. A fundamental mistake may be described as a mistake in relation to the transaction and this is to be distinguished from a mistake as to a motivating fact. On the

---

[91] [1938] 1 K.B. 49.
[92] [1988] Crim. L.R. 762. See also *Re Att.-Gen.'s Reference (No 1 of 1983)* [1985] Q.B. 182 and *R v. Stalham* [1993] Crim. L.R. 310.
[93] [1988] Crim. L.R. 465.
[94] [1977] C.L.J. 62. For the purposes of the law of theft the article would now have to be read in the light of *R. v. Gomez* [1993] 1 All E.R. 1. See also the useful synthesis of views by W.J. Swadling [1994] *Restitution Law Review* at 80–85.

Glanville Williams analysis a mistake in relation to the transaction means a material mistake as to the identity of the transferee, as to the identity of the property transferred or as to the quantity of the property transferred but not as to the quality of property transferred.[95] The authorities cited in support of this proposition are not however decisive and even Williams recognises "the flux of judicial opinion". He cites *R v. Hehir*[96] in support of the proposition that a mistake as to the identity of the thing being transferred prevents property from passing. *Cundy v. Lindsay*[97] is referred to in connection with the identity of the transferee point.

Some of the lack of clarity that has occasionally permeated judicial thought in this area is manifest in *Norwich Union Fire Insurance Society v. W.H. Price Ltd.*[98] This is a case where the plaintiff insurance company paid out on a policy insuring lemons in the mistaken belief that the lemons had been damaged in circumstances that were covered by the policy whereas in fact they were damaged by reason of an event that was not covered by the policy. Recovery was allowed by the Privy Council but in his judgment Lord Wright runs together a number of different themes. He said[99]:

> "The mistake being of the character that it was, prevented there being that intention which the common law regards as essential to the making of an agreement or of the transfer of money or property . . .[proof] of mistake affirmatively excludes intention. It is, however, essential that the mistake relied on should be of such a nature that it can be properly described as a mistake in respect of the underlying assumption of the contract or transaction or as being fundamental or basic."

The flux in judicial opinion is of course most acute when one is talking about mistakes as to the amount transferred or cases of mistaken double payments. *R. v. Gilks*,[1] the *Chase Manhattan Bank* Case,[2] and *R. v. Shadrokh-Cigari*[3] point in the direction of saying that no property passes or else that the payer retains an equitable proprietary interest. *Moynes v. Coopper*[4] and *R. v. Davis*,[5] on the other hand, suggest that property does pass. The confusion is compounded by the fact that in no case has all the relevant authorities from both the civil and criminal sphere been analysed though there was a fairly full discussion in the Australian High Court case *Ilich v. The Queen*.[5a] Some support for the Professor Glanville Williams line of analysis

---

[95] [1977] C.L.J. 62 at 64.

[96] (1895) 18 Cox 267.

[97] (1878) 3 App. Cas. 459. This is a well known case discussed *supra* where a mistake as to identity rendered a contract void. The mistaken identity cases pose particular problems of reconciliation where the parties are dealing *inter praesentes*. In this connection *Lake v. Simmons* [1927] A.C. 487 and *Ingram v. Little* [1961] 1 Q.B. 31 should be contrasted with *Phillips v. Brook* [1919] 2 K.B. 243 and *Lewis v. Averay* [1972] 1 Q.B. 198.

[98] [1934] A.C. 455.

[99] *ibid* at 463. Lord Wright also said at 461–462: "The facts which were misconceived were those which were essential to liability and were of such a nature that on well-established principles any agreement concluded under such mistake was void in law, so that any payment made under such mistake was recoverable. The mistake, being of the character that it was, prevented there being that intention which the common law regards as essential to the making of an agreement or the transfer of money or property."

[1] [1972] 1 W.L.R. 1341.

[2] [1981] Ch 105.

[3] [1988] Crim. L.R. 465.

[4] [1956] 1 Q.B. 439.

[5] [1988] Crim. L.R. 762.

[5a] (1987) 162 C.L.R. 1100. For a general discussion of this whole area see D. Fox "The Transfer of Legal Title to Money" [1996] *Restitution Law Review* 60.

derives from this decision. Because of the comparative lack of authority in this area and the relatively full discussion in the case it seems appropriate to give the decision in *Ilich v. The Queen* extended treatment.

The case concerned a locum veterinary surgeon who was overpaid by the principal of the practice. The payment had been made to discharge a debt owed to the locum but when the latter discovered the overpayment he retained the excess. He was charged with stealing the surplus under the relevant provisions of the Western Australian Criminal Code. The conviction was quashed unanimously by the High Court of Australia but different strands are visible from the various judgments delivered by members of the court. Gibbs C.J. spoke of serious errors in the summing up but he thought that the jury were entitled to find that the property in the surplus had not passed to the locum creditor. Wilson and Dawson JJ. took a somewhat different view. In their opinion there was no mistake of a fundamental kind which would have operated to prevent ownership in the money passing at the time when it was handed by the principal to the locum. The judges spoke of a mistake having to be of a sufficiently fundamental kind to preclude the passage of property. They said that a mistake would be of that kind if it was as to the identity of the transferee or as to the identity of the thing delivered or as to the quantity of the thing delivered though there was some hesitation expressed about the exhaustiveness or otherwise of this catalogue of circumstances. Moreover, Wilson and Dawson JJ. suggested that the third category—mistake as to the quantity of the thing delivered— required some qualification where the thing was money. Reference was made to the observations of Lord Mansfield in *Miller v. Race*[5b]:

> "It has been quaintly said, 'that the reason why money can not be followed is, because it has no ear-mark': but this is not true. The true reason is, upon account of the currency of it: it can not be recovered after it has passed in currency. So, in case of money stolen, the true owner cannot recover it, after it has been paid away fairly and honestly upon a valuable and bona fide consideration: but before money has passed in currency, an action may be brought for the money itself."

Wilson and Dawson JJ. opined that money passed into currency when it was negotiated and in this case, upon the locum's view of the facts, the transaction in which the money changed hands was both bona fide and for value. He was unaware of the overpayment when it was made and consequently there was no reason to doubt the bona fide character of the transaction. Therefore the notes or coins ceased to be the subject of specific title as chattels and passed as currency, that is it say, passed "from hand to hand in point, not merely of possession, but of property". Somewhat surprisingly the relevance of the *Chase Manhattan Bank* case to this analysis was not discussed. The proprietary dimensions of that case do not seem to have been appreciated; it being cited simply in support of the proposition that a civil action to recover money paid under a mistake of fact may be available.

Deane J. expressed his general agreement with what was said by Wilson and Dawson JJ. He said that what was involved from the locum vet's point of view was the honest receipt of currency which was delivered and received as representing, in its entirety, payment of an outstanding debt. That being so, the legal property

---

[5b] (1758) 1 Burr. 452; 97 E.R. 398 at 401.

in all of the notes passed to the locum by and on delivery and receipt.

Brennan J. also took the line that a fundamental mistake vitiated the passing of property but his conception of fundamental mistake was somewhat different from that of Wilson and Deane JJ. He was prepared to accept that when a person in possession of money in the form of currency hands it to another intending the latter to be the owner of it and the other receives it with the same intention, prima facie the other acquires ownership of the money. But there were exceptions to the general proposition. The prima facie conclusion about property passing might be displaced in some cases where the intention was formed on the basis of a fundamental mistake. It is unclear however why Brennan J. felt it necessary to explore the exceptions. In his veiw, where the exceptions applied the payer was only entitled to recover money *in specie* before it was disbursed. In this particular case there was no evidence that the money had been preserved *in specie*. Be that as it may, the judge observed that when the relevant transaction was the transfer of possesssion or ownership of property, a fundamental mistake must relate to the knowledge of the owner of the property as to what he was doing, what the property was, and to whom he was transferring possession or ownership.

The judge noted that minds might differ on the character to be attributed to a particular mistake. *R. v. Ashwell* [5c] was a case in point. In that case the prosecutor, intending to loan Ashwell a shilling, gave him a sovereign by mistake. Ashwell thought it was a shilling but when he subsequently discovered it to be a sovereign, kept it for himself. He was tried and convicted. A case was stated and the appeal court which consisted of 14 judges was evenly divided which meant that the conviction stood. On one view since there was a mistake as to the identity of the coin no property passed. On the other hand as Brennan J. states it is at least arguable that the relevant transaction was not the loan of a shilling but the delivery of the coin, the value, but not the identity of which, was mistaken.[5d] He quoted the observations of a judge in an earlier case that there was no mistake as to the identity of the particular metal disc handed over but rather there was a mistake about its value and perhaps about its kind.[5e]

In this particular case Brennan J. suggested that there was no evidence of the principal of the veterinary practice being mistaken as to what he was doing, or what he was handing to the locum or who the locum was. The only mistake was as to the number or value of the notes needed to discharge the debt owed to the locum. The judge observed that when a debtor pays out money to discharge his debt, he has but one intention with respect to the money paid, namely, to transfer ownership in discharge of the debt. It was artificial to ascribe to a debtor an intention to transfer ownership of some only of the notes and coins he pays. Brennan J. accepted that a payee was obliged to refund an overpayment made by mistake. The payee was indebted to the payer in the amount of the overpayment, but that did not affect the payee's ownership of the notes and coins he had received.

Given Brennan J.'s adherence to the concept of fundamentality as forming the basis of a proprietary claim to mistaken payments resides somewhat uneasily with his later denunciation of the notion of fundamentality as lacking sufficient specificity in *David Securities Pty Ltd v. Commonwealth Bank of Australia*.[5f] Admittedly the two fact situations are somewhat different. The latter case was concerned

[5c] (1885) 16 Q.B.D. 190.
[5d] (1987) 162 C.L.R. 110 at 140.
[5e] Bray C.J. in *R. v. Patisk* (1973) 6 S.A.S.R. at 395.
[5f] (1992) 175 C.L.R. 353; (1992) 66 A.L.J.R. 768 at 785.

with a personal restitutionary action to recover mistaken payments and the proprietary consequences of such payments were not an issue in the case. Be that as it may if "fundamentality" was too vague in one context it is difficult to see how it acquires precision in another different but related context. The analysis adopted by Professor Glanville Williams goes some way towards providing clarifications by categorising mistakes. This classification exercise however runs up against the difficulty that different minds may put the same type of mistake into a different box. The end-result of the categorisation exercise would be a radically different outcome in terms of proprietary effect.

What about the principle apparently recognised in *Ilich v. The Queen* that money behaves differently, *i.e.* that when money is used as currency title passes with possession? In other words where money is received honestly and for valuable consideration title to the money goes to the recipient notwithstanding the fact that there may have been an element of overpayment. The question arises how far this apparent exception extends. How big may the overpayment be? If the overpayment is say 100 times greater than the amount of the original debt does this bring the case outside the pale of the exception? In these circumstances given the amount of the overpayment there is a strong temptation to hold that the payer retains a proprietary interest. Why should the payee's general creditors benefit from sheer chance? Does it encompass mistaken double payments as distinct from over-payments *i.e* where the same debt is paid twice over rather than there being a surplus payment the first time of asking? In this situation it could hardly be said that there is any consideration for the second payment. Moreover, and perhaps more importantly, how does the exception cope with modern payment methods? What about the telegraphic transfer of funds? Here there is no physical transfer of cash. All that passes, to borrow words used in the *Agip* case, is a stream of electrons.

As long ago as 1820 in *Wookey v. Pole*[5g] it was spoken of as well established that a person who receives money in the form of currency in good faith and for valuable consideration acquires a good title to the money even though the person who gave him possession of the notes or coins had no title to them. But as Brennan J. pointed out in *Ilich v. The Queen* a person who receives money in the form of currency without consideration gets no better title than the person from whom the money was received. One might argue that the last principle should be widened to say that even if the payer has good title the payee should not get good title to mistaken payments made without consideration. After all it has long been recognised that an owner of notes and coins may recoup them from a person who has obtained possession of them in bad faith. So mere transfer of possession is not enough to transfer ownership even if the payer has good title.

THE NOTION OF AN UNDESTROYED PROPRIETARY BASE

Professor Peter Birks has argued that the only satisfactory basis for raising a restitutionary proprietary right in assets is by showing that the circumstances of the original receipt by the defendant must be such that, either at law or in equity, the plaintiff retained or obtained the property in the assets received by the defendant.[6] The plaintiff is mounting a claim in the second measure of restitution to the amount of the surviving enrichment in the hands of the

---

[5g] (1820) 4B & Ald. 1 at 7; 106 E.R. 839 at 841.
[6] See generally Birks, *Introduction to the Law of Restitution* (1985), pp. 378–389.

defendant but in Birks' view a proprietary base is a necessary starting point to such a claim. On this analysis there are two situations where a proprietary claim is justified[7]:

"One is where the recipient did receive legal title to the original enrichment but where the circumstances were such as to detach the equitable title and to vest it in the plaintiff, thus creating a trust-like relationship between them. The other is where the recipient obtained no title at all by virtue of the transfer to him, so that the plaintiff remained the legal owner until, the legal title being defeated by some intermixture, equitable rules had to be invoked in order to identify the assets in which the original value survived. In both cases the plaintiff has the necessary proprietary base, at the moment after the original enrichment of the defendant; on that base there can be raised a new equitable interest in those different assets in which the original enrichment is, by the process of tracing, identified as surviving."

Birks distinguishes these situations from a third situation, in which no proprietary right can be asserted in the surviving enrichment. The third situation arises where wealth belonging to the plaintiff passes to the defendant in circumstances in which, though he may come under a restitutionary obligation to repay its value, he does, as far as rights in rem are concerned, become fully entitled, legally and beneficially. One might argue that this whole approach is somewhat question-begging since it does not say anything expressly about the circumstances in which the plaintiff has a proprietary base. At one point though Birks talks about a mistake being sufficiently fundamental to prevent property from passing.[8] So we are back to the notion of "fundamentality". This concept has been criticised. For instance the majority judges in the High Court of Australia in *David Securities Pty Ltd v. Commonwealth Bank of Australia*[9] said the idea of "fundamentality" was extremely vague. Insistence upon this factor only served to focus attention in a non-specific way on the nature of the mistake, rather than the fact of enrichment. Brennan J. thought that the term "fundamental" lacked sufficient specificity to be invoked as a working criterion.[10]

A PRESUMPTIVE PROPRIETARY CLAIM

In the leading practitioner text on the law of restitution by Sir Robert Goff and Professor Gareth Jones it is argued that the scope of the proprietary remedy should depend on such factors as whether the contest is between the plaintiff and a solvent or an insolvent defendant and whether the defendant knows, or does not know, the facts which form the basis of the restitutionary claim.[11] At another point they argue that a person who confers a benefit, normally a money

---

[7] *ibid* at 384.
[8] *ibid* at 379. He says: "By contrast, if the mistake is insufficiently fundamental to prevent the property passing then, always supposing that it does, nevertheless, have the effect of giving the plaintiff a personal claim to the value received by the defendant, there can be no question of recognising a right in rem in any surviving enrichment since, apart from the neutral or contingent fact of intermixture or substitution, the facts are *ex hypothesi* such as to reduce the plaintiff to a purely personal claim."
[9] (1992) 66 A.L.J.R. 768 at 777.
[10] *ibid* at 785.
[11] (4th ed., 1993), p. 101. This approach has been criticised by Birks on the basis that the question whether the plaintiff has or has not got a right in rem is not something to be decided from case to case on the basis of abstract reasonableness or justice.

payment, under mistake, compulsion, necessity or in consequence of another's wrongful or unconscionable conduct should be deemed to have retained the equitable title in the money paid.[12] Unlike the general creditors of the recipient, the payer has not taken the risk of the recipient's insolvency. By contrast where he had paid money under an ineffective contract, intending to advance credit to the defendant, then the proprietary claim should fail.

A somewhat similar approach is favoured by Professor Roy Goode who asks why should a mistaken double payment be impressed with a trust in favour of the payer when a payment made under a contract in the mistaken belief that the recipient will perform his part of the bargain is recoverable only by a personal action?[13] Professor Goode proceeds to answer the question by saying that a debtor who mistakenly receives a double payment clearly has no right to retain it. The argument continues[14]:

"It would be unjust enrichment of the estate for the court to hold that a title to goods which was voidable prior to bankruptcy should become converted into an indefeasible title upon bankruptcy. By contrast, a seller who sells goods without reserving title or taking security for the price cannot complain of his status as an unsecured creditor, for if he has intentionally given up his proprietary rights before the buyer's bankruptcy there is no reason why these should be restored to him gratuitously by the law upon such bankruptcy."

Goode recognises that equitable proprietary rights arising otherwise than by way of security are usually invisible to creditors, who might be misled by the debtor's possession into thinking that he is the beneficial owner of the asset. On the other hand the reputed ownership doctrine never applied to companies and was laid to rest completely by the Insolvency Act reforms of 1985–1986 insofar as personal bankruptcy is concerned.[15] As long ago as 1957 the Blagden Committee were of the opinion that the practice of procuring on hire purchase almost every article used in trades and businesses made it very difficult for the trustee in bankruptcy to claim goods belonging to other parties.[16] The committee considered that the doctrine had become obsolete and served no useful purpose, while drawing attention to the non-existent perils of a creditor being induced to give credit by an assumption that all goods in the possession of the debtor were his own property.

There has been some criticism of the Goff and Jones/Goode line of reasoning on the ground that it is doubtful whether all ordinary creditors consciously take the risk of their debtors' insolvency.[17] Even if this were the case it is contended that this does not make the case for inferior treatment. The argument proceeds as follows[18]:

"After all the risk argument would mean that if the plaintiff makes a foolish mistake and pays £100 to the defendant he will have a proprietary restitutionary remedy to recover the £100 whereas the plaintiff who is the victim of the defendant's contractual

---

[12] *ibid* at 94.
[13] (1987) 103 L.Q.R. 433 at 439.
[14] *ibid* at 440.
[15] See now Insolvency Act 1986, s. 283; see also Insolvency Act 1985, s. 130.
[16] Cmnd. 221 at para. 110.
[17] See Burrows, *The Law of Restitution* (1993), 42.
[18] *ibid*.

promise to repay a loan of £100 will be confined to a mere personal restitutionary remedy for £100... [I]t should be remembered that in one sense there is no question of the creditors receiving a windfall. Each of them is prima facie entitled to recover to the extent of his personal claim against the insolvent defendant. They are all potential 'losers' and the sole issue is the extent to which their loss can be wholly or partly avoided."

Be that as it may, it is clearly the case that pre-insolvency property entitlements survive a liquidation or other form of insolvency procedure. If a particular event rules out the passing of property then this state of affairs should be respected in an insolvency. That much is established. So we are back to the concept of the passing of property. Notwithstanding the various judicial vacillations and fluctuations in view it is settled that certain types of mistake such as mistakes as to identity and as to the thing being transferred have the effect of impairing fatally the passage of property. The proprietary consequences of other kinds of mistakes are not clearcut. Should only mistakes that may be dubbed "fundamental" preclude the transfer of full legal and equitable ownership or should any kind of causative mistake suffice? In other words should the law distinguish between different categories of mistakes with one category generating a proprietary resitutionary claim and the other type merely a personal restitutionary entitlement. If so, what would be the extra element that brings into being a proprietary claim? It is difficult to think of anything concrete apart from some rather amorphous notion of fundamentality and the unsatisfactory nature of this concept has been explored at an earlier stage.

CONCLUSION

In *Chase Manhattan Bank v. Israel-British Bank*[19] Goulding J. held that person who pays money under a fundamental mistake of fact retains an equitable proprietary interest and the payer is thereby able at least in principle to trace the moneys through subsequent changes of property provided that it remains identifiable. Issues relating to the passing of property were not however explored in any detail and in particular there was no consideration of the criminal law cases. The judgment is to that extent unsatisfactory. Was the mistake deemed sufficiently fundamental to prevent property from passing? Or is the fact that the moneys were recoverable in a personal restitutionary action enough to ground a proprietary claim. In this chapter the proposition has been advanced that causative mistakes generate a personal right of action and also prevent property from passing though there is strong support in the authorities to cover cases where an overpayment has been made and honestly received to discharge a debt. This exception stems from the old principle that money behaves differently from chattels, etc., in that it has no earmark. The transfer of full legal and equitable ownership to the recipient is the key. If this has not occurred the payer will have priority in the event of the recipient's insolvency.[20] Ultimately

[19] [1981] Ch 105.
[20] Other restitution-generating events like duress and undue influence should be treated in the same way as mistakes. If property does not pass because of the duress, etc., then the transferor of the property should have priority in the event of the recipient's insolvency. The effect of duress on the passsing of property and consequential priority in insolvency has not however been the subject of extensive judicial consideration—see Goff and Jones, *The Law of Restitution* (4th ed., 1993), p. 275.

Conclusion

it is a question as to how far the law should recognise proprietary claims. Passing of property questions in mistake cases also have ramifications in the criminal sphere but in the United Kingdom that matter has been tackled by legislation specific to the criminal arena namely section 5(4) of the Theft Act 1968. If full legal and equitable ownership is held not to have passed in mistake cases arguably the legislation is unnecessary at least in the generality of cases. Nevertheless the statute does reflect a legislative belief that such behaviour (*i.e.* the payee holding on to excess or mistaken payments in certain circumstances) should be deemed criminal. Recognising a proprietary claim on the part of the payer does not in any way undermine that legislative policy as reflected in the criminal context but rather is an issue specific to the policy of the law of insolvency. Any resolution of the policy question must involve full consideration of the position of unsecured creditors of the payee. All too often they have been left out of the equation. While proprietary claims may deserve their place in the sun this cannot eclipse consideration of unsecured creditors and their rival claims to assets still in the hands of the payee's insolvency office-holder.

It remains to be seen however whether the judges will feel able to weight up all the competing considerations. In *Westdeutsche*[21] Lord Goff suggested that it was no part of the judicial function to rewrite the agenda for the law of restitution nor even to identify the role of proprietary claims in the law. He thought that the courts were ill-equipped for performing this role. Lord Browne-Wilkinson acknowledged no such limit on judicial capabilities. Moreover, he was of the opinion that full legal and equitable title passed to the recipient of a mistaken payment irrespective of the gravity of the mistake that precipitated the transfer. This view was reached without the benefit of a detailed review of the authorities or of the various policy factors and was not necessary for a decision in the case at hand. In the circumstances, it is questionable whether it will carry decisive weight in subsequent judicial deliberations.

---

[21] [1996] 2 W.L.R. 802 at 810–811.

CHAPTER EIGHT

Fundamental Principles of Tracing Misapplied Assets

It is often the case that a person or company to whom property has been transferred under a mistake, or a recipient of trust property or a dishonest fiduciary, has become insolvent. The liability to repay the value received is established subject to certain conditions and qualifications that have been discussed elsewhere in this book. But what if what has been received has been in some way transformed in character or altered in form? How does this affect the entitlement to recover? Issues of identifiability becomes acute in this context. At all times a person is asserting that "it's property" should be kept out of the hands of general creditors notwithstanding the fact that the property originally transferred may not quite be what remains in the clutches of the insolvent at this stage. The matter is usually discussed under the rubric of tracing[1] and is a question of some complexity. The complexity is compounded by a lack of terminological consistency and also by the fact that there are both legal and equitable principles of tracing. Tracing issues have come before the courts on many occasions in recent years. One might cite as an example the *Westdeutsche* case. This case arose out of the the *ultra vires* interest rate "swap" transactions entered into by local authorities in an attempt to get around controls imposed by central government on spending and borrowing.

On another note a leading Chancery judge in a caustic expression has described commercial fraud as a growth industry.[2] The well publicised collapses of the Barlow Clowes and Maxwell group of companies seemingly attest to that proposition. These business failures have thrown the spotlight on the identification rules of equitable tracing. The principles governing identification will be examined in the succeeding chapter of this book in the light of the recent case law. This chapter will focus on common law tracing and the preconditions necessary to mount an equitable tracing claim. First however it is useful to analyse what exactly is meant by the use of the expression "tracing" and to provide an example which throws the matter into sharper relief.

TRACING: DEFINITION AND EXAMPLE

By "tracing" is essentially meant the process of following property through

---

[1] For periodical literature on tracing see *inter alia* R.H. Maudsley "Proprietary Remedies for the Recovery of Money" (1959) 75 L.Q.R. 234; M. Scott "The Right to Trace at Common law" (1966) 7 Univ. of W.A.L.R. 63; F.O.B. Babafemi "Tracing Assets: A Case for the Fusion of Common Law and Equity in English law" (1971) 34 M.L.R. 12; R. Pearce "A Tracing Paper" [1976] *Conveyancer* 277; R.M. Goode "The Right to Trace and its Impact on Commercial Transactions" (1976) 92 L.Q.R. 360, 528; S. Khurshid and P. Matthews "Tracing Confusion" (1979) 95 L.Q.R. 98. See also A. Burrows *The Law of Restitution* (1993), pp. 57–76.
[2] See the comments by Sir Peter Millett (1991) 107 L.Q.R. 71.

changes into form.[3] With tracing we are concerned with locating value through a series of substitutions. We cease to be concerned with the original object and instead are focussed upon the value that was derived from the original asset and locating it. The expression "tracing" when applied in the context under discussion may seem somewhat strange to continental legal brethren. The term in their eyes might denote the process of locating criminal suspects but to a common lawyer it refers to the identification of misapplied property through one or more substitutions.[4] There was an extremely useful explanation of the nature of tracing by Millett L.J. in *Boscawen v. Bajwa*.[5] The learned Lord Justice pointed out that equity lawyers habitually use the expressions "the tracing claim" and "the tracing remedy" to describe the proprietary claim and the proprietary remedy which equity makes available to the beneficial owner who seeks to recover his property in specie from those into whose hands it has come. Millett L.J. went on to say[6]:

"Tracing properly so-called, however, is neither a claim nor a remedy but a process. Moreover, it is not confined to the case where the plaintiff seeks a proprietary remedy; it is equally necessary where he seeks a personal remedy against the knowing recipient or knowing assistant. It is the process by which the plaintiff tracers what has happened to his property, identifies the persons who have handled or received it, and justifies his claim that the money which they handled or received (and if necessary which they still retain) can properly be regarded as representing his property. He needs to do this because his claim is based on the retention by him of a beneficial interest in the property which the defendant handled or received."[7]

The acknowledgement by the judge that tracing constituted a process of identification rather than a remedy in itself, compelled rejection of an argument advanced by one of the parties that, since tracing and subrogation were both remedies, a claimant could not claim to recover its money using both of them at the same time. According to Millett L.J. a claimant is mot merely entitled but was positively obliged to trace its money into the discharge of a security before it could lay claim to that security via subrogation.

In *Boscawen v. Bajwa*[8] one Bajwa who was in straightened financial circumstances was in the process of selling his house which was mortgaged to the Halifax Building Society. The would-be purchaser arranged a mortgage with the Abbey National and the latter used the same solicitors as the purchaser. The Abbey National sent the solicitors the mortgage moneys on terms which obliged them to use it for completion of the purchase or to return it if, for any reason, completion did not take place. The solicitors moved a little precipitately and sent the money to the seller, Bajwa's lawyers believing that the sale was

---

[3] It has been argued most forcefully by Professor P.B.H. Birks that tracing should be viewed in this light rather than as a right or remedy: see (1992) (2) 45 C.L.P. 69; (1993) (1) 46 C.L.P. 157 and [1993] L.M.C.L.Q. 218. Professor Birks' views on the subject have been cogently restated in Birks (ed.), *Laundering and Tracing* (1995), p. 289. See also the comments of Millett J. in *Agip (Africa) Ltd v. Jackson* [1989] 2 W.L.R. 1367 at 1382.
[4] See paper "The Legal and Moral Limits of Common law Tracing" by Paul Matthews in Peter Birks ed. *Laundering and Tracing* (1995).
[5] [1995] 4 All E.R. 769.
[6] *ibid.* at 776.
[7] "Knowing receipt" and "knowing assistance" are discussed in the penultimate and final chapters of this book respectively.
[8] The case is discussed by Birks [1995] *Trust Law International* 124 and by Mitchell [1995] L.M.C.L.Q.

bound to go ahead, and the latter in turn paid it over to the Halifax. The purported contract of sale was however void because of non-compliance with the formalities required by section 2 of the Law of Property (Miscellaneous Provisions) Act 1989 and the sale never went ahead. In essence the moneys advanced by Abbey National was used to discharge the Halifax mortgage and the question in the case was whether Abbey National were entitled to be subrogated to this security.[9] Millett J. held that Abbey National were so entitled and by this means they obtained priority over Bajwa's judgment creditors who had obtained a charging order against the house.

Boscawen v. Bajwa serves as an instance of tracing in action, so to speak. Another example serves to widen the field of discourse and to lend a further air of topicality to the discussion. X, a dishonest company director, misappropriates company assets by transferring them to "dummy" companies that he controls in return for an illusory consideration. Company funds are transferred electronically from London to accounts maintained by the "dummy" companies in New York. There follows a series of electronic fund transfers into and out of "off-shore" jurisdictions with tough bank secrecy laws like Liechtenstein and the Cayman Islands. The funds are mixed in the course of these progressions with the fraudster's own moneys and with other moneys that he has swindled. Some of the fund is dissipated through expenditure on ordinary everyday expenses whereas some more is gambled away in the casinos of Monte Carlo. Part of the fund finds its way back to London where it is used to finance the acquisition of expensive properties in Knightsbridge and Buckinghamshire. Another part of the fund is utilised to discharge a loan that was taken out by the fraudster to purchase shares in an English registered company.[10]

COMMON LAW AND EQUITY

A big barrier to practical understanding is the wedge that is sometimes said to exist between common law and equitable tracing. The points of distinction between the two are usually encapsulated in the comment that, unlike in the common law, a fiduciary relationship between the parties is required as a precondition of equitable tracing while the common law but not equity is deficient when it comes to tracing through a mixed bank account. Moreover, until recently it has been true to say that common law tracing has not been developed to any great extent. For instance one judge has written extra-judicially that the common law's remedies are inadequate and its jurisprudence defective.[11]

---

[9] The case is further discussed in the context of subrogation in Chapter 9.

[10] This chapter does not purport to address conflict of law issues arising from the tracing of assets. It might well be asked whether the English court's jurisdiction to order the return of (or declare a constructive trust of charge over) property acquired by a trustee with funds misappropriated from the trust depend on (a) the trustee being—or having been—subject to the jurisdiction of the English courts, (b) the act of misappropriation having been commited in England, (c) the trust being, as it were, governed by English law, or the trust instrument providing for the English courts to have jurisdiction, (d) the asset being in England, or (e) the asset being held in the custody of a person subject to the jurisdiction of the English courts (for example, Eurobonds held at the Zurich office of a Swiss bank which has a branch in London)? These are interesting questions but lie beyond the scope of the present Chapter. For a "taster" see *Barclays Bank v. Glasgow City Council* [1994] 4 All E.R. 865.

[11] See the article by Sir Peter Millett (1991) 107 L.Q.R. 71 and also *Agip (Africa) Ltd v. Jackson* [1992] 4 All E.R. 385 (Millett J.) and [1992] 4 All E.R. 451 (Court of Appeal).

His thesis is that in all but the simplest cases recourse to the common law should be abandoned and that attempts to rationalise and develop the common law rules are unlikely to succeed and should no longer be pursued.[12] Far greater attention has been directed at equitable tracing though one must note the important decision of the House of Lords in *Lipkin Gorman v. Karpnale Ltd*[13] which has led to a resuscitation of interest in common law tracing.

COMMON LAW RIGHT TO TRACE

The *locus classicus* of common law tracing is *Taylor v. Plumer*.[14] In this case one Walsh was entrusted by Sir Thomas Plumer with money for investment in exchequer bills. Walsh instead purchased bullion and American stock with which he attempted to abscond. In this attempt he was unsuccessful and was forced to surrender the property to Plumer. An action in trover was brought by Walsh's assignees in bankruptcy to recapture the property from Plumer but the action failed. According to Lord Ellenborough C.J.[15]:

> "He has repossessed himself of that, of which, according to the principles established in the cases I have cited, he never ceased to be the lawful proprietor; and having so done we are of opinion, that the assignees cannot in this action recover that which, if an action were brought against them, the assignees, by the defendant, they could not have effectually retained against him, inasmuch as it was trust property of the defendant, which, as such, did not pass to them under the commission."

Taylor v. Plumer has given rise to the "exchange-product" theory of common law tracing.[16] Under this theory legal title to the exchange product vests in the owner of the original goods.[17] Certain passages from the judgment of Lord

---

[12] The judge argues for the development of a unified restitutionary remedy based on equitable principles.

[13] [1991] 2 A.C. 548. The decision may fairly be described as truly seminal from the point of view of the development of a coherent and rational law of restitution. See generally on this point Birks "The English Recognition of Unjust Enrichment" [1991] L.M.C.L.Q. 473 and also Birks [1992] L.M.C.L.Q. 218 and Birks [1993] C.L.P. 157. Note too Cornish [1991] C.L.J. 407; Watts (1991) 107 L.Q.R. 521; McKendrick (1992) 55 M.L.R. 377; Halliwell [1992] Conv. 124.

[14] (1815) 3 M. & S. 562.

[15] *ibid.* at 579. Lord Ellenborough referred to cases including *L'Apostre v. Le Plaistrier* (1708) 1 P. Wms. 318 and *Scott v. Surman* (1743) Willes 400.

[16] Certain commentators, *e.g.* Khurshid & Matthews (1979) 95 L.Q.R. 78, have argued that throughout his judgment Lord Ellenborough was referring to equitable rather than common law tracing. Certainly there are plentiful references therein to "trust property". Moreover, Jessel M.R. in *Re Hallett's Estate* (1880) 13 Ch.D. 696 was critical of Lord Ellenborough's ignorance of equitable developments with respect to tracing. Hence the latter's derogatory remarks about the constraints of tracing. The Kurshid & Matthews theory has now received powerful support from Lionel Smith [1994] L.M.C.L.Q. 240 who argues that the defendant's success in *Taylor v. Plumer* was based on the assertion of equitable proprietary rights in the proceeds of a disposition by a faithless fiduciary and that the case is no authority for any rule of common law property. See also Lionel Smith "The Stockbroker and the Solicitor-General: The Story behind *Taylor v. Plumer*" (1994) 15 *Journal of Legal History* 1.

[17] See generally Kurshid and Matthews *op. cit.*, Goode [1976] 92 L.Q.R. 360 at 365–368. The "exchange product" theory has been given a new lease of life by the decision of the House of Lords in *Lipkin Gorman v. Karpnale Ltd* [1991] A.C. 548 which is discussed below. The implications of the case for the theory are examined by Burrows, *The Law of Restitution* (1993), pp. 65–69.

Ellenborough can be read as supporting the exchange product theory. At one point he said[18]:

> "It makes no difference in reason or law into what other form, different from the original, the change may have been made ... for the product of or substitute for the original thing still follows the nature of the thing itself, as long as it can be ascertained to be such, and the right only ceases when the means of ascertainment fail, which is the case when the subject is turned into money, and mixed and confounded in a general mass of the same description."

The difficulty with this analysis is that property passes to the person to whom the transferor intended it to pass, even if the person with whom he deals has falsely assumed the identity of another.[19] Therefore, a right to trace based on legal ownership of the product exchanged for the original goods would seem to have little scope for application.[20] One possible way out of the problem is by recourse to the doctrine of ratification. It may be argued that the principal has impliedly ratified the initially unauthorised acts of the agent and thereby acquired title to the exchange product.[21] There is somewhat ambiguous textual support for this proposition in *Taylor v. Plumer* itself. According to Lord Ellenborough[22] "if the property in its original state and form was covered with a trust in favour of the principal, no change of that state and form can divest it of such trust, or give the factor, or those who represent him ... any other more valid claim in respect to it, than they respectively had before such change." Be that as it may the theory of implied ratification does not explain the actual decision in *Taylor v. Plumer* itself. Towards the end of his judgment the Chief Justice opined[23]:

> "If this case had rested on the part of the defendant on any supposed adoption and ratification on his part of the act of converting the produce of the draft or bank-notes of the defendant into these American certificates, we think, it could not have been well supported on that ground, inasmuch as the defendant, by taking a security by bond and judgment to indemnify himself against the pecuniary loss he had sustained by that very act, must be understood to have disapproved and disallowed that act instead of adopting and confirming it ..."

The doctrine of ratification also runs up against the formidable obstacle of the decision of the House of Lords in *United Australia Ltd v. Barclays Bank Ltd*[24] and in particular the observations of Lord Atkin therein. The latter was very concerned to exorcise the ghosts of the old forms of action. He said that when these ghosts of the past stand in the path of justice clanking their medieval

---

[18] (1815) 3 M. & S. 562 at 575.

[19] See *Lewis v. Averay* [1972] 1 Q.B. 198.

[20] See Hayton and Marshall *Cases and Commentary on the Law of Trusts* (9th ed. 1991) at p. 533 "The better view is that if C has not passed title to A directly via B's agency then title has passed to B so that unless B specifically appropriates the property to A, thereby passing title to A, then A has no title to the property nor sufficient right to immediate possession to enable him to bring a claim in tort. This is a significant limitation upon the common law position."

[21] In *Re Diplock* [1948] 2 All E.R. 318 at 345 Lord Greene M.R. said that common law tracing "proceeded on the basis that the unauthorised act of purchasing was one capable of ratification by the owner of the money." See also the comments of Lord Parker in *Sinclair v. Brougham* [1914] A.C. 398 at 441.

[22] (1815) 3 M. & S. 562 at 574.

[23] *ibid.* at 579.

[24] [1941] A.C. 1.

chains the proper course for the judge is to pass through them undeterred.[25] Lord Atkin observed that if a plaintiff in truth treats the wrongdoer as having acted as his agent, overlooks the wrong, and by consent of both parties is content to receive the proceeds this will be a true waiver. In the ordinary case however, the plaintiff has never the slightest intention of waiving, excusing or in any palliating the tort. To bring the discussion closer to home, it was said that if a thief had stolen securities and was in possession of the proceeds, legal action against the thief did not mean excusing him. The plaintiff was protesting violently that he was a thief and because of the theft was instituting proceedings.[26]

Professor R.M. Goode has argued eloquently that the right to follow an asset at common law is not a proprietary right but rather a right to assert against another a personal right of some kind (whether possessory or purely personal) by reason of his receipt and retention or disposal of the asset.[27] In Goode's view each movement of the asset from one recipient to another brings into existence a distinct personal right of the original owner against that recipient and a separate new duty of account by the recipient to the owner. The right to follow an asset at common law may be lost though. One such situation is where a subsequent transferee has given value at a time that he is unaware that the transmission is in breach of the transferor's duty of account to the original owner. On this analysis the right to follow also denotes a right to trace the asset into a changed form, so that if the asset is exchanged for cash or other proceeds, a person has the same right to follow the proceeds as he had to follow the original asset.[28]

The "exchange-product" analysis of common law tracing derives however strong support from the Court of Appeal decision in *Banque Belge pour L'Etranger v. Hambrouck*.[29] This is a case where the plaintiffs by their statement of claim asked for an order that the sum of £315 paid into court should be paid out to them. Basically we had an employee, Hambrouck, who obtained by fraud from his employer, Pelabon, a number of cheques purporting to be drawn by the employer upon the plaintiff bank. These cheques Hambrouck paid into an account with his bankers, who collected the cheques and credited Hambrouck's account with the amounts. Against the amount credited Hambrouck drew cheques and handed some to Ms Spanoghe, a woman with whom he was living.[30] She in turn paid some of what she received into an account with her

---

[25] *ibid.* at 29. See also the article by Lord Denning (1949) 65 L.Q.R. 37.

[26] *ibid.* at 28–29. See also *Keighley Maxsted & Co. v. Durant* [1901] A.C. 240 which is authority for the proposition that a contract made by a person intending to contract on behalf of a third party, but without his authority, cannot be ratified by the third party so as to render him able to sue or liable to be sued on the contract, where the person who made the contract did not profess at the time of making it to be acting on behalf of a principal.

[27] See Goode, *op. cit.*, at 369–370.

[28] See also the following passage from Hayton and Marshall, *Cases and Commentary on the Law of Trusts* (1991), p. 552: "If A's original property is in B's hands and B disposes of such property in return for new property in such circumstances that the new property belongs to A then, if B goes bankrupt, the title to the new property does not belong to B's trustee in bankruptcy. However, if he attempts to hold on to the property he can be personally sued for wrongful interference with goods so that he must either deliver the new property to A or pay damages to their value to A. Thus A obtains priority over B's creditors."

[29] [1921] 1 K.B. 321.

[30] As some commentators quaintly put it this may have been done "in consideration of the continuance of their illicit cohabitation": see Goff and Jones, *The Law of Restitution* (3rd ed., 1993), p. 79.

bankers. When Hambrouck's frauds were discovered Ms Spanoghe had £315 standing to her credit in this account which sum was paid into court. According to Bankes L.J. the money which the plaintiff bank sought to recover was capable of being traced.[31] Ms Spanoghe never paid any money into her bank except money which was part of the proceeds of Hambrouck's frauds, and her bank had paid all money standing to her credit into court. Heavy reliance was placed on *Taylor v. Plumer*[32] and Bankes L.J. talked about the right of an owner to recover property in the common law courts from a person who could show not title to it, where the property was capable of being traced, whether in its original form or in some substituted form.[33] Atkin L.J. suggested that the common law rights were large and had been admirably stated in *Taylor v. Plumer*. On his assessment of the situation it would follow that as the money paid into the bank could be identified as the product of the original money, the plaintiffs had the common law right to claim it, and could sue for money had and received.[34]

Common law tracing has come very much back on the agenda with the decision of the House of Lords in *Lipkin Gorman v. Karpnale Ltd*[35] which decision also gives a new lease of life to the exchange product theory. The facts of the case are relatively straightforward. Basically a firm of solicitors had a partner, Cass, who was a compulsive gambler. To compound matters Cass had authority to draw cheques on his sole signature on the firms clients account. The main method employed by Cass to obtain money from the clients account was to persuade the firm's cashier, whom he had corrupted, to make out a cheque payable to cash drawn on the account which Cass then signed. The cashier then cashed the cheque and handed the money to Cass who exchaged it for chips at a casino, the Playboy Club in Mayfair, and thus the money was gambled away. The question was whether the solicitors could recover this money from the Playboy Club. The House of Lords answered affirmatively and in doing so the doctrine of unjust enrichment attained a full flowering in English law.[36] Lord Goff pointed out that the House of Lords was not concerned with an equitable tracing claim in the present case, since no such case was advanced by the solicitors, who had been content to proceed at common law by a personal action for money had and received.

According to Lord Templeman the law imposes an obligation on the recipient of stolen money to pay an equivalent sum to the victim if the recipient has been "unjustly enriched" at the expense of the true owner.[37] The club was enriched as and when Cass staked and lost to the club money stolen from the solicitors. Lord Templeman explained that the Playboy Club received stolen money by way of gift from the thief; the club, being a volunteer, had been unjustly enriched

---

[31] [1921] 1 K.B. 321 at 328.
[32] (1815) 3 M. & S. 562.
[33] [1921] 1 K.B. 321 at 327.
[34] [1921] 1 K.B. 321 at 335–336.
[35] [1991] A.C. 548. For a recent example of the use of common law tracing see *FC Jones & Sons v. Jones* [1996] *The Times* May 13, 1996.
[36] For a comparative perspective see *Degelman v. Guaranty Trust* (1981) 117 D.L.R. (3d) 289 (Canada); *Pavey and Matthews v. Paul* (1986) 162 C.L.R. 221 (Australia); *East Cork Foods v. O'Dwyer Steel* [1978] I.R. 103 (Ireland).
[37] He quoted the following words of Lord Wright in *Fibrosa Spolka Akcyjna v. Fairbairn Lawson Combe Barbour Ltd* [1943] A.C. 32 at 61: "It is clear that any civilised system of law is bound to provide remedies for cases of what has been called unjust enrichment or unjust benefit, that is, to prevent a man from retaining the money of, or some benefit derived from, another which it is against conscience that he should keep."

at the expense of the solicitors from whom the money had been stolen and the club must reimburse the solicitors. Reference was made to the decision of the High Court of Australia in *Black v. Freedman & Co.*[38] where it was held that money stolen by a husband and handed over to his wife by way of gift to her could be recovered by the victim. In that case O'Connor J. said[39]:

> "Where money has been stolen, it is trust money in the hands of the thief, and he cannot divest it of that character. If he pays it over to another person, then it may be followed into that other person's hands. If, of course, that other person shows that it has come to him bona fide for valuable consideration, and without notice, it then may lose its character as trust money and cannot be recovered. But if it is handed over merely as a gift, it does not matter whether there is notice or not."

Lord Templeman observed that while the decision in *Black v. Freedman & Co.* was made on the basis of a trust, the reasoning applied equally to a claim for money had and received.

The relevant principles were more fully developed by Lord Goff who delivered the only other full judgment. He pointed out that the court were not concerned with an equitable tracing claim in the present case, since no such case was advanced by the solicitors, who were content to proceed at common law by a personal action, *viz.* an action for money had and received. There were however two Privy Council cases *Union Bank of Australia Ltd v. McClintock*[40] and *Commercial Banking Co. of Sydney Ltd v. Mann*[41] which seemed to present an insuperable obstacle to a common law tracing action. These cases stood as authority for the proposition that where a partner obtained money by drawing on a partnership account in an unauthorised fashion that partner alone got legal title to the money thereby obtained.[42] Lord Goff eliminated these decisions from the reckoning by holding that since the partnership account was in credit the bank became the debtor of the partnership. In his view this debt constituted a legal chose in action belonging to the solicitors and on the basis of *Taylor v. Plumer* they had power to follow this chose in action into its proceeds, namely the cash drawn by Cass from the client account and gambled away.[43]

What about legal title to exchange products? Lord Goff observed that it was well established that a legal owner was entitled to trace his property into its product, provided that the latter was indeed identifiable as the product of his property. He added that tracing property into its product involved a decision by the owner of the original property to assert his title to the product in place of his original property. In other words, the solicitors had the option of vesting title to the money in the gambler's possession in themselves by their own election. The use of the expression "ratification" was eschewed to describe this

---

[38] (1910) 12 C.L.R. 105.
[39] *ibid.* at 110.
[40] [1922] 1 A.C. 240.
[41] [1961] A.C. 1.
[42] For criticism of this reasoning see Halliwell [1992] Conv. 124 who writes: "According to the two Privy Council decisions, it must follow that legal title to the chose in action would immediately vest in Cass when he withdrew the money for his own unauthorised purposes, in the same way as did the legal title to the cash itself. The inescapability of this conclusion is affirmed by the fact that the two Privy Council decisions actually applied to cheques drawn on partnership accounts."
[43] For a somewhat sceptical approach to this analysis see Birks [1991] L.M.C.L.Q. 473 at 476–481; McKendrick (1992) 55 M.L.R. 379 and Smith (1991) 11 O.J.L.S. 480.

operation but it was said to have at least one feature in common with ratification, namely that it could not be relied upon so as to render an innocent recipient a wrongdoer.[44] One commentator has drawn an alternative analogy with the common law power to revest held by one who has parted with property as the result of a fraudulent misrepresentation.[45] So how is common law tracing to be described? Perhaps as a power hovering over a series of substitutions? The person tracing had the power to switch its legal title from the original property to one of a series of substitutions and this exercise of the power had retrospective effect. In this particular case the firm of solicitors did not discover the frauds perpetrated by their partner Cass until the money had been gambled away. Once the true facts emerged, the firm could lay claim to the product of its chose in action.[46]

The "power of election" analysis eliminates the so-called geometric multiplication problem that is part and parcel of the exchange-product theory of common law tracing. The problem becomes apparent if one considers the following set of facts. A fiduciary defrauds his principal of a power boat and swaps the power boat for a motor car. The exchange takes place with X who is at all times aware of the fraud. The defrauded principal cannot claim ownership of both the power boat and the car. He has however a power to choose between them which power may be exercised retrospectively.[47]

As we have seen the original asset may have altered in form or become unidentifiable thereby making necessary a claim to the proceeds of the assets instead. A big question is when the "means of ascertainment" of proceeds fails. This is the major difficulty associated with common law tracing. Commentators have talked about the materialism of the common law. The common lawyer has been depicted as the "poor mutt ... able to grasp the identity of specific coins but retiring mouth agape in baffled amazement once they are mixed with other coins".[48]

The judgment of Lord Ellenborough in *Taylor v. Plumer* contributes to this characterisation. He suggests that the means of ascertainment fail and with that the right to trace is lost when the subject is turned into money and mixed and confounded in a general mass of the same description.[49] He explained the earlier case of *Scott v. Surman*[50] by pointing out that the difficulty was one of fact and not of law. The *dictum* that money has no earmark must be understood as predicated on the existence only of an undivided and undistinguishable mass of current money. He went on to say that money marked or kept apart from other money could be followed. Money which remained as a debt and so was

---

[44] Reference was made to the statemement by Cotton L.J. in *Bolton Partners v. Lambert* (1889) 41 Ch.D. 295 at 307 that "an act lawful at the time of its performance [cannot] be rendered unlawful, by the application of the doctrine of ratification."

[45] See Birks [1991] L.M.C.L.Q. 473 at 478–479.

[46] See generally Andrew Burrows, *The Law of Restitution* (1993), pp. 67–68.

[47] Burrows, *op. cit.*, at p. 68 points out that the facts of *Lipkin Gorman* itself did not raise any geometric multiplication problem because, although a case of tracing by substitution, there was factually no possibility of the firm being entitled to both the original chose in action underpinning the bank account and the money drawn out from that account. It was the case that the very process of substitution destroyed the original property. As money was abstracted from the account the value of the chose in action automatically diminished.

[48] See Scott, *op. cit.*, at 470; see also Lord Greene M.R. in *Re Diplock* [1948] Ch. 465 at 520.

[49] (1815) 3 M. & S. 562 at 575.

[50] (1743) Willes 400. See in particular the statement of Lord Willes at 404.

identifiable could also be traced and so was money laid out in the purchase of specific goods.[51]

The matter of identifiability becomes acute when the proceeds of the original goods are mixed in a bank account with other moneys. The traditional view is that the common law is helpless in this respect.[52] The *locus classicus* is *Banque Belge pour L'Etranger v. Hambrouck*[53] where the judgments of Bankes and Scrutton L.JJ. seem to be to the effect that mixing of moneys in bank account defeats a common law tracing action. There is a degree of tentativeness about the expressions of opinion however. For instance all that Scrutton L.J. said on the subject was[54]: "at common law this would be a good answer to a claim for money had and received ... if the money was mixed in Hambrouck's bank with other money." Professor R.M. Goode, for one, takes a different view about the apparent inadequacy of common law remedies.[55] He has contended forcefully that the inability of the common law to allow money to be followed into a mixed fund is a myth and that in the common case of mixing in a bank or other account the rule in *Clayton's case*,[56] which will be discussed later, should apply. Others have argued for application of the principles operative in the case of a mixture of goods.[57] According to *Spence v. Union Marine Insurance Co. Ltd*,[58] where it is impossible to identify or separate the goods the original owners are treated as tenants in common of the mixed whole in proportion to the value of their contributions to it.

The point is, nonetheless, that the common law right to trace has not been relied upon to any great extent in recent times with the admittedly quite big exception of *Lipkin Gorman*.[59] Incidentally, one might have thought that the claim of the solicitors in *Lipkin Gorman* might have been defeated through the mixing by the fraudulent partner Cass of the cash with other moneys in a bank account. Yet the Playboy Club conceded that, if the plaintiffs could "establish legal title to the money in the hands of Cass, that title was not defeated by the mixing of the money with other money of Cass while in his hands."[60] Thus the common law tracing claim succeeded. Generally speaking however, equitable intervention is the order of the day. Consequently, in the words of Goff and Jones[61] the courts have not had the opportunity to develop "mature and consistent" common law rules for tracing money into a mixed fund in a bank account. *Agip (Africa)*

---

[51] See *Ryall v. Rolle* (1749) 1 Atk. 165.

[52] The *locus classicus* is *Banque Belge pour L'Etranger v. Hambrouck* [1921] 1 K.B. 321. In *Agip (Africa) Ltd v. Jackson* [1992] 4 All E.R. 451 Fox L.J. said: "Both common law and equity accepted the right of the true owner to trace his property into the hands of others while it was in an identifiable form. The common law treated property as identified if it had not been mixed with other property. Equity, on the other hand, will follow money into a mixed fund and charge the fund."

[53] [1921] 1 K.B. 321.

[54] *ibid.* at 330.

[55] Goode, *op. cit.*, at 378 *et seq.*

[56] (1816) 1 Mer. 572.

[57] See Pearce, *op. cit.*, at 282–283.

[58] (1868) L.R. 3 C.P. 427.

[59] [1991] 2 A.C. 339.

[60] As McKendrick has pointed out (((1992) 55 M.L.R. 377 at 380) this concession by counsel appears astonishing. There may have been something of a trade-off with the plaintiffs limiting their submissions with respect to the monetary amount that the defendants had actually been enriched. See generally on this point Birks [1991] L.M.C.L.Q. 473 at 476 and 495–496.

[61] Goff and Jones, *Law of Restitution* (3rd ed., 1986), p. 71, n. 66. The statement does not appear in the fourth edition of the work.

Ltd v. Jackson[62] is a case where the courts had such an opportunity yet spurned it.

Prior to *Agip* a lot of commentators looked upon the judgment of Atkin L.J. as the fountain from which more fully developed common law tracing principles might spring.[63] The judge talked about situations when the means of ascertainment failed and added[64]:

> "But if in 1815 the common law halted outside the bankers door, by 1879 equity had had the courage to lift the latch, walk in and examine the books: *Re Hallett's Estate*. I see no reason why the means of ascertainment so provided should not now be available both for common law and equity proceedings."

In *Agip* Fox L.J., who spoke with the concurrence of his brethren, said that Atkin L.J.'s approach in the *Banque Belge* case amounted virtually to saying that there was now no difference between the common law and equitable remedies. Indeed, the common law might conceivably be wider because of the absence of any requirement of a fiduciary relationship. Fox L.J. ventured the observation that this suggestion went well beyond the views of Bankes and Scrutton L.JJ. and in the 70 years since *Banque Belge* had never been applied.[65]

The plaintiff company in *Agip*, which was incorporated under the laws of Jersey, was involved in oil exploration. A senior employee, Zidri, managed to defraud it systematically of large sums of money. Zidri was an authorised signatory of the plaintiffs U.S. dollar account which it maintained with Banque du Sud in Tunis. He fraudulently altered legitimate payment orders by substituting the name of a different payee, Baker Oil. The new payee maintained an account with an English bank in London, Lloyds Bank. One such forged payment order was for an amount in excess of 518,000 U.S. dollars which payment order Zidri took to the Tunis bank. The latter executed it by debiting the plaintiff's account and sending instructions by telex to the London bank to credit Zidri's account with the sum of 518,000 U.S. dollars and to its correspondent bank in New York, Citibank, to reimburse the London bank for the same amount. The London bank made this payment before it had been reimbursed in New York. Ultimately, the money was transferred out of London and 45,000 US dollars found its way into an account maintained by Jackson & Co. in the Isle of Man. Was this amount traceable at common law? Both Millett J. and the Court of Appeal refused an affirmative answer to the question but for somewhat different reasons.

With respect, it must be said that the judgment of Millett J. seems rooted in the pre-technological age. Not for him the intricacies of modern payment methods and the notion that the common law must keep pace with sophisticated banking techniques. Essentially he denied the availability of common law tracing because the payment from Banque du Sud to Lloyds Bank was by telegraphic transfer.[66] No cheque or other physical asset was presented. In his words[67]:

---

[62] [1991] Ch. 547.
[63] See Birks [1993] C.L.P. 157 at 181.
[64] [1921] 1 K.B. 321 at 335.
[65] [1992] 4 All E.R. 451 at 466.
[66] It has been suggested that the judgment is barely intelligible in this respect except as part of a concerted attack on the strict common law liability: see [1989] L.M.C.L.Q. 296 at 340.
[67] [1992] 4 All E.R. 385 at 399.

"Nothing passed between Tunisia and London but a stream of electrons." Whilst not expressly disapproving of this opinion, the Court of Appeal appeared more receptive to the proposition that the common law must keep in step with technological advance. Fox L.J. opined[68]:

"The inquiry which has to be made is whether the money paid to Jackson & Co's account 'was the product of, or substitute for, the original thing.' In answering that question I do not think that it matters that the order was not a cheque. It was a direction by the account holder to the bank."

But this victory for the plaintiffs on the common law front in the Court of Appeal, if victory it can be called, was certainly a Phyrric one. The court took the view that the plaintiff's common law claim failed because Lloyds Bank had paid out Baker Oil before it had been reimbursed by Citibank in New York. This advance crediting meant that it was necessary to trace through the New York clearing bank system which the common law was incapable of doing. The money that was received by Lloyds Bank could not be equated with the money that left Citibank without going through the clearing system and in the system a process of mixing with other money must have been undergone. Fox L.J. said[69]:

"Baker Oil was paid by Lloyds, which had not been put in funds from New York. It was subsequently recouped. But it was not possible to show the source from which it was recouped without tracing the money through the New York clearing system."

It is submitted that reliance on the advance crediting analysis to defeat the plaintiff company's claim is not easy to reconcile with the approach adopted by the earlier Court of Appeal in the *Banque Belge* case.[70] Remember in that case a rogue employee Hambrouck had paid cheques into an account with Farrow's bank. He drew cheques against this account. Some of these he paid to a woman friend Ms Spanoghe who in turn lodged them with her bank and there stood to her account with the bank what survived of the frauds of Hambrouck. This amount was held to be traceable and there was no enquiry about whether Farrow's Bank had allowed Hambrouck to draw against the cheques before Farrows collected them. Such an enquiry assumed crucial significance in *Agip* but points of differentiation with *Banque Belge* in this respect were nowhere pointed out in the judgments.[71]

Another discordance between *Agip* and *Banque Belge* emerges if one focusses on the identity of the plaintiff in both cases. In both cases we had frauds perpetrated on employers. In *Banque Belge* the bank that paid out under a fraudulent pretence was suing whereas in *Agip* it was the company defrauded that was at the forefront of proceedings. How does one explain the discrepancy?[72] In *Banque Belge* Scrutton L.J. observed that it was "clear ... that the money actually obtained by Hambrouck was the Bank's money, even if they might

---

[68] [1992] 4 All E.R. 451 at 465.
[69] [1992] 4 All E.R. 451 at 466.
[70] [1921] 1 K.B. 321.
[71] See the comment by McKendrick [1991] L.M.C.L.Q. 378 at 384: "The matter was treated as being irrelevant and, if it was irrelevant in *Banque Belge*, it is not at all clear why it should be a relevant factor in *Agip*."
[72] See generally McKendrick [1991] L.M.C.L.Q. 378 at 379–381, Burrows *op. cit.* at 64.

debit their payments to the account of another."[73] The relationship between banker and customer is that of debtor and creditor so that property in the money has passed to the bank. Moreover, a bank has no right to debit its customer's account on a forged instruction since in such a case it has no mandate from the customer to do so. In *Agip* the plaintiff company may have been entitled to require the bank to recredit the money to their account and to treat the sums as paid with the bank's own money, but they tried to do so and failed. Agip sued in the Tunisian courts to have their account recredited—Tunisian law apparently being the proper law of the banking relationship between Agip and Banque du Sud—but no relief was granted. In the Court of Appeal Fox L.J. said that in those circumstances to regard Agip as not having paid Baker Oil was highly unreal.[74] Agip must be entitled to pursue such remedies as there were for the recovery of what was in substance its money.[75]

ADVANTAGES OF COMMON LAW TRACING

It is fair to say that common law tracing has advantages not associated with its equitable equivalent. One drawback, however, is that the common law does not take cognisance of equitable interests in property. Hence a beneficiary under a trust could not at common law follow the property in the hands of the trustee. The big plus is the absence of any requirement of a fiduciary relationship as a foundation of the right to trace which equity unlike the common law, requires.

It is possible to conceive of two situations at least where reliance might be placed on common law tracing remedies in preference to their equitable counterparts. One instance might be where property that represents the product of the plaintiff's original property is identified as being in the hands of a receiver appointed to a company. The receiver ignores demands to hand over this property or its monetary equivalent to the plaintiff. Instead he sells the property to a bona fide purchaser and uses the proceeds in the ordinary course of running the business of the company by paying employee wages, etc., the right to trace in equity would be lost and so the plaintiff would have had to fall back on the personal common law remedy against the receiver in an action for money had and received.[76]

The second situation I have in mind comes from the reservation of title context. Say a purchaser of goods subject to a reservation of title clause sub-sells without authorisation, express or implied, from the original seller. Payment for the goods is set off against a previous debt owed by the "Romalpa-type" purchaser to the sub-purchaser.[77] It is difficult to conceive of the availability of an equitable proprietary remedy in this situation for such a remedy assumes the existence of assets in the hands of the defendant and a set-off can hardly constitute this.

---

[73] [1921] 1 K.B. 321 at 329.
[74] [1992] 4 All E.R. 451 at 462.
[75] For criticism see McKendrick [1991] L.M.C.L.Q. 378 at 380 who asks whether a bank can now use *Agip* as authority to justify a refusal to re-credit a customer's account on the ground that, where it does so refuse, the customer has a cause of action against the recipient of the money or persons who knowingly assist in its dissipation.
[76] Goode (1976) 92 L.Q.R. 528 at 551.
[77] See I. Davies "Reservation of Title Clauses: A Legal Quagmire" (1985) L.M.C.L.Q. 49 at 70.

EQUITABLE TRACING

The concept of equitable tracing has been extensively discussed in numerous judicial decisions. Much of the heat and controversy has turned on the question of a fiduciary relationship. It is a strongly entrenched proposition that the equitable right to trace is not available to every owner. The remedy obtains only where the owner can show that a fiduciary duty is owed to him by the person to whom he has entrusted his property. Some have argued to the contrary[78] and suggested that it is possible to interpret the leading case, *Re Diplock*,[79] in a way which does not require, as a general rule, the finding that there is a fiduciary relationship. However, this view has been dismissed as an ingenious rationalisation not present in the mind of the Court of Appeal.[80] Furthermore, the proponent of this idea has mended the error of his ways.[81]

Re Diplock is a (in)famous case where a testator, Caleb Diplock, directed his executors to apply his residuary estate "for such charitable institution or institutions or other charitable or benevolent object or objects in England" as they in their absolute discretion should select. Caleb Diplock died in 1936 and by 1939 pursuant to the direction in the will the executors had paid over £200,000 to 139 charitable institutions. Certain of the testator's next of kin challenged the validity of the direction and in 1944 the House of Lords held that the residuary bequest was void for uncertainty.[82] In this particular action the Court of Appeal held that the next of kin had, subject to certain defences, an equitable proprietary claim to the money in the hands of the charities that had been mistakenly paid out by the executors.[83] Lord Greene M.R. spoke of the necessity of establishing, as a precondition of an equitable tracing claim, the existence of a fiduciary or quasi-fiduciary relationship or of a continuing right of property recognised in equity.

The fiduciary relationship requirement was accepted as inviolable by Goulding J. in *Chase Manhattan Bank N.A. v. Israel-British Bank (London) Ltd.*[84] The judge, however, gave a generous interpretation to the phrase. In this case the plaintiff bank paid some 2 million dollars by mistake to the defendant bank, which later was the subject of a winding up order. The plaintiffs discovered their mistake and sought to trace the sum paid. They also claimed for it in the winding up proceedings on the basis of an action for money had and received. As the defendant bank was insolvent, the latter claim, being a purely personal one, was

---

[78] See Pearce [1976] Conv. 277 at 287 *et seq*. See also Oakley "The Prerequisites of an Equitable Tracing Claim (1975) 28 C.L.P. 64.

[79] [1948] Ch. 465.

[80] See Goff and Jones, *The Law of Restitution* (4th ed., 1993), p. 85, n. 71.

[81] See Pearce "Reservation of Title on the Sale of Goods in Ireland" (1985) 20 Irish Jurist (New Series) 264 at 288.

[82] *Chichester Diocesan Fund and Board of Finance (Inc.) v. Simpson* [1944] A. C. 341. The use of the word "or" rather than "and" proved to be be a fatal flaw.

[83] The Court of Appeal also held in the case that where the estate of a deceased had been wrongfully distributed to persons an unpaid or underpaid creditor, legatee or next of kin had a personal claim in equity against those persons. This personal claim however only operated where the person had first exhausted his claim against the personal representatives responsible for the mistake. In *Ministry of Health v. Simpson* [1951] A.C. 251 the House of Lords affirmed the reasoning and conclusions of the Court of Appeal on this point.

[84] [1981] Ch. 105.

insufficient to compensate the plaintiffs, so they pressed ahead with their tracing action. The action proved successful.

Goulding J. observed that there was no judicial decision in England on the question whether a person who mistakenly paid money could be granted the restitutionary proprietary remedy of tracing.[85] He then proceeded to examine *Re Diplock*[86] to see if it supported the argument of counsel for the defendants that there was no equitable right to trace property unless some initial fiduciary relationship existed. The judge's conclusion was that, in order to be traced, a fund need not have been the subject of fiduciary obligations before falling into the wrong hands: it was enough that the payment into the wrong hands itself gave rise to a fiduciary relationship.[87] *Sinclair v. Brougham*[88] was mentioned in support of this proposition. There did not have to be any consensual arrangement involved. Applied to the facts of the *Chase Manhattan* case this principle meant that "a person who pays money to another under a factual mistake retains an equitable property in it and the conscience of that other is subjected to a fiduciary duty to respect his proprietary right."

Sinclair v. Brougham is a case where a building society carried on a banking business that was beyond its powers. The House of Lords held that persons who had made deposits to the society in connection with the *ultra vires* banking business could trace into the assets of the now insolvent society. Moreover they were entitled to share these assets *pari passu* with shareholders of the society. Lord Greene, speaking for the Court of Appeal in *Re Diplock*[89] said that the court would be lacking in candour rather than showing respect if it refrained from saying that it found the speeches in *Sinclair v. Brougham* not only difficult to follow but also difficult to reconcile with one another. Be that as it may, the object of the depositors in that case was to establish contractual relationships between themselves and the society. Given however, the limitations on the building society's powers the depositors retained an equitable property in the funds they parted with and this was enough to establish the right to trace.

The same analysis commended itself to Hobhouse J. at first instance and to the Court of Appeal in *Westdeutsche Landesbank Girozentrale v. Islington L.B.C.*[90] Tracing issues were not however explored to any great extent in the judgments of the Court of Appeal. The case arose out of an interest rate "swap" contract entered into by Islington with the German bank that was beyond the powers of the local authority. A swap contract has been described as follows[91]:

"an agreement between two parties by which each agrees to pay the other on a specified date or dates an amount calculated by reference to the interest which would have accrued over a given period on the same notional principal sum assuming different rates of interest are payable in each case. For example, one rate may be fixed

---

[85] *ibid.* at 116. But see *Barclays Bank Ltd v. W.J. Simms Son & Cooke (Southern) Ltd* [1980] 2 W.L.R. 218.

[86] [1948] Ch. 465.

[87] [1981] Ch. 105 at 119.

[88] [1914] A.C. 398.

[89] [1948] Ch. 465.

[90] [1994] 4 All E.R. 890; on which see Swadling [1994] *Restitution Law Review* 73.

[91] The quote is from the judgment of Lord Templeman in *Hazell v. Hammersmith and Fulham London BC* [1992] 2 A.C. 1. This quote was used by Dillon L.J. in *Westdeutsche Landesbank* as a convenient working defintion of an interest rate swap contract.

at 10 per cent and the other rate may be equivalent to the six-month London Inter-Bank Offered Rate (LIBOR). If the LIBOR rate over the period of the swap is higher than 10 per cent then the party agreeing to receive 'interest' in accordance with LIBOR will receive more than the party entitled to receive the 10 per cent. Normally, neither party will in fact pay the sums which it has agreed to pay over the period of the swap but instead will make a settlement on a 'net payment basis' under which the party owing the greater amount on any day simply pays the difference between the two amounts due to the other."

Under the particular arrangement between the bank and the local authority Westdeutsche was the fixed rate payer at a rate of 7.5 per cent per annum and Islington was the floating rate payer at the domestic sterling LIBOR rate.[92] The agreement ran for a period of ten years and the bank paid the local authority £2.5 million at its commencement. This initial sum was the only payment that the bank made to the local authority. Interest rate fluctuations worked to the disadvantage of the local authority. Due to this fact the four payments between the parties before the invalidity of the contract was discovered were made by the local authority to the bank. These payments totalled approximately £1.3 million leaving the bank out of pocket to the tune of over a £1 million. It was held that the bank was entitled to recover this money in a personal restitutionary action. Hobhouse J. in his first instance judgment also considered the equitable proprietary angle.[93]

In his view the constituents of the right to trace in equity and the equitable remedy were firstly the identification of some fiduciary relationship between the plaintiff and the recipient of the money and secondly the ability to trace the payment into the assets of the recipient (or his representative) as they exist at the time of trial. In his view the present case was indistinguishable from *Sinclair v. Brougham*.[94] The fiduciary relationship came into existence and the equity was created at the time that the payee received the money under a void contract. Thereafter the question became one of ability to trace and of the continued existence of the equity. In the Court of Appeal Leggatt L.J. seemed to take the same view stating that in equity the money remained the property of Westdeutsche and that receipt by Islington of money which was not theirs constituted them fiduciaries.[95]

The holding that Islington were fiduciaries in respect of the receipt of the money carried an important practical consequence in that Islington thereby became subject to the possibility of having to pay compound interest as distinct from simple interest on the money unlawfully retained.[96] Leggatt L.J. explained that where money has been withheld by a person in a fiduciary position the court has power to award compound interest.[97] He said that the court was concerned to ensure that the fiduciary did not make a profit from the use of

---

[92] It should be noted that the bank entered into a parallel swap transaction with a second bank in order to hedge its potential liabilites under the arrangement with the local authority. Under the parallel swap contract with the second bank, Morgan Grenfell, Westdeutsche was the floating rate payer and Morgan Grenfell the fixed rate payer.

[93] [1994] 4 All E.R. 890 936–940.

[94] [1914] A.C. 398.

[95] [1994] 4 All E.R. 890 at 969.

[96] The *Westdeutsche* case has been appealed to the House of Lords on the simple versus compund interest point. At the time of writing judgment on the appeal is awaited.

[97] [1994] 4 All E.R. 890 at 969. Leggatt L.J. referred to *Burdick v. Garrick* (1870) L.R. 5 Ch. App. 233 and also to the observations of Scarman L.J. in *Wallerstiener v. Moir (No. 2* [1975] Q.B. 373.

money that was not his.[98] Dillon L.J. adopted the same view and added that in considering what profit a person is to be taken to have made, the court takes into account the economic and financial conditions of the time.[99]

The view advanced in *Westdeutsche Landesbank* that a fiduciary relationship existed between payer and payer has been criticised on the basis that, generally speaking, the invalidity of a contract does not of itself prevent property from passing.[1] Examples may be cited from the law pertaining to illegal contracts.[2] The demarcation line between property and restitution is not however marked out with precision.[3] Different types of invalidities are not treated consistently by the courts insofar as their proprietary effects are concerned.[4] The decision of the Court of Appeal in *Westdeutsche* has now been overturned by the House of Lords. The House of Lords took the view that payments made pursuant to an *ultra vires* contract did not give rise to any relationship of trust between payer and recipient. In other words the payee obtained full legal and equitable ownership and all that the payer had was a personal restitutionary right of action to recover the *ultra vires* payment. There was no equitable proprietary claim available. Consequently the grounds for awarding compound interest that found favour with the Court of Appeal fell away. Lord Browne-Wilkinson who spoke for the majority of the House of Lords in *Westdeutsche* suggested that *Sinclair v. Brougham* should be overruled and the law developed in accordance with principle and commercial common sense. He said[5]:

> "[A] claimant for restitution of moneys paid under an *ultra vires*, and therefore void, contract has a personal action at law to recover the moneys paid as on a total failure of consideration; he will not have an equitable proprietary claim which gives him either rights against third parties or priority in an insolvency; nor will he have a personal claim in equity, since the recipient is not a trustee."

The various judgments in *Sinclair v. Brougham* were dissected at some length by Lord Browne-Wilkinson. In his view, while all the reasoning therein was open to serious objection, it was only intended to deal with cases where there were no trade creditors in competition and the reasoning should be regarded as incapable of application where there were such creditors.

---

[98] As Andrew Burrows has pointed out in [1995] *Restitution Law Review* 15 at 27 the consequence of the *Westdeutsche* case would appear to be that, even where the payee is solvent, it will always be in a payer's interests in seeking restitution to claim a resulting trust or fiduciary relationship in equity rather than bringing a common law action for money had and received. The common law remedy is confined to permitting recovery of the amount paid and does not attract compound interest.

[99] [1994] 4 All E.R. 890 at 965. In the particular circumstances of this case the Court of Appeal took the view that an award of compound interest was appropriate. The local authority had spent the money on its ordinary purposes and moreover, if it had not received the "up-front" payment pursuant to the *ultra vires* swap contract, it would have had to borrow an equivalent sum at compound interest so as to meet its expenditures.

[1] See Swadling [1994] *Restitution Law Review* 73 at 80–82.

[2] See for instance *Singh v. Ali* [1960] A.C. 167 where the parties entered into an illegal contract for the sale of a lorry. Notwithstanding that fact that the contract of sale was unlawful and void, the Privy Council took the view the view that when, in pursuance of the contract, the lorry was sold and delivered to the buyer, the property in it passed to him.

[3] See Swadling, *op. cit.*, at p. 80.

[4] In *Barclays Bank Ltd v. W.J. Simms, Son and Cooke (Southern) Ltd* [1980] 1 Q.B. 677 at 689 Robert Goff J. said that property will almost invariably pass in the case of a mistaken payment. The whole issue of passing of property in cases of mistake is considered in Chapter 7.

[5] [1996] 2 W.L.R. 802 at 836–837.

REQUIREMENT OF A FIDUCIARY RELATIONSHIP AS PRODUCTIVE OF
INJUSTICE

There may still be one situation where the requirement of a fiduciary
relationship as a prerequisite to equitable tracing is capable of causing practical
problems.

While there may have been a sufficient proprietary base for a tracing claim.
Take the case of thief who steals a car from a full legal and beneficial owner
and then sells the car in circumstances that confer on the purchaser a good title
thereto. The thief mixes the sale proceeds with other moneys in a bank account
thereby defeating a common law tracing action. Later on, the thief withdraws
money from the bank account which money he invests in real estate. Finally he
becomes bankrupt. Are we to suppose that the victim of the theft is left with a
mere claim to a dividend in the bankruptcy? It is difficult to accept that an
English court would follow this analysis. It seems more likely that they would
grant an equitable tracing remedy against the thief where the legal remedies fell
down on the adequacy score thereby stretching the concept of fiduciary
relationship to breaking point.[6] This supposition is strengthened by reference to
the judgment of Lord Templeman in *Lipkin Gorman v. Karpnale Ltd.*[7] Lord
Templeman cited the decision of the High Court of Australia in *Black v.
Freedman & Co.*[8] where it was held that money stolen by a husband and handed
over to his wife by way of gift to her could by recovered by the victim. O'Connor
J. said[9]:

> "Where money has been stolen, it is trust money in the hands of the thief, and he
> cannot divest it of that character. If he pays it over to another person, then it may be
> followed into that other person's hands. If, of course, that other person shows that it
> has come to him bona fide for valuable consideration, and without notice, it then may
> lose its character as trust money and cannot be recovered. But if it is handed over
> merely as a gift, it does not matter whether there is notice or not."

In *Westdeutsche*, counsel for the bank, in arguing for the proposition that the
transferor of the property under the *ultra vires* contract, retained an equitable
proprietary interest, invoked the spectre of the thief. Essentially counsel for the
bank was arguing that the victim of the theft should have an equitable proprietary
interest. If such relief was denied to the payer under a *ultra vires* contract, it was
difficult to see how it could be available in the theft situation. Lord Browne-
Wilkinson did not accept this analogy and considered that proprietary relief
could be available to the theft victim while denied to the bank. He said[10]:

> "I agree that the stolen moneys are traceable in equity. But the proprietary interest
> which equity is enforcing in such circumstances arises under a constructive not a
> resulting trust."

---

[6] See the Canadian case *Lennox Industries v. The Queen* (1986) 34 D.L.R. (4th) 304 and also the article
by Sir Peter Millett "Tracing the Proceeds of Fraud" (1991) 107 L.Q.R. 71 at 76.
[7] [1992] 4 All E.R. 512 at 522.
[8] (1910) 12 C.L.R. 105.
[9] *ibid.* at 110.
[10] [1996] 2 W.L.R. 802 at 838–839. Lord Browne-Wilkinson referred to *Bankers Trust Co. v. Shapiro*
[1980] 1 W.L.R. 1274 and *McCormick v. Grogan* (1869) L.R. 4 H.L. 82. Somewhat surprisingly he
did not mention *Lipkin Gorman*.

The wise words of Robert Goff L.J., as he then was, in *Clough Mill Ltd v. Martin*[11] should also be borne in mind in this connection. He said that concepts like fiduciary duty are our tools and not our masters. Much the same sentiments appealed to Millet J. in *El Ajou v. Dollar Land Holdings*.[12] This case was concerned partly with the question whether moneys that had been paid over pursuant to voidable contracts could be traced in equity. The judge answered the question in the affirmative, and did so quite summarily, but the issue merits more extended treatment.

TRACING IN EQUITY AFTER RESCISSION OF VOIDABLE CONTRACTS

El Ajou v. Dollar Land Holdings arose out of a massive fraudulent share pushing operation that was managed by three Canadians based in Amsterdam. The plaintiff had entrusted considerable funds for investment to a fiduciary agent based in Geneva and the latter was bribed by the rogue Canadian to invest the funds in worthless shares. Could the plaintiff trace the funds in equity? The judge said "yes". The judge observed that the agent had committed a gross breach of his fiduciary obligations to the plaintiff and that was sufficient to enable the plaintiff to invoke the assistance of equity.[13] But as he also pointed out other victims were in a sense less fortunate. They employed no fiduciary and were simply swindled. The judge suggested that it would be an intolerable reproach to our system of jurisprudence if the plaintiff were the only victim who could trace and recover his money. Lo and behold, in his view, this was not the case. The other victims, having been induced to purchase the shares by false and fraudulent misrepresentations, were entitled to rescind the transaction and revest the equitable title to the purchase money in themselves, at least to the extent necessary to support an equitable tracing claim. The observations of Brennan J. in *Daly v. Sydney Stock Exchange Ltd*[14] were cited in support of this proposition.

These observations were specifically directed to the position of a fiduciary transferee but carry a more general import. Brennan J. said[15]:

> "If the transfer is set aside, the fiduciary transferee (and, no doubt, a volunteer or a purchaser with notice of the circumstances) holds the property transferred on a constructive trust for the transferor which a court of equity will enforce subject to any accounts or inquiries that may be necessary to do equity to the transferee. The transferor may elect to avoid the contract and to assert his title to the land or other property transferred assuming it still exists in specie, or being, can be traced. He may invoke the assistance of equity to recover the land or other property in specie or to trace the money."

[11] [1985] 1 W.L.R. 111 at 116.
[12] [1993] 3 All E.R. 717. It should be noted that the decision of Millett J. was actually reversed by the Court of Appeal but nothing was said in the Court of Appeal about tracing resulting from rescisssion of voidable contracts. Furthermore, while the issue of tracing in this particular context was not specifically addressed by the House of Lords in *Westdeutsche*, the general thrust of the judgment of Lord Browne-Wilkinson seems hostile to the proposition that such a claim should succeed.
[13] [1993] 3 All E.R. 717 at 734.
[14] (1986) 160 C.L.R. 371 at 387–390.
[15] *ibid* at 387–388.

The judge added that where property has been sold and conveyed, the purchaser's beneficial title must be ascertained by reference to the sale so long as it stands; the vendor cannot insist on an equitable interest in the property if he does not choose to enforce his equity to avoid the sale. In other words the contract of sale must be rescinded before a vendor can assert equitable tracing rights. This is essentially what Millett J. was saying in *El Ajou v. Dollar Land Holdings.*

It is possible to cite other authorities in support of broadly the same proposition from an Edwardian world of Sale of Goods and personal bankruptcy. A case in point is *Re Eastgate.*[16] In this case it was held that where a sale of goods is induced by the fraud of the purchaser, the vendor, on discovering the fraud, was entitled within a reasonable time to disaffirm the sale and retake possession of the goods. This may be done even though the vendor has notice of an act of bankruptcy on which the purchaser is subsequently adjudicated bankrupt. In such a case the trustee in bankruptcy had no higher or better title than the bankrupt. According to Bigham J. the trustee acquired the interest of the bankrupt in the property subject to the rights of third parties. One of those rights in this case was the right of the vendors of the goods to disaffirm the contract and to retake possession of the goods.

Re Eastgate was applied in *Tilley v. Bowman*[17] which is again a sale of goods case. The contact had been induced by the fraud of the purchaser and the latter had been given a period of credit. Upon obtaining the goods he proceeded to pledge them with a pawnbroker. The purchaser paid part of the purchase price and later a receiving order was made against him. When the vendor discovered the fraud he disaffirmed the contract and retook possession of the goods having paid to the pawnbroker the sum advanced upon them. The purchaser was adjudicated bankrupt and the question arose whether the rescission of the contract was effective against the trustee in bankruptcy. This question was answered in the affirmative. Hamilton J. held that the vendor had a right to disaffirm the contract after the date of the receiving order and that therefore the trustee was not entitled to recover the goods or their value.

So one falls back on the old principle that a liquidator or trustee in bankruptcy must take the goods and property of an insolvent company or individual as he finds them. Pre-insolvency entitlements of others *vis-a-vis* the goods must be respected. The liquidator stands in no better position than the insolvent.

It has been suggested that the principle enunciated by Millett J. in *El Ajou v. Dollar Land Holdings* may require reconsideration in the light of the decision of the Privy Council in *Re Goldcorp Exchange Ltd.*[18] Somewhat surprisingly *El Ajou* does not appear to have been cited in the *Goldcorp* case so that we are deprived of the benefit of hearing the views of the Privy Council on the apparent tensions between the two holdings. The *Goldcorp* case arose out of the collapse of a New Zealand company which dealt in gold and other precious metals. Various persons purchased bullion from the company for future delivery. It was understood by the investors that they were purchasing "non-allocated metal" which would be stored and insured free of charge by the company. The company represented that bullion purchased was not set aside as a customer's metal but was instead

---

[16] [1905] 1 K.B. 465.
[17] [1910] 1 K.B. 745.
[18] [1994] 2 All E.R. 806.

stored in safe-keeing as part of the company's overall stock of bullion and was insured by the company. It was further represented that the stock of bullion held by the company from which customers could call for delivery if they so wished would always be sufficient to meet the company's obligations under all outstanding contracts of sale. No appropriation of specific and segregated parcels of bullion to the individual purchase contacts of non-allocated claimants was made. The company became insolvent and it was held by the Privy Council that the non-allocated claimants were not entitled to assert any proprietary rights over the stocks of bullion then in the company's premises.

As Lord Mustill pointed out most of the arguments for the non-allocated claimants were premised on the assumption that each contract of sale and collateral promises together created a valid and effective transaction coupling the ordinary mutual obligations of an agreement for the sale of goods with special obligations stemming from a trust or fiduciary relationship. The claimants however also argued the contrary proposition that the transactions were rendered ineffectual by the presence of vitiating factors such as misrepresentation. The misrepresentations invoked were that (in fact) the company intended to carry out the collateral promise to establish a separate stock and and also that (in law) if this promise was performed the customer would obtain a title to bullion. Lord Mustill would have no truck with the submission. He said[19]:

> "The customers have never rescinded the contracts of sale, but have throughout the proceedings asserted various forms of proprietary interest in the bullion, all of them derived in one way or another from the contracts of sale. This stance is wholly inconsistent with the notion that the contracts were and are so ineffectual that the customers are entitled to get their money back. As a last resort the non-allocated claimants invited the Board to treat the contracts as rescinded if their claims for a proprietary interest in bullion were rejected. There is however no mechanism which would permit the claimants to pause, as it were, half-way through the delivery of the present judgment and elect at last to rescind; and even if such a course were open, the remedies arising on rescission would come too late to affect the secured rights of the bank under its previously crystallised floating charge."

Put simply the applicants could not both approbate and reprobate and there is nothing said in *El Ajou* that controverts this proposition. So the ratio of *Re Goldcorp Exchange Ltd* and the observations of Millett J. in *El Ajou* are compatible but certain comments by Lord Mustill generate a degree of tension between the two cases. His Lordship opined that while it was convenient to speak of the customers "getting their money back" this expression was misleading. The customers would not recover "their" money on rescission of the contracts of purchase but rather an equivalent amount. Lord Mustill had no hesitation in rejecting the proposition that where a purchaser was misled into buying goods he was automatically entitled upon rescinding the contract to a proprietary superior to those of all the vendor's other creditors, exercisable against the whole of the vendors's property. The judge described this proposition as an extreme one and declined to follow *Re Eastgate*[20] if insofar as the case lent it any support though he doubted whether or not this was in fact the situation.[21]

---

[19] [1994] 2 All E.R. 806 at 825.
[20] [1905] 1 K.B. 465.
[21] [1994] 2 All E.R. 806 at 825–826.

Certainly the proposition is an extreme one as it purports to disregard completely the identification principles of equitable tracing. If a proprietary claim is in principle available to a person induced by misprepresentation to enter into a contract the property handed over must remain identifiable for the claim to succeed. Equity has an elaborate set of principles for determining whether property is sufficiently identifiable and these principles must be satisfied. In fact as was later pointed out by Lord Mustill in *Goldcorp* the moneys paid by the investors were paid into an overdrawn account and therupon ceased to exist.[22] Millett J. in *El Ajou v. Dollar Land Holdings* was not in the business of rewriting completely the identification principles of equitable tracing so again there is no necessary inconsistency between *El Ajou* and *Goldcorp*. The claimed incompatibility between the two cases derives simply from two passages from the judgment of Lord Mustill where he stated[23]:

"Upon payment by the customers the purchase moneys became, and rescission or no rescission remained, the unencumbered property of the company. What the customers would recover on rescission would not be 'their' money, but an equivalent sum."

All judicial observations must be read *secundam subjectam materiam*. *Re Goldcorp Exchange Ltd* was a straightforward case of contractual non-performance. The default of the company was the simple contractual breach of failing to deliver goods ordered and paid for before it became insolvent. This was the kernel of the complaint and not that of a misrepresentation or misrepresentations inducing the contract.

CONCLUSION

It is submitted that a plaintiff should be able to "trace" or to follow assets through changes in form whenever he has got a proprietary base at the outset, when the facts on which the claim to trace is based occur. Legal or equitable ownership should be irrelevant. Talk of fiduciary relationships or not, have diverted attention away from the real question, which is, whether the plaintiff has retained property, whether legal or equitable, in the subject matter of the tracing claim. Focussing on the issue of the plaintiff's proprietary base does not necessarily make the resolution of concrete cases any easier. The proprietary consequences of particular transactions are not clearcut. It is now clear as a result of the *Westdeutsche* case that full legal and equitable ownership passes where property has been handed over pursuant to a contract that is flawed due to lack of *vires* on the part of one of the contracting parties. Uncertainties however still arise in relation to contracts that are voidable due to fraud or misrepresentation on the part of the contracting party who has obtained goods on foot of the contract. The proprietary effect of payments made on the basis of a mistake which caused the payment has also yet to receive thorough judicial consideration. So a switch from the notion of fiduciary relationships to that of a proprietary base does not provide an easy answer to thorny questions. It may however enable judges and commentators to see the competing interests at stake in a clearer light.

[22] See his comments at [1994] 2 All E.R. 806 at 827.
[23] [1994] 2 All E.R. 806 at 825.

CHAPTER NINE

The Identification Principles of Equitable Tracing

The greatest contribution of equity to the law of tracing has been in fashioning principles that assist in the identification of misapplied property. In other words, Equity, unlike the common law, has been able to follow property with some ease through changes in form. To use contemporary terminology from the law of Restitution Equity has been good identifying the surviving enrichment.[1] A famous Victorian judge said in a colourful phrase that whereas the common law may have stopped at the banker's door, equity was able to open the latch, walk in and inspect the books.[2] To use the language of Lord Greene M.R. in *Re Diplock* equity adopted a more metaphysical approach than the common law. It had no difficulty in regarding a composite fund as an amalgam consisting of the mixture of two or more funds, each of which could be regarded as having, for certain purposes, a continued separate existence. Equity was able to draw up a balance sheet, on the right hand side of which appears the composite fund and on its left hand side the two or more funds of which it is deemed to consist.[3] Equity may order the restoration of an unmixed sum of money or property acquired through the use of this money. Alternatively, it may declare a charge on a mixed fund or on any property that has been acquired through the use of such a fund. In this chapter the identification principles of equitable tracing will be discussed in detail as well as the limitations on their application. The chapter also considers calls that have been made for the extension or even the abrogation of these principles.

EQUITABLE TRACING PRINCIPLES—A SUMMARY

If the property that forms the subject matter of the original tracing claim has been used to purchase another asset, the original owner may adopt the purchase and claim the purchased property entirely as his own.[4] Alternatively, he may claim a lien on the property to secure recoupment of the value of his original asset. Normally, what the fiduciary receives in return for the goods is money and he may mix this money with his own money in a bank or other running account. The original owner is entitled to a charge on the account to secure recoupment of the proceeds of his asset.[5]

Usually withdrawals from a bank account are taken as representing the earliest credit item. This is the rule in *Clayton's Case*.[6] However, the principle is not

---

[1] See Birks, *Introduction to the Law of Restitution* (1985), p. 358.
[2] *Banque Belge Pour L Etranger v. Hambrouck* [1921] 1 K.B. 321 at 335 *per* Atkin L.J.
[3] *Re Diplock* [1948] Ch. 465 at 520 *per* Lord Greene M.R. The Master of the Rolls stated that it was the metaphysical approach of equity coupled with and encouraged by the far-reaching remedy of a declaration of charge that enabled equity to identify money in a mixed fund.
[4] *Re Hallett's Estate* (1880) 13 Ch.D. 696 at 709 *per* Sir George Jessel M.R.
[5] *ibid.* It was explained that the charge was quite independent of the fact of the amount laid out by the fiduciary. The moment you got a substantial portion of it furnished by the fiduciary, the right to a charge followed.
[6] (1817) 1 Mer. 572.

applied in the tracing situation that we have outlined. The presumption is that the fiduciary did not intend to commit a breach of trust. Consequently, in working out which funds have been expended *Clayton's Case* is inapplicable and the moneys remaining in the account will be taken to be the moneys belonging to the original owner. This is known as the rule in *Re Hallett's Estate*.[7] In that case Jessel M.R. said[8]:

> "[In] the case of a trustee who has blended trust moneys with his own, it seems to me perfectly plain that he cannot be heard to say that he took away the trust money first when he had the right to take away his own money.... No human being ever gave credit to a man on the theory that he would misappropriate trust money, and thereby increase his assets. No human being ever gave credit, even beyond that theory, that he should not only misappropriate trust moneys to increase his assets, but that he should pay the trust moneys so misappropriated to his own banking account with his own moneys, and draw out after that a larger sum than the first sums paid in for the trust moneys."

THE LOWEST INTERMEDIATE BALANCE PRINCIPLE

The presumption against a breach of trust is not carried very far. If subsequently, the trustee were to replenish the fund there is no assumption that in doing so he intended to replace the moneys withdrawn in breach of trust.[9] The defrauded beneficiary is entitled to a charge on the bank account only to the extent of the lowest intermediate balance. This principle was formulated in *James Roscoe (Bolton) Ltd v. Winder*.[10] Here Sargant J. held that payments into a general account cannot, without proof of express intention, be appropriated to the replacement of trust money which has been improperly mixed with that account and drawn out. The rationale of this principle has been explained by one U.S. jurist in the following terms:

> "[T]here is no reason for subjecting other property of the wrongdoer to the claimant's claim any more than to the claims of other creditors merely because the money happens to be put in the same place where the claimant's money formerly was unless the wrongdoer actually intended to make restitution to the claimant."[11]

Evidentiary principles are however applied strictly against a wrongdoer in the context of the tracing exercise. Certain observations of Millett J. in *El Ajou v. Dollar Land Holdings plc*[12] clearly demonstrate this proposition. The judge said[13]:

> "The victims of a fraud can follow their money in equity through bank accounts where it has been mixed with other moneys because equity treats the money in such accounts

---

[7] (1880) 13 Ch.D. 696. The Court of Appeal (Thesiger L.J. dissenting) on this point refused to follow the earlier decision in *Pennell v. Deffell* (1853) 4 De G.M. & G. 372.

[8] *ibid.* at 729–730.

[9] The evidence of such an intention on the part of a defaulting trustee may be available on the facts of a particular case. See in this connection *Re Lewis's of Leicester Ltd* [1995] BCC 514.

[10] [1915] 1 Chap. 62.

[11] A.W. Scott, *The Law of Trusts*, Vol. 5 (3rd ed., 1967), p. 3638.

[12] [1993] 3 All E.R. 717.

[13] *ibid.* at 735. In the court of appeal these remarks were not specifically considered but the general tenor of Millett J.'s judgment in this respect was approved: see [1994] 2 All E.R. 685 at 692–693 (Nourse L.J.), at 699 (Rose L.J.) and at 701 (Hoffmann L.J.).

as charged with the repayment of their money. If the money in an account subject to such a charge is afterwards paid out of the account and into a number of different accounts, the victims can claim a similar charge over each of the recipient accounts. They are not bound to choose between them. Whatever may be the position as between the victims *inter se*, as against the wrongdoer his victims are not required to appropriate debits to credits in order to identify the particular account into which their money has been paid."

In *El Ajou v. Dollar Land Holdings plc (No. 2)*[14] the defendant tried to resist an equitable tracing claim by invoking the rights of third parties. The plaintiff had been defrauded by being deceitfully induced to buy worthless shares as part of a fraud operated from Amsterdam by three Canadians. There were thousands of other victims of the fraud with most of them being small investors. A Mr Van Apeldoorn was appointed by a Dutch court as trustee in bankruptcy of the Canadians' companies. The plaintiffs managed to trace part of their moneys to moneys invested in the acquisition of a site in Battersea. They sought an order that this money should be paid over to them. None of the other victims of the fraud had sought to trace their investment to identifiable money or property and it had been agreed between the plaintiffs and Mr Van Apeldoorn, on behalf of the other victims, that the proceeds of the present action should be divided 70:30 with the larger share going to the plaintiffs.

In effect, the defendant was contending that the plaintiff should not receive 70 per cent of the recoveries since this would potentialy be unfair to other victims of the fraud who might similarly be able to trace their losses into the funds used for the acquisition of the Battersea property. The judge, Robert Walker J., said that there was no general rule as to whether a defendant can ever plead a sort of equitable *ius tertii* in this type of case. In his view, a rigid rule of universal application either way or the other would be inappropriate. He gave the following example from the field of family trusts[15]:

"Suppose that a tenant for life's interest is charged in equity with two annuities, one payable to A of £700 a year and the other payable to B of £300 a year but subject to an overall restriction that the total annuities payable should not exceed half the annual income of the trust property, and that half the annual income is for the time being only £500. If, after there has been no annuity payment to anyone for over a year, A sues the tenant for life for £500, B not being a party to the proceedings, should A get judgment for £500 or £350. Normally the answer would be that he should get only his proper proportion, that is £350, but if it appeared from strong (though not conclusive evidence) that B had disappeared and might be dead and that before he disappeared he had indicated that he had no wish to receive his annuity, the position would be different. In those circumstances, the court might well order the tenant for life to pay to A the full amount available for the annuities, on A giving him a suitable indemnity against any possible claim by B."

According to the learned judge the court's inclination to take such a course might be considerably stronger if the defendant in question is not a beneficiary and simultaneously a trustee under a properly constituted trust, but like in this case, a person who knowingly received the proceeds of fraud and so with no claim to retain the traceable money subject to the equitable charges. In this

---

[14] [1995] 2 All E.R. 213.
[15] *ibid.* at 223–224.

particular case Robert Walker J. refused to allow the rights of third parties to be raised by way of defence to the tracing claim. It was almost inconceivable that any of the other victims of the fraud would now try to mount an individual action. Their official representative under Dutch law was supporting the plaintiff's claim. The court concluded that the other victims, apart from the hard core of those who never read or respond to any official communications, even when directly touching on their own financial affairs, either actively supported or willingly accepted or acquiesced in the trustee in bankruptcy's attitude.

Issues of identification of misapplied assets also arose in *Westdeutsche Landesbank Girozentrale v. Islington London Borough Council*[16] As explained before the case arose out of the interest rate swap transactions that were entered into by local authorities in the late 1980s as a way of circumventing central government limits on borrowing. It was held by the House of Lords in *Hazell v. Hammersmith and Fulham B.C.*[17] that such swap transactions were outside the powers of local authorities. The question then arose how might the effect of such *ultra vires* agreements be unravelled. To instance only one case, Westdeutsche had paid a large sum of money to Islington pursuant to a swap agreement. Was such money recoverable by Westdeutsche? Both Hobhouse J. at first instance and the Court of Appeal answered the question in the affirmative. It was held that the sum was recoverable. Otherwise the local authority as recipient of the money under a void contract would be unjustly enriched at the expense of the bank. What had happened to the money since its receipt by Islington? Hobhouse J. at first instance felt it appropriate to explore this issue albeit tentatively. He relied on *Sinclair v. Brougham*[18] as authority for the proposition that a fiduciary relationship came into existence at the time that the payee received the money. In his view the question therefore became one of ability to trace and of the continued existence of the equity. The judge suggested that where no question of insolvency arises and where the claimant is simply asking that the fiduciary account for the money that he has received, the fiduciary cannot, by failing to account, escape liability.[19] Various cases were mentioned as illustrating the grant to a plaintiff of a general tracing remedy in the nature of an equitable charge upon the defendant's assets notwithstanding the inability to trace individual specific sums through the accounts of the defendant (or the recipient) down to the date of trial.[20] In the judge's view, the position might be different where the claimant is seeking to share in the increased value of assets which the fiduciary has acquired or, in a case where there are competing claims on an inadequate fund, the claimant is having to assert his right to a prior claim on that fund. Hobhouse J. quoted the observations of Ungoed-Thomas J. in *Re Tilley's Will Trusts*[21] to the effect that if a trustee mixes trust assets with his own, the onus is on the trustee to distinguish the separate assets and, to the extent that he fails to do so, they belong to the trust. Hobhouse J. added that the mere fact that a given bank account or group of bank accounts may not be in credit does not mean that the right of a beneficary to trace through the assets of a fiduciary has been

---

[16] [1994] 4 All E.R. 890.
[17] [1992] 2 A.C. 1.
[18] [1914] A.C. 398.
[19] [1992] 4 All E.R. 890 at 938.
[20] Such as *Sinclair v. Brougham* [1914] A.C. 398 and *Re Tilley's Will Trusts* [1967] Ch. 1179.
[21] [1967] Ch. 1179 at 1183. See also the observations of Stuart V.-C. in *Cook v. Addison* (1869) L.R. 7 Eq. 466 at 470.

lost. If the fiduciary wishes to say that the relevant moneys have been dissipated, the fiduciary must prove that that is the only possible conclusion on the evidence.[22] One may argue that this is no different from recognising a personal remedy against Islington. The judge himself recognised this fact.[23]

The Court of Appeal in the case did not find it necessary to investigate tracing issues. Dillon L.J. pointed out that Islington was undoubtedly solvent. Irrespective of whether or not some particular or general charge came into being, there was a personal liability in equity to make reimbursement.[24] In the circumstances this was an efficacious remedy as far as Westdeutsche was concerned. The House of Lords in *Westdeutsche*[24a] did not consider the tracing question. This was not necessary in view of its prior holding that full legal and equitable title in the payment had passed to the recipient.[24b]

A CHARGE ON THE ENTIRETY OF THE MIXED FUND

Re Hallett's Estate does not take away from the fundamental principle that the original owner has an entitlement to a charge on the mixed fund or any property which is purchased thereout. A case in point is *Re Oatway*[25] where the trustee had mixed his own and trust moneys in a banking account. The account was drawn upon to further the purchase of shares but a balance was left that exceeded the amount of trust moneys paid in. Further drawings were made which exhausted the account. Therefore, it was useless to proceed against the account. These later drawings were dissipated and did not result in any assets which could be traced. The court took the view that the *cestuis que trust* had a charge on the shares from the trust money paid into the account. It was held that the original charge on the mixed fund continued on each and every part thereof, despite changes of form unless and until the restoration of the trust money paid into the mixed account and reinstatement of the trust fund by the proper investment of the money in the joint names of the appropriate trustees. Joyce J. put the matter bluntly. He said[26]:

"It is, in my opinion, ... clear that when any of the money drawn out has been invested, and the investment remains in the name or under the control of the trustee, the rest of the balance having been afterwards dissipated by him, he cannot maintain that the investment which remains represents his own money alone, and that what has been spent and can no longer be traced and recovered was the money belonging to the trust."

If the entirety of a mixed fund is used in the acquisition of property which increases in value, then according to the opinion expressed by Ungoed Thomas

---

[22] [1994] 4 All E.R. 890 at 939.
[23] *ibid.* at 940.
[24] [1994] 4 All E.R. 890 at 966. See also Leggatt L.J. at 969. Kennedy L.J. agreed with the judgments of both Dillon L.J. and Leggatt L.J.
[24a] [1996] 2 W.L.R. 802.
[24b] There was a suggestion from Lord Browne-Wilkinson that he found the identification principles of equitable tracing very much pro-plaintiff: see [1996] 2 W.L.R. 802 at 828.
[25] [1903] 2 Ch. 356.
[26] *ibid.* at 360.

J. in *Re Tilley's Will Trusts*[27] the claim will be for a proportionate part of the enhanced value and not just for the amount of the trust money expended in the purchase. So, in general, the beneficiary may claim a proportionate share of a new asset purchased out of the trust money. The judge held that this right of election by a beneficiary also applied where an asset was purchased by a trustee in part out of his own money and in part out of the trust money. The beneficiary could, if he wished, require the asset to be treated as trust property with regard to that proportion of it which the trust moneys contributed to its purchase.[28]

If a dispute arises between two claimants to a mixed fund consisting of moneys held on behalf of the two of them and mingled together by the trustee, they share *pari passu*. Moreover, if property is acquired by means of the mixed fund, each is entitled to a charge rateably. Neither gains over the other. The same principle holds if the property of the original owner and an innocent volunteer are mixed. In *Re Diplock* it was said[29]:

> "It would be inequitable for the volunteer to claim priority for the reason that he is a volunteer: it would be equally inequitable for the true owner of the money to claim priority over the volunteer for the reason that the volunteer is innocent and cannot be said to act unconscionably if he claims equal treatment for himself. The mutual recognition of one another's rights is what equity insists upon as a condition of giving relief."

"FIRST IN, FIRST OUT"—AN INNOCENT VOLUNTEER OR ANOTHER VICTIM IN COMPETITION WITH THE TRACING CLAIMANT

As was discussed earlier and confirmed by Jacob J. in the recent case *Brinks Ltd v. Abu-Saleh*[30] if a trustee mixes trust assets with his own money, to the extent that the assets can not be distinguished, they belong to the trust. The onus of distinguishing the two sets of assets lies with the wrongly acting trustee. Where however the funds of two separate trusts or the funds of one trust and those of an innocent volunteer are mixed in the context of an active banking account then the rule in *Clayton's Case* has traditionally been held to apply.[31] The principle enunciated in *Clayton's Case* is one of "first in, first out" with bank withdrawls taken as representing the earliest credit item. Application of this principle tends to produce unjust results causing loss to fall on the shoulders of one or other

---

[27] [1967] 1 Ch. 1179. See also *Lord Provost of Edinburgh v. Lord Advocate* (1879) 4 App. Cas. 823 and *Scott v. Scott* (1963) 37 A.L.J.R. 345.

[28] *ibid.* at 1189. Ungoed-Thomas J. said: "It seems to me that if, having regard to all the circumstances of the case objectively considered, it appears that the trustee has in fact, whatever his intention, laid out trust moneys in or towards a purchase then the beneficiaries are entitled to the property purchased and any profits which it produces to the extent to which it has been paid for out of the trust moneys." The judge concluded however, that, even on this objective test, the trust moneys were not in this case so laid out. This factual conclusion has been described as "rather surprising in Hanbury & Martin, *Modern Equity* (14th ed., 1993), p. 663.

[29] [1948] Ch. 465 at 539.

[30] [1995] 4 All E.R. 65 at 72. Reference was made by Jacob J. in this connection to *Re Tilley's Will Trusts* [1967] Ch. 1179.

[31] (1817) 1 Mer. 572; 35 E.R. 781. See *Re Diplock* [1948] Ch. 465 at 554. See also Fry J. in *Hallett's Case* (1880) 13 Ch.D. 696 at 699 and North J. in *Re Stenning* [1895] 2 Ch. 433. The justification advanced for not treating two claimants rateably was that this would lead to the greatest difficulty and complication in practice.

innocent party.[32] The American judge, Learned Hand has stated that to adopt the fiction of first in, first out, is "to apportion a common misfortune through a test which has no relation whatever to the justice of the case."[33] *Re Stenning*[34] is a case where such injustice occurred. Basically in the case we had a solicitor who paid money which he had received for a client to his own banking account. From that time up to the date of the death of the solicitor there was always to the credit of the account a balance so exceeding the sum so paid in. The solicitor however, also paid other client moneys into his private account and made various withdrawals therefrom. North J. held that the rule in *Clayton's Case* applied. Therefore the money of the first client must be taken to have been drawn out by the solicitor in the earliest withdrawal from the account and so it did not form part of the balance to the credit of the account at the time of his death.

Recent authority indicates that the principle propounded in *Clayton's Case* based as it is on presumed intention is not one of universal application and may be departed from in the circumstances of a particular individual case. Such a departure occurred in *Barlow Cowes International Ltd v. Vaughan*.[35] The dispute arose following the well-publicised collapse of certain deposit-taking companies that had promoted and managed various investment plans. At the time of the collapse the companies had a total liability of over £115 million but the amount available for distribution to investors was far less. The question arose whether the available assets should be distributed on the basis that withdrawals from the investment fund and its consequent depletion had been made on a "first in, first out" basis so that the late investors were those most likely to be repaid.[36] The Court of Appeal said that judicial decisions had established and recognised a general rule of practice that *Clayton's Case* was to be applied when several beneficiaries moneys had been blended in one bank account and there was a deficiency.[37] The rule would not be applied however where its application would be contrary to the intention, express or implied, of the investors. In this particular case because of the plan to establish a collective investment pool the presumed intention must have been that the rule would not apply and that all the assets available for distribution would be shared rateably amongst the investors in

---

[32] For a critical perspective see Goff and Jones, *The Law of Restitution* (4th ed., 1993) at p. 89.
[33] *Re Walter J. Schmidt & Co.* (1923) 298 F. 314, 316. See also the New Zealand case *Re Registered Securities Ltd* [1991] 1 N.Z.L.R. 545.
[34] [1895] 2 Ch. 433.
[35] [1992] 4 All E.R. 22. In *El Ajou v. Dollar Land Holdings plc (No. 2)* [1995] 2 All E.R. 213, Robert Walker J. said that when, as in cases like *Barlow Clowes*, a court-appointed fiduciary has taken control of what is left of the proceeds of a massive fraud and is seeking directions as to its division between all or some of the would-be investors who were defrauded, it is natural to view the divisible assets as a trust fund and the victims as the beneficiaries, whose identities and whose proper shares must be established. But he went on to say that the analogy with a properly constituted and properly managed trust fund was far from exact. Changes in the "state of investment" of the fund which is being traced might occur in a totally random way and may, except where a bona fide purchaser for value without notice appears on the scene, present the tracing claimant with an election as to which of two assets to claim against. Moreover, the tracing claimants' position was not the same as that of beneficiaries of a properly constituted trust fund since changes in the composition of the fund might alter their rights as between themselves. The rule of "first in, first out" may be applied as between rival claimants seeking to trace through an active bank account.
[36] In other words in accordance with the rule in *Clayton's Case*.
[37] See in particular the statement of Dillon L.J. [1992] 4 All E.R. 22 at 33.

proportion to the amounts due.[38] Reference was made by Dillon L.J. to the decision of Astbury J. in *Re British Red Cross Balkan Fund, British Red Cross Society v. Johnson*.[39] This is a case where a special fund had been brought into being through the collection of subscriptions that were intended to be expended on those sick or wounded in the 1912 Balkan War. When the war ended moneys remained in the fund. The court arrived at the decision that the remaining amount belonged to the subscribers rateably as the subscriptions had been made to the fund en bloc. Astbury J. said *a propos* the rule in *Clayton's Case*[40]:

> "It is a mere rule of evidence and not an invariable rule of law, and the circumstances of any particular case may or may not afford ground for inferring that the transactions of the parties were not intended to come under the general rule."

As was pointed out by Dillon L.J. the actual decision in *Re British Red Cross Balkan Fund, British Red Cross Society v. Johnson* seems somewhat questionable since the objects of the fund would seem to have been charitable. If they were charitable the surplus should have been applied *cy-pres* for other charitable purposes. The decision was however applied in the case of a winding up of a non-charitable fund by Cohen J. in *Hobourn Aero Components Air-Raid Distress Fund*.[41] Dillon L.J. applied these cases by analogy and accepted that what he called the narrow submission of counsel that all investors who contributed to the investment portfolios in question were contributing to common funds in which all investors were to participate.[42] Thus *Clayton's Case* should not be applied. Leggatt L.J. took much the same approach. He said the investors contributed to what they thought was a collective investment fund. Such investors cannot be presumed to have intended that losses incurred would be borne other than rateably.[43] Application of the principle of "first in, first out" would be capricious and arbitrary and to use this fiction for the amelioration of a common misfortune would not be justifiable. The judge concluded by saying that since all the investors had equitable charges, and their equities were equal and they presumably intended their money to be dealt with collectively, they should share rateably what was left in the pool as did the claimants in *Sinclair v. Brougham*.[44]

Woolf L.J. took a somewhat broader approach. He went along with his brethren in holding that the documentation contemplated the creation of a collective investment scheme which necessarily rendered the rule in *Clayton's Case* inapplicable. He also said however that he would refuse to apply the rule even if the documents indicated that Barlow Clowes International were obliged to create separate funds for each investor.[45] What actually happened was that Barlow Clowes did not create separate funds but a common pool into which all

[38] [1992] 4 All E.R. 22 at 39. As explained in the text Woolf L.J. appeared to go somewhat further than his brethren, Dillon and Leggatt L.JJ., by suggesting that irrespective of whether the fund was or was not a common investment fund the rule in *Clayton's Case* should not be applied.
[39] [1914] 2 Ch 419.
[40] *ibid.* at 421.
[41] [1946] Ch. 194. The decision of Cohen J. was affirmed by the Court of Appeal but the only issue for the court was whether or not the fund was charitable.
[42] [1992] 4 All E.R. 22 at 33.
[43] [1992] 4 All E.R. 22 at 46.
[44] [1914] A.C. 398.
[45] [1992] 4 All E.R. 22 at 41.

the investors moneys were collected. In this situation of common misfortune it was correct to assume that the investors intended that what could be salvaged should be shared rateably. It was not safe to infer an intention that those who had invested with Barlow Clowes longest should receive least which result application of the "first in, first out" principle would produce.[46]

The Court of Appeal were unanimous in rejecting the application of the so-called North American "rolling charge" solution in the particular case.[47] This solution involves regarding credits to a bank account made at different times and from different sources as a cocktail with the consequence that upon a withdrawl being made from the account it was regarded as a withdrawl in the same proportions as the different interests in the account bore to each other at the instance before the withdrawl was made. In this particular case, Dillon L.J. pointed out that because of the large number of depositors and even with the benefits of modern computer technology, the cost of having recourse to this method of distribution would be disproportionate to the amounts at stake. Thus its use was impracticable.[48]

TRACING INTO THE PAYMENT OF DEBTS

It has been argued that where money is used to pay a debt, it is traceable into what was acquired in exchange for the incurring of the debt. Take the situation where a dishonest fiduciary buys a car on credit and then mis-appropriates trust moneys which he uses to discharge the debt. The fiduciary then becomes bankrupt. The suggestion is that the trust fund beneficiaries should have a claim to the car in preference to the general creditors of the fiduciary.[49] There is in fact some support, albeit scant support, for this view in *Re Diplock.*[50] In this case money paid to the Heritage Craft Schools was used to repay a Colonel Warren a like sum advanced by him to the Schools for the purpose of executing improvement to buildings. It was held that as a matter of substance the money had been used to pay for the improvements. Lord Greene M.R. said *a propos* the point[51]:

"The payment to Colonel Warren can only have operated to extinguish the debt owing to him and the money which he had advanced was consequently available for use by the charity for the purposes indicated without there being any obligation to repay it. The case cannot, we think, be regarded as a case of subrogation. [In] such a

---

[46] See also *Re Eastern Capital Future Ltd* [1989] B.C.L.C. 371 which is a case involving futures transactions. In the case Morritt L.J. said at p. 375 with regard to the possible application of *Clayton's Case*: "Obviously the court does not apply a rule which leads to substantial expense but to nowhere else. There is no suggestion that any client or class of client is more or less innocent than any other; thus the equities are equal between all clients and they are entitled to the funds *pari passu*: compare *Sinclair v. Brougham* [1914] A.C. 398."

[47] It should be noted that Dillon L.J. in *Barlow Clowes* ([1992] 4 All E.R. 22 at 33) described the rolling charge solution as more logical than the rule in *Clayton's Case* and it was described by Woolf L.J. as likely to produce the "most just result". It may be argued that these *dicta* open the way for the North American method to be used in simpler insolvencies than *Barlow Clowes*.

[48] [1992] 4 All E.R. 22 at 27–28.

[49] See Lionel Smith, "Tracing into the payment of a Debt" (1995) 54 C.L.J. 290, and also see Smith [1994] *Trust Law International* 102.

[50] [1948] Ch. 465. See also *Agricultural Credit Corp. of Saskatchewan v. Pettyjohn* [1991] 3 W.W.R. 689.

[51] [1948] Ch. 465.

case the debt was extinguished so that, in order to give effect to the equitable doctrine said to be applicable, it would be necessary to revive the debt in some way. We do not see how it can be said to be unconscientious on the part of the charity to object to this being done. In substance, the Diplock money was used for the purpose of carrying out works on the land of the charity ..."

When discussing *Re Diplock* in this context it must be remembered that the tracing claim was refused where the charities had spent money on improvements to buildings—in a sense a recognition of the defence of change of position. Therefore the case is very weak authority for saying that tracing into the payment of debts is permissible at all.

There are considerable practical problems with allowing tracing into the payment of debts. To return to the situation of the dishonest fiduciary, say before misappropriating the trust moneys he had been granted a bank loan and used the car that was acquired on credit as security. Do the trust fund beneficiaries take the car subject to this security? On a more general level, it might be argued that as a matter of substance the car has not been acquired with the money of the beneficiaries. Rather, it was acquired free of any encumbrance through the willingness of the vendor to extend credit.

In *Bishopsgate Investment Management Ltd v. Homan* Leggatt L.J. was adamantly opposed to tracing into the payment of debts.[52] He said that there could be no equitable remedy against an asset acquired before misappropriation of money takes place, since *ex hypothesi* it could not be followed into something which existed and so had been acquired before the money was received and therefore without its aid. The concept of a composite transaction was fallacious. Nevertheless the judge saw some force in the submission that if an asset were used as security for an overdraft which was then discharged by means of misappropriated money, the beneficiary might obtain priority by subrogation. But ordinarily there could be no tracing into an asset which was already in the hands of the defaulting trustee when the misappropriation occurs.

Dillon L.J. was more favourably disposed to backward tracing.[53] Two examples were supplied of this phenomenon. One was where an asset was acquired by MCC with moneys borrowed from an overdrawn or loan account and there was an inference that when the borrowing was incurred it was the intention that it should be repaid by misappropriations of Bishopsgate moneys. Another possibility was that moneys misappropriated from Bishopsgate were paid into an overdrawn account of MCC in order to reduce the overdraft and so make finance available within the overdraft limits for MCC to purchase some particular asset. Following the approach adopted by Vinelott J. at first instance, Dillon L.J. suggested that if the connection postulated between a particular misappropriation of Bishopsgate money and the acquisition by MCC of a particular asset was sufficiently clearly proved, it was at least arguable, depending on the facts, that there ought be an equitable charge in favour of Bishopsgate on the asset in question.

Clearly, there is an obvious divergence between the judgments of Dillon L.J. and Leggatt L.J. with respect to "backward tracing". Dillon L.J. thinks that backward tracing is possible whereas Leggatt L.J. denies that possibility. Notwithstanding the inconsistency Henry L.J. agreed with both judgments. Therefore

[52] [1994] B.C.C. 868 at 874.
[53] [1994] B.C.C. 868 at 870–871.

the case is somewhat unsatisfactory as an authority on this point. It is submitted that "backward tracing" should not be possible. After all, initially the asset was acquired through the willingness of a lender to extend credit and not by reason of any misappropriation of funds.

The observations of Dillon L.J. in the *Bishopsgate* case countenance a restricted form of "backward tracing". On his analysis, when an asset was acquired on credit it must have been intended by the borrower that the loan should be repaid through the use of misappropriated money before the tracing exercise is possible. Such intention may be very difficult to prove and may involve very complicated factual inquiries. While the state of the late Robert Maxwell's mind at any particular point of time may have been just as much a fact as the state of his indigestion, ascertaining and verifying information about his mental state is certainly more difficult than about his digestive state. Moreover, Maxwell may not have intended to pay particular creditors or at least carried on business at a time when he realised that there was no reasonable prospect of them being paid.[54] These facts do not bring about a general equitable lien in favour of creditors who have suffered as a result. There seems no good and sufficient reason for treating the tracing claimant more favourably.

SUBROGATION

It may be suggested however that a beneficiary whose funds have been misappropriated and used to discharge a debt owed by the trustee could have a remedy under the doctrine of subrogation.[55] If for instance a trustee has acquired an asset on credit and used the misappropriated money to pay off the debt the argument is that the beneficiary is subrogated to the rights of the unpaid vendor of the asset. The leading House of Lords pronouncement on subrogation to an unpaid vendor's lien is *Orakpo v. Manson Investments Ltd.*[56] Here Lord Diplock observed that the mere fact that money has been expended upon discharging a secured liability of the borrower does not give rise to any implication of subrogation unless the contract under which the money was borrowed provides that the money is to be applied for this purpose. He suggested that the origin of the right of subrogation is the contract between borrower and moneylender for the loan of money by the moneylender to the borrower. If there was no contractual obligation upon the borrower to apply the moneys in discharging a security on the the property of the borrower in favour of a third party, the expectation of the parties that the money would in fact be used for

---

[54] Under s. 214 of the Insolvency Act 1986 once a director or shadow director knows or ought to have concluded that there was no reasonable prospect that a company would avoid going into insolvent liquidation he must take every step with a view to minimising potential loss to company creditors. Otherwise he runs the risk of being declared personally liable for the debts and liabilities of the company. Any recoveries under the section go however, to swell the assets of the company available for distribution to all creditors. The court cannot direct payment to particular creditors who have suffered during the period of "wrongful trading". The position was different under the old fraudulent trading jurisdiction embodied in s.332 of the Companies Act 1948: see *Re Cyona Distributors Ltd* [1967] Ch. 889.

[55] See generally on subrogation C. Mitchell [1992] L.M.C.L.Q. 483. See also Mitchell, *The Law of Subrogation* (Oxford University Press 1995).

[56] [1978] A.C. 95.

this purpose did not give rise to any right of subrogation in the moneylender, even if the money was so applied.[57]

How does this statement fit in with the present example? Obviously the context is completely different. In the one situation we have a contract of loan and an obligation to apply the moneys for a specific purpose. In the other, we have the misappropriation of money and then its subsequent use to discharge a particular liability. There appears to be no authority precisely in point but the question of principle arises whether the doctrine of subrogation should be used to circumvent limitations on equitable tracing. Lord Edmund Davies in *Orakpo* said[58]:

"Apart from specific agreement and certain well-established cases, it is conjectural how far the right of subrogation will be granted, though in principle there is no reason why it should be confined to the hitherto-recognised categories"

According to Lord Salmon in the same case[59]:

"The test as to whether the courts will apply the doctrine of subrogation to the facts of any particular case is entirely empirical. It is ... impossible to formulate any narrower principle than that the doctrine will be applied only when the courts are satisfied that reason and justice demand that it should be."

Lord Diplock was somewhat more cautious in his approach. He referred to subrogation as a convenient way of describing the transfer of rights from one person to another, without assignment or assent of the person from whom the rights are transferred. Such a transfer of rights took place in a whole variety of widely different circumstances. The judge went on[60]:

"This makes particularly perilous any attempt to rely upon analogy to justify applying to one set of circumstances which would otherwise result in unjust enrichment a remedy of subrogation which has been held to be available for that purpose in another and different set of circumstances."

It should be noted that in *Orakpo* Lord Diplock also observed that there was no general doctrine of unjust enrichment in English law. Clearly this view is no longer tenable in the light of *Lipkin Gorman v. Karpnale Ltd*[61] where the House of Lords were unanimous in affirming the existence of an independent principle of unjust enrichment in English law. Lord Templeman quoted approvingly the words of Lord Wright in *Fibrosa Spolka Akcyjna v. Fairbairn Lawson Combe Barbour*

---

[57] Lord Keith was of the same opinion. He said at p. 119 that if a person had simply borrowed money without any strings attached and then voluntarily used it to complete contracts for the purchase of land or to pay off the holders of existing charges, no question of subrogation would have arisen.

[58] [1978] A.C. 95 at 112.

[59] *ibid.* at 110.

[60] *ibid.* at 104. In *Boscawen v. Bajwa* [1995] 4 All E.R. 769 the Court of Appeal denied the existence of a general rule which, irrespective of the circumstances, required the party claiming subrogation to a creditor's security to prove that he intended his money to discharge the security in question and that he intended to obtain the benefit of the security by subrogation. In this particular case the party claiming subrogation did not intend to become an unsecured creditor. Rather, it's intention was to retain a beneficial interest in the loan moneys advanced unless and until it obtained a charge over the property whose acquisition the loan was intended to finance.

[61] [1991] A.C. 548.

Ltd[62] that "any civilised system of law is bound to provide remedies for cases of what has been called unjust enrichment or unjust benefit, that is, to prevent a man from retaining the money of, or some benefit derived from, another which it is against conscience that he should keep."

It must be remembered however that in the situation under discussion it is not simply a matter of obtaining redress from a wrongdoer. It is a question of preferring the plaintiff who has admittedly been wronged over general creditors of the wrongdoing trustee. The trustee has insufficient funds to satisfy all his creditors. The plaintiff is in competition for scarce resources, as it were, with other creditors. Essentially the plaintiff is seeking priority over other creditors. Where the identification principles of tracing deny him such priority and there is a policy justification for this result there seems no good reason for reaching precisely the opposite conclusion through the vehicle of subrogation.

LOSS OF THE TRACING REMEDY

Tracing rights subsist only so long as the fund can be followed, in the legally understood sense of that term. Dissipation may occur leaving no traceable assets. In *Re Diplock* itself the court spoke thus[63]:

> "The equitable remedies presuppose the continued existence of the money either as a separate fund or as part of a mixed fund or as latent in property acquired by means of such a fund. If ... such continued existence is not established, equity is as helpless as the common law itself. If the fund, mixed or unmixed, is spent upon a dinner, equity, which dealt only in specific relief and not in damages, can do nothing."

Lord Greene M.R. gave the example of a fund of money, mixed or unmixed, being spent on a dinner. In this situation equity could do nothing.

Re Diplock is also important in highlighting equitable bars to a tracing claim. The remedy awarded by equity is a declaration of charge enforceable by sale. If an innocent volunteer has spent the trust money on altering or improving his own land or buildings, it would not be equitable to allow the claimant to trace the moneys. A charge on the land or buildings is backed up by a power to compel a sale. This would mean the volunteer being forced to exchange his land or buildings for money and often their market value will not have increased in line with the monetary amount of the alterations.[64]

Certain jurisdictions have moved towards acknowledgement of a wider defence to restitutionary claims of change of position. For instance, in the United States the American Law Institute's *Restatement of the Law, Restitution*[65] defines the defence in the following terms:

> "(1) The right of a person to restitution from another because of a benefit received is terminated or diminished if, after the receipt of the benefit, circumstances have

---

[62] [1943] A.C. 32 at 61.

[63] [1948] Ch. 465 at 521.

[64] See generally, *op. cit.*, at 546–550. Goff and Jones, *The Law of Restitution* (4th ed., 1993), p. 91 allude to to the fact that in certain circumstances it may not be inequitable to impose a lien. They give the example of an innocent volunteer who happens to be a rich banker and who has used the money wisely to increase the value of his country house. Furthermore, the person has ample liquid assets to discharge any lien imposed over the property.

[65] (1937) at para. 142. See also *Palmer on Restitution* (1978) vol. 3, para. 16.8.

so changed that it would be inequitable to require the other to make full restitution.

(2) change of circumstances may be a defence or a partial defence if the conduct of the recipient was not tortious and he was no more at fault for his receipt, retention or dealing with the subject matter than was the claimant."

The House of Lords were much influenced by these developments in *Lipkin Gorman v. Karpnale Ltd*[66] when articulating a general defence of change of position in English law. Lord Goff opined[67]:

"[W]here an innocent defendant's position is so changed that he will suffer an injustice if called upon to repay or to repay in full, the injustice of requiring him so to repay outweighs the injustice of denying the plaintiff restitution. If the plaintiff pays money to the defendant under a mistake of fact, and the defendant then, acting in good faith, pays the money or part of it to charity, it is unjust to require the defendant to make restitution to the extent that he has so changed his position. Likewise ... if a thief steals my money and pays it to a third pary who gives it away to charity, that third party should have a good defence to an action for money had and received. In other words, bona fide change of position should of itself be a good defence in such cases as these."

Lord Goff went on to stress that the mere fact that the defendant has spent the money, in whole or in part, did not of itself render it inequitable that he should be called upon to repay. After all the expenditure might in any event have been incurred by him in the ordinary course of things.

RELEVANCE OF TRADITIONAL TRACING RULES IN CONTEMPORARY CONDITIONS

The relevance of equity's traditional rules for following property, given that we are now in the age of electronic transfer of funds, has been questioned by Professor Gareth Jones.[68] Professor Jones suggests that it may no longer be necessary, to "identify" in accordance with Equity's traditional rules and presumptions, assets in the hands of the defendant and points to the fact that the rules may be found wanting in the context of a volatile and active banking. Elsewhere, in their highly influential treatise on *The Law of Restitution*, Professor Jones along with his co-author Lord Goff of Chieveley, talk about equity's rules and presumptions as having been conceived in the horse-and-buggy world of trifling sums paid into relatively passive banking accounts.[69]

Chase Manhattan N.A. v. Israel-British Bank (London) Ltd[70] is cited as exemplifying the deficiencies in the traditional approach. In this case the defendant had traded for over a month after it had been mistakenly paid the sum of $2 million

---

[66] [1992] 4 All E.R. 512.
[67] *ibid.* at 533. See also the Supreme Court of Canada case *Storthoaks Rural Municipality v. Mobil Oil Canada Ltd* (1975) 55 D.L.R. (3d) 1. Lord Goff is of course the co-author of Goff and Jones, *The Law of Restitution* the publication of which has had a seminal influence on the shaping of the modern law of restitution.
[68] "Tracing Claims in the Modern World" [1988] King's Counsel 15. See also Goff and Jones, *The Law of Restitution* (4th ed., 1993) at pp. 98–102.
[69] See Goff and Jones (4th ed., 1993) at p. 98.
[70] [1981] Ch. 105.

twice over. Daily inflows and outflows from the bank's coffers ran into the millions of pounds. While holding that tracing was theoretically possible Goulding J. left aside for another day the question of whether any part of the *corpus* of the mistaken payment remained to form the subject matter of a tracing order.[71] Professor Jones reasons that the other day never dawned in the Chancery Division for the very probable reason that there was no unsecured assets over which a lien could be imposed in favour of the plaintiff.[72] The arguments advanced by Professor Jones for a wholescale liberalisation of the identification rules of equitable tracing have received some judicial support from Lord Templeman when giving the advice of the Privy Council in *Space Investments Ltd v. Canadian Imperial Bank of Commerce Trust Co.*[73] It should be borne in mind however that his comments were purely *obiter* and moreover seemed to have been grounded on the misapprehension that they fairly reflected the state of existing law. Furthermore the comments were made without full consideration of the case law. This is a case where a bank acting as a trustee, pursuant to a power in the trust instrument and therefore lawfully, deposited money as a loan with the bank itself. The bank went into liquidation and it was held that the claims of the beneficiaries were merely those of unsecured creditors.

By way of contrast Lord Templeman drew attention to the hypothetical situation where a bank trustee misappropriated trust money for its own benefit but it was impossible for the beneficiaries to trace their money to any particular asset belonging to the trustee bank. He suggested that equity would allow the beneficiaries to trace the trust moneys to all the assets of the bank and to recover the trust money by the exercise of an equitable charge over all the assets of the bank. In his opinion[74]:

> "This priority is conferred because the customers and other unsecured creditors voluntarily accept the risk that the trustee bank might become insolvent and unable to discharge its obligations in full. On the other hand, the settlor of the trust and the beneficiaries interested under the trust, never accept any risks involved in the possible insolvency of the trustte bank. On the contrary, the settlor could be certain that if the trusts were lawfully administered, the trustee bank could never make use of trust money for its own purposes and would always be obliged to segregate trust money and trust property in the manner authorised by law and by the trust instrument free from any risks involved in the possible insolvency of the trustee bank."

The prescription of Jessel M.R. in *Re Hallett's Estate*[75] might also be thought to lend some support to the arguments of Professor Jones. The Master of the Rolls in that case pointed out that the rules of Court of Equity were not established from time immemorial. On the contrary he said that they had been established from time to time as well as altered, improved and refined from

---

[71] *ibid.* at 128.
[72] Jones, *op. cit.*, at 16.
[73] [1987] 1 W.L.R. 1072. Professor Goode points out: "The implication in Lord Templeman's speech seems to be that all the assets of the bank constitute one enormous fund so that the infusion of any part of the trust property into those assets impresses the totality of the assets with a charge in favour of the beneficiaries" (1987) 103 L.Q.R. 433 at 447.
[74] [1987] 1 W.L.R. 1072 at 1074.
[75] (1880) 13 Ch.D. 696 at 710.

time to time. In addition, to discover the principles of equity one had to refer to the more modern rather than the more ancient cases.[76]

On the other hand the rules have been firmly established over the past 100 years. It would require an extremely daring judge to cast these principles aside and to go back to the drawing board. Moreover, the traditional approach has been vigorously defended. In the words of one commentator there seems no good reason to prefer a tracing claimant to an insolvent's general creditors where it could not be proved at the time of the action that the insolvent's assets consisted wholly or in part, of funds originally provided by the plaintiff.[77] Professor R.M. Goode has persuasively argued[78]:

"When the route taken by the money or property is clearly visible and leads to its dissipation, the notion that the claimant's proprietary rights are then replaced by an new equitable charge over the defendant's free assets at the expense of his unsecured creditors surely cannot be countenanced either in principle or in policy, for their infusion of funds against a defeated expectation is as much a contribution to the swelling of the debtor's estate as the infusion of the tracing claimant."

Both the Privy Council in *Re Goldcorp Exchange Ltd*[79] and the Court of Appeal in *Bishopsgate Investment Management Ltd v. Homan*[80] were extremely cautious when deliberating upon the breadth of Lord Templeman's observations. It is fair to say that they have almost been distinguished out of existence. Consideration of the issue was but a peripheral part of the decision in *Goldcorp* however. In *Re Goldcorp Exchange Ltd* a bank holding a debenture had appointed a receiver over the assets of a company, Goldcorp. Some of the claimants had purchased from the company gold bullion for future delivery but at the date when the receivers were appointed there had not been any appropriation of specific and segregated parcels of bullion to the individual purchase contracts. At first blush this would seem to suggest that the bullion was swallowed up as it were by the bank's charge but the claimants invoked a number of arguments including that of the constructive trust. The Privy Council refused to accede to any of these arguments.

There was a group of claimants nevertheless—the Walker & Hall claimants— who were able to demonstrate sufficient appropriation to establish a shared interest in the pooled bullion. On a conventional tracing analysis though their claim was limited to the lowest balance of metal held by Goldcorp between the accrual of their rights and the commencement of receivership.[81] They attempted to circumvent this limitation by arguing for the existence of a general equitable lien on the basis of the observations of Lord Templeman in the *Space Investments* case. Lord Mustill who spoke for the Privy Council refused however to declare

---

[76] The approach adopted by Hobhouse J. in the *Westdeutsche* case [1994] 4 All E.R. 890 at 938– 940 might indicate a more flexible and expansive approach towards the identification principles of equitable tracing. *Space Investments* is not expressly referred to in the judgment but was cited by counsel in the case. It must be remembered that the person against whom a tracing order was sought, Islington Borough Council, was at all times solvent. Conceding a claim based on tracing was, in the circumstances, no different from recognising a personal remedy. Hobhouse J. himself acknowledged (at p. 938) that stricter principles might apply in situations of insolvency.

[77] *Law of Trusts* (3rd ed., 1967) Vol. 5, s.521 quoted by Jones, *op. cit.*, at 16.

[78] (1987) 103 L.Q.R. 433 at 447.

[79] [1994] 2 All E.R. 806. On the case see generally McKendrick (1994) 110 L.Q.R. 509.

[80] [1994] B.C.C. 868.

[81] *James Roscoe (Bolton) Ltd v. Winder* [1915] 1 Ch. 62.

such a lien on the grounds that it would be inequitable in the particular circumstances of the case. There was no reason for granting the Walker & Hall claimants rights superior to those enjoyed by other claimants. The Walker & Hall claimants received the same certificates and trusted the company in a manner no different from other bullion customers. There was no material from which it might be suggested that the debenture holders and the unsecured creditors at the date of the receivership benefited directly or indirectly from the breaches of trust committed by the company or that Walker & Hall bullion continued to exist as a fund latent in property vested in the receivers. In the circumstances the court did not find it necessary or appropriate to consider the scope and ambit of the *dicta* in *Space Investments* or their application to trustees other than bank trustees.[82]

Traditional tracing principles were also applied in the only too real modern situation of *Bishopsgate Management Ltd v. Homan*.[83] After the controversial publishing tycoon Robert Maxwell went to a watery demise it was discovered that he had systematically defrauded pensions funds maintained in respect of companies under his control of vast sums. To cut a complicated and involved story short, Maxwell moved pension fund assets belonging to Bishopsgate into bank accounts of Maxwell Communications Corporation ("MCC") that were overdrawn or subsequently became overdrawn. These bank accounts nevertheless carried a substantial credit balance when administrators were appointed to MCC. Applying traditional principle as expounded in *Roscoe v. Winder*[84] any tracing claim by the pension funds was extinguished by the payments into the overdrawn account and by the fact that the other accounts became overdrawn. The only way around this problem on an conventional analysis would be to argue that Maxwell intended to replenish the pension fund trusts by the subsequent payments into the bank accounts. According to the Court of Appeal there was no such evidence. Dillon L.J. stated that in the absence of clear evidence of intention to make good the depredations on Bishopsgate it was not possible to assume that the credit balance had been clothed with a trust in favour of Bishopsgate and its pension fund beneficiaries. Leggatt L.J. was of the same view. He referred to the observations of Buckley L.J. in *Borden v. Scottish Timber*[85] that "it is a fundamental feature of the doctrine of tracing that the property to be traced can be identified at every stage of its journey through life." Henry L.J. agreed with both judgments.

More generally the pension fund beneficiaries argued for a wide interpretation of the remarks of Lord Templeman in *Space Investments*. The argument proceeded along the lines that the beneficiaries under the pension schemes never took the risk that their pension funds would be misappropriated and paid into the overdrawn bank account of an insolvent company, whereas all the banks which lent money to MCC gambled, as a commercial risk, on MCC's solvency.

This submission was rejected by reference to *Re Goldcorp Exchange Ltd.* According to Dillon L.J. equitable tracing, though devised for the protection of trust moneys misapplied, could not be pursued through an overdrawn and therefore non-existent fund. The observations in *Space Investments* on which so much

---

[82] [1994] 2 All E.R. 806 at 831–832.
[83] [1994] B.C.C. 868; on the case see generally Lionel Smith [1994] *Trust Law International* 102.
[84] [1915] 1 Ch. 62.
[85] [1981] Ch. 25 at 46.

reliance was placed should be read in the context of a mixed and not a non-existent fund.

CONCLUSION

The idea of following assets through changes in form has been the subject of intense judicial scrutiny in recent cases. The decision of the House of Lords in *Lipkin Gorman* has revived interest in common law tracing. While the impact of that decision may be revolutionary in terms of its forthright recognition of the principle of unjust enrichment and its acknowledgement of the defence of change of position there has been no revolution so far in the common law rules for identifying misapplied assets. Recent cases have also shone the spotlight on the traditional principles of equity used to indentify assets that have been altered in form. These principles have been the subject of incremental change as occurred in the *Barlow Clowes* case but the courts have eschewed the option of wide ranging revision as was canvassed in in *Re Goldcorp Exchange Ltd* and *Bishopsgate Investment Management Ltd v. Homan*. The requirement of an undestroyed proprietary base remains. The court in the *Bishopsgate* case neatly encapsulated this proposition when they endorsed the observations of the Court of Appeal in *Re Diplock*[86]:

"The equitable remedies pre-suppose the continued existence of the moeny either as a separate fund or as part of a mixed fund or as latent in property acquired by means of such a fund. If, on the facts of any individual case, such continued existence is not established, equity is as helpless as the common law itself."

The Privy Council in *Att.-Gen. for Hong Kong v. Reid*[87] and the House of Lords in *Lord Napier and Ettrick v. Hunter*[88] recognised the existence of proprietary remedies in situations that formerly were not thought by many commentators to give rise to that possibility. Some writers have criticised the decisions for confusing property and obligation and for transforming mere contractual claims into proprietary claims.[89] Be that as it may, there is the chance that the assets over which property rights might now legitimately be asserted have been dissipated. So one is left with property rights over now non-existent assets. In such circumstances, according to the *Goldcorp* and *Bishopsgate* cases equity is helpless and the claimant emerges with nothing. Hopes of recovery have been built up only to be suddenly deflated. Given however, the somewhat discursive nature of the discussion in this chapter it seems appropriate to attempt to sum up the identification principles of equitable tracing. The following is a summary of the applicable principles:

---

[86] [1948] Ch. 465 at 521.
[87] [1994] A.C. 324. In *Reid* the Privy Council refused to follow the long standing English Court of Appeal decision in *Lister v. Stubbs* (1890) 45 Ch.D. 1. The case has and the resulting controversy controversy over the proprietary status of bribes obtained in breach of fiduciary duties has generated an enormous welter of articles and comment. For just some of the literature see Birks [1988] L.M.C.L.Q. 128 and [1993] L.M.C.L.Q. 30; Goode "Property and Unjust Enrichment" in *Essays on the Law of Restitution* (Burrows ed., Oxford: Clarendon Press, 1991) p. 225; Millett [1993] *Restitution Law Review* 7; Crilley [1994] *Restitution Law Review* 57; J.C. Smith (1994) 110 L.Q.R. 180; Nolan (1994) 15 Co Law 3; Pearce [1994] L.M.C.L.Q. 189; Allen (1995) 58 M.L.R. 87.
[88] [1993] A.C. 713.
[89] See, *e.g.* McKendrick (1994) 110 L.Q.R. 509.

The Identification Principles of Equitable Tracing

1. If the original asset, the misappropriation or misdirection of which has generated the equitable tracing claim, has been exchanged for another asset the tracing claimant may adopt the exchange and claim the fresh article, so to speak, as his own.

2. Alternatively, the person mounting the tracing action may lay claim to a lien on the new article.

3. If misdirected funds are mixed with the fiduciary's own funds in a bank account and then drawings are made from the account the presumption is that the fiduciary intended to spend his own funds first and that the funds which remain in the account belong to the tracing claimant.

4. If the funds that remain in the original mixed account are later dissipated the beneficiary has a charge on any property that was purchased out of the original mixed fund. As far the tracing claimant and the defaulting fiduciary are concerned, it is a question of "Heads I win, tails you lose".

5. If a mixed fund has been used in the acquisition of property that has increased in value the claimant may stake out an entitlement to a proportionate part of the added value.

6. The same principle applies where a fiduciary has purchased property partly out of his own funds and partly out of funds in respect of which he is a fiduciary.

7. Where the funds of two "innocent parties" have been mixed by a fiduciary in a bank or other running account the general principle still appears to be that debits from the account are taken as representing the earliest payment into the account. This principle of "first in, first out" is known as the rule in *Clayton's Case*.

8. In a comparatively simple cases the court may decide to adopt the so-called rolling charge solution by regarding credits to the account at different times and from different sources as a cocktail. This has the result that if a withdrawal is made from the account it is regarded as a withdrawal in the same proportions as the different interests in the account bear to each other at the instance before the withdrawal is made.

9. The rule in *Clayton's Case* is subject to the contrary intention of the parties. Where therefore investors have contributed to what they thought was a common investment fund the presumption is that any losses from the fund should be shared proportionately amongst the investors.

10. In certain circumstances a defendant to an equitable tracing action may be able to conjure up and invoke the rights of third parties as a defence though the courts will not tolerate such a *ius tertii* as a matter of course.

11. The courts do not countenance backward tracing. If property has been acquired on credit which means that a debt has been incurred in the course of the property acquisition and then misdirected moneys are used to discharge the debt, then, generally speaking, this does not generate any entitlement on the part of the tracing claimant to the property.

12. There were suggestions however from Dillon L.J. in *Bishopsgate Investment Management Ltd v. Homan* that "backward tracing" may be acceptable in restricted situations.

13. If a person against whom a tracing claim is brought has changed his position as to make it inequitable to allow the claim to succeed then the plaintiff may be denied relief against that particular defendant in whole or in part.

Conclusion

14. A tracing claim will fail if assets that form the subject matter of the claim have ceased to exist. An example would be where funds are paid by a defaulting fiduciary into an overdrawn bank account. Susbsequent payments into the account are only impressed with a trust in favour of the tracing claimant if there is specific evidence that the fiduciary intended to replenish the depleted funds.

CHAPTER TEN

Knowing Receipt of Trust Property: Liability of Recipient to make Restitution

It is often stated that persons who knowingly receive trust property or those who are party to a dishonest and fraudulent design on the part of a trustee may become liable as a constructive trustee.[1] The seminal statement in this area of law is generally taken to be the judgment of Lord Selborne in *Barnes v. Addy* who said[2]:

> "[S]trangers are not to be made constructive trustees merely because they act as the agents of trustees in transactions within their legal powers, transactions, perhaps, of which a Court of Equity may disapprove, unless those agents receive and become chargeable with some part of the trust property, or unless they assist with knowledge in a dishonest and fraudulent design on the part of the trustees."

What exactly does this statement mean and what are its ramifications for the law of insolvency? At first blush the implications of the pronouncement for the law of insolvency would appear to be enormous. Constructive trusteeship or indeed any form of trusteeship equals priority in the event of insolvency equals recovery before other creditors. In this context however the use of the expression "constructive trusteeship" is apt to cause confusion.[3] While the phraseology has acquired respectability through long usage it is positively misleading if read more generally than the particular area in which it appears. What we are talking about is personal accountability rather than proprietary remedies. The judgment of Megarry V.C. in *Re Montagu's Settlement Trusts*[4] contains considerable explanatory force in this direction and it is to this judgment that I now turn.

TRACING VERSUS CONSTRUCTIVE TRUSTEESHIP——*RE MONTAGU'S SETTLEMENT TRUSTS*

Re Montagu's Settlement Trusts arose out a family settlement made in 1923 by

---

[1] For a comprehensive if now somewhat dated account of this area of laws see Harpum (1986) 102 L.Q.R. 114 and 267. Note now Harpum "Knowing Assistance and Knowing Receipt" in *The Frontiers of Liability: volume 1* (Peter Birks ed., 1993) and also Gardner (1996) 112 L.Q.R. 56. See too the section on "knowing assistance and knowing receipt" in one of the standard textbooks on the law of trusts. The area has benefited from some thoroughgoing academic treatment by Professor Peter Birks: see, *e.g.* [1989] L.M.C.L.Q. 296; [1991] L.M.C.L.Q. 473; [1992] L.M.C.L.Q. 218 and "Trusts in the Recovery of Misapplied Assets: Tracing, Trusts and Restitution" in *Commercial Aspects of Trusts and Fiduciary Obligations* (E. McKendrick ed., 1992).
[2] (1874) 9 Ch. App. 244 at 251–252. It has been argued however with some force that this statement should be abandoned as one of the cornerstones of the modern law: see Loughlan (1989) 9 O.J.L.S. 260; Sales [1990] C.L.J. 491.
[3] See generally the essay by Birks in *Commercial Aspects of Trusts and Fiduciary Obligations* (E. McKendrick ed., 1992) pp. 153–156.
[4] [1987] Ch. 264; [1992] 4 All E.R. 308.

the future tenth Duke of Manchester. Basically there was assigned to the trustees of the settlement certain chattels on trust to select those which were suitable for inclusion in the settlement as heirlooms, to make an inventory of the selected chattels and to hold the residue in trust for the tenth Duke absolutely. The tenth duke succeeded to the dukedom in 1947 but no selection of heirlooms or inventory was ever made by the trustees. All the settled chattels were treated as being the absolute property of the tenth duke and were released to him. After the tenth duke's death in 1977 the eleventh duke brought an action against the executor of the tenth duke's will and the surviving trustees of the 1923 settlement alleging, *inter alia*, that the trustees had acted in breach of trust in failing to make any selection and inventory of heirlooms and in releasing all the chattels to the tenth duke. It was claimed that the tenth duke had become a constructive trustee of the settled chattels. That claim was in fact rejected for reasons that will become apparent later[5] but the case is noteworthy also for the differentiation made by Megarry V.C. between the equitable doctrine of tracing and that of the constructive trust. The judge said that the equitable doctrine of tracing and the imposition of a constructive trust by reason of the knowing receipt of trust were governed by different rules and must be kept distinct. Tracing was primarily a means of determining the rights of property, whereas the imposition of a constructive trust created personal obligations that went beyond mere property rights.

Megarry V.C. gave the example of a trustee who transferred trust property to a person who took it in all innocence, believing that he was entitled to it as a beneficiary. He might have believed that he was a beneficiary within a testamentary, discretionary trust whereas in fact he was not. He could not claim to be a purchaser for value without notice, for he was a mere volunteer. The judge continued[6]: "If when the truth emerged he still has the property he must restore it, whereas if he no longer had either the property or its traceable proceeds he was under no liability, unless he had become a constructive trustee." Megarry V.C. also said[7]:

> "It should be remembered that the doctrines of purchaser without notice and constructive trusts are concerned with matters which differ in important respects. The former is concerned with the question whether a person takes property subject to or free from some equity. The latter is concerned with whether or not a person is to have imposed upon him the personal burdens and obligations of trusteeship. I do not see why one of the touchstones for determining the burdens of property should be the same as that for deciding whether to impose a personal obligation on a man. The cold calculus of constructive and imputed notice does not seem to be an appropriate instrument for deciding whether a man s conscience is sufficiently affected for it to be right to bind him by the obligations of a constructive trustee."

The principle articulated in *Re Montagu* deserves further elaboration. If property has been transferred to a person in breach of trust and that property or its traceable equivalent is still in the hands of that person the property can generally be reclaimed by the beneficiaries under the trust. The proposition

---

[5] Principally because the tenth Duke had no actual knowledge that the property had been transferred in breach of trust nor was he recklessly indifferent to that possibility.
[6] [1992] 4 All E.R. at 318.
[7] [1992] 4 All E.R. at 320.

follows from the application of ordinary principles of property law.[8] The recipient is however protected if he is a bona fide purchaser of a legal estate in the property without notice of prior beneficial interests therein. Alternative protection is available if the disposition has been made within the scope of the overreaching provisions in the 1925 property legislation or some provision of the Factors Acts, Sale of Goods Acts or Hire Purchase Acts applies which contains an exception to the *nemo dat quod non habet* principle. The phrase "overreaching " refers to a mechanism whereby in the case of land if certain conditions are fulfilled a purchaser from the trustees will get a good title to the land. The interests of the beneficiaries under the trust thereafter attach to the proceeds arising from the transaction.

The doctrines of the bona fide purchaser for value without notice is now of somewhat peripheral importance when it comes to land because of two factors. The first is the overreaching mechanism contained in the 1925 property statutes. The second is the system of registration of title to property which was given a fillip in 1925[9] and has since spread, albeit slowly, across the entire country. Since 1990 the whole of England and Wales is an area of compulsory registration of title.[10] According to section 20 of the Land Registration Act 1925 a disposition of registered land for valuable consideration shall, when registered, confer on the transferee an estate absolute subject to (a) interests protected by an appropriate entry on the register of title and (b) so-called overriding interests.[11] The most notable example of an overriding interest is mentioned in section 70(1)(g) of the 1925 Land Registration Act as the "rights of every person in actual occupation of the land or in receipt of the rents and profits thereof, save where enquiry is made of such person and the rights are not disclosed."[12] So a purchaser for value of registered land will take free of the rights of beneficiaries under trusts that encompass the registered land unless either the trusts are protected by an entry on the register or the beneficiary is in actual occupation of the land and his interest is one capable of subsisting as an overriding interest.

To qualify as a bona fide purchaser one must be without notice, actual, constructive or imputed, of the beneficial interest in question.[13] Imputed notice

---

[8] See generally Harpum (1986) 102 L.Q.R. at 267–273.

[9] Land Registration Act 1925. The system of registration of title in England dates from as far back as 1862 but at that time it existed only on an optional footing. See generally Gray, *Elements of Land Law* (2nd ed., 1993), Chap. 8.

[10] Registration of Title Order 1989 (S.I. No. 1347 of 1989). The effect of the Order is that all conveyances on sale taking effect in England and Wales on or after December 1, 1990 must be recorded in the Land Register pursuant to the Land Registration Act 1925.

[11] See also s. 59(6) of the Land Registration Act 1925 which provides that a purchaser acquiring title under a registered disposition shall not be concerned with any pending action, writ, order, deed of arrangement, or other document, matter or claim (not being an overriding interest) which is not protected by a caution or other entry on the register, whether he has or has not notice thereof, express, implied or constructive.

[12] This paragraph has generated a vast volume of case law. The following trilogy of cases in the House of Lords is particularly noteworthy; *Williams & Glyn's Bank Ltd v. Boland* [1981] A.C. 487; *City of London Building Society v. Flegg* [1988] A.C. 54; *Abbey National Building Society v. Cann* [1991] 1 A.C. 56.

[13] s. 199 of the Law of Property Act 1925 provides:
"(1) A purchaser shall not be prejudicially affected by notice of—
(i) any instrument or matter capable of registration under the provisions of the Land Charges Act... which is void or not enforceable as against him under that Act... by reason of the non- registration thereof;
(ii) any other instrument or matter or any fact or thing unless—

refers to the actual or constructive notice of an agent who is acting for the purchaser in connection with the particular transaction. A person is said to have actual notice of matters that are within his own knowledge while one has constructive notice of matters that you would have discovered had you made reasonable inquiries. The concept of reasonable inquiries varies considerably according to context. Reasonablenes has to be understood with reference to a particular kind of transaction. The duty to make inquiries is at its most onerous insofar as land is concerned whereas with the sale of goods the courts has been resistant to the notion that there is any obligation to inquire in the absence of suspicious circumstances. This stance emerges clearly from the well known *dicta* of Lindley L.J. in *Manchester Trust v. Furness*.[14] He said[15]:

> "The equitable doctrines of constructive notice are common enough in dealing with land and estates, with which the Court if familiar; but there have been repeated protests against the introduction into commercial transactions of anything like an extension of those doctrines, and the protest is founded on perfect good sense. In dealing with estates in land title is everything, and it can be leisurely investigated; in commercial transactions possession is everything and there is not time to investigate title; and if we were to extend the doctrine of constructive notice to commercial transactions we should be doing infinite mischief and paralysing the trade of the country."

These *dicta* were applied by Neill J. in *Feuer Leather Corpoaration v. Frank Johnstone & Sons*.[16] He emphasised the fact that there was no general duty on a buyer of goods in an ordinary commercial transaction to make inquiries as to the right of the seller to dispose of the goods.[17]

INSOLVENCY AND CONSTRUCTIVE TRUSTEESHIP

Given the fact that the assertion of property rights and priority in the event of insolvency are qualitatively different from personal accountability as a so-called constructive trustee for knowing receipt of trust property or knowing assistance in its disposition, one might ask why consider the latter. The answer is comprehensiveness in the discussion of remedies. The original trust property or its traceable equivalent may have disappeared beyond hope of discovery. Nevertheless, in the course of its journey the property may have passed through the hands of a still solvent person or such a person may have lent assistance in its dissipation. It is worth recounting the observations of Lord Nicholls in the

(a) it is within his own knowledge, or would have come to his knowledge if such inquiries and inspections had been made as ought reasonably to have been made by him; or
(b) in the same transaction with respect to which a question of notice to the purchaser arises, it has come to the knowledge of his counsel, as such, or of his solicitor or other agent, if such inquiries and inspections had been made as ought reasonably to have been made by the solicitor or other agent."

[14] [1895] 2 Q.B. 539.
[15] *ibid.* at 545.
[16] [1981] Com. L.R. 251.
[17] See also *Greer v. Downs Supply Co.* [1927] 2 K.B. 28; *Goodyear Tyre & Rubber Co. (G.B.) v. Lancashire Batteries* [1958] 1 W.L.R. 857; *Wilts United Dairies v. Robinson (Thomas) Sons & Co.* [1957] R.P.C. 220; *Panchaud Freres v. Etablissements General Grain Co.* [1970] 1 Lloyd's Rep. 53; *Worcester Works Finance v. Cooden Engineering Co.* [1972] 1 Q.B. 210.

recent Privy Council case *Royal Brunei Airlines v. Tan*[18] in this context. He said that increasingly plaintiffs have recourse to equity for an effective remedy when the person in default, typically a company, is insolvent. He went on[19]:

> "Plaintiffs seek to obtain relief from others who were involved in the transaction, such as directors of the company or its bankers or its legal or other advisers. They seek to fasten fiduciary obligations directly onto the company's officers or agents or advisers, or to have them held personally liable for assisting the company in breaches of trust or fiduciary obligations."

While not strictly speaking proprietary remedies the claims against such persons arguably merit attention for the sake of completeness even in the context of a book devoted almost exclusively to a discussion of proprietary remedies and insolvency. Before moving on to a consideration of the substantive issues it is useful to say something about terminology.

AN ACCESSIBLE TERMINOLOGY?

Given the fact that the institution of the trust grew up historically in English law based around the notion of a divide between the technical legal and practical beneficial enjoyment of property, it might be argued that a trust can only exist if it relates to specific identifiable property in being. The same principle should obtain for the constructive trust if it is a species of trust at all.[20] In this context the observations of Kekewich J. in *Re Barney*[21] bear quotation. He said[22]:

> "... it is essential to the character of a trustee that he should have trust property actually vested in him or so far under his control that he has nothing to do but require that, perhaps by one process, perhaps by another, it should be vested in him."

In a string of cases however persons have been talked about as constructive trustees notwithstanding the fact they they never had any trust property vested in them.[23] According to Slade J. in *English v. Dedham Vale Properties Ltd*[24] constructive trusteeship was no more than a formula for granting equitable relief. He referred to the observations of Ungoed-Thomas J. in *Selangor United Rubber Estates Ltd v. Cradock (No. 3)*[25] to the effect that a person is made liable in

---

[18] [1995] 3 All E.R. 97.

[19] *ibid.* at 99.

[20] See generally A.J. Oakley, *Constructive Trusts* (2nd ed., 1987), Chap. 4 particularly at pp. 87–88.

[21] [1892] 2 Ch. 265.

[22] *ibid.* at 273.

[23] Liability for knowing assistance and knowing receipt should be distinguished from trusteeship de son tort. A.L. Smith L.J. said in *Mara v. Browne* [1896] 1 Ch. 199 at 209: "if one, not being a trustee and not having authority from a trustee, takes upon himself to intermeddle with trust matters or to do acts characteristic of the office of trustee he may thereby make himself a trustee of his own wrong, *i.e.* a trustee de son tort, or as it is also termed, a constructive trustee." In *Selangor United Rubber Ltd v. Cradock (No. 3)* [1968] 2 All E.R. 1073 at 1095 Ungoed-Thomas J. also discussed the issue of trustees de son tort. He said that trustees de son tort do not claim to act in their own right but for the beneficiaries. Their assumption to act was not of itself a ground of liability (save in the sense of liability to account and for any failure in the duty so assumed) and so their status as trustees precedes the occurrence which may be the subject of a claim against them.

[24] [1978] 1 All E.R. 381 at 398.

[25] [1968] 2 All E.R. 1073 at 1097.

equity as trustee because it was equitable that he should be held liable as though he were a trustee. So use of the language of constructive trusteeship in this context may fairly be described as a fiction which supplies a useful remedy in instances where no remedy is available in contract or in tort.[26] The use of legal fictions is not to all tastes especially when it is capable of clouding understanding. Professor Peter Birks, for one, has made a plea for more accessible terminology. He argues that it would help if the question could always be put with the crutch of "constructive trusteeship" simply thrown away.[27] Moreover, recipient liability is usually named by reference to the facts which are supposed to generate it by being called liability for "knowing receipt". In Birks' view that term contains an obvious *petitio principii* for it is a controversial issue whether or not the recipients liability turns on his knowing of the misdirection.[28] Furthermore, liability for knowing assistance might more logically be dubbed accessory liability and viewed as the equitable analogue of the tort of inducing a breach of contract.[29] The response of more traditional theorists is to say that in some hands, the law of restitution has acquired an unhelpful jargon that is impenetrable to the outsider.[30] The contention is that if it is really to become part of the mainstream of English legal thinking, it must adopt mainstream thinking.

It may be that there is something to be said for both of the competing viewpoints. While if one was starting from scratch it might be more logical and appropriate to use straightforwardly restitutionary terminology, the fact is that a considerable corpus of authority has built up invoking the language of constructive trusteeship. While it may be necessary and useful to pare away at the edges of unhelpful, and obscure, linguistic and conceptual usages, a wholescale reinterpretive process would be too great a divorce from the ideas of the case law and more traditional treatments of the subject. The decision of the Privy Council in *Royal Brunei Airlines v. Tan*[31] perhaps signifies progress along the path of incremental change. In that case Lord Nicholls separated out recipient liability and accessory liability and said unequivocally that different considerations applied to the two heads. Recipient liability was restitution-based whereas accessory liability was not.

KNOWING RECEIPT

A bank that is party to a money laundering scheme is potentially at risk under the knowing receipt head of constructive trusteeship. Such liability may arise if say a cheque received from the launderer is applied in reduction of an

---

[26] (1985) 27 *Malaya Law Review* 313 at 314.

[27] This point has been addressed by Birks throughout his numerous writings on the subject but for a general discussion of the issue see Birks in *Commercial Aspects of Trusts and Fiduciary Obligations* (E. McKendrick ed., 1992) at pp. 153–156. It is argued that the language of trusteeship is a nuisance which is rooted in the days of the institutional separation of common law and equity, and it reflects the fact that equity frequently extended the scope of the relief that it could offer by working outwards from the central case of the trustee. The idea that this liability arises "as a constructive trustee" he contends, is not only surplusage. Furthermore, it forces us into the additional falsehood of talking all the time about "trust money", thus disguising the true scope of the liability.

[28] See Peter Birks, *Restitution—The Future* (1992), p. 26.

[29] See generally Sales P.J. Sales [1990] C.L.J. 491.

[30] See n. 97 of "Knowing Assistance and Knowing Receipt, The Basis of Equitable Liability" by Charles Harpum in *The Frontiers of Liability: volume 1* (Peter Birks ed., 1993).

[31] [1995] 3 All E.R. 97.

overdrawn bank account. A lot of confusion in the authorites has been generated by reason of the fact that this ground of liability and that of knowing assistance have not been kept distinct. Tradition however would seem to favour the view that a person who receives for his own benefit trust property transferred to him in breach of trust and has since parted with it, is liable to account as a constructive trustee if he received the property with notice, actual or constructive, that it was trust property and that the transfer to him was in breach of trust.[32] Such liability should also obtain if the person received the property without the appropriate notice but discovered the facts before he spent or parted with it. It does not seem to matter whether the original breach of trust was fraudulent or not. In *Re Montagu's Settlement Trusts*[33] Megarry V.C. muddied the waters somewhat by deciding that dishonesty or want of probity was essential to liability on the basis of knowing receipt.

Whatever view is accepted liability for "knowing receipt" seems defendant-sided and fault-based. The dispute rages over the degree of fault required. Is constructive notice of the defect in entitlement sufficient or is some dishonesty or want of probity necessary? Strict liability seems to be shut out of the equation. There is however powerful academic and extra-curial judicial support for the proposition that a recipient of trust property, transferred in breach of trust, should be under a strict personal restitutionary obligation to refund what has been received subject to defences such as bona fide purchase and change of position.[34] Millett L.J., writing extra-judicially, has contended that since the liability is receipt-based, it should logically be strict.[35] The argument proceeds as follows[36]:

"The absence of notice on the part of a volunteer is normally irrelevant. It does not help him if he retains the property. Why should it provide him with a defence if he has parted with it, albeit in breach of a trust of whose existence he had no reason to be aware? The answer, it is suggested, is that this is not the true nature of the volunteer's defence. His defence is based on having parted with the property, not on the absence of constructive notice. That is a necessary, but necessarily a sufficient, condition for the defence to operate. The defence itself is based on change of position."

This reference to a change of position defence anticipates in many ways the judgments of the House of Lords in *Lipkin Gorman v. Karpnale Ltd*[37] which were delivered after the article was written. Cutting through a lot of the older authorities the House of Lords enunciated the general proposition that the law

---

[32] *Selangor United Rubber Estates v. Cradock (No. 3)* [1968] 1 W.L.R. 1555; *International Sales and Agencies Ltd v. Marcus* [1982] 3 All E.R. 551; *Belmont Finance Ltd v. Williams Furniture (No. 2)* [1980] 1 All E.R. 393.

[33] [1987] Ch. 264. See also *Carl Zeiss Siftung v. Herbert Smith and Co. (No. 2)* [1969] 2 Ch. 176.

[34] Birks [1992] L.M.C.L.Q. 218 at 228 argues that the courts should recognise that, whether the receipt is from misdirecting personal representatives of from other misdirectors, honest or dishonest, the recipient's personal restitutionary liability in equity and in law is in principle strict. See also Birks [1989] L.M.C.L.Q. 296. Fennell contends (1994) 57 M.L.R. 34 at 55 that the defendant should be liable under a proprietary constructive trust if it could be shown that property belonging to the plaintiff is still in his hands but where the plaintiff claims that the defendant once had his property but has subsequently parted with it, liability should be strict, subject to the defences of bona fide purchase, change of position and estoppel.

[35] (1991) 107 L.Q.R. 71.

[36] *ibid.* at 82.

[37] [1992] 1 A.C. 548; [1992] 4 All E.R. 512.

imposes an obligation on the recipient of stolen money to pay an equivalent sum to the victim if the recipient had been unjustly enriched at the expense of the true owner.[38] The defence of change of position was available however to a person whose position had so changed that it would be inequitable in all the circumstances to require him to make restitution, or alternatively to make restitution in full. According to Lord Goff the defence of change of position was akin to the defence of bona fide purchase, but bona fide purchase was not merely a species of change of position. Change of position only availed a defendant to the extent that his position had changed, whereas when bona fide purchase was invoked, no inquiry was made, in most cases, into the adequacy of the consideration.[39]

It has been argued that *Lipkin Gorman* has precipitated a legal revolution and it is the *only* relevant authority ushering in a brave new world with a general regime of strict liability for restitutionary claims.[40] Moreover, while the exercise smacks completely of *ex post facto* rationalisation, it is submitted that authorites such *Cowan de Groot Properties* and *SBC Securities* which are discussed *infra* could be fitted comfortably into a "strict liability subject to defences" analysis. After all in both cases the defendants had given value. Therefore they could avail of the defence of change of position. On the other hand, it has been recognised this approach necessitates the abandonment of a vast corpus of authority and could not be attained without the pain of considerable litigation.[41] While the conception might be fun and the offspring healthy the birth pangs could be excruciating. It may be more in keeping with the incremental approach that is characteristic of the common law to say that the House of Lords decision in *Lipkin Gorman*, while of general import when it comes to the affirmation of the principle of unjust enrichment as embedded in English law and the recognition of the defence of change of position, should be viewed through the prism of it being a common law tracing action.[42] One commentator has persuasively argued that a regime of strict liability subject to defences would be too pure for the realities of life and that the traditional requirement of notice serves to reconcile the law with the latter.[43] The knowledge requirement on the part of the recipient

---

[38] See the statment of Lord Templeman [1992] 4 All E.R. 512 at 517.

[39] [1992] 4 All E.R. 512 at 534. For a general analysis of the change of position defence see Key (1995) 58 M.L.R. 505.

[40] See paper by Charles Harpum "Knowing Assistance and Knowing Receipt: The Basis of Equitable Liability" in *The Frontiers of Liability: volume 1* (Peter Birks ed., 1993).

[41] *ibid.* at n. 174.

[42] In one of his earlier articles Birks [1989] L.M.C.L.Q. 296 at 313–316 invokes the fate of the *Re Diplock* personal action to mount an argument for a general restitutionary regime of strict liability with respect to the recipient of trust property. In *Re Diplock* [1948] Ch. 465 which was affirmed by the House of Lords *sub nom. Ministry of Health v. Simpson* [1951] A.C. 251 it was held that where personal representatives have paid money from the estate of the deceased to a person not entitled to it, the next-of-kin or legatees entitled under the will, or any creditor of the estate, can recover the money from a recipient, other than a bona fide purchaser. It appears that no action will hold good until remedies against the defaulting personal representatives has first been exhausted. This limitation is not accepted by Birks who tries to rely on the somewhat weak authority of *G.L. Baker Ltd v. Medway Building & Supplies Ltd* [1958] 1 W.L.R. 1216 to generalise notwithstanding the fact that the House of Lords seem to confine it to the administration of estates. Some commentators profess to see the addiction of Professor Birks to so quaint a line of authorities as being deeply puzzling; see for instance Harpum "Knowing Assistance and Knowing Receipt: The Basis of Equitable Liability" in *The Frontiers of Liability: volume 1* (Birks ed., 1993), n. 169.

[43] See generally Gardner (1996) 112 L.Q.R. 56 at 85–93.

serves to protect the security of receipts and this is an important policy consideration.

> "[K]nowing receipt provides, albeit at the price of some incoherence with the surrounding areas, a reminder that a recipient's interest in broad security of wealth is not inconsequential; and that it is not inconceivable for the law to lean towards protecting that interest."[44]

Also a change of position defence is not necessarily capable of dealing with all possible problems. In real life, fact situations often arise that are much murkier than the examples usually posited of the application of the change of position defence. In addition, a principle of prima facie strict liability might generate a torrent of claims that at the moment would fail to get off the starting block. But what is the basis of liability at the moment? In other words, what degree of knowledge on the part of the recipient is necessary to sustain liability? That issue will now be examined.

CONSTRUCTIVE NOTICE OR WANT OF PROBITY?

A convenient starting point for analysis is the lengthy judgment of Megarry V.C. in *Re Montagu's Settlement Trusts*.[45] This decision contains a detailed treatment of the authorities and comes down on the "want of probity" side of the line for the imposition of a knowing receipt constructive trust. The judge enunciated the principle that in considering whether a constructive trust had arisen in this context, the basic question was whether the conscience of the recipient was sufficiently affected. This depended primarily on the knowledge of the recipient and not on notice to him. Knowledge, for this purpose, was not confined to actual knowledge, but encompassed knowledge of types (ii) and (iii) on the *Baden* scale, *i.e.* actual knowledge that would have been acquired but for shutting one's eyes to the obvious, or wilfully and recklessly failing to make such inquiries as a reasonable and honest man would make. These situations illustrated a want of probity but no such absence was demonstrated in cases of knowledge of types (iv) and (v) on the *Baden* scale.[46] Moreover, a person was not to be taken to have knowledge of a fact that he once knew but had genuinely forgotten. The test was whether the knowledge continued to operate on that person's mind at the time in question. Furthermore, the doctrine of imputed notice did not apply so as to fix a donee or beneficiary with all the knowledge that his solicitor had, at

---

[44] *ibid.* at 89.

[45] [1987] Ch. 264; [1992] 4 All E.R. 308.

[46] [1992] 4 All E.R. 308 at 329–330. It should be noted that in the related field of liability for knowing assistance Lord Nicholls suggested in *Royal Brunei Airlines v. Tan* [1995] 3 All E.R. 97 at 109 that the *Baden* scale of knowledge was best forgotten. The *Baden* scale is as follows:

(i) actual knowledge;

(ii) wilfully shutting one's eyes to the obvious;

(iii) wilfully and recklessly failing to make such inquiries as an honest and reasonable man would make;

(iv) knowledge of circumstances which would indicate the facts to an honest and reasonable man;

(v) knowledge of circumstances which would put an honest and reasonable man on inquiry and failure to make such inquiries.

See also Gardner (1996) 112 L.Q.R. 56 at 57–64 who endeavours to explain the knowledge/notice distinction. He suggests that knowledge could be identified with the first three categories on the *Baden* scale and notice with the remaining two.

all events if the donee or beneficiary had not employed the solicitor to investigate his right to the bounty, and had done nothing else that could be treated as accepting that the solicitor's knowledge should be regarded as his own.[47]

The underlying rationale of the judgment of Megarry V.C. has been searchingly examined. Why is it regarded as some special hardship to the defendant to give up something that he should never have received in the first place? What about the hardship and injustice suffered by the plaintiff beneficary whose property has been spirited away without his knowledge or consent? The defendant is not being punished. All that is done is making sure that the plaintiff regains what is justly his. The position of the defendant is protected by the defences that are available.[48]

There is in fact a body of authority predating *Montagu* that suggests that constructive notice is enough for the knowing receipt limb of constructive trusteeship though a problem with many of the cases is that they do not draw a distinction between knowing assistance and knowing receipt. *Selangor United Rubber Estates Ltd v. Cradock (No. 3)*[49] and *Karak Rubber Co. Ltd v. Burden (No. 2)*[50] are cases that fall within this category. According to Ungoed-Thomas J. in *Selangor* equity[51] "will hold a purchaser for value liable as constructive trustee if he had actual or constructive notice that the transfer to him was of trust property in breach of trust..."

The overall approach of the judge was to say that a person with actual or constructive notice of equitable rights should be fixed with knowledge of them. To the same effect is the judgment of Brightman J. in the *Karak* case. Also in line with this attitude is the judgment of Denning J., as he then was, in *Nelson v. Larholt*.[52] In this case the executor of a will drew cheques on the executors account signing "G.A. Potts, Executor of William Burns, dec." and paid the cheques to a bookmaker.[53] It was held that the bookmaker was liable to repay the money by reason of the fact that an honest and reasonable man in his position should have known of the want of authority.[54]

The judgments of Buckley and Goff L.JJ. in *Belmont Finance Corp. Ltd v. Williams Furtniture Ltd (No. 2)*.[55] are also in line with the principle that constructive notice warrants liability. So too the observations of Lawson J. in *International Sales and Agencies Ltd v. Marcus*[56] who said:

---

[47] *ibid.* at 323.
[48] [1992] L.M.C.L.Q. 218 at 225–228.
[49] [1968] 1 W.L.R. 1555; [1968] 2 All E.R. 1073.
[50] [1972] 1 W.L.R. 602; [1972] 1 All E.R. 1210.
[51] [1968] 2 All E.R. 1073 at 1098.
[52] [1948] 1 K.B. 339. The case is examined by Denning at (1949) 65 L.Q.R. 37. According to Lord Denning this article contains the material on which the statements of law in *Nelson v. Larholt* were based: see (1949) 65 L.Q.R. 37 at 50.
[53] There was evidence, which Denning J. apparently accepted, that the cheques were used to settle gambling debts.
[54] Denning J. said [1948] 1 K.B. 339 at 343: "He must, I think, be taken to have known what a reasonable man would have known. If, therefore, he knew or is to be taken to have known of the want of authority, as, for instance, if the circumstances were such as to put a reasonable man on inquiry, and he made none, or if he was put off by an answer that would not have satisfied a reasonable man, or, in other words, if he was negligent in not perceiving the want of authority, then he is taken to have notice of it."
[55] [1980] 1 All E.R. 393 at 405, 412. A somewhat different interpretation was put on these observations by Megarry V.C. in the *Re Montagu* case: see [1992] 4 All E.R. 308 at 326.
[56] [1982] 3 All E.R. 551 at 558.

"... in my judgment, the knowing recipient of trust property for his own purposes will become a constructive trustee of what he receives if either he was in fact aware at the time that his receipt was affected by a breach of trust, or if he deliberately shut his eyes to the real nature of the transfer to him ... or if an ordinary reasonable man in his position and with his attributes ought to have known of the relevant breach."

Millett J. said much the same thing in *Agip (Africa) Ltd v. Jackson*[57]:

"He is liable as a constructive trustee is he received it with notice, actual or constructive, that it was trust property and that the transfer to him was in breach of trust, or if he received it without such notice but subsequently discovered the facts."

There are however contradictory authorities. In this connection *Carl-Zeiss Stiftung v. Herbert Smith & Co. (No. 2)*.[58] merits citation. Here Sachs L.J. said that some element of dishonesty or of consciously acting improperly was required whereas Edmund Davies L.J. talked about want of probity as an essential.

COMMERCIALLY UNACCEPTABLE CONDUCT

Constructive liability *qua* recipient failed to be established also in *Cowan de Groot Properties Ltd v. Eagle Trust plc.*[59] In this case it was claimed that company property had been sold at a gross undervalue by two directors of the company as part of a fraudulent scheme and in breach of their fiduciary duties to the company. It was further claimed that the purchaser of the property knew or ought to have known of this fraudulent breach of fiduciary duty and was therefore liable as a constructive trustee *qua* recipient of the property. Knox J. rejected this argument on the basis that the purchaser had not been dishonest or, on the assumption but without deciding that this was enough, guilty of commercially unacceptable conduct that fell short of dishonesty. The case may be criticised on the basis that it is not clear whether it imports a different test for commercial and non-commercial transactions.

Knox J. stated that the position of a person dealing as purchaser with a vendor company's directors on a sale as regards potential breaches of fiduciary duty by the directors was in many ways similar to that of a person to whom a payment was made in discharge of an obligation. Knowledge within categories (i), (ii) or (iii) of the *Baden* classification was what was required in the case of a commercial transaction. Moreover, it would not be appropriate for the court to be astute to find circumstances which could indicate knowledge by a purchaser of breaches of fiduciary duty on the part of directors of the vendor company. It was up to those acting for the purchasing company to buy as cheaply as they could in the light of the mode and terms of the proposed sale.

---

[57] [1992] 4 All E.R. 385 at 403; [1990] Ch. 265 at 291. See also *Thomson v. Clydesdale Bank Ltd* [1893] A.C. 282 and the New Zealand case *Westpac Banking Corp. v. Savin* [1985] 2 N.Z.L.R. 41 which is another authority in favour of objective knowledge. In this case Richardson J. said: "Clearly courts would not readily import a duty to inquire in the case of commercial transactions where they must be conscious of the seriously inhibiting effects of a wide application of the doctrine. Nevertheless there must be cases where there is no justification on the known facts for allowing a commercial man who has received funds paid to him in breach of trust to plead the shelter of the exigencies of commercial life."
[58] [1969] 2 Ch. 276; [1969] 2 All E.R. 367.
[59] [1992] 4 All E.R. 700.

In one sense one might contend that the preference expressed by Knox J. for the "want of probity" principle was immaterial to the actual decision in the case. He went on to hold that even if constructive notice was appropriate for liability the claim was still unsuccessful because of the particular fact situation. The judge spoke of an underlying broad principle which permeated the authorities on commercial transactions that the court would impute knowledge, on the basis of what a reasonable person would have learnt, to a person who was guilty of commercially unacceptable conduct in the particular context involved.[60] It is not altogether apparent whether this statement imports a different test for commercial and non-commercial transactions.

EAGLE TRUST PLC V. SBC SECURITIES LTD (NO. 2)

Many of the foregoing authorities were reviewed by Mary Arden J. in *Eagle Trust plc v. SBC Securities Ltd (No. 2)*. This case arose out of the Stock Market collapse on Black Monday in October 1987. The plaintiff, Eagle, had made a takeover bid for the shares of a group of companies, the Samuelson Group. The stock market failure wrecked the the overall takeover arrangement and threw a lot of financial liability onto the shoulders of the defendant underwriters, SBC, and the sub-underwriters amongst whom were Ferriday, the chief executive of Eagle, and a firm of provincial stockbrokers, Earnshaw Haes. SBC received a sum of £13.5 million from a Panamanian company to discharge the obligations of Ferriday and Earnshaw Haes as sub-underwriters. Eagle alleged that this sum was its own money and that it had been misappropriated by Ferriday. It sought to make the defendant, SBC, liable *qua* recipient. The principal allegation was that SBC should have been aware of the danger that Ferriday would seek to cover his sub-underwriting obligations from whatever funds he had access to, most obviously the plaintiff's funds. Nevertheless, SBC had made no inquiry as to the source of the £13.5 million or how Ferriday had managed to meet his liabilities as a sub-underwriter. Initially the constructive trust claim failed on the basis that there was nothing in the pleadings to indicate knowledge of the kind required to sustain liablity *qua* recipient. The pleadings were however redrafted and the matter then came before Arden J. She took the view that in a "knowing receipt" case where receipt occurred in the discharge of a lawful debt (at least one arising out of a transaction which did not itself constitute a breach of trust) dishonesty as indicated by the first three categories in the *Baden* scale was required.

Applying that principle to the present case there was no constructive trust liability. The defendants did not know or suspect that Ferriday had taken money from the company to meet his sub-underwriting commitments. The defendants regarded him as an honest and trustworthy man. So far as they were aware, there was no reason why he should not have been able to raise the requisite funds from his business associates or on the security of his other assets. The loss that he was to suffer was a large one in absolute terms but not in the context of a person with major business assets. There was no motive shown for the defendants to become knowingly involved in Ferriday's fraud. The reverse was the case. It was not shown that they either knew that the money was the company's money, or even that it was probably the company's money, or that

---

[60] [1992] 4 All E.R. 700 at 761.

it wilfully shut its eyes to the obvious or that it knowingly and recklessly failed to make the inquiries that a reasonable and honest man would make.

The judgment however went on to say that even if constructive notice sufficed as a condition of liability the defendants were not implicated. A hypothetical honest and reasonable person in their position when it received the sums totalling £13.5 million would not have been put on inquiry that the moneys were probably Eagle's moneys.

The judgment of Arden J. is very much in line with that of Knox J. in *Cowan de Groot Properties Ltd v. Eagle Trust plc* and Vinelott J. in *Eagle Trust plc v. SBC Securities Ltd (No. 1)*. It appears to draw a distinction between commercial transactions where value is given as in this case and other types of dealing.[61] It should be noted that Vinelott J. in *Eagle Trust plc v. SBC Securities Ltd (No. 1)* was hesitant in accepting *Re Montagu* as an authority of universal application finding it unnecessary to express any opinion on the question whether a defendant who had received trust property in breach of trust but who has parted with it and who has no identifiable proceeds in his hands can never be made liable unless it is shown that he actually knew that the property was trust property and was being transferred in breach of trust. The Arden judgment does not purport to resolve the question conclusively of whether dishonesty is a prerequisite to receipt-based liability.

MINISTERIAL RECEIPT[62]

According to Millett J. in *Agip (Africa) Ltd v. Jackson*[63] an agent who receives trust property ministerially, *i.e.* not for his own benefit, is not under any liability for knowing receipt. There may be cases however where a person receives trust property ministerially and then applies it for his own benefit in which instance there is a potential liability for knowing receipt. An example would be where a banker purports to set off a trust account against the trustee's own personal account. Furthermore, if an agent having received trust property ministerially, obtains knowledge of a fraudulent breach of trust, proceeds to apply the property in accordance with the instructions of the principal and ignoring the breach of trust, then there is potential liability *qua* accessory.

CONCLUSION

There are many criticisms that one might make of the current state of the law pertaining to liability for knowing assistance and knowing receipt. First, the terminology employed in this area is something of a historical legacy and does nothing to enlighten one as to what is actually happening on a factual level. To call a defendant a trustee while he is no such thing seems somewhat strange, if not positively misleading. In many of the cases a real trustee is nowhere in sight. The insight, widely shared, that liability for knowing assistance does not involve

---

[61] See also on commercial and non-commercial transactions Millett J. in *Macmillan Inc. v. Bishopsgate Investment Trust Plc* [1995] 1 W.L.R. 978 at 1000–1001 and Gardner (1996) 112 L.Q.R. 56 at 61.
[62] See generally Y.L. Tan [1991] L.M.C.L.Q. 357 and also William Swadling "Ministerial Receipt" in *Laundering and Tracing* (Peter Birks ed., 1995).
[63] [1990] Ch. 265 at 291–292.

a constructive trust should obtain equally with respect to liability for knowing receipt.

A second problem arises from the fact that the two forms of liability have not always been understood as essentially distinct. Cases from one sphere have sometimes been indiscriminately cited and applied in the other. With knowing receipt one is talking about a personal restitutionary remedy which depends on the defendant having received property for his own benefit. With knowing assistance one is concerned about a form of secondary liability which is dependent on the defendant having acted as an accessory to a fraudulent breach of trust. Where liability is imposed the defendant is being penalised for the infliction of a wrong on the plaintiff and the latter compensated for the wrong done to him. We are talking about compensation for wrongs and not restitution for the defendant who may never have received any of the property that was mis-appropriated. Of course the same fact situation may throw up the two forms of liability. A defendant may have received trust property for his own benefit and also, in some way, aided the wrongdoing fiduciary in the perpetration of the breach of trust.

The third problem springs from the fact that the tests for determining liability have not been worked out with exactitude. As far as knowing receipt is concerned there is some uncertainty as to the degree of knowledge required to make a defendant liable. The situation is quite fluid when it comes to the receipt-based liability with judicial opinion fluctuating between the proposition that dishonesty is a precondition of liability and the alternative hypothesis that carelessness on the part of the defendant is enough. To complicate matters more there have been recent judicial suggestions of a via media between dishonesty and carelessness and the idea that this is the foundation stone of liability. The long standing reluctance of the courts to extend the doctrine of constructive notice to commercial transactions is well known. In the last century in *Manchester Trust v. Furness*[64] Lindley L.J. ventured the view that to do this would be to do infinite mischief and paralyse the trade of the country. While the sentiments are less robustly expressed manifestations of this attitude are to be found in the recent case law on liability of a recipient of misappropriated property. Where the defendant has given value the courts are especially reluctant to interfere. It must be remembered however that the concept of reasonable notice is not an inflexible, absolute standard. It is capable of being tailored to the particular circumstances of the case. It asks no more than reasonableness in the light of the peculiar facts of an individual situation. That antromorphic conception of justice—the reasonable person—is invoked. It is submitted that the refusal of the judiciary as evidenced in cases like *Eagle Trust plc v. SBC Securities Ltd (No. 2)* to embrace the criterion of constructive notice as a touchstone of liability is somewhat misguided. Insistence on actual dishonesty may be too limiting a principle. Constructive notice deserves its place in the sun.

[64] [1895] 2 Q.B. 539.

CHAPTER ELEVEN

Assisting in a Breach of Trust: Principles of Accessory Liability

As Lord Nicholls pointed out in *Royal Brunei Airlines v. Tan*[1] the proper role of equity in commercial transactions is a topical question. Persons have recourse to equity for an effective remedy when the person in default, typically a company, is insolvent. Relief is sought from others who were involved in the transaction, such as directors of the company or its bankers or its legal or other advisers. An attempt is made to hold such persons personally liable for assisting the company in breaches of trust or fiduciary obligations. The starting point for this head of liability is usually taken to be the judgment of Lord Selborne in *Barnes v. Addy*[2] who said:

> "[S]trangers are not to be made constructive trustees merely because they act as the agents of trustees in transactions within their legal powers, transactions, perhaps, of which a Court of Equity may disapprove, unless those agents receive and become chargeable with some part of the trust property, or unless they assist with knowledge in a dishonest and fraudulent design on the part of the trustees."

In this chapter the principles used for determining liability under the "knowing assistance" head will be discussed.

FOUNDATIONS OF LIABILITY

In order to establish liability under the "knowing assistance" head four elements were identified by Peter Gibson L.J. in the *Baden Delvaux* case.[3] These were first, the existence of a trust; secondly the presence of a dishonest and fraudulent design on the part of the trustee; thirdly, the assistance by the agent in that design and finally the knowledge of the agent. The *Baden Delvaux* approach requires re-examination in the wake of the decision of the Privy Council in *Royal Brunei Airlines v. Tan*. In that case the view was taken that while dishonesty was both a necessary and a sufficient ingredient of accessory liability the breach of trust which was a prerequisite for accessory liability need not itself be a dishonest and fraudulent breach of trust by the trustee. Be that as it may it is useful to retain the quodropartite division adopted in *Baden Delvaux* as the starting point of analysis whilst remembering that it is not the finishing point.

---

[1] [1995] 3 All E.R. 97.
[2] (1874) 9 Ch. App. 244 at 251–252.
[3] *Baden Delvaux and Lecuit v. Societe General pour Favouriser le Developpement du Commerce et de L'Industrie en France SA* [1983] B.C.L.C. 325; [1992] 4 All E.R. 161.

THE *ACTUS REUS* OF ACCESSORY LIABILITY

One of the most common criticisms levelled with respect to the "knowing assistance" head of liability has been the traditional preoccupation with issues of *mens rea* to the comparative neglect of questions of *actus reus*.[4] For instance it has been asked why should the design assisted have to be fraudulent? Proving fraud is a difficult process at the best of times but can the operation be lightened by construing the concept of fraud flexibly. Ungoed-Thomas J. in the *Selangor* case appeared to leave some room for latitude in interpretation.[5] He said that it was unnecessary and indeed undesirable to attempt a definition of "dishonest and fraudulent design" in the abstract. He said that the words themselves were not terms of act and were not taken from a statute or other document demanding construction. The words connoted conduct which was morally reprehensible but what was morally reprehensible was best left open to identification and not to be confused by definition.

This broad brush approach did not commend itself to Buckley L.J. in *Belmont Finance Ltd v. Williams Furniture Ltd*.[6]

In this case the plaintiff contended that the court should consider whether the conduct in question was so unsatisfactory, whether it could be strictly described as fraudulent or dishonest in law, as to make accountability on the footing of a constructive trust equitably just. The Lord Justice refused to accept this idea on the ground that it would introduce an undesirable degree of uncertainty to the law. He was concerned about the absence of any other logical stepping stone to liability and asked if dishonesty was not to be the criterion, what degree on unethical conduct was to be sufficient?[7] In the *Baden Delvaux* case Peter Gibson J. accepted the views expressed by Buckley L.J. and these are generally understood as representing the current state of English law. Peter Gibson J. added that for present purposes no distinction should be drawn between the two adjectives "dishonest" and "fraudulent".[8] He also took as a relevant description of fraud "the taking of a risk to the prejudice of another's rights, which risk is known to be one which there is no right to take".[9]

In New Zealand there has been some judicial tinkering with the requirement that the breach of trust be dishonest but this departure from precedent has attracted the ire of later judges. In *Powell v. Thompson*[10] Thomas J. suggested that it did not matter whether the trustees conduct was fraudulent or negligent, devious or foolish, heinous or indifferent. He said that if the third party's conduct had been unconscionable, then irrespective of the degree of impropriety in the trustee's conduct, the third party was liable to be held accountable to the beneficiary as if he or she were a trustee.[11] Subsequent New Zealand courts

---

[4] See the paper by Harpum "Knowing Assistance and Knowing Receipt: The Basis of Equitable Liability" in *The Frontiers of Liability: volume 1* (Birks ed., 1993).
[5] [1968] 2 All E.R. 1073 at 1105.
[6] [1979] Ch. 250.
[7] *ibid.* at 267.
[8] [1992] 4 All E.R. 161 at 234. The judge added that while the standard of proof of an allegation of fraud was no higher than a balance of probabilities, the more serious the allegations, the more cogent was the evidence required to overcome the unlikelihood of what was alleged and thus to prove it.
[9] Reference was made to *R. v. Sinclair* [1968] 1 W.L.R. 1246 in this connection.
[10] [1991] 1 N.Z.L.R. 597.
[11] *ibid.* at 613.

have been unimpressed and this has not passed muster because of its vagueness. For example, in *Marshall Futures Ltd v. Marshall*[12] Tipping J. said that he preferred the herald of equity to be wearing more distinctive clothing that that suggested by the formulation which appealed to Thomas J.

The traditional insistence on a fraudulent breach of trust has been questioned by some. One commentator argues[13]:

"When the analogy of this form of liability with other types of secondary liability in the civil law is emphasised, the requirement that the breach of trust which is assisted in should be dishonest appears superfluous. What is important is that there should have been an actionable civil wrong (whether dishonest or not), and a sufficient nexus between the loss suffered by the plaintiff as a result of that wrong and the person who has encouraged or assisted in its commission. That nexus is established by the plaintiff showing that the person inducing or assisting in the commisssion of the wrong acted knowing that he was assisting in the commission of that wrong."

Such sentiments appealed to the Privy Council in *Royal Brunei Airlines v. Tan*.[14] In this case the airline appointed a travel company to act as its general travel agent in various places in Malaysia for the sale of passenger and cargo transportation. The company was obliged to account to the airline for all amounts received from sales of tickets and received commission on sales. The agency agreement declared that all moneys received by the company for sales on behalf of the airline were the property of, and to be held in trust for, the airline and were to be paid to it within 30 days. In actual fact the company paid all moneys received for sales on behalf of the airline into the current account used for the conduct of its business, out of which payments were made for salaries, overheads and other expenses and to reduce the company's bank overdraft. This was a breach of trust and the respondent, as managing director and principal shareholder of the company, had caused or permitted it to apply the money in this way. The airline sought to recover the unpaid money from the respondent contending that he was liable as a constructive trustee because he had knowingly assisted in a fraudulent and dishonest design on the part of the company as trustee for the airline.

In the Privy Council they were successful with this attempt. The authorities were reviewed and the court concluded that a liability in equity to make reparation for resulting loss attaches to a person who dishonestly procures or assists in a breach of trust or fiduciary obligation. This conclusion was reached as a matter of principle. Lord Nicholls gave the example of an honest trustee and a dishonest third party. One situation of this would be where a dishonest solicitor persuaded a trustee to apply trust property in a way which the trustee

---

[12] [1992] 1 N.Z.L.R. 316 at 325. See also *Equiticorp Industries Group Ltd v. Hawkins* [1991] 3 N.Z.L.R. 700.

[13] See P.J. Sales [1990] C.L.J. 491 at 508. See also the paper by Charles Harpum "Knowing Assistance and Knowing Reciept: The Basis of Equitable Liability" in *The Frontiers of Liability: volume 1* (Birks ed., 1993). Harpum talks about the absence of compelling reasons why liability for knowing assistance should be confined to cases where the trustee's breach was fraudulent. In his view the weight of authority was not so strong as to prevent establishment of a more rational rule and he suggested that any breach of trust, whether unethical or not, should suffice for liability for knowing assistance. These comments are of course prophetic in the light of the decision of the Privy Council in *Royal Brunei Airlines v. Tan* [1995] 3 All E.R. 97.

[14] [1995] 3 All E.R. 97.

honestly believed was permissible but which the solicitor knew full well was a clear breach of trust. Lord Nicholls added[15]:

> "It cannot be right that in such a case the accessory liability principle would be inapplicable because of the innocence of the trustee. In ordinary parlance, the beneficiaries have been defrauded by the solicitor.... Indeed, if anything, the case for liability of the dishonest third party seems stronger where the trustee is innocent, because in such a case the third party alone was dishonest and that was the cause of the subsequent misapplication of the trust property."

The judge was adamant that what matters was the state of mind of the third party sought to be made liable and not the state of mind of the trustee. The trustee's state of mind was essentially irrelevant to the question of whether the third party should be made liable to the beneficiaries for the breach of trust. The alternative hypothesis would mean that a dishonest third party was liable if the trustee was dishonest but if the trustee did not act dishonestly that of itself would excuse a dishonest third party from liability. The court said, and it is submitted rightly, that this made no sense.

There are however a couple of comments that may be made. First, in the generality of cases, a trustee or fiduciary will be acting dishonestly where the third party who is assisting him is acting dishonestly. Indeed one could argue that the whole exegesis about liability in *Royal Brunei Airlines v. Tan* was immaterial to the actual decision in the case for the travel agent company was found to have acted dishonestly. According to the court, Tan was the company and his state of mind was to be imputed to the company.[16] Secondly, the authority of the case is somewhat weakened by the absence of any reference to *Air Canada v. M & L Travel Ltd*.[17] The judgment in the latter case was handed down in late 1993 and the facts of the case are very similar to those in *Royal Brunei Airlines v. Tan*. There were two conflicting lines of Canadian authorities. One of these lines followed the English approach as adumbrated in *Barnes v. Addy*[18] whereas the second stream of cases flowed in a different direction holding that a person who was the directing mind of a corporate trustee could be liable for a non-fraudulent breach of trust if the person knowingly assisted in the breach of trust.[19] The Supreme Court of Canada, speaking through Iacobucci J., plumped for what they perceived to be the predominant English position. It was said that generally there were good reasons for requiring participation in a fraudulent and dishonest breach of trust before imposing liability on agents of the trustees. The reasons adduced for such insistence seem less than convincing.[20]

---

[15] [1995] 3 All E.R. 97 at 101.

[16] See generally on attribution theory Celia Wells, *Corporations and Criminal Responsibility* (1993) and James Gobert (1994) 14 *Legal Studies* 393 and [1994] Crim. L.R. 722. See also Clarkson (1996) 59 M.L.R. 557.

[17] (1994) 108 D.L.R. (4th) 592.

[18] Representative of the first stream of authority are *MacDonald v. Hauer* (1976) 72 D.L.R. (3d) 110; *Scott v. Riehl* (1958) 15 D.L.R. (2d) 67 and *Wawanesa Mutual Insurance Co. v. Chalmers & Co.* (1969) 7 D.L.R. (3d) 283.

[19] *Horsman Bros Holdings Ltd v. Panton* [1976] 3 W.W.R. 745; *Trilec Installations Ltd v. Bastion Construction Ltd* (1982) 135 D.L.R. (3d) 766; *Andrea Schmidt Construction Ltd v. Glatt* (1979) 104 D.L.R. (3d) 130 and *Austin v. Habitat Development Ltd* (1992) 94 D.L.R. (4th) 359.

[20] (1994) 108 D.L.R. (4th) 592. Iacobucci J. was in fact quoting from an article by Ruth Sullivan "Strangers to the Trust" (1986) 8 *Equity & Trusts Quarterly* 217 at 246.

"Unlike the stranger who takes title, an agent who disposes of trust property has no choice in the matter. He is contractually bound to act as directed by his principal the trustee. It is one thing to tell an agent that he must breach his contract rather than participate in a fraud on the part of his principal. It is quite another to tell him that he must breach his contract any time he believes his principal's instructions are contrary to the terms of the trust. This is to tell the agent that he must first of all master the terms of his principal's undertaking and, secondly, enforce his own understanding of what that undertaking entails. In effect, it burdens him with the duties of trusteeship upon the mere receipt of trust property as agent."

Surely though this rationale cannot count for anything if the accessory is dishonest. Dishonesty must render unnecessary any considerations of alleged hardship for the accessory in having to master the terms of the trusts.

A BREACH OF TRUST

Clearly the so-called trust need not be a formal one. All that is required is fiduciary relationship between the alleged trustee and the property of another person. Peter Gibson J. explained in the *Baden Delvaux* case that if A is placed in possession of or continues to exercise command or control over the property of B while it remains B's property and A can deal with B's property only for the benefit of B or for purposes authorised by B, A is a trustee of that property for the purposes of constructive trusteeship.[21] Because of the fiduciary responsibilities of company directors they are treated as if they were trustees of the company's property under their control. Likewise with the acquisition of information. In *Consul Development Pty. Ltd v. D.P.C. Estates Pty. Ltd*[22] it was held in Australia that a senior corporate executive may owe a fiduciary duty to the company with respect to information he acquires in that capacity so as to constitute the executive a trustee for the purpose of accessory liability.

The necessity for the existence of a breach of trust so as to establish liability has been questioned by some commentators. Liability for knowing assistance has been viewed as the equitable analogue of the tort of interference with contractual relations. In the analogous domain interference with contractual relations falling short of breach is enough to ground liability. Why should the position be any different in the equitable sphere? A counter-argument might be that removing the requirement of a breach of trust eviscerates the equitable basis of the liability and that this step should not be taken in the absence of an integrated law of civil wrongs.[23]

[21] [1992] 4 All E.R. 161 at 233.
[22] (1975) 132 C.L.R. 373.
[23] The case for a new law of civil wrongs pertaining to secondary liability has been eloquently put by Professor Peter Birks in, *e.g.* [1996] L.M.C.L.Q. 1 at 5. Birks points out many of the cases on knowing assistance involve straightforward example of acquisitive dishonesty and says: "The law has chosen to solve the civil problems associated with that kind of behaviour by appealing to and extending the law relating to trusts. And now we find that that historical practice is arming defendants, for the moment effectively, with the curious and substantially irrelevant argument that somehow or other, in order to sustain the associated liabilites, the plaintiff must convince the court that there is indeed a trust and a wrongdoing trustee. It is manifest that a cleaner break has to be made with the trust origins of these instruments of restitution and reparation. The context is not trusts. It is wrongdoing, usually of a commercial or financial kind." See also Birks "Civil Wrongs: A New World" *The Butterworth Lectures for 1990–91* (London, 1992), pp. 99–101.

ASSISTANCE

Again there has not been a great deal of judicial focus on what degree of assistance in the dishonest scheme is necessary to render an accessory liable. There was some discussion of the issue in the *Baden Delvaux* case however. Peter Gibson J. said that it was a simple question of act whether or not there had been assistance.[24] The payment by a bank on the instructions of fraudulent directors of a company of company moneys to another person could constitute such assistance. The judge rejected the gloss that there could not be assistance for this purpose unless what was done by the stranger inevitably had the consequence that a loss was suffered.

The issue of what degree of assistance sufficed to establish liability surfaced again in *Brinks Ltd v. Abu-Saleh (No. 3)*.[25] The case arose out of the well-known Brinks Mat gold bullion robbery in which gold and other valuables worth approximately £26 million had been stolen from a warehouse at Heathrow. In the course of the robbery a breach of trust had been committed in that a Brinks employee had betrayed the confidences of his employer and generally participated in the planning and execution of the robbery. Brinks Ltd brought civil proceedings against 57 defendants who had allegedly been involved in the robbery and subsequent laundering operations in an endeavour to recover the money. The present case related to proceedings against a Mrs Elcombe. Her husband had acted as a courier in transporting robbery proceeds abroad and his wife had accompanied him on these trips. Brinks Ltd contended that in this way she had provided "relevant assistance" in the furtherance of the dishonest and fraudulent breach of trust. She had provided an important element of cover intended to deter the suspicious from regarding the various journeys as other than commonplace and honest. Rimer J. adopted a different interpretation. While not wishing to minimise the benefit to a husband of being able to enjoy the company of his wife, he did not regard her presence on such trips as constituting relevant "assistance" in the breach of trust.

Somewhat more controversially however, the judge also held that, in order for a person to be liable in equity as an accessory to a breach of trust it was necessary for him to have given the relevant assistance in the knowledge of the existence of the trust or, at least, of the facts which give rise to the trust. It is submitted that if a defendant has been dishonest there is little merit in requiring knowledge of the existence of the trust. Furthermore, the judgment of Rimer J. in *Brinks Ltd v. Abu-Saleh (No. 3)* in this respect is a little difficult to reconcile with the views expressed by Millett J. in *Agip (Africa) Ltd v. Jackson*.[26] According to Millett J. in that case it was no answer for a man charged with having knowingly assisted in a fraudulent and dishonest scheme to say that he thought it was "only" a breach of exchange control or "only" a case of tax evasion. It was not necessary that he should have been aware of the precise nature of the fraud or even the identity of its victim. Millett J. observed that a man who consciously assisted others, by making arrangements which he knew were calculated to conceal what was happening from a third party, took the risk that they were part of a fraud practised on that party. This statement of principle is

---

[24] [1992] 4 All E.R. 161 at 234.
[25] (October 10, 1995) [1995] *The Times* October 23, 1995.
[26] [1990] Ch. 265.

difficult, if not impossible, to reconcile with the requirement of knowledge of the breach of trust insisted upon by Rimer J. in *Brinks Ltd v. Abu-Saleh (No. 3)*.

THE *MENS REA* OF LIABILITY

In *Royal Brunei* the Privy Council made it clear that dishonesty on the part of the accessory to a breach of trust was both a necessary and a sufficient condition of liability. Prior to this decision there had been considerable judicial disagreement over whether dishonesty was a necessary condition of liability. The view that it was was propounded with some force by Millett J. in *Agip (Africa) Ltd v. Jackson*.[27] In this case the plaintiff company which had been incorporated under the laws of Jersey was engaged in oil exploration in Tunisia. A senior employee of the plaintiffs systematically defrauded it of large sums of money. It was claimed in the action that the defendant accountants had assisted the dishonest employee in this endeavour by setting up nominee companies on his behalf so as to conceal the various transactions. The plaintiffs contended that the defendants were liable to account in equity for the moneys that had passed through their hands because they were knowing participants in the furtherance of a fraudulent and dishonest breach of trust.

Millett J. at first instance accepted this submission. He said that in cases of "knowing assistance" which were concerned with the furtherance of fraud (as distinct from cases of "knowing receipt" of trust property), constructive notice of the fraud was not sufficient to sustain liability on the part of a stranger to the trust. Dishonest furtherance of the dishonest scheme of another was the basis for liability. Thus a person's negligent but honest failure to appreciate that someone else's scheme was dishonest did not make that person a constructive trustee. In this particular case Millett J. pointed out that the defendants were professional men. He said that they obviously knew that they were laundering money. They were consciously helping their clients to make arrangements designed for the purpose of concealment. According to the judge it must have been obvious to them that their clients could not afford their activities to see the light of day. Secrecy was the badge of fraud. It was no answer for a man charged with having knowingly assisted in a fraudulent and dishonest scheme to say that he thought it was "only" a breach of exchange control or "only" a case of tax evasion. It was not necessary that he should have been aware of the precise nature of the fraud or even the identity of its victim. Millett J. opined that a man who consciously assisted others by making arrangements which he knew were calculated to conceal what was happening from a third party, took the risk that they were part of a fraud practised on that party. Unfortunately, the judgment of the Court of Appeal is not so clearcut. It was held that the defendants were dishonest and in consequence liable for their participation in a dishonest and fraudulent breach of trust. It is not so clear whether the Court of Appeal thought that dishonesty was a necessary condition of liability.[28]

---

[27] [1990] Ch. 265.

[28] In a brief reference ([1991] Chap. 547 at 567) Fox L.J. apparently affirms the statement of Ungoed-Thomas J in *Selangor United Rubber Estates Ltd v. Cradock (a bankrupt) (No 3)* [1968] 1 W.L.R. 1555 at 1590 that the degree of knowledge required was knowledge of circumstances which would indicate to an honest and reasonable man that a fraudulent design was being committed or would put him on inquiry whether it was being committed. See also the observations of Brightman J. in *Karak Rubber Co Ltd v. Burden (No 2)* [1972] 1 W.L.R. 602 at 633–638.

At one point Fox L.J., who delivered the only substantive judgment, approved the formulation put forward by Peter Gibson J. of the requisite states of knowledge[29]:

"(i) actual knowledge; (ii) wilfully shutting one's eyes to the obvious; (iii) wilfully and recklessly failing to make such inquiries as an honest and reasonable man would make; (iv) knowledge of circumstances which would indicate the facts to an honest and reasonable man; (v) knowledge of circumstances which would put an honest and reasonable man on inquiry."[30]

Writing extra-judicially Mr Justice Millett has argued cogently against acceptance of constructive notice as being sufficient to establish liability on the part of an accessory though he concedes that the authorites on the question are in a state of some disarray.[31] He suggests that given that the breach of trust must be a fraudulent and dishonest one, it followed logically that constructive notice of the fraud was not enough to make the accessory liable. In his view, there was no sense in requiring dishonestly on the part of the principal while accepting negligence as sufficient for his assistant.[32] There is however a considerable corpus of authority predating *Agip* that supports the existence of an objective test for knowledge and some of this body of case law will now be dissected.[33]

THE CASE LAW ON KNOWING ASSISTANCE—*SELANGOR UNITED RUBBER ESTATES LTD V. CRADOCK (NO. 3)*

The first of the modern cases that is usually mentioned is *Selangor United Rubber Estates Ltd v. Cradock (No. 3)*. This is a case where one Cradock launched a takeover bid for the plaintiff company using essentially its own funds. The end-result involved a breach of what is now section 151 of the Companies Act 1985 for as a general proposition a company is forbidden from giving financial assistance for the purchase of shares in itself. The particular scheme employed was a complicated one but the essential facts are as follows. The plaintiff company had been engaged in the rubber business in Malaysia but following nationalisation of the rubber estates by the Malaysian government was left with no business but substantial liquid assets including £232,500 on credit with the National Bank. Contanglo, a banking concern, made an offer for all the shares in the company in the capacity of an agent for an undisclosed principal, Cradock. The offer was accepted by 79 per cent of the shareholders. How could Cradock pay for these shares as his own bank account with District Bank at the London Oxford St. branch was barely in credit? The total amount payable was

---

[29] [1992] 4 All E.R. 161 at 235.
[30] One commentator at least feared that the Court of Appeal in *Agip* thought that constructive knowledge was sufficient to establish liability: see Harpum [1991] C.L.J. 409.
[31] (1991) 107 L.Q.R. 71 at 83–85.
[32] See generally Helen Norman, "Knowing Assistance, A Plea for Help" (1992) 12 *Legal Studies* 332. See also Gareth Jones, "Knowing Receipt and Knowing Assistance" in *Equity and Contemporary Legal Developments* (S. Goldstein ed., Jerusalem, 1992), 374.
[33] Simon Gardner in (1996) 112 L.Q. R.56 at 72–73 has argued that the invocation of logic by Sir Peter Millett was misplaced. In Gardner's view it is entirely intelligible to impose liability for negligently assisting in the dishonest causing of loss. He suggests that is an exact definition of the liability of store detectives and security personnel. The function of such persons is to guard against loss caused to their hirers by thieves and they incur liability if, negligently, they fail to do this.

£195,000. Cradock told the Oxford St. branch manager that he might influence the transfer of the plaintiff company's bank account to District and thereby persuaded the manager to let Contanglo have a banker's draft for £195,000. It was promised that an immediate counterdraft would be forthcoming from another bank. The takeover was completed and the Selangor account transferred to the District Bank. This transfer occurred by reason of the fact that the board of directors of Selangor was now under the control of Cradock. Selangor now resolved to lend £232,500 to a company called Woodstock. This was done simply by drawing a cheque on its account with District Bank and Woodstock in turn lent the same sum to Cradock merely by endorsing the cheque. Cradock then paid the cheque into his account with District Bank and thereby covered the banker's draft which had been used to pay for the shares. At the end of the day the District Bank had enabled Cradock to purchase the majority of shares in Selangor using Selangor's own money in a way that was contrary to what is now section 151 of the Companies Act 1985. The assets of Selangor had been paid out in breach in trust. Officials of the District Bank were ignorant of the true state of affairs but could the bank be made liable as an accessory to the fraud and illegality that had been perpetrated? Ungoed-Thomas J. answered in the affirmative and in so doing formulated an objective test for determining liability. He said[34]:

> "The knowledge required to hold a stranger liable as constructive trustee in a dishonest and fraudulent design, is knowledge of circumstances which would indicate to an honest and reasonable man that such a design was being committed or would put him on enquiry, which the stranger failed to make, whether it was being committed."

Applying the law as he perceived it to be to the facts of the case Ungoed-Thomas J. held that a reasonable banker would have no hesitation in concluding, before debiting the plaintiff company's account with the Woodstock cheque payment, that the plaintiff's moneys were being used for the purchase of shares in the plaintiff by Cradock. The District Bank was therefore liable for "knowing assistance" even though the bank officials dealing with the transaction in question did not then realise that the payment was being used for this purpose. The officials were completely without any experience in take-over transactions. The judge saw no substantial difficulty in banks providing against such exceptional transactions, involving substantial amounts, as in this case, being carried through by officials completely inexperienced in such transactions and unqualified to deal with them.

The judgment of Ungoed-Thomas J. has been subjected to severe criticism for his indiscriminate application of principles derived from cases on knowing receipt to the situation of knowing assistance. The cases relied on for the proposition that dishonesty on the part of the accessory was not necessary were all cases on knowing receipt.[35] Moreover, some cases that involved the issue of liability for knowing assistance were dismissed as irrelevant.[36] There was no judicial recognition of the fundamentally different bases of the two types of liability. The "knowing receipt" head of liability is essentially restitutionary

---

[34] [1968] 2 All E.R. at 1104.
[35] See *Gray v. Johnston* (1868) L.R. 3 H.L. 1; *Re Blundell* (1888) 40 Ch. D. 370; *Gray v. Lewis* (1869) L.R. 8 Eq. 526; *Thomson v. Clydesdale Bank Ltd* [1893] A.C. 282.
[36] [1942] 1 Ch. 219.

whereas arguably the liability of an accessory is unintelligible unless based on fault. To compound matters it has been persuasively contended that *Selangor* could be argued on the basis of knowing receipt.[37] The District Bank credited to the account of Cradock a cheque that had been drawn by Selangor. This cheque cleared what would otherwise have been an overdraft of £195,000. A bank has clearly been enriched where it applies a cheque in reduction of an overdrawn bank account.

Despite these criticisms *Selangor* was applied by Brightman J. in *Karak Rubber Co. Ltd v. Burden (No. 2)*. The facts of this case were essentially similar to those in *Selangor*, *i.e.*, the application of a company's own moneys for the purchase of shares in itself contrary to statute. The same result was also reached in the case with the judge holding that a bank by negligence on its part was accessory to a fraudulent and dishonest design on the part of a trustee. The bank was therefore liable under the "knowing assistance" head of constructive trusteeship. Brightman J. denied that want of probity was essential to liability. In his view it was sufficient to show constructive knowledge, *i.e.*, that the third party had knowledge of circumstances which would have indicated to an honest reasonable man that such a design was being committed or would have put him on enquiry whether it was being committed.[38] The judge was distinctly unimpressed with the suggestion that *Selangor* was fatally flawed because (a) important and decisive authorities had not been cited[39] and (b) it had been impliedly overruled by the Court of Appeal in *Carl-Zeiss Stiftung v. Herbert Smith & Co.*[40]

CARL-ZEISS STIFTUNG V. HERBERT SMITH & CO.

The *Carl-Zeiss* case has a quaintly historical air arising as it does out of the post Second World War partition of Germany. Basically, there were rival Carl-Zeiss foundations in the two Germanies. In the main suit the East German foundation contended that the assets of the West German foundation, including its property in England were held by that foundation in trust for the East German foundation. The East German foundation then instituted proceedings against the solicitors of the West German foundation claiming that when they were put in funds by their client, they had notice from the pleadings in the main action, that such money belonged to the East German foundation. The claim was that the solicitors were accordingly accountable as constructive trustees. Essentially the case comes under the rubric of knowing receipt though some of what the judges say appears directed across the totality of so-called constructive trusteeship. At the same time however the judges were careful not to cast direct aspersions on the judgment of Ungoed-Thomas J. in *Selangor* since an appeal, later abandoned, was then pending in that case. That said, Sachs L.J. was inclined to the view that an element other than constructive notice was

---

[37] See Harpum (1986) 102 L.Q.R. 114 at 151.

[38] The judge also pointed out that equitable doctrines have developed over the passage of time and it would not be right to assume that principles expressed two centuries ago were being fully and exhaustively enunciated for all ages to come; see [1968] 2 All E.R. at 1239.

[39] Brightman J. dealt with in detail one pre *Selangor* authority: *Williams v. Williams* (1881) 17 Ch. D. 437.

[40] [1969] 2 Ch. 276; [1969] 2 All E.R. 367.

necessary to render an accessory liable.[41] He stated that that factor was one of dishonesty, or of consciously acting improperly, as opposed to an innocent failure to make what what a court may later decide to have been a proper enquiry. Edmund Davies L.J. seemed to think that want of probity was the hallmark of constructive trusts, however created, and that nothing short of this would do. The Court of Appeal as a whole rejected the action by the East German foundation on the basis that mere notice of a claim asserted by a third party was insufficient to render an agent guilty of a wrongful act in dealing with property derived from his principal in accordance with the latter's instructions unless the agent knew that the third party's claim was well founded.[42]

The decision of Peter Gibson J. in the *Baden Delvaux*[43] case also supports an objective test for determining accessory liability. The facts of this case are extremely complicated which is not surprising given the fact that it was described in the Court of Appeal as involving "what was probably the biggest financial fraud of this century."[44] The fraudulent scheme was perpetrated by one Vesco and entailed the transfer of investors funds to jurisdictions such as Panama were they would be irrecoverably by the original investors and could be used by Vesco for his own purposes. To cut a long and entangled story short a court order was made under which the defendant bank received some $7 million on deposit from BCB, a Panamanian company that was controlled by Vesco. The bank knew that the funds were to be held on trust for the plaintiffs from whom they had originated and also that they were the subject of an ongoing investigation by the U.S. Securities and Exchange Commission. Through the machinations of Vesco the schedule to a later court order was altered and equipped with this court order BCB persuaded the defendant bank to transfer $4 million of the deposit to a Panamanian bank where it was misappropriated by Vesco. The later court order, fraudulently altered, was used to induce the defendant bank to believe that only $3 million was subject to the trust. The question was whether the defendants were liable as accessories to the fraudulent breach of trust by Vesco and BCB. The contested ground in the case was quite small. Counsel on both sides were at one in accepting that any of the following different types of knowledge justified the imposition of liability

"(1) actual knowledge;
(2) wilfully shutting one's eyes to the obvious;
(3) wilfully and recklessly failing to make such inquiries as an honest and reasonable man would make;
(4) knowledge of circumstances which would indicate the facts to an honest and reasonable man;
(5) knowledge of circumstances which would put an honest and reasonable man on inquiry and failure to make such inquiries."

Peter Gibson J. reviewed the authorities extensively and decided that the

---

[41] He also cited with approval the following proposition "where the agent of the trustees acts honestly and confines himself to the duties of an agent then, though he will not be accountable to the beneficiaries, they will have their remedy against the persons who are the trustees": see [1969] 2 Ch. 276 at 299.

[42] [1969] 2 Ch. 276 at 303–304.

[43] [1983] B.C.L.C. 325; [1992] 4 All E. R. 161.

[44] *Per* Lawton L.J. The decsion of Peter Gibson J. was affirmed by the Court of Appeal in an unreported decision (February 27, 1985) which has been noted [1985] B.C.L.C. 258. See generally Harpum (1986) 102 L.Q.R. 114 at 154.

concessions by counsel were well made.[45] He said that it was little short of common sense that a person who actually knew all the circumstances from which the honest and reasonable man would have knowledge of the relevant facts should also be treated as having knowledge of the facts. The judge added that it would be illogical not to apply a similar objective test in circumstances where the honest and reasonable man would be put on inquity.

In a sense the defendants had their "pay-off" for the concessions made when Peter Gibson J. went to say that the court should not be astute to impute knowledge where no actual knowledge exists. He explained that it was only in exceptional circumstances that the court should impute type (5) knowledge to an agent like a bank acting honestly on the instructions of its principal. If an explanation was offered, the presumption of honesty was strong and the court would not require the agent to be hypercritical in examing that explanation. There were thus limits to what inquiries a banker was under a duty to make. The banker could not be expected to play the detective. In this particular case it was held that there were two specific situations in which a duty to inquire arose. Once was when it received instructions to treat the $4 million as released from the trust and the second instance occcured when an inhouse accountant employed by the Investors body IOS claimed that the $4 million belonged to trust funds. The defendant bank was held not to have failed in its duty however because it relied on the court order which it was entitled to assume was duly obtained. Moreover it had been assured by the plaintiffs that they had no claim to the $4 million and the latter failed to institute proceedings to block the transfer to Panama.

While the judgment as well as being a blockbuster in terms of sheer length and marshalling of facts, contains much in the way of lucid and careful legal analysis, it may suffer from an element of internal inconsistency. At one point Peter Gibson J. said it was important not to lose sight of the requirement that the court must be satisfied that the alleged constructive trustee was a party or privy to dishonesty on the part of the trustee.[46] Furthermore, favourable reference was made to *Belmont Finance Corp Ltd v. Williams Furniture Ltd.*[47] In this case, which is another allegedly involving the grant by a company of financial assistance for the purchase of shares in itself, the Court of Appeal enunciated the proposition that subjectivity was the order of the day when it came to the test for accessory liability. Both Buckley and Goff L.JJ. were of the opinion that constructive notice was insufficient. Buckley L.J. said the knowledge of the fraudulent design on the part of the party sought to be made liable may be actual knowledge. If the person wilfully shuts his eyes to dishonesty or wilfully or recklessly fails to make such enquiries as an honest and reasonable man would make, he may be found to to have involved himself in the fraudulent character of the design, or any rate to be disentitled to rely on lack of actual knowledge of the design as a

---

[45] See the statement at [1992] 4 All E.R. 161 at 242; "Because of the judicial controversy to which the *Selangor* and *Karak* cases have given rise and the full citation to me of authorites by counsel on each side I have thought it right to review the authorities even though counsel effectively are at one in accepting that all five types of knowledge are relevant for the purposes of constructive trusteeship and neither has sought to submit that there should be or is any distinction on this point between the "knowing receipt or dealing" category and the "knowing assistance" category. I agree with counsel."

[46] [1992] 4 All E.R. 161 at 232–233.

[47] [1979] Ch. 250.

defence. But otherwise he should not be held to be affected by constructive notice.[48]

To the same effect is the first instance judgment of Alliott J. in *Lipkin Gorman v. Karpnale Ltd*[49] who observed:

> "in knowing assistance, the stranger to the trust must be proved subjectively to know of the fraudulent scheme of the trustee when rendering assistance, or to shut his eyes to the obvious, or to have wilfully and recklessly failed to make such inquiries as a reasonable and honest man would make."

When the case went to the Court of Appeal the parties changed tack a little and argued the case somewhat differently.[50] Nicholls L.J. opined however[51]:

> "... a plea that a defendant knew or ought to have known that transactions were part of a fraudulent and dishonest design can be an adequate plea of knowledge if, but only if, the plea is girded with appropriate particulars of all the allegation that the defendant "knew" of the matters in question."

Recent cases have tended towards acceptance of the proposition that the knowledge of the accessory has to be assessed subjectively.[52] In *Polly Peck v. Nadir (No 2)*[53] Scott L.J. spoke of:

> "a general consensus of opinion that, if liability as a constructive trustee is sought to be imposed, not on the basis that the defendant has received and dealt in some way with trust property (knowing receipt) but on the basis that the defendant has assisted in the misapplication of trust property (knowing assistance), 'something amounting to dishonesty or want of probity on the part of the defendant must be shown' (see *per* Vinelott J. in *Eagle Trust Plc v. SBC Securities*[54])."

Moreover in *Cowan de Groot Properties Ltd v. Eagle Trust Plc*[55] Knox J. adverted to a measure of consensus between the parties that liability had to be based on the first three points of the *Baden Delvaux* scheme.

The Supreme Court of Canada has recently come down in favour of the same line in *Air Canada v. M & L Travel Ltd*[56] though the point is not extensively discussed. In this case the appellant was one of two directors and shareholders of a travel agency. He was not active in the business, but was fully aware of the details of its operations. The respondent airline entered into an agreement with the agency which permitted the agency to sell tickets on behalf of the airline. The agreement laid down that all moneys, less commissions collected by the

---

[48] It should be noted however that it was not strictly necessary for the court to decide the point and that his opinion was merely a provisional one.
[49] [1992] 4 All E.R. 331 at 349. The judgment was actually handed down in 1986.
[50] For the Court of Appeal judgment see [1992] 4 All E.R. 409.
[51] *ibid.* at 450.
[52] *Polly Peck International plc v. Nadir (No. 2)* [1992] 4 All E.R. 769 (Mareva injunction application); *Polly Peck International plc v. Nadir (No. 3)*, *The Times*, March 22, 1993 (application for service out of the jurisdiction); *Eagle Trust plc v. SBC Securities Ltd* [1992] 4 All E.R. 488 and *Cowan de Groot Properties Ltd v. Eagle Trust plc* [1992] 4 All E.R. 700 and see generally Birks [1992] L.M.C.L.Q. 218 and Fennell (1994) 57 M.L.R. 38 at 50–54.
[53] [1992] 4 All E.R. 769 at 777.
[54] [1992] 4 All E.R. 488 at 499.
[55] [1992] 4 All E.R. 700 at 754.
[56] (1994) 108 D.L.R. (4th) 592.

agency for tickets sold by it, would be held in trust by the agency until it accounted for them to the airline. The agency had an operating line of credit from a bank. The moneys advanced thereon and interest on advances constituted a loan repayable on demand. Repayment of the loan was personally guaranteed by the directors. The agency established trust accounts with the bank for the deposit of the proceeds of ticket sales but it never used them. Instead, it deposited the proceeds into its general operating account with the bank. Subsequently the bank demanded repayment of its loan and when it was not paid withdrew the amount of the loan from the general operating account. Thereupon the airline sued *inter alia* the two directors for the amount owed to it in respect of ticket sales. The Supreme Court of Canada held that the agency had breached its trust arrangements with the airline by failing to account to it for moneys received in respect of ticket sales. Moreover the appellant along with the other director were personally liable for the breach of trust because, according to the court, they were constructive trustees under the *Barnes v. Addy* principle. Iacobucci J. who spoke for the majority of the court said that the kind of knowledge required for "knowing assistance" was actual knowledge of the trust and its breach, or reckless disregard for or wilful blindness to the obvious. Constructive knowledge was insufficient. The judge added that if the accessory received a benefit as a result of the breach of trust, this may ground an inference that the accessory knew of the breach.

One comment about the case is that the relevant principles are discussed very shortly in the judgment. Not all the English authorities are examined nor is there any great analysis or discussion of principle. The judgment is cast very much in the old language of constructive trusteeship and there is no consideration of the underlying basis of liability insofar as this point is concerned. Moreover, as McLachlin J. pointed out in her concurring judgment, the evidence in the case met the higher standard of subjective knowledge given that the appellant was wilfully blind. She preferred to postpone consideration of the degree of knowledge required until a later case where the issue squarely arose.[57]

The Privy Council in *Royal Brunei Airlines v. Tan*[58] were of the opinion that dishonesty on the part of the participant in the breach of trust was both a necessary and a sufficient condition of accessory liability. Perhaps the most noteworthy holding in the case, contrary to the prevailing orthodoxy, is that the breach of trust to which the defendant is an accessory need not be fraudulent or dishonest. The court said that a liability in equity to make good resulting loss attaches to a person who dishonestly procures or assists in a breach of trust or fiduciary obligation. It was not necessary that, in addition, the trustee or fiduciary was acting dishonestly, although this would usually be so where the third party who was assisting him was acting dishonestly.

Specifically on the dishonesty versus negligence as the *mens rea* of acccessory liability issue the judgment is firmly in the dishonesty camp. The *Baden Delvaux* scale of knowledge was discarded in favour of a more straightforward dishonesty/negligence dichotomy with dishonesty being the operative test. The expression "dishonesty" was preferred to "unconscionability" partly because the latter was not a word in everyday use by non-lawyers. Dishonesty, according to Lord Nicholls, meant in this context simply not acting as an honest person

[57] *ibid.* at 595.
[58] [1995] 3 All E.R. 97.

would in the circumstances. For the most part dishonesty was to be equated with conscious impropriety. The subjective characteristics of honesty did not mean however that individuals were free to set their own standards of honesty in particular circumstances. It was said[59]:

> "Honest people do not intentionally deceive others to their detriment. Honest people do not knowingly take others property. Unless there was a very good and compelling reason, an honest person does not participate in a transaction if he knows it involves a misapplication of trust assets to the detriment of the beneficiaries. Nor does an honest person in such a case deliberately close his eyes and ears, or deliberately not ask questions, lest he learn something he would rather not know, and then proceed regardless."

The Privy Council went on to focus on the taking of risks.[60] It was stressed that imprudence was not dishonesty, although imprudence might be carried recklessly to lengths which called into question the honesty of the person making the decision. Tensions with the test were to be resolved by bearing in mind that an individual was expected to attain the standard which would be observed by an honest person placed in those circumstances. Lord Nicholls said[61]:

> "Acting in reckless disregard of others' rights or possible rights can be a tell-tale sign of dishonesty. An honest person would have regard to the circumstances known to him, including the nature and importance of the proposed transaction, the nature and importance of his role, the ordinary course of business, the degree of doubt, the practicability of the trustee or the third party proceeding otherwise and the seriousness of the adverse consequences to the beneficiaries. The circumstances will dictate which one or more of the possible courses should be taken by an honest person."

THE CASE FOR A WIDER PRINCIPLE OF ACCESSORY LIABILITY

While acknowledging the trend of recent authority that dishonesty is necessary to render an accessory liable it would be useful for the sake of clarity, above all else, if old objective knowledge cases like *Selangor* were cleared from the path of precedent. This step has been taken by the Privy Council in *Royal Brunei Airlines v. Tan* but not in a domestic English forum. Perhaps, the most convincing rationale for confining liability to cases of dishonesty has been put forward by Millett J. He says[62]:

> "There is no sense in requiring dishonesty on the part of the principal while accepting negligence as sufficient for his assistant. Dishonest furtherance of the dishonest scheme of another is an understandable basis for liability; negligent but honest failure to appreciate that someone's scheme is dishonest is not."

[59] [1995] 3 All E.R. 97 at 106. Lord Nicholls said that if a person knowingly appropriates another's property, he will not escape a finding of dishonesty simply because he sees nothing wrong in such behaviour.
[60] Favourable reference was made to the observations of Peter Gibson J. in *Baden Delvaux* [1992] 4 All E.R. 161 at 234 that fraud includes taking a risk to the prejudice of another's rights, which risk is known to be one which there is no right to take. Peter Gibson J. was in turn invoking the judgment of the Court of Appeal in *R. v. Sinclair* [1968] 1 W.L.R. 1246 at 1249.
[61] [1995] 3 All E.R. 97 at 107.
[62] In *Agip (Africa) Ltd v. Jackson* [1990] Ch. 265 at 293. See also his article in the *Law Quarterly Review* (1991) 107 L.Q.R. 71 at 83–85.

While this may be true as a matter of logic it is a truism to say that the life of the law has not been logic but experience. Furthermore, the logic of the proposition may be questioned to some extent. Making a helper for negligently not realising that somebody else was committing a negligent breach of trust would seem to be going too far. It may be argued however that in cases of fraud more stringent duties are appropriate. Fraud is so special yet heinous that additional steps are needed to avert its occurrence and furtherance. Penalising a helper for failing to take reasonable precautions to avoid being implicated in the fraud would not seem to be excessive. One commentator argues that as beneficiaries under trusts are vulnerable, third parties who deal with trustees or other fiduciaries should be required to minimise the risk to beneficiaries by exercising reasonable care when they deal with fiduciaries.[63]

Moreover, the criterion of liability is one of context-sensitive fault.[64] As the reasoning of Peter Gibson J. in the *Baden Delvaux* case makes plain the only requirement is that the defendant should act reasonably in the light of the usual course of honest business. A banker is not forced into the role of a bloodhound nor is there any obligation to make futile inquiries.

The case for a wide principle of accessory liability has not appealed to all academics. Professor Peter Birks for one contends that if there is an argument someone who facilitates or assisted should be liable for carelessness, it is better that such liability should come about through the tort of negligence or perhaps through contract.[65] But why this doctrinal divide? All the law cannot be subsumed within the tort of negligence. Accessory liability in situations of breach of trust belongs historically to the realm of equity rather than to the common law. Saying that all knotty legal problems can be resolved through the tort of negligence seems somewhat ahistorical as well as being at variance with the views propounded by the Privy Council in *Downsview Nominees Ltd v. First City Corp Ltd.*[66] That case was concerned with the duties said to be owed by a mortgagee of property and by a receiver appointed by the mortgagee to subequent incumbrancers and to the mortgagor. The Privy Council took the view that the duties owed were based on historical equitable principles and rejected the existence of an additional or alternative duty of care based on negligence.

Moreover the impact of the Criminal Justice Act 1993 and the Money Laundering Regulations 1993 must not be ignored. At the risk of gross over-simplification it may fairly be said that the combined effect of this legislation is to impose on financial institutions a duty to take reasonable precautions to forestall or prevent money laundering. Failure to take such steps results in criminal penalties. Helping to conceal or disguise trust assets or to spirit such assets out of the jurisdiction would be a classic case of money laundering. The Criminal Justice Act 1993 in section 18 creates a new offence of failing to disclose knowledge or suspicion of money laundering. A person is guilty of the offence if he knows or suspects that another person is engaged in drug money laundering on the basis of information that came to him in the course of his

---

[63] See generally, Loughlan (1989) 9 O.J.L.S. 260 at 268 and see also Gardner (1996) 112 L.Q.R. 56.

[64] See G. Elias, *Explaining Constructive Trusts* (Oxford 1990), p. 81.

[65] [1992] L.M.C.L.Q. 218 at 224. He refers to the case of *Stransbie v. Troman* [1948] 2 K.B. 48.

[66] [1993] A.C. 295.

trade, profession, business or employment and he fails to disclose the information to the police as soon as is reasonably practicable.

During the parliamentary debates preceding the legislation disquiet was expressed at the fact that there is an obligation to report mere suspicions.[67] The argument was that it is all too easy to prove a suspicion but very difficult indeed to refute it. The official response was that if "belief" was substituted for "knowledge" this would be quite a large step towards undermining the objective of bringing money launderers to justice. It would take away the incentive to report the merely suspicious and thus reduce the number of reports that were actually made.[68] The Criminal Justice Act 1993 has been complemented by the Money Laundering Regulations 1993 which regulations impose on financial institutions the obligation of putting in place systems to deter money laundering and to assist the relevant authorities in detecting money laundering actitvities. Given this climate of criminal punishment, imposing civil liability on a person who has assisted in a breach of trust and has negligently failed to appreciate that such breach of trust was fraudulent does not seem unduly harsh.

While the matter was not discussed in any great detail, these sentiments did not seem to appeal to the Privy Council in *Royal Brunei Airlines v. Tan*.[69] The court expressly considered the position where third parties were acting for, or dealing with, dishonest trustees. It was pointed out that in such cases the trustees would have no claims against the third party because the trustee would suffer no loss by reason of the third party's failure to discover what was going on. Did the third party owe a duty of care to the beneficiaries to, in effect, check that a trustee was not misbehaving? Lord Nicholls said that in agreement with the preponderant view dishonesty was an essential ingredient here. While this statement may seem dogmatic there were signs of a softening in approach. He added[70]:

"There may be cases where, in the light of the particular facts, a third party will owe a duty of care to the beneficiaries. As a general proposition, however, beneficiaries cannot reasonably expect that all the world dealing with their trustees should owe them a duty to take care lest the trustees are behaving dishonestly."

While there is no open acknowledgement of the academic writings of Professor Peter Birks at this juncture the reasoning of the Privy Council smacks very much of the idea advanced by Birks that the call for additional liability with respect to a person who assists in a misapplication of trust funds should be answered in contract and tort.[71] In Birks' view that attempt to work out, in these established categories, the circumstances in which one person sould be liable when his negligence has facilitated a wrong by someone else can hardly be helped by any contribution from the much less understood category of constructive trusts.[72] But equitable liability for carelessly facilitating a fraudulent breach of trust is no new fangled creation. Moreover, the principle of liability

[67] See comments by Lord Richard at H.L. Deb., col 1380, (December 3, 1992).
[68] H.L. Deb., col 1487, (December 3, 1992).
[69] [1995] 3 All E.R. 97.
[70] [1995] 3 All E.R. 97 at 108.
[71] [1989] L.M.C.L.Q. 296 at 335. This article by Birks is in fact mentioned by Lord Nicholls but at an earlier stage in the reasoning process.
[72] *A propos* tort Birks refers to *Smith v. Littlewoods Organisation plc* [1987] A.C. 241 and the article by Markesinis (1989) 105 L.Q.R. 104.

has recently received statutory reinforcement albeit with no direct civil law implications. With respect to the specific observations of the Privy Council one might retort by saying that one is not talking about liability of an indeterminate class. Take the particular facts of *Royal Brunei Airlines v. Tan*.[73] The trustee or person owing fiduciary obligations was a company and the person sought to be made liable was a director of that company. Furthermore, liability is conditioned by the particular circumstances. In *Macmillan Inc. v. Bishopsgate Investment Trust Plc*[74] Millett J. recently remarked that "account officers are not detectives" and moreover, "unless and until they are alerted to the possibility of wrongdoing, they proceed, and are entitled to proceed, on the assumption that they are dealing with honest men". As has been pointed out the money laundering legislation has made such statements erroneous. Any bank or similar institution which trained its officials on the assumption that such pronouncements accurately represented the law would be committing a crime.[75]

As might be expected the judgment of Lord Nicholls in *Royal Brunei Airlines v. Tan* has provoked a mixed response from academic commentators, at least on the *mens rea* point. The decision has been enthusiastically applauded by Professor Peter Birks[76] who suggests that the judgment of Lord Nicholls has a strong claim to be included in any anthology of great judgments. Birks is firmly of the view that an accessory should not be made liable as such except on the basis of his own dishonesty. He says[77]:

"The importance of this point should not be underestimated. It represents a move to a more rational organisation of the law, and one long overdue. If and so long as "knowing assistance" could be based on carelessness as opposed to dishonesty, it constituted an example of negligence-based liability outside the tort of negligence. The contradictions inherent in that situation could be explained only by the failure to advance the project of integrating common law and equity. The Judicial Committee is now in effect insisting, and rightly, that all negligence liabilities be brought together and subjected to the same enquiry into duty, breach and damage."

Simon Gardner has argued that the general modern leniency in restricting liability for knowing assistance may be an aspect of the wide tendency, visible in the last 10 or 15 years, to curb the liabilities of banks and other commercial undertakings.[78] His argument is developed as follows[79]:

"Such curbing of liabilities evidently cannot be a goal in itself, but must be a facilitator of one or more further goals. The latter presumably include considerations such as mimimising the costs of such undertakings, perhaps as a means of encouraging their economic performance, thereby in turn benefiting the economic performance, and so the wealth, of the nation; that, at any rate, was the message of the political rhetoric with which such legal developments were coeval."

[73] [1995] 3 All E.R. 97.
[74] [1995] 1 W.L.R. 978 at 1014.
[75] See Gardner (1996) 112 L.Q.R. 56 at 83.
[76] [1996] L.M.C.L.Q. 1. See also Stevens [1995] *Restitution Law Review* 105; Harpum (1995) 111 L.Q.R. 545; Nolan [1995] C.L.J. 505.
[77] [1996] L.M.C.L.Q. 1 at 3. Birks also argues that there may be more occasions in the near future for driving this lesson home, to prevent renewed subversion of the tort of negligence by spurious sorties from fiduciary obligation.
[78] (1996) 112 L.Q.R. 56 at 71–85.
[79] *ibid.* at 78.

But as Gardner also demonstrates the policing of their clients has become part of professional agents' work in recent years. He refers not only to the money laundering legislation but also the codes of relevant professional bodies. The procedures of banks, etc., are not set in stone but are the product of various demands placed upon them. If such a demand was to take care to prevent fraud by their trustee clients, there was no reason why their procedures should not reflect this fact.[80] Furthermore, the suggested liability was one of taking care, rather than of achieving the impossible. It is submitted that these considerations have much force.

CONCLUSION

A person such as a solicitor, accountant or banker who has helped in some way the commission of a fraudulent breach of trust such as the misappropriation of pension fund assets may be civilly liable. Conventional terminology talks about liability as a constructive trustee though such language can engender confusion since the helper may not have handled the trust property. The Privy Council in *Royal Brunei Airlines v. Tan* laid down that dishonesty on the part of the accessory is both a necessary and sufficient condition of liability. It is submitted that this is a welcome development insofar as it removes the absolute requirement that the breach of trust to which the defendant is a party be fraudulent. It has been argued in this chapter however that where the breach of trust is a dishonest one, liability should also extend to situations where the accessory is merely negligent. The case for a wider principle of accessory liability has been advanced on the basis of the existing authorities and by reference to principle. The argument is reinforced by the new legislative measures in place to prevent money laundering. These provisions essentially impose a duty on a financial institution to take reasonable care to prevent its facilities being used for the purpose of money laundering.

[80] *ibid.* at 80–81.

INDEX

Index

Index

Index

Index

Index

Index

Index

Index